Date Due

M. 10170

THE LITERATURE OF THE
MIDDLE WESTERN
FRONTIER

THE LITERATURE OF THE MIDDLE WESTERN FRONTIER

BY

RALPH LESLIE RUSK, PH.D.

ASSOCIATE PROFESSOR OF ENGLISH
IN COLUMBIA UNIVERSITY

VOLUME II

New York
COLUMBIA UNIVERSITY PRESS
1926

THE TORCH PRESS
CEDAR RAPIDS
IOWA

CONTENTS OF VOLUME II

CHAPTER IX

THE VOGUE OF BRITISH AND EASTERN WRITERS

The uneven exchange of influence between the West and older communities, 1-4; the vogue of the earlier British writers on the frontier, 4-9; the British sentimentalists, 9-11; Scott and Byron, 11-23; Wordsworth, Coleridge, Shelley, and Keats, 23-29; the Victorians, 29-30; the writers of the Atlantic states, 30-38.

BIBLIOGRAPHIES

Introductory note, 39-41.

CHAPTER I: Foreign elements, 42-45; means of communication, 46-47; principal towns (municipal records, directories, etc.), 47-53; churches (minutes of conventions, synods, conferences, etc.), 53-65; auxiliary religious societies, 65-68; public schools, 68-69; private academies, 69-70; colleges and universities, 70-82; educational associations, 82-84; societies for promoting history, science, and art, 84-85; libraries and bookstores, 85-88; political parties, 88-91; antislavery societies, 91-93; miscellaneous societies, 93-95.

CHAPTER II: Accounts of captivity among the Indians, 96-100; narratives of adventurers and travellers from the Eastern states and from Europe, 101-129; travel and observation by Western writers, 129-136; guidebooks and gazetteers, 136-144; foreign travel by Western writers, 144.

CHAPTER III: Newspapers, 145-153; weekly publications

other than newspapers, 153-159; semimonthlies, monthlies, and quarterlies, 159-184; periodicals not definitely assigned to any of the three preceding groups, 184.

CHAPTER IV: Political pamphlets and speeches, 185-230; religious polemics and sermons, 231-270; popular accounts of trials and public appeals relating to them, 270-273; miscellaneous debate and propaganda, 273-280.

CHAPTER V: History, 281-288; biography, 289-293; science, 293-305; addresses before agricultural and mechanical societies, 305-306; college addresses and discussions of educational problems, 306-329; schoolbooks, 329-340; popular manuals, 340-344; almanacs, 344-350.

CHAPTER VI: Fiction, 351-353.

CHAPTER VII: Songbooks, 354-356; miscellaneous verse, 357-362.

CHAPTER VIII: Published plays, 363.

CHAPTER IX: Bibliographical note, 364.

INDEX

Explanatory note, 365; index to Chapters I-IX, 365-419.

CHAPTER IX

THE VOGUE OF BRITISH AND EASTERN WRITERS

"Pray," said I, . . . "do they ever read the Quarterly at English Prairie?"

"The Quarterly! Lord bless you — they read nothing but Tom Paine. I never saw any other book in all the Western country."

"Not read the Quarterly!" exclaimed I — "Ah, that accounts for their barbarity." — Paulding, *John Bull in America; or, the New Munchausen.*

Dallas's nephew (son to the American Attorney-general) is arrived in this country, and tells Dallas that my rhymes are very popular in the United States. These are the first tidings that have ever sounded like *Fame* to my ears — to be redde on the banks of the Ohio! — Byron, "Journal."

I

The West, as a pioneer country, received the impress of various outside influences without exerting a very great direct influence in return. The streams of immigration poured into it but did not flow back. The newly arrived settlers sometimes carried with them a certain respect for the cultural ideals of the older states and countries; but, until the growth of population had made the frontier politically powerful, there was no noticeable backwash of influence from the West upon the East. Nowhere was the exchange more uneven than in literature. There, the whole force of a tradition centuries old bore in one direction. Notwithstanding occasional protestations of sectional loyalty, Western writers kept their faces turned toward the East and toward England.

1

The vogue of the principal English authors of the time, which would probably have been considerable even under less favorable circumstances, was greatly aided by the laxity of copyright restrictions. Everywhere in America it was possible for publishers to reproduce English books more cheaply than they could print the works of native authors. "The fact, that an American publisher can get an English work without money," wrote James Fenimore Cooper,

must, for a few years longer (unless legislative protection shall be extended to their own authors), have a tendency to repress a national literature.[1]

Fearon's assertion that Byron's *Manfred* "was received, printed, and published all in one day"[2] testifies to the amazing facility with which the newly imported books of popular contemporary authors might be reproduced in America. Western presses, especially those of Cincinnati, performed their part in this wholesale distribution.[3]

Bristed's statement, about the same time, that

the best English poets are as much read here as in Britain; and Milton, Cowper, Burns, Scott, Southey, Byron, Campbell, and Moore, are formidable rivals to our American bards,[4]

did not, at any rate, overestimate the popularity in either East or West of English writers. Harriet Martineau, who

---

[1] James Fenimore Cooper, *Notions of the Americans*, 1828, II, 140.

[2] H. B. Fearon, *Sketches of America*, second ed., 1818, p. 35. For an account of a parallel achievement in the reproduction of one of Scott's novels by an American publisher a few years later, see J. Henry Harper, *The House of Harper*, 1912, p. 23. See also, in Earl L. Bradsher, *Mathew Carey*, 1912, pp. 79 ff., a valuable study of the influence on American literature of the exploitation of foreign authors by American publishers.

[3] See, for example, Charles Cist, *Cincinnati in 1841*, 1841, p. 262.

[4] John Bristed, *The Resources of the United States of America*, 1818, p. 356.

thought that "If the American nation be judged of by its literature, it may be pronounced to have no mind at all,"[5] found in this country, nevertheless, a considerable following for almost every English writer of any importance.[6]

The popularity of British authors among critics throughout America was doubtless due in no small measure to the wide circulation of the chief British reviews. Both *The Edinburgh* and *The Quarterly*, current numbers of which were reissued from American presses,[7] were included in the list of less than a dozen periodicals received at the principal popular library in Cincinnati in 1838;[8] and it is altogether likely that these famous arbiters of literary taste were read in every important town in the West. Nor was Foster's reprint of *Blackwood's* wholly unknown on the frontier.[9] Western school readers, the more advanced of which, in spite of some attempt at sectional and national loyalty by their compilers, usually contained numerous selections from the contemporary as well as the older British authors, were a much more popular means of extending the same kind of influence. The very general circulation of the foreign

---

[5] Harriet Martineau, *Society in America*, 1837, II, 301.

[6] *Ibid.*, pp. 310-311.

[7] Fearon, *loc. cit.* For reviews of *The Edinburgh* and *The Quarterly*, see *The Western Monthly Review*, III, 76-91 (Aug., 1829) and 487-496 (Mar., 1830).

[8] See *A Catalogue of Books Belonging to the Young Mens'* [sic] *Mercantile Library Association of Cincinnati*, n. d. (1838), p. 39. Both *The Edinburgh* and *The Quarterly* also appear in the very scanty collection listed in *A Catalogue of the Books Contained in the Library of Miami University*, 1833, p. 14.

[9] For an advertisement showing that various numbers of this reprint were for sale by the Detroit Book Store in 1836, see *Detroit Daily Free Press*, Aug. 6, 1836. For mention of both *Blackwood's* and *The Edinburgh* as among "the current works of the day" at Cincinnati at a much earlier date, see James Flint, *Letters from America*, 1822, p. 272.

keepsakes and annuals, especially about 1830 and later, was also significant.[10] Magazines published in the West devoted a generous amount of space to a discussion of contemporary British authors, and the frontier newspapers commonly copied both verse and prose derived from abroad.[11]

II

There was scarcely an important writer in the whole range of English literature from Chaucer [12] to Tennyson who did not achieve some slight vogue in the pioneer West; but only a few stand out as significant. Among the earliest of these were Shakespeare and Milton, who were accepted as an established tradition. Notices of both are to be found in Western prints even earlier than the end of the eighteenth century; [13] and their works were accessible, no doubt, in almost all such libraries as the frontier could boast.[14] Milton, to be sure, was laid under tribute by the epic vagaries of Emmons and Genin; but elsewhere the influence

---

[10] See, for example, St. Louis Beacon, Jan. 30, 1830, where no fewer than eight English annuals for 1830 are advertised for sale; and Daily Lou. Pub. Adv., Feb. 27, 1834, where an equal number are listed. The latter list consists of The Keepsake, The Amulet, The Literary Souvenir, Forget me not, New Year's Gift, Landscape Annual, Hood's Comic Annual, and Juvenile Forget me not. For an advertisement of several native American annuals, see St. Louis Beacon, Dec. 19 ff., 1829.

[11] See above, Chapter III.

[12] E. g., for one occurrence of Chaucer's "Truth" in a modernized version, see The Supporter (Chillicothe), Aug. 15, 1815.

[13] For early parodies on passages in Hamlet, see The Kentucke Gazette, Aug. 25, 1787 (probably the first verse printed in the West), and Cent. N.-W. Ter., Mar. 8, 1794; and for an almost equally early advertisement of Milton's works as offered for sale by John Bradford in Lexington, see Ky. Gaz., July 4, 1795.

[14] For catalogues of libraries and booksellers of the early West, see below, bibliography to Chapter I. Nearly all of the twenty-two catalogues there listed include titles by Shakespeare and Milton.

of his poetry was scarcely perceptible except in brief imitated passages. The great poet might even be made to suffer the indignity of being used as an authority by eccentrics engaged in debates on church ritual; and the prose works were found apt for quotation by the propagandists of radical social theory.[15] Homage, indeed, was done him in one extraordinary article, written, it seems, as a protest to a too negligent public. It was the duty of an editor of periodicals or a contributor to them, said this writer, "to keep in public view the genius and the works of those who are preeminently the classics of his language."[16] For the most part, however, it is likely that Milton was respected rather than known.

Something more, however, must be said for Shakespeare, whose name was familiar, not only to persons versed in the English classics, but to the much larger number of people who saw something of the drama. Of the more than seven thousand performances noticed in the preceding chapter, no less than one in every eighteen was, as has been shown, of a Shakespearean play. From the time when the prologue was pronounced at the opening of the first Cincinnati theatre worthy of the name,[17] Shakespeare was acclaimed

---

[15] For citation of Milton in a debate on psalmody, see above, Chapter IV, footnote 24. A series of extracts from *The Doctrine and Discipline of Divorce* were printed in *The New-Harmony Gazette*, June 11, 18, and 25; and July 2, 9, 16, and 23, 1828.

[16] "Thoughts upon the Poetry of Milton," *The Western Monthly Magazine*, V, 387-397 (July, 1836).

[17] The prologue spoken at the reopening of the Cincinnati Theatre, Nov. 19, 1821, includes an account of the earlier days in Cincinnati, when

The Drama's noble art was scarcely known
and when
With lyres unstrung the Scenic Muses slept,
While Shakespeare's genius saw the scene, and wept
(see Thomas Peirce, *The Odes of Horace in Cincinnati*, 1822, pp.

the genius of drama on the frontier, as elsewhere in English-speaking countries; and what was perhaps the finest theatre projected in the West toward the end of the period was to have as its most conspicuous ornament a statue of the great poet.[18]   Pioneer publishers and booksellers were able to offer Shakespeare's works in a variety of forms;[19] and, though in the magazine sections of newspapers he was not so much favored as were many lesser writers, especially the authors of patriotic or sentimental verse, it is clear that he was, much more than they, the source of casual illustrative passages which might lend an air of respectability to the borrower.[20]   There were even slight signs of a more or less popular interest in Shakespeare scholarship.[21]

Meantime, the tradition of Pope and other early eight-

98-100).   At the first opening of the same theatre (then unfinished), in the preceding year, a prologue explained that it was the purpose of the new establishment

to adorn the stage
With the bright sterling Ore of SHAKESPEAR'S page
(*Liberty Hall*, Mar. 21, 1820).

[18] Thomas and Wild, *The Valley of the Mississippi*, 1841, p. 23.

[19] Truman, Smith & Co., of Cincinnati, advertised in the *Cinc. Daily Gaz.*, May 7, 1834, Shakespeare's dramatic works for sale in seven different forms.   It seems clear, however, that these books were not published by the Western firm, though they might well have been. For a manifestly exaggerated account of the frequency with which Shakespeare's works were to be found in the cabins of the frontier, see Alexis de Tocqueville, *Democracy in America. Part the Second*, 1840, p. 57.

[20] For one example of the industrious use of Shakespeare in this way, see *Detroit Free Press*, for July, 1838, *passim*, where several editorials begin with quotations from Shakespeare, used in each case merely as a starting point for discussion.

[21] For a notice concerning early Shakespeare quartos (1609-1612) owned in America, see *The Cincinnati Mirror and Ladies' Parterre*, Jan. 21, 1832.   It may be worthy of note that *The Western Monthly Review* (III, 234-252, Nov., 1829) published "A Literary Essay on Shakespeare," translated from the French of Villemain.

eenth century writers of the neo-classical school exerted a
great influence, constantly lessening, but by no means
ended even during the period of romantic triumph.   The
heroic couplets common throughout the first four decades
of the nineteenth century were made in the image of Pope;
and the satirical versifiers of the West were, in particular,
his followers.   Thomas Peirce placed only Milton and
Thomson by Pope's side on the throne of English poetry:

> fresh shall bloom
> Their laurels in the Muse's page,
> And each historian's pen engage.[22]

The earliest critical review of the West refused, even while
heralding the triumph of a new generation of poets, to deny
the greatness of Pope:

> We are not enemies, but are admirers of Pope, and take
> unceasing pleasure in reading his numbers.   We have never
> paid the least regard to the silly attempts which have been
> made to prove, that the author of the Essay on Man, and of
> the Rape of the Lock, was no poet.[23]

For the orator, Pope's couplets supplied pointed illustra-
tion.[24]   What was probably the first magazine issued in the

---

[22] Peirce, *The Muse of Hesperia*, 1823, p. 43.

[23] *The Western Review and Miscellaneous Magazine*, II, 5 (Feb.,
1820).   For a later magazine article devoted entirely to Pope but not
an original Western production, see the translation of Villemain's
"Essay on the Life and Writings of Pope," in *The Western Monthly
Review*, III, 205-215 (Oct., 1829).   In a brief prefatory note, the
translator or editor characterizes Pope as "one of the first poets
the world has seen."   Curiously enough, Mrs. Trollope makes Flint,
the editor of this magazine and, no doubt, the translator of Villemain's critique, say of Pope: "He is so entirely gone by, that in
our country it is considered quite fustian to speak of him" (Frances
Trollope, *Domestic Manners of the Americans*, New York, 1832, p.
87).

[24] E. g., Charles Caldwell, *A Discourse on the Genius and Character of the Rev. Horace Holley*, 1828, pp. 20 and 55.

West included biographical sketches, on the ground that

The proper study of Mankind is Man.[25]

Among the early publications of the Lexington press, then the most important on the frontier, was *An Essay on Man*;[26] and the fact that Pope's influence had not wholly ceased at the end of the pioneer period is proved by the publication in the same town of a lengthy analysis of this poem by a Kentucky author, William C. Bell.[27] This volume, called *Analysis of Pope's Essay on Man* (1836), devoted more than two hundred pages to quotation and explication of the poem almost line by line. It was, however, simply the didactic quality of the *Essay* which attracted this writer. He found in it an effective sermon on the text "private good is only to be found in the public good":

It was for the preservation and propagation of this sentiment, applied to all the social relations of citizen, countrymen, neighbors and friends, to the still more endearing ones of husband, wife, father and child, and all the various ties of society, that Pope wrote his Essay on Man.[28]

Like Shakespeare and Milton, Pope was in every library worthy of the name; and there are evidences, too, of the lesser fame of his predecessor, Dryden, and of his successor, Samuel Johnson. Perhaps, however, a no less important influence of these writers and of their imitators was exerted through the vogue of classical literature in English translation, which was largely due to them. When Kentucky was still little more than a wilderness open to the attacks of savages, the Latin and Greek authors were on sale at

---

[25] From prospectus of *The Medley* in *Ky. Gaz.*, Oct. 1, 1802.

[26] Advertised in *Ky. Gaz.*, Sept. 4, 1804.

[27] According to the *Observer & Reporter*, Mar. 19, 1836, Bell was a resident of Lexington.

[28] William C. Bell, *Analysis of Pope's Essay on Man*, 1836, p. vi.

Lexington. As early as 1793 we hear of English versions of Homer and Aristotle, and of Cornelius Nepos, Sallust, Virgil, Horace, and Ovid, along with a medley of British writers.[29] Homer seems always to have appeared in Pope's dress. Virgil was, of course, known in Dryden's translation.[30] Not only the schoolbooks already noticed,[31] but numerous minor attempts at original English versions and imitations, showed a marked interest in classical literature which seems to have been at its height during the first decade of the nineteenth century. Anacreon [32] and Horace [33] were for a time the favorites. The almost universal practice, at this period, of turning the latter author's method to account on subjects of contemporary interest or in making local satire, was illustrated by the appearance of a set of verses called "Horace in Lexington," [34] and of Thomas Peirce's volume *The Odes of Horace in Cincinnati* (1822). There were some attempts at original translations of both Ovid [35] and Virgil.[36]

III

The British writers who aroused the greatest enthusiasm in the West were, however, the contemporary poets and novelists. Among these, perhaps the most conspicuous for

---

[29] Advertised among books just arrived at a Lexington store, *Ky. Gaz.*, July 27, 1793.

[30] See, for example, *Catalogue of the Books in the Lexington Library*, 1815, pp. 56 and 63.

[31] See above, Chapter V.

[32] For some translations and imitations of the odes, see *Ky. Gaz.*, Mar. 26, 1805; and for 1806, Aug. to Nov., *passim*. For a translation of Anacreon by Samuel Johnson, see *Liberty Hall*, Sept. 23, 1806.

[33] See, for example, *Cent. N.-W. Ter.*, July 12, 1794, and July 25, 1795; *Ky. Gaz.*, Nov. 21, 1805, and Oct. 2, 9, and 27, 1806; and *Liberty Hall*, July 12, 1809.

[34] See *Ky. Gaz.*, Aug. 13, 1811.

[35] *Ibid.*, Dec. 19, 1805.

[36] *Ibid.*, Oct. 24, 1805.

widespread popular favor were the group of romantic sentimentalists, with "the English songstress of the heart, the
unequalled Felicia Hemans," as Flint characterized her,[37]
and Thomas Moore at their head. Hannah More, who,
according to Harriet Martineau, was more popular in
America than any other British author,[38] was certainly not
so on the frontier. The moral tone to which Miss More's
rank was attributed, doubtless had no small part, however,
in determining the vogue of Mrs. Hemans, who, with Thomas
Moore, held the front rank among favorites in the poetical
corners of newspapers and other weekly periodicals.
Scarcely a paper in the West during the decade following
1825 was without its quota of verses by Mrs. Hemans,[39]
which, according to Mrs. Trollope, the merchant was wont
to scan as he held out his hand for an invoice.[40] Moore's
notoriety, manifested in the same way, but evidently due to

[37] Timothy Flint, *The Shoshonee Valley*, 1830, II, 251.   For
further proof of Flint's devotion to Mrs. Hemans, see *The Life and
Adventures of Arthur Clenning*, 1828, I, 59-60.

[38] Martineau, *op. cit.*, II, 310.

[39] See, for example, *Ky. Gaz.*, Apr. 6, May 4, June 1 and 8, 1827,
and Apr. 2, 1830; *Liberty Hall*, Mar. 6, 1827; *Daily Cinc. Gaz.* (with
slight change of name), Sept. 29, 1827, Apr. 23 and July 10, 1829,
Jan. 28, 1830, Jan. 28 and May 31, 1833, May 13, Aug. 8, and Sept.
6, 1834, and May 3 and 20, 1836; *Lou. Pub. Adv.* (with slight changes
in title), Nov. 19, 1825, Feb. 22, June 17, and Nov. 1 and 18, 1826,
Oct. 20 and Nov. 10, 1827, Jan. 17, Mar. 14, May 20, Sept. 5, and
Oct. 1, 1829, Jan. 19, June 25, Aug. 27, and Nov. 23, 1830, May 22
and Sept. 16, 1833, Sept. 6, 1834, and July 29, 1835; *Mo. Rep.*, Feb.
23, June 1 and 15, Sept. 14, and Oct. 19, 1826, Feb. 22, Mar. 15, Apr.
5, June 7, and Oct. 11, 1827, Apr. 1, June 10, and Nov. 11, 1828,
Nov. 29, 1831, and May 29, 1832; *Detroit Gaz.*, Jan. 10, Aug. 8, and
Nov. 28, 1826, and Jan. 7 and Feb. 18, 1830; *Detroit Journal and
Michigan Advertiser*, Oct. 26, 1831, Mar. 1 and 8, and Sept. 4 and 18,
1833; *The New-Harmony Gazette*, Nov. 15, 1826, Jan. 24, Feb. 14
and 21, Apr. 4, May 23, Oct. 24, and Dec. 12, 1827, Jan. 23, May 28,
Aug. 27, Sept. 3, and Oct. 1, 1828.

[40] Trollope, *op. cit.*, p. 88.

his sentimental quality and to his success as a song-maker, rather than to any moral tendency, began much earlier,[41] yet fell a little short of that achieved by Mrs. Hemans. Letitia E. Landon, who may be regarded as a member of the same group, was at the height of her popularity on the frontier at about the same time with Mrs. Hemans.

IV

Far more remarkable than the vogue of these writers, however, was the phenomenal growth of the cult of the romanticists of action, Scott and Byron, who were regarded as the chief literary figures of the age by those who set themselves up as authoritative critics. Thomson,[42] Cowper,[43] and Burns, pioneers of the new era in English poetry, had each won no small applause, even from readers in the backwoods of the West; and it is a noteworthy fact that Burns was well enough known to be imitated in verses published in a Cincinnati newspaper some years before his death.[44] Southey, of a later generation, was remarkable

---

[41] For early evidences of Moore's Western fame, see copies of his verse in *Ky. Gaz.*, Apr. 16, 1805; Feb. 6, and Aug. 11 and 25, 1806; Dec. 5, 1809; and Feb. 19, 1811. See also *Liberty Hall*, Mar. 28, 1810; and Jan. 30, 1811.

[42] As early as 1788 "A Hymn on the Seasons," in slightly altered form, was made to do duty in describing Western scenery (see *The Kentucke Gazette*, Nov. 22, 1788).

[43] Cowper, like Burns, was known in the West during his own lifetime. An early copy of some verses from *The Task* appeared in *The Palladium* (Frankfort), Aug. 9, 1798. Five years earlier, at least the *Olney Hymns* were to be had at a Lexington store (see *Ky. Gaz.*, July 27, 1793). Both Thomson and Cowper were recommended as models by perhaps the most noteworthy lyrical poet of the West as late as 1833 (see *The Cincinnati Mirror and Ladies' Parterre*, for Mar. 2 of that year).

[44] A poem in the style of "The Holy Fair" occupies two columns in *Cent. N.-W. Ter.*, May 31, 1794. For copies of Burns's own verse appearing in a frontier newspaper of early date, see *Ky. Gaz.*, Nov.

both for his early fame and for the high regard in which
he was held by critics of a certain religious bias.[45]

But all praise of such writers was lost in the great din
which greeted the triumph of Scott and Byron. The
rapidity with which the former, from about 1810, and the
latter, from a few years after, became known throughout
the frontier country was unparalleled. *The Lady of the
Lake* was so much in demand at Lexington within a few
months after its publication in Edinburgh that the owner
of a copy had to advertise for its return.[46] By about the
same time the fame of this poem had reached Cincinnati.[47]
The novels were still more eagerly received. By 1815, not
only the poetry of both Byron and Scott, but the anonymous
Waverley, which first appeared in 1814, were in the possession of the Lexington Library.[48] The later novels likewise
experienced little delay in finding their way into the hands
of the small body of cultured readers in backwoods places.

8 and Dec. 20, 1797. For a review of Carlyle's criticism published
in *The Edinburgh Review* on Lockhart's *Life*, see *The Western
Monthly Review*, III, 81-91 (Aug., 1829). Aside, however, from
imitations of some popular Scotch stanza forms used by Burns, perhaps the most remarkable proof I have noted of the poet's popularity
during later years in the West was an anniversary celebration held
in his honor at Detroit in 1836 (see *Detroit Daily Free Press*, Jan.
30, 1836).

[45] For an early reproduction of Southey's poetry, see *The Palladium*, Jan. 15, 1799. As for Southey's reputation as poet toward the
end of the pioneer period, it may be remarked that as late as 1836
and by as good a critic as James H. Perkins, he was ranked with
Milton, the author of Job, and the prophets (see *The Western Messenger*, I, 460, Jan., 1836).

[46] *The Reporter*, Apr. 13, 1811. For a notice of this work offered
for sale in the same town, see *Ky. Gaz.*, July 16, 1811.

[47] The song ''The heath this night must be my bed'' is copied in
Liberty Hall, Apr. 17, 1811.

[48] See *Catalogue of the Books in the Lexington Library*, 1815, pp.
54, 65, and 68.

Rob Roy, issued in Edinburgh early in 1818, was actually
for sale in Lexington before the end of March the same
year.[49]   *Kenilworth* was to be had in Detroit before the end
of 1821.[50]   So great was public interest that booksellers in
some instances even notified readers in advance of the time
when the latest Scotch novel was expected to arrive.[51]
James Flint, who visited the Ohio River towns in 1818-
1820, found Scott's novels still the literary sensation of the
day.   At Cincinnati *The Monastery* was in the public eye.
''When lately at Louisville,'' he wrote in a letter of October
13, 1820,

I found an acquaintance reading Ivanhoe; during my stay
with him, which was only about an hour, two persons applied for a loan of the book.   He told me that there were
seven or eight copies of it in that town, and that they are
no sooner read by one than they are lent to another.   Two
copies of the Monastery had just then arrived in town,
and were, if possible, more in request than the former.[52]

Meantime Byron's fame had spread with equal rapidity.
Hebrew Melodies, published in April, 1815,[53] were to be had
in Kentucky within a few months.[54]   And more than a
year earlier Byron had recorded ''the first tidings that have
ever sounded like *Fame* to my ears — to be redde on the
banks of the Ohio!''[55]   Both *Manfred* and *The Lament of*

---

[49] See *Ky. Gaz.,* Mar. 27, 1818.

[50] *Detroit Gaz.,* Nov. 2, 1821.

[51] See, for example, *Ky. Reporter,* July 8, 1829, where *Anne of
Geierstein* is so announced.

[52] James Flint, *op. cit.,* p. 272.   *Cf.* William N. Blane, *An Excursion through the United States and Canada,* 1824, p. 196.

[53] For this and other citations of definite dates of Byron's publications, see *The Encyclopædia Britannica,* eleventh ed., 1910.

[54] *Ky. Gaz.,* Dec. 11, 1815, contains the poem ''She walks in
beauty.''

[55] *The Works of Lord Byron.   .   .   .   Letters and Journals,* ed.
Rowland E. Prothero, 1898, II, 360.   The date of this entry is Dec.
5, 1813.

Tasso were for sale in Western bookstores within a few
months after their first publication.[56] *Beppo* (February
28, 1818) was known as early as the following July.[57] Near
the beginning of 1820, we hear of the opening cantos of *Don
Juan;*[58] and before the end of the following year, the third,
fourth, and fifth cantos, which had not appeared till August,
were advertised in Louisville.[59] A few months later *The
Two Foscari, Sardanapalus,* and *Cain* were likewise avail-
able.[60] The stanzas on Boone in the third series of *Don
Juan* promptly became current on the frontier.[61] *The
Island* was known by October, 1823.[62] Captain Marryat,
writing at the close of the pioneer period, reported that,
although the present number of editions of Byron appearing in America made it impossible to form more than a
rough estimate of the total number of volumes, it was likely
that from a hundred and fifty to two hundred thousand had
been sold throughout the United States.[63] The English

[56] See, for example, *Ky. Reporter* (Lexington), Nov. 19, 1817.
Manfred was published June 16 and *The Lament of Tasso,* on July
17 of that year.

[57] See stanzas quoted in *Ky. Reporter,* July 29, 1818.

[58] E. g., *Detroit Gaz.,* Mar. 24, 1820. These cantos were first published July 15, 1819.

[59] *Lou. Pub. Adv.,* Dec. 19, 1821.

[60] *Ibid.,* Apr. 20, 1822. The three were first published Dec. 19,
1821, on the same day when the second series of *Don Juan* was advertised in Louisville.

[61] See, for example, *Detroit Gaz.,* Oct. 10, and *Illinois Intelligencer,*
Nov. 1, 1823. None of cantos VI-XVI had been published till July
15, 1823.

[62] A notice of this poem, copied from an Eastern paper, is to be
found in the *Mo. Rep.,* Oct. 8, 1823. For extensive quotations and
criticism of *The Island,* see *The Cincinnati Literary Gazette,* Jan.
24, 1824. *The Island* had first appeared on June 26, 1823.

[63] Frederick Marryat, *Second Series of a Diary in America,* 1840,
p. 70.

novelist seems to have been most surprised, however, at
Byron's penetration to the extreme frontier of the West.
At Sault Ste. Marie, "the Ultima Thule of this portion of
America," he was particularly impressed by the evidences
of the poet's fame. "In two instances," he wrote, "I
found in the log-houses of this village complete editions of
Lord Byron's works." [64] As a matter of fact, however, an
edition of Byron in eight volumes had been on sale at no
great distance from the Sault within little more than two
years after the poet's death. [65]

Before the end of the pioneer period the fame of both
Byron and Scott was, indeed, everywhere in the West.
Steamboats plying on the Ohio and Mississippi were named
the "Lady of the Lake," the "Ellen Douglas," the "Marmion," the "Corsair," the "Mazeppa" and the "Medora." [66] Doubtless names from the same sources were
commonly given to children and to slaves as well. In a
novel called *East and West*, by a Cincinnati writer, a negro
servant is named Waverley. Such great names were given
to negroes, says the author, according to a custom which
acknowledges the nearness of the sublime to the ridiculous;
"or, as the boy was a great pet . . . it may have been
to display . . . admiration of the greatest genius of
the age." [67] One may suppose that it was a commonplace
proceeding at Western taverns to drink such toasts as
"*Byron*: His works are imperishable" and "*To the Mem-
ory of Sir Walter Scott.*" [68] Until 1827 a good deal of

[64] Marryat, *A Diary in America*, Philadelphia, 1839, I, 97.

[65] Such an edition is advertised for sale in *Detroit Gaz.*, Aug. 29,
1826.

[66] See *Picture of Cincinnati*, for 1839, pp. 75 ff.; and for 1840,
pp. 70-76.

[67] Frederick W. Thomas, *East and West*, 1836, I, 69.

[68] *Detroit Daily Free Press*, Jan. 30, 1836.

popular interest was manifested in the debate regarding the authorship of the Waverley novels.[69]   Thereafter, as more intimate facts regarding the novelist became known, much attention was given in the public prints to his character and personal affairs.   His death was memorialized in verse;[70] his family life was praised;[71] anecdotes of his experience as a lawyer were recalled;[72] his relations with the Ballantynes were discussed.[73]   Byron, on the other hand, attracted much attention on account of the scandals connected with his name.   His separation from his wife[74] and the whole question of his character and of the moral or immoral tendency of his poetry were the subjects of much comment about the time of his death.[75]

---

[69] E. g., *Ky. Reporter*, Nov. 4, 1818; *The Cincinnati Literary Gazette*, Jan. 17, 1824; and *Liberty Hall*, May 1, 1827.

[70] E. g., in *Cinc. Daily Gaz.*, Dec. 5, 1832; and Feb. 15, 1833.

[71] Hogg's account of ''Sir Walter Scott's Family'' was reproduced in the *Detroit Journal and Courier*, Feb. 18, 1835.

[72] A story of Scott's first client was printed by the *Detroit Daily Advertiser*, May 15, 1837.

[73] An article on the subject in *Cinc. Daily Gaz.*, Nov. 28, 1838, deals with Lockhart's account and the rejoinder by the Ballantyne family.   Scott's business affairs had even before his death been a topic of some interest in the West (see, for example, *Detroit Journal and Michigan Advertiser*, Jan. 26, 1831).

[74] See, for example, *Ky. Gaz.*, July 15, 1816; and *Liberty Hall*, Aug. 3, 1824.

[75] For anecdotes of Byron, see *Detroit Gaz.*, May 29, 1818; and *Mo. Rep.*, July 26, 1827.   A poem entitled ''Lord Byron's Exit from Earth, (a Report)'' was contributed to the *Detroit Gaz.*, Dec. 25, 1818.   Shortly after the poet's death, a good deal of space was given to accounts of his last days and to general comment on him (see, for example, *Liberty Hall*, July 13, Aug. 3, Oct. 22, and Nov. 9 and 16, 1824).   Even in one of the most liberal journals published in the West, it was held that the poet's character was the central fact in the Byron episode, and that his genius must therefore be regarded as wasted (*The New-Harmony Gazette*, Dec. 20, 1826).   For a later

The influence of both Scott and Byron on the literature of more pretentious sort was quite equal to the measure of the popular enthusiasm aroused by them. Allusions, quotations, and imitations were the order of the day. In a single travel account written toward the end of the period by Edmund Flagg, a cultured immigrant to the frontier, there are more than a score of quotations or allusions which testify to Byron's fame — and especially to the vogue of *Childe Harold* and *Manfred* — and a few which show that Scott was also fresh in the mind of the author.[76] James Hall, whose books on the West may be regarded, with Flint's, as the most valuable early accounts of the new country by a resident observer, though much less discursive than Flagg, does not fail to find in his subject many things suggestive of Scott. His mild ridicule of the curious exotic place names he encounters in Illinois is expressed ironically in the opinion that they would admirably set off the verses of that poet.[77] The new country's barrenness of well-established popular superstitions, he considers discouraging to the creative artist; for he has in his mind the author of *Waverley* as the ideal creative artist.[78] Aaron Burr, whose conspiracy in the West, Hall, as a historian, discussed, could make Hamilton experience

> The stern joy that warriors feel,
> In foeman worthy of their steel; [79]

---

discussion of Byron's character (this article, like several others mentioned, is borrowed material), see *ibid.*, Feb. 20, 1828.

[76] Edmund Flagg, *The Far West*, 1838, *passim*. The devotion to Byron is here the more remarkable because the book — principally a record of observations made in parts of Illinois and Missouri — had properly nothing at all to do with Byron or Scott.

[77] James Hall, *Letters from the West*, 1828, p. 196.

[78] *Ibid.*, pp. 328 and 337.

[79] Hall, *Sketches of History, Life, and Manners, in the West*, 1835, II, 45.

certain young women of Kentucky, whose adventure with the Indians is narrated, were not so well skilled in navigation as was the Lady of the Lake; [80] the first settlers of the country were men who, like Fitz-James, found sufficient lure in danger alone; [81] Indian tactics remind Hall again inevitably of the Highlanders in *The Lady of the Lake*:

When Colonel Hardin and his detachment had passed into the ambushed spot, the enemy rose, discovering themselves on all sides, like the followers of Roderic Dhu, in the splendid conception of Scott.[82]

In such manner, with only scanty literary allusion of any other sort, did this author give point to what was intended as a sober historical account.

Western writers of fiction often drew their inspiration partly or largely from Scott; and, at the same time, their works testify eloquently to the vogue of Byron. Perhaps the use of historical materials in such novels as Flint's *Francis Berrian* and, especially, M'Clung's *Camden*, affords the best examples of Scott's impress on fiction. Byron, without such fundamental influence, was, nevertheless, so much in the atmosphere of the time that he was echoed by the novelists as well as by the poets. The most striking instance is in F. W. Thomas's *Howard Pinckney*, whose hero, himself compounded of what was intended to pass as Byronic brilliancy and Byronic melancholy, is an enthusiastic worshiper of the poet. Even when engaged in making love, he cannot forbear the pleasure of delivering learned harangues on the life and character of his literary idol. " 'What a great admirer you are of Byron, Mr. Pinckney,' " his companion ventures to interrupt on one such occasion. " 'Yes, Miss Fitzhurst,' " he replies, " 'I

---

[80] *Ibid.*, II, 63.

[81] *Ibid.*, II, 85.

[82] *Ibid.*, II, 134.

love his poetry as much as ever lady loved himself.' ''
Presently he halts the conversation in order to appeal to a
eulogy on Byron in a recent number of *The Edinburgh*;
and, having armed himself with this authority, he launches
into a dissertation on the poet which is continued through
no less than nine pages of the novel.[83] With Thomas's
hero it is, however, not merely a matter of ardent admiration, but an attempt to imitate the poet's personal idiosyn-
crasies. " 'You're in a moody, Byronic way, again,' ''
Pinckney is told by Miss Atherton, another of his sweet-
hearts; " 'plague take my lord of poets, for the fancies he
has engendered in young gentlemen's brains.' '' [84]

Once the popularity of Scott and Byron had begun,
scarcely a frontier verse-maker escaped their influence.
There were many tributes in rime, equally numerous
echoes of favorite passages, and several pieces of some
length patterned upon the longer poems of these writers.
Gorham Worth had discovered as early as 1819 that Byron
had already been "made a pack-horse for the follies of
others;" [85] and Worth's own satire, *American Bards*, is
clearly a frontier adaptation of *English Bards and Scotch
Reviewers*. About the same time Angus Umphraville, who,
in his preface to *Missourian Lays*, warned the reader not to
expect the genius of "a Byron, a Moòre, a Scott, a Campbell, or a Barlow," inscribed his "Lines Written on the
Bank of the Mississippi" "as an humble tribute of American respect to the poetical genius of Lord George Byron." [86]
Thomas Peirce, whose *The Odes of Horace in Cincinnati*
contains many echoes of Byron, followed him most closely
in "City Poets," designed to chastise the poetasters of the

---

83 Thomas, *Howard Pinckney*, 1840, I, 96-104.

84 *Ibid.*, II, pp. 32-33.

85 Gorham Worth, *American Bards*, 1819, p. viii.

86 Angus Umphraville, *Missourian Lays*, 1821, pp. 5 and 21-23.

West. Even Peirce's rimes are significant of influence from this source, for they recall the slipshod cleverness of Byron's later style.[87] Another work by the same author, called "Billy Moody," was a satirical poem of travels in imitation of *Don Juan*. For F. W. Thomas's verse travelogue reflections in *The Emigrant, Childe Harold* was the model. W. D. Gallagher included in his second *Erato* a poem which he entitled "Childe Harold" in Byron's honor; and his example was followed by William Ross Wallace a little later. For Wallace, Byron is the "Great Bard," whose "deathless name" is crowned with glory:

> ITALIA brightly breathes of thee,
> And SCIO with her coral sea!—
> Immortal GREECE hath caught the tone,
> The ALPS repeat it on their throne![88]

Scott's influence on Whiting's Indian metrical romances, *Ontwa* and *Sannillac*, has been noticed at some length. Beach's *Escalala* was scarcely less indebted to the same model. Imitation descended even to parody in such verse as Hall's dedicatory lines "Oh! a new SOUVENIR is come out of the west."[89] Mrs. Hentz's *Lamorah* afforded, on the stage, an example of plain plagiarism in the Indian girl's song of warning, on the model of Blanche of Devan's.[90] Gallagher, who had done honor to Byron in a "Childe Harold," nevertheless placed Scott first, though not for his poetry. In an ode to "the Author of Waverley" he prophesies for Scott future glory as a twin star in greatness with the "Man of Destiny."[91] James H. Perkins, in his praise of the power of literature to transform

---

[87] Peirce, *The Odes of Horace in Cincinnati*, 1822, pp. 51-55.

[88] William Ross Wallace, "Childe Harold," in *The Battle of Tippecanoe, Triumphs of Science, and Other Poems*, 1837, p. 87.

[89] *The Western Souvenir*, ed. James Hall, n. d. (1829), p. 10.

[90] *The Western Monthly Magazine*, I, 64 (Feb., 1833).

[91] *The Cincinnati Mirror and Ladies' Parterre*, Mar. 16, 1833.

reality into a world of the imagination, names Scott as one
of the chief masters of this kind of magic:

> In her great name we need but call
> Scott, Schiller, Shakspeare, and, behold! [92]

Both Scott and Byron, moreover, received not only the
tribute of popular applause and the praise of the writers
of fiction and of poetry, but also the suffrage of the reviewers, especially during the early years of their fame.
The Western Review and Miscellaneous Magazine, which
was at this time the only important critical journal in the
West, had little but admiration to express for the author
of the Waverley novels. Every volume of Scott's fiction
which appeared in 1819 and from that time till the *Review*
ceased publication, in 1821, was discussed at length in the
pages of this early censor of literary taste on the frontier.
Something of the importance which the editor attached to
the Scotch novels is shown by the promptness with which
the reviews followed the appearance of the books — every
one of these articles, in fact, appeared in the same year with
the publication of the work on which it was based. *Ivanhoe*
was reviewed in May, 1820; *The Monastery*, in July; and
The Abbot, in October and December. *Kenilworth* was
praised in April of the following year; and specimens of
The Pirate were printed in the number for July — the last
issue of the magazine — before the novel had been published
in America, we are told. The criticisms, not all by the
same hand, are unanimous in their praise of Scott. "We
do not hesitate," wrote the author of one of them,

to avow the sentiment of congratulation, which we cherish
toward the present period of the world on account of the
appearance of Waverley and its successors. There is no
thing in ancient literature, which the classical scholar can

---

[92] "Poverty and Knowledge," in William T. Coggeshall, *The
Poets and Poetry of the West*, 1860, p. 160.

bring forward as an offset for these delightful and masterly productions of modern genius. . . .

We cannot dismiss our miscellaneous comments upon the Abbot, without expressing our gratitude to the author for the reiterated and accumulating pleasure, which his works afford us. If this man be Walter Scott, it is his own fault that we are made to forget his poetry in the superior interest of his prose. We would rather have the fame, acquired by these novels and justly due to them, than that of any living bard whatever; not that talents equal to Byron's are shown, but the former are pure and holy, while the latter are corrupt and damning.[93]

Byron, whose *Mazeppa* was appreciated in the same *Review* for October, 1819, though praised only with some reserve, was willingly granted supreme genius. The writer of the criticism of *Mazeppa* found the poem "spirited and excellent" and took occasion to protest against the attacks of Eastern papers on Byron.[94] The early cantos of *Don Juan*, which were reviewed in the same magazine some months later, evoked, however, less decided praise. The spectres of Byron's immorality and irreverence haunted the mind of the critic. "Much good, or much evil," he ventured to predict, "may be drawn from Don Juan, and will be drawn by readers of different ages and tastes."[95] The *Review*, whose final issue contained an appraisal of *The Prophecy of Dante*, was not succeeded during Byron's lifetime by any critical periodical of like importance; but in such minor writings of the kind as did appear at that time it is clear that the question of morality, as raised by *Don Juan*, troubled the poet's admirers, who entertained only a faint hope that he might return to his earlier manner. In

---

[93] *The Western Review and Miscellaneous Magazine*, III, 255 and 260 (Dec., 1820).

[94] *Ibid.*, I, 164-170 (Oct., 1819).

[95] *Ibid.*, II, 16 (Feb., 1820). *The Prophecy of Dante* was reviewed in July, 1821 (IV, 321-328).

the year of Byron's death, a writer in the most prominent Western literary journal wrote thus of *The Island*:

His Lordship has here returned, with some success, to the heroic measure of "THE CORSAIR;" but we fear he has too long been debasing himself with the splendid ribaldry of *'Don Juan,'* ever wholly to regain the purer power and pathos of his earlier muse. Some portions of the present poem, however, are not unworthy of the genius which painted in such glowing colours the loves and sufferings of *Conrad* and *Medora*.[96]

V

The other great romantic poets — Wordsworth, Coleridge, Shelley, and Keats — were little noticed in the midst of the excitement attending the triumphal reception of Byron and Scott. So far as it may have been intended to apply to the West, Harriet Martineau's declaration that "Byron is scarcely heard of" but that "Wordsworth lies at the heart of the people" could hardly have been wider of the mark. Wordsworth's name, she wrote,

may not be so often spoken as some others; but I have little doubt that his influence is as powerful as that of any whom I have mentioned. It is less diffused, but stronger. His works are not to be had at every store; but within people's houses they lie under the pillow, or open on the work-box, or they peep out of the coat-pocket: they are marked, remarked, and worn.[97]

Such an estimate must have resulted, not from careful observation, but from the writer's own enthusiasm for Words-

---

96 *The Cincinnati Literary Gazette*, Jan. 24, 1824. For evidence that Western reviewers continued in later years to regard Byron in the same light, see *The Western Monthly Magazine*, I, 293 (July, 1833), where Byron is classed among those writers who have been "fearfully profane, and scandalously immoral," while Scott is, in contrast, placed among those "who dare to write like gentlemen and christians."

97 Martineau, *op. cit.*, II, 311.

worth. "Coleridge," she added, with much better judgment, "is the delight of a few." And the reputation of Shelley and Keats was, as a matter of fact, not only later, but even much less. *Lyrical Ballads* was to be found in the Lexington Library as early as 1815,[98] seventeen years after its appearance in England; but there were few other signs of either one of its authors until much later. "We are Seven" (with the original opening line) became, after 1825, a somewhat popular newspaper gem;[99] and Coleridge's "Love" enjoyed a similar notoriety.[100] It is a more striking fact, however, that the volume containing "Christabel," "Kubla Khan," and "The Pains of Sleep" was to be had in Lexington by January, 1818.[101] In libraries and sales collections during the period ending in 1840, there is only scant testimony to the fame of Wordsworth, Coleridge, Shelley, and Keats. In the forty-page list of books advertised by one of the chief Ohio booksellers in 1831, none of these four authors was included;[102] and from the catalogue of the same firm for 1833, Wordsworth was still absent. Two years later a minor list of Detroit booksellers, sufficiently large to include Coleridge, Shelley, and Keats, showed the same disregard of Wordsworth.[103] Curiously enough, a number of libraries exhibited exactly the same interest in Coleridge, Shelley, and Keats and lack of attention to Wordsworth.[104] Perhaps the vogue of the three

[98] *Catalogue of the Books in the Lexington Library*, 1815, p. 68.

[99] See, for example, *Ky. Gaz.*, July 15, 1825; and *Cinc. Daily Gaz.*, Nov. 28, 1839.

[100] "Love" was printed, for example, in the *Detroit Gaz.*, Feb. 25, 1820; *Liberty Hall*, June 28, 1820; *The Cincinnati Literary Gazette*, Feb. 26, 1825; *Mo. Rep.*, Oct. 7, 1828.

[101] Advertised in *Ky. Reporter*, Jan. 14, 1818.

[102] *A Catalogue of Valuable Books, for Sale by Isaac N. Whiting*, 1831.

[103] Snow & Fisk's list, *Detroit Daily Free Press*, Dec. 5, 1835.

[104] See *A Catalogue of Books Belonging to the Library of the*

former, small as it was, was due in part to the fact that all of these poets were early to be had together in a single volume. It was, at all events, this one-volume edition that was usually contained in the lists mentioned. In the library of perhaps over four thousand volumes owned by the State of Ohio in 1840, it is again the same collection of the three poets which appears; but in this case Wordsworth too is represented.[105]

It is, indeed, clear that the fame of these great romanticists was only beginning to make itself felt in the West, and that their reputation was still in the hands of the reviewers, who praised them in an apologetic tone but were sometimes openly hostile. As early as 1820 we find such timid recommendation of the older poets of the group as this:

We can see very great poetical excellencies, not only in SOUTHEY, SCOTT, and CRABBE, but in WORDS-WORTH, HOGG, LEIGH HUNT, and even in COLE-RIDGE. The short piece, entitled "Pains of Sleep," by the last writer, is an admirable picture of mental distress in a dream.[106]

In later years the critics were especially concerned about the obscurity of Coleridge's prose, but at the same time grew bolder in their praise of his poetry. The author of

Philomathesian Society of Kenyon College, 1834; _A Catalogue of the Honorary and Ordinary Members of the Erodelphian Society of Miami University, with a List of the Books Belonging to the Society's Library_, 1835; and _A Catalogue of Books Belonging to the Young Mens' Mercantile Library Association of Cincinnati_, n. d. (1838). All of these lists include Coleridge, Shelley, and Keats; but none of them mentions Wordsworth.

[105] See _Catalogue of the Ohio State Library_, 1840, pp. 56-57. _Cf._ also the catalogue of this library for Dec., 1832, pp. 26-27, where the same editions of these authors are listed.

[106] _The Western Review and Miscellaneous Magazine_, II, 5 (Feb., 1820). For bare mention of the Duddon sonnets, see _ibid._, II, 316 (June, 1820).

verses "To Coleridge, after Reading Some of his Darker Writings" [107] regrets the attempts at prose which occupy the attention of one who should devote himself to poetry alone. "His imagination," said another commentator, writing in the year following Coleridge's death,

flew meteorlike athwart his calmer and more starlike philosophy. His mind might be said, to use his own language, to be "self-dazzling, because of its own exceeding brightness." But this brightness was not the light of noon-day. Coleridge was a MYSTIC — a beautiful, wonderful one, but still a Mystic.[108]

The publication in 1836, at both New York and Cincinnati, of *Letters, Conversations and Recollections*, aroused new interest in this author. W. D. Gallagher found in these pages proof that Coleridge was

forever grumbling, because of a petulant and jealous disposition, and dissatisfied with existing canons of criticism, existing forms of government, existing administrations of justice, and existing philosophies.

Nor did the critic have a high opinion of Coleridge as philosopher. "We confess at once," he said, "that we do not comprehend him." Yet Gallagher granted him the possession of great genius:

for Coleridge the Poet, as we have known him from boyhood, and Coleridge the Man, as we behold him in parts of the volume before us, our respect borders on veneration.[109]

A somewhat lengthy appreciation which appeared in an important periodical exactly three years later showed the continued growth of Coleridge's reputation at the end of the pioneer period.[110]

---

[107] *The Western Monthly Magazine*, I, 214 (May, 1833).

[108] *The Western Messenger*, I, 221 (Sept., 1835).

[109] This and the preceding quotation are from *The Western Literary Journal, and Monthly Review*, I, 199 and 203-204 (Aug., 1836).

[110] See *The Western Messenger*, VII, 258-264 (Aug., 1839).

No doubt Byron and the British reviews were responsible for the fashion which was prevalent among frontier critics of overemphasizing the simplicity of Wordsworth. As early as 1828 we hear of him as "that celebrated poet" the admirers of whose simplicity are challenged "to point out, in all his works, or in those of his disciples, a single verse, which is as simple, as descriptive, or which contains so much matter in small compass" as some of the songs of the Western river men.[111] In later years a few voices of enthusiastic praise were, indeed, to be heard. James H. Perkins, in *The Western Messenger*, reproached "that poor school of critics of which Francis Jeffrey walked foremost" and asserted Wordsworth's right to stand beside Milton in the front rank of the English poets.[112] But Perkins frankly admired Wordsworth more as "a great Christian philosopher" than as a poet. Probably no finer tribute to the glory of the earlier Wordsworth was paid by a Western writer than Christopher P. Cranch's poem "To my Sister M., with Wordsworth's Poems." [113] At length, the poet of "Tintern Abbey" received homage; the young priest of nature was recommended as a "thoughtful sage and poet" and "a hallowed name." Doubtless Wordsworth became better known in the West after Professor Reed's American edition of 1837, of which, at any rate, there are some notices.[114] But what is perhaps the last important critical

---

[111] Hall, *Letters from the West*, 1828, p. 92. For a very brief notice of Wordsworth, half a dozen years later, in which the poet's quality of "devout simplicity" is emphasized, see *The Western Monthly Magazine*, II, 311-312 (June, 1834). An earlier and more favorable comment on Wordsworth, inspired by the "Song at the Feast of Brougham Castle," occurs in Timothy Flint, *Francis Berrian*, 1826, I, 188.

[112] *The Western Messenger*, I, 460-465 (Jan., 1836).

[113] *Ibid.*, IV, 375-376 (Feb., 1838).

[114] See, for example, *ibid.*, III, 783 (June, 1837); and *Mo. Rep.*, Nov. 3, 1837.

comment on his poems during the pioneer period returns to the old formula of Byron and Jeffrey. In the writings of the group among whom Wordsworth is chief, declares Otway Curry,

both poetry and doggerel are so constantly and ludicrously intermingled that there is a good deal of difficulty in determining which is the predominating material.[115]

"Strange fits of passion have I known" is offered as an example of Wordsworth's shortcomings.

Aside from his appearance in the same volume with Coleridge and Keats, there seems to be no evidence that Shelley was known at all until long after his death.[116] Even then his fame was almost wholly confined to two reviews. The *Messenger* condemned with measure his extravagant behavior and radical opinions, but admired his poetry. He was a "much reprobated, little read, and less understood son of the Muses," who was, nevertheless, without a superior in power of imagination.[117] *The Hesperian* accorded him even more generous praise, contrasting him favorably with Wordsworth.[118]

Almost the only recognition which Keats received was, it would seem, due to the circumstance of his brother's residence in Louisville and acquaintance with the editor of the *Messenger*. The publication, for the first time, of some of Keats's verse and prose in this magazine [119] marks the point of closest connection between the great English poets and Western periodicals. Moreover, James Freeman Clarke,

---

[115] *The Hesperian*, II, 444 (Apr., 1839).

[116] The earliest sign of Shelley I have come upon is a copy of his posthumous "Song" beginning "Rarely, rarely, comest thou," in *The New-Harmony Gazette*, May 14, 1828.

[117] *The Western Messenger*, III, 474-478 (Feb., 1837).

[118] *The Hesperian*, II, 440-447 (Apr., 1839).

[119] See above, Chapter III, footnotes 150-152.

at that time in charge of the *Messenger*, deserves recognition as one of the first critics to realize the value of the poet's prose. "We wished," he wrote,

to say a word of the prose writings of Keats.

These have not hitherto been published, but it appears to us, from the specimens which we have seen of them, that they are of a higher order of composition than his poems. There is in them a depth and grasp of thought; a logical accuracy of expression; a fulness of intellectual power, and an earnest struggling after truth, which remind us of the prose of Burns.[120]

The praise in the *Messenger* was echoed the following year by *The Western Monthly Magazine, and Literary Journal*, where a lengthy criticism did honor to Keats as a poet of no ordinary power, and, unfortunately, helped perpetuate the misconception of him already spread abroad by *Adonais*. "The subject of this article," it was declared,

is a striking instance of the melancholy effects of ill-natured and malicious criticism upon a sensitive mind conscious of its own powers; it may be truly said, that it brought him to an untimely grave.[121]

VI

If the philosophical poets and the more subtle masters of verse and imagery among the great romantic writers were only tardily recognized in the West, the most important early Victorians experienced a very different fortune. Tennyson had received the tribute of a review in the *Messenger* within half a dozen years after he had first come before the public. The author of this enthusiastic encomium had, he tells us, transcribed half the volume of *Poems, chiefly Lyrical* into his commonplace book, "as no other copy

[120] *The Western Messenger*, I, 773 (June, 1836).

[121] *The Western Monthly Magazine, and Literary Journal*, I, 259-264 (May, 1837).

could be found in any book store."[122] The same periodical published a formidable commentary on Thomas Carlyle as a German scholar,[123] and later noticed the same author as a historian.[124] *The Hesperian* gave even more space to this new writer.[125] Miss Martineau had already reported, indeed, that in America "No living writer, . . . exercises so enviable a sway, as far as it goes, as Mr. Carlyle;"[126] but according to Captain Marryat, a few years later, American publishing houses estimated that not more than six hundred copies of Carlyle had been printed and sold in the whole country.[127] Dickens was already an important name in the Western reviews,[128] and his fiction had begun to appear serially in frontier periodicals.[129]

VII

The literary influence of the Atlantic states in the West was widely diffused and of great significance. Eastern critics must often have furnished the mould in which Western literary estimates were formed. Especially was this true after the establishment of *The North American Review*, which became the official spokesman for American taste on points of difference from British opinion. Yet the hegemony of East over West was not marked by the extraordinary vogue of any important author belonging to

---

[122] *The Western Messenger*, II, 323-325 (Dec., 1836).

[123] *Ibid.*, IV, 417-423 (Feb., 1838). For earlier, but brief, comment on Carlyle, see *The Western Monthly Magazine*, V, 563-565 (Sept., 1836).

[124] *The Western Messenger*, V, 5-6 (Apr., 1838).

[125] *The Hesperian*, II, 5-20 (Nov., 1838).

[126] Martineau, *op. cit.*, II, 311.

[127] Marryat, *Second Series of a Diary*, 1840, p. 70.

[128] See *The Hesperian*, I, 257 (July, 1838).

[129] See, for example, *The Daily Chronicle* (Cincinnati), 1840, *passim*. For a suggestion of the already widespread borrowings from Dickens, see *The Rose of the Valley*, I, 240 (Oct.? 1839).

the older section of the country. The enthusiasm for the most popular poets and novelists of New England or New York was inconsiderable in comparison with that displayed for British writers.

Of the older colonial authors, perhaps none enjoyed any considerable following. *Essays to Do Good* were, it is true, reprinted at Lexington, and published by subscription, as late as 1822. But there is no substantial evidence that Cotton Mather or any other writer of his time was widely read. Among the earliest national writers, none but Joel Barlow seems to have been much known. During the first decade of the nineteenth century some of his verses were copied into the newspapers.[130] His works were to be found in a number of libraries, and so staunch was the patriotism of the West that *The Vision of Columbus* found even in one of the smaller backwoods towns a publisher willing to reproduce it.[131] There were some poetasters who, like Umphraville, could rank Barlow with Byron and Scott;[132] but no doubt the most pernicious effects of the epic bombast of the Eastern writer are to be found in the works of Emmons and Genin.

For the rest, there were the popular triumphs of such insignificant sentimental moralists as Selleck Osborn and Hannah Gould; the ephemeral reputation of James Gates Percival, N. P. Willis, and Fitz-Greene Halleck; the still uncertain allegiance to Washington Irving and James Fenimore Cooper; the more solidly established distinction of Bryant; and the beginnings of the fame of Holmes, Whittier, and Longfellow. Hawthorne attracted the attention

---

[130] See, for example, *Liberty Hall*, Mar. 24, 1807; and Nov. 22, 1809. A copy of the Lexington edition of Mather mentioned above is in the possession of Dr. Carl Van Doren.

[131] John C. Stockbridge, *A Catalogue of the Harris Collection of American Poetry*, 1886, p. 20.

[132] Umphraville, *op. cit.*, p. 5.

of a few critics. Emerson was scarcely a name. Poe was almost wholly unknown.

Perhaps nothing could better testify to the generally low state of public taste as interpreted or represented by pioneer journalists than that Selleck Osborn was admired for a score of years and that Hannah Gould succeeded to his honors.[133] Though Gorham Worth, in 1819, excepted Osborn alone from the wholesale condemnation of native poets,[134] there seems to have been no serious praise of the Eastern poetaster in the critical journals, the first of which was founded about this time. Miss Gould's reputation had likewise little support from the reviewers. Yet it is a reasonable conjecture that the products of these two New England writers, together with the even more popular banalities of such English authors as Moore and Mrs. Hemans, had no small share in the inspiration of the vast deal of mediocre verse published in the West before 1840.

Percival, whose example, as an early critic pointed out, may have influenced Gallagher's *Erato*,[135] was certainly known on the frontier within a short time after the appearance of the second *Clio*.[136] N. P. Willis was undoubtedly

[133] Osborn was probably the most popular American poet of the whole period if one may judge by the number of copies of his verses in the poetry corners of the newspapers. I have noted quotations from him as early as 1806 (*Liberty Hall*, Sept. 15 and 30; *Ky. Gaz.*, Nov. 6) and as late as 1825 (*The National Republican and Ohio Political Register*, Sept. 30; *Mo. Rep.*, Oct. 24). Miss Gould's vogue, of exactly the same kind, seems to have been greatest from 1830 to 1836. For a number of original contributions by her, see *The Western Monthly Magazine, passim*.

[134] Worth, *op. cit.*, p. 42.

[135] W. H. Venable, *Beginnings of Literary Culture in the Ohio Valley*, 1891, p. 446.

[136] For some early copies of his verse, see *Liberty Hall*, Sept. 14, 1824; *The National Republican and Ohio Political Register*, June 24 and July 8, 1825; *Detroit Gaz.*, Aug. 30, 1825; *Lou. Pub. Adv.*, Dec. 28, 1825.

among the most widely known of all Eastern authors.[137]
His writings served, in 1838, as the text for a notable plea
by Gallagher directed against the general neglect of American literature.[138] In comparison with Willis, Halleck
received slight attention in the West.

Irving was known on the frontier from the time of the
first parts of *The Sketch Book*, but praise of his work was
not unanimous.   Gorham Worth satirized him sharply, but
clearly with little claim to be heard:

If newspaper and magazine eulogies were to be admitted as
evidence in an estimate of literary merit, Mr. Irvine [*sic*]
and his coadjutors would outrank even the great classics of
antiquity. But alas! the arts of puffing and book-making,
the notorious co-partnership of authors and reviewers.[139]

Irving, he declared, might perhaps be considered "a very
pretty birth-day poet;" but "as a writer, claiming notoriety
and rank in the republic of letters, he is lamentably defi-
cient."   Worth had, he confessed, not yet read *The Sketch
Book*; but the specimens of it which he had seen in the
gazettes were, he believed, "surpassed, in the same department of writing, by at least fifty female novelists that might
be named."   In the following year, however, *The Sketch
Book* received a tribute from the Kentucky review which
was the chief purveyor of critical opinion at that time in
the West.[140]   The success of *The Spectre Bridegroom* and
Rip Van Winkle as adapted for the theatre [141] was a further
sign of Irving's growing reputation; and during his visit
to the West the author himself was "hailed with acclama-

---

[137] I have noticed fourteen copies of his verses in the *Lou. Pub.
Adv.* and *Mo. Rep.* alone from 1828 to 1837.

[138] *The Hesperian*, I, 263-277 (Aug., 1838).

[139] For this and the following quotations from the same critic, see
Worth, *op. cit.*, pp. 50-51.

[140] *The Western Review and Miscellaneous Magazine*, II, 244-254
(May, 1820).

[141] See above, Chapter VIII.

tion in the theatre of Cincinnati."[142] Gallagher, a little later, gave him rank, indeed, with Longfellow and Hawthorne; but found all three of these writers lacking in "force, comprehensiveness, intensity."[143]

As early as 1823 Cooper was heralded in the West as an American novelist who seemed to be running the career of the author of *Waverley*.[144] Yet the writer of the first important critical estimate of the native romancer, five years later, declared him worthy of respect only "as a man, whom we consider capable of doing far more than he has yet done," and was distressed to find, in the fiction which had then appeared, not only a lack of probability, but also a lack of moral aim. Cooper was afterwards attacked on the ground that in *The Prairie* he had failed lamentably to catch the true spirit of the West;[145] and some, who, like Governor Cass, were champions of the less attractive view of savage life, stoutly denied the veracity of his delineation of the Indians, though acknowledging his genius. "With the powers of invention and description displayed by this writer," Cass declared,

it is a source of regret that he did not cross the Allegany, instead of the Atlantic, and survey the red man in the forests and prairies, which yet remain to him. . . . His Uncas, and his Pawnee Hardheart, . . . have no living prototype in our forests. . . . They are the Indians of Mr Heckewelder, and not the fierce and crafty warriors and hunters, that roam through our forests.[146]

In spite of the strictures of such critics, however, Cooper's influence upon Western fiction was of importance, especially

---

[142] *The Western Monthly Magazine*, III, 333 (June, 1835).

[143] *The Hesperian*, III, 420 (Oct., 1839).

[144] See *Mo. Rep.*, Apr. 2, 1823; and *cf. The Western Monthly Review*, I, 604 and 606 (Feb., 1828).

[145] Daniel Drake, *Discourse on the History, Character, and Prospects of the West*, 1834, p. 55.

[146] *The North American Review*, XXVI, 373-376 (Apr., 1828).

in the case of M'Clung, who aspired, he says, to "wing a flight a little below Cooper;" [147] and the echo of the earlier novelist's fame in the frontier theatres has already been noticed.

Bryant began to be known in the West about 1825; [148] and, although he enjoyed no great popularity there, he soon became an important influence on such writers as Flint and Gallagher. Flint, who declared that his school was "the contemplation, and the study of nature," [149] and who demanded of his own critics an "imagination to admire" and a "heart to feel simple nature, as I have communed with her," [150] did not think of Wordsworth, but of Bryant, as his teacher. Even many American poets, he wrote, in 1829, were better known; but his own taste was for Bryant, "the poet of our country, if we might not say, of the age." [151] It is altogether likely that Bryant's example was also in Gallagher's mind when he wrote the best of his verses in the three numbers of *Erato*. The fact that letters which Bryant wrote during a visit to the West in 1832 show no evidence of his reception there as a famous poet [152] may, perhaps, be due to the incompleteness of the record or to his desire to avoid popular applause. There is, however, no very good reason to suppose that his name was widely known.

---

[147] John M'Clung, *Camden*, 1830, I, ix.

[148] For some early copies of his verse, see *Detroit Gaz.*, Nov. 21, 1823; *The National Republican and Ohio Political Register*, Jan. 14, 1825; *Ky. Gaz.*, Jan. 20, 1825; *Lou. Pub. Adv.*, Sept. 9, 1826.

[149] *The Western Monthly Review*, I, 18 (May, 1827).

[150] Timothy Flint, *The Shoshonee Valley*, 1830, I, iii.

[151] *The Western Monthly Review*, II, 483 (Feb., 1829).

[152] See *Prose Writings of William Cullen Bryant*, ed. Parke Godwin, 1884, II, 6-22. A few months after his visit, he was described in a Western review as a "poet of acknowledged originality and power" and "emphatically a poet of nature" (*The Western Monthly Magazine*, I, 85 and 87, Feb., 1833).

In 1830, the year of its first appearance, "Old Ironsides" was copied into a Western paper;[153] and others of Holmes's poems, first published in *The New-England Magazine*, were to be found in a frontier print two years later.[154] But there is little evidence that this poet's reputation increased greatly before 1840. William Ross Wallace, as we have seen, wrote an imitation of "Old Ironsides." In *The Western Messenger*, always sympathetic with New England literary opinion, or even in advance of it, the *Poems* of 1836 were reviewed with generous praise; and in the same periodical there appeared some stanzas contributed by Holmes and not previously published.[155]

Of the great quantity of Whittier's youthful journalistic verse, the West early received some share. "Spirit of the Pestilence," printed in *The Daily Cincinnati Gazette*, of June 21, 1830, was described as an unpublished poem, from manuscript.[156] To another Cincinnati paper he sent verses in honor of Clay,[157] with whose political fortunes he was soon to be more intimately connected through George Dennison Prentice, Whittier's predecessor in the editorial chair of *The New England Review*. Among Western critics, Gallagher was early to recognize the Quaker poet's genius. He not only copied some of Whittier's poetry in 1832,[158]

---

[153] *Daily Lou. Pub. Adv.*, Oct. 5, 1830.

[154] *Mo. Rep.*, Feb. 28 and Apr. 10, 1832.

[155] For the review, see *The Western Messenger*, III, 684-689 (May, 1837); for the poem contributed to the *Messenger*, see above, Chapter III, footnote 155.

[156] So far as I am aware, this poem is not among the large number of Whittier's which have, in recent years, been salvaged from the files of obscure newspapers. It seems to have remained unknown.

[157] Samuel T. Pickard, *Life and Letters of John Greenleaf Whittier*, 1895, I, 74. For what is presumably a copy of the same verses, see *Ky. Reporter*, Sept. 7, 1831.

[158] *The Cincinnati Mirror and Ladies' Parterre*, Jan. 7, 1832.

but pointed him out as a "man whom his countrymen will yet delight to honor." [159]

Longfellow, though not wholly unknown as early as 1826,[160] gained the suffrage of few critics until 1839, when, with the publication of *Voices of the Night,* his popularity began. As late as the preceding year, *The Hesperian* had found, as has been seen, that Longfellow was, like Irving, lacking in certain cardinal qualities of literary greatness. The *Louisville Literary News-letter,* of which Edmund Flagg, a fellow collegian of Longfellow's, had recently been editor, was perhaps the first journal in the West to begin the enthusiastic praise of the author of *Voices of the Night.*[161]

Hawthorne, still in the period of *Twice-told Tales,* was, of course, very little esteemed. The best we hear of him is that he belongs to "the Irving and Longfellow school of writers; and without possessing the sparkling fancy or original genius of either of these authors, is eminently worthy of being called their disciple." [162] A year later the same review again classed Hawthorne as a member of this school and a sharer in its faults and virtues.

Emerson's contributions to *The Western Messenger* have already been noticed.[163] There is, perhaps, no other evidence that he was known at all on the frontier; but in one instance, at any rate, among a remarkable group of New England men who were missionaries not only of religion but of literature among the Ohio River towns, he was

---

[159] Venable, *op. cit.,* p. 444.

[160] For a reprint of "Burial of the Minnisink," published as a specimen of *The Atlantic Souvenir,* for 1827, see *Mo. Rep.,* Dec. 7, 1826.

[161] *Louisville Literary News-letter,* Jan. 25, 1840.

[162] *The Hesperian,* I, 416 (Sept., 1838).

[163] See above, Chapter III.

praised generously and intelligently. The *Messenger* was even a partisan of the persecuted author of the Divinity College address. For the Western editor there was nothing objectionable in this bold pronouncement; the address was rather a cause for delight.[164] Of the hitherto unpublished verses which Emerson sent — "The Humble-bee" and others of his best — the editor knew the true value. He found in them the "same antique charm, the same grace and sweetness, which distinguish the prose writings of our author."[165]

---

[164] See "R. W. Emerson, and the New School," and a supplementary article, *The Western Messenger*, VI, 37-47 (Nov., 1838).

[165] *Ibid.*, VI, 229 (Feb., 1839).

BIBLIOGRAPHIES

The bibliographies which follow are intended as a record (necessarily incomplete) of works published before 1841 either by citizens of the Middle West or by travellers who described the Middle West from their own observation. A few titles, however, not strictly within the limits thus defined have been included on account of their special significance. On the other hand, certain classes of publications, such as legal compilations, public documents, broadsides, and newspapers of no considerable importance, I have omitted so far as it was convenient to do so. Critical authorities later than 1840 or of other than Western origin are excluded from the lists here given; but those which have served in any way as a basis of the present study are cited in the footnotes of various chapters and are to be found in the index.

Usually only the first American or English edition of any work is recorded in the bibliographies. Minor variations among copies contained in different libraries are not, except in a few instances, indicated. Unimportant irregularities in the numbering of pages have likewise been disregarded for the sake of brevity. Separate series of pagination are noted, but only one number is given when numerals of different styles are arranged consecutively or approximately so.

Except where the source is explicitly stated, the titles are from the originals (I have attempted to reproduce peculiarities of spelling and punctuation). Nothing has been drawn from Sabin or other such general bibliographies, where a few additional items are, however, to be found. Whenever possible I have named at least one library where each work listed is to be had, but I have made no attempt to supply a complete finding list. I have not been able to describe in detail the periodical and newspaper files in the possession of every library mentioned as possessing them; the record of issues included or lacking is often necessarily a very general one, and is sometimes based wholly upon information derived from card catalogues or printed check lists not cited below.

Besides those employed throughout this study for certain newspapers frequently cited, the following abbreviations are used below:

AmericanAS (American Antiquarian Society), Brigham (Clarence S. Brigham, "Bibliography of American Newspapers, 1690-1820," in *Proceedings of the American Antiquarian Society*, New Series, *passim*), BrownU (Brown University), BurColl (the Burton Historical Collection of the Public Library, Detroit), ChHist (Chicago Historical Society), ChPL (Chicago Public Library), ChU (University of Chicago), CinPL (Cincinnati Public Library), ColU (Columbia University), DaytonPL (Dayton Public Library and Museum), DePauwU (DePauw University), DetroitPL (Public Library, Detroit, general library), GrandRPL (Grand Rapids Public Library), Harvard (Harvard College), Henry (Edward A. Henry, *The Durrett Collection, now in the Library of the University of Chicago*, n. d. — a newspaper check list), HistPSO (the Historical and Philosophical Society of Ohio), IllStHist (Illinois State Historical Library), IllU (University of Illinois), IndStL (Indiana State Library), IU (Indiana University), JCrerar (the John Crerar Library), KyStHist (the Kentucky State Historical Society), KyStL (the Kentucky State Library), LaneTS (the Lane Theological Seminary), LexPL (Lexington Public Library, Lexington, Ky.), LC (Library of Congress), LC card (printed card of the Library of Congress), LouPL (Louisville Public Library), LWI (Library of the Workingmen's Institute, New Harmony, Ind.), MercLStL (St. Louis Mercantile Library), MiamiU (Miami University), MoHist (Missouri Historical Society, St. Louis), MoStHistS (the State Historical Society of Missouri, Columbia, Mo.), NewL (Newberry Library, Chicago), NYPL (New York Public Library), OhioStL (Ohio State Library), Smith (from original in stock of Smith Book Company, Cincinnati), Smith catalogue (trade list of Smith Book Company, Cincinnati — copy not made from the original), StLPL (St. Louis Public Library), TerreHautePL (Terre Haute Public Library), Thomson (Peter G. Thomson, *A Bibliography of the State of Ohio*, 1880), TransylvaniaU (Transylvania University, now Transylvania College), UMich (University of Michigan), USBurEd (United States Bureau of Education), USGeoS (United States Geological Survey), WRHist (the Western Reserve Historical Society), WisH (the State Historical Society of Wisconsin), WisU (University of Wisconsin), YMML (the Young Men's Mercantile Library, Cincinnati).

MS. copyright records of the old Western district courts for the period before 1841 now in the Copyright Office, Washington, D. C., are as follows: for District of Illinois, MS. book, 1821-1848; for District of Indiana, MS. book, 1822-1841; for District of Michigan, MS.

book, 1824-1857; for District of Ohio, MS. book, with numerous printed title-pages inserted, 1806-1828. The MS. entries have, with a few exceptions, been disregarded; but several of the printed title-pages inserted in the MS. book for Ohio have been copied below as evidence — not quite conclusive — of actual publication.

CHAPTER I

CULTURAL BEGINNINGS

I. Foreign Elements

A. *French and German Imprints*

1. French

a. Works of European Authorship

L'ame penitente ou le nouveau pensez-y-bien; consideration sur les ve'rite's eternelles, avec des histoires & des exemples. Nouvelle edition revue & augmentée par l'auteur de L'ame élevée à Dieu. 214, [2, badly mutilated] pp. Au Detroit, Imprimé par Jacques M. Miller, 1809. BurColl (incomplete copy). Complete copy in Diocesan Library at Detroit is said to contain 220 pp.

Epitres et evangiles; pour tous les dimanches et fetes de l'anne'e. Nouvelle edition. 396 pp. Detroit, Imprimé par T. Mettez, 1812. (French and English on opposite pages.) BurColl.

The Family Book, or Children's Journal. Consisting of Moral & Entertaining Stories, . . . From the French of M. Berquin. . . . New edition. 252 pp. Detroit, Printed by Theophilus Mettez, 1812. (French and English on opposite pages; French title-page lacking.) BurColl.

Neuvaine a l'honneur de St. François Xavier, de la Compagnie de Jesus; apotre des Indes, et du Japon. Nouvelle edition, avec l'ordinaire de la messe, prières pour la confession & . . . les vêpres du D—— [mutilated].

42

72 pp. Detroit, Imprimé par A. Coxshaw, 1810. BurColl; Diocesan Library, Detroit.

Petit catachisme historique, contenant en abregé l'histoire sainte . . . Par M. Fleury . . . Nouvelle edition. 201, [6] pp. Detroit, Imprimé par Theophile Mettez, 1812. (French and English on opposite pages.) BurColl.

Les ornemens de la memoire; ou les traits brillans des poetes francois les plus celebres; avec des dissertations sur chaque genre de style, pour perfectionner l'education de la jeunesse. 132 pp. Au Detroit, Imprime' par A. Coxshaw, 1811. BurColl.

Table generale des fetes d'obligation. Fetes de devotion. Jeunes d'obligation. Jours d'abstinence & fetes mobiles accompagne'e de la priere pour le Pape. Qui doit étre placée à la tête du Nouveau pensez-y bien, des Neuvaines de S. Fr. Xavier, de Recueil des prieres pour la messe. &c. xii pp. Au Detroit, Imprime' par A. Coxshaw, 1811. From transcript in BurColl made from copy in Diocesan Library, Detroit.

b. Miscellaneous Broadsides

(Selected to illustrate the use of the French language in public proclamations, etc.)

Camp au Detroit le 16 d'août 1812. Capitulation pour la reddition du Fort Detroit, faite entre le Major General Brock, commandant les forces de sa Majeste' Britannique, d'une part: & le Brigadier Ge'ne'ral Hull, commandant l'arme'e du Nord-ouest des Etats-Unis, d'autre part. Broadside. BurColl.

Nous, les soussignes, habitants de la Cote des Poux, de la Riviere Rouge . . . Broadside, circular. BurColl.

Par William Hull, gouverneur du territoire de Michigan. Proclamation. . . . 19e jour d'octobre A. D. 1809,

. . . Jacques M. Miller, Imprimeur . . . Detroit.
Broadside. BurColl.

2. German

Eine kleine Sammlung harmonischer Lieder als die erste
Probe der anfangenden Druckerey anzusehen. Pagination incomplete. [75] pp. Gedruckt in Harmonie, Indiana, 1824. IndStL.

Herzens Opfer, eine Sammlung geistreicher Lieder, aus den
mehrsten jetzt üblichen Gesangbücher gesammlet; zum
öffentlichen und privat Gebrauch für Liebhaber des gött-
lichen Lebens. . . . [2], 352, [26] pp. Lancaster,
O., Gedruckt bey Eduard Schäffer, 1816. LC, WRHist.

B. *Writings in Foreign Languages by Members of French and German Colonies*

1. By Frenchmen

Badin, Stephen Theodore. Origine et progrès de la mission
du Kentucky, (Etats-Unis d'Amérique); par un témoin
oculaire. . . . 32 pp. Paris, chez Adrien le Clere,
1821. WRHist.

Du Bourg, Louis Guillaume. Officia propria pro Diœcesi
Ludovicenensi. Illmi ac Rmi. D. Ludovici Guillelmi du
Bourg Episcopi ejusdem diœcesis nec non Floridarum
jussu edita. 313 pp. S. Ludovici, apud Jacobum Cummins, 1821. MercLStL.

Lezay-Marnezia, Cl. Fr. Ad. de. Lettres écrites des rives
de l'Ohio, . . . viii, 144 pp. Fort-Pitt, an IX de
la République. HistPSO.

2. By Germans

Hoher Zweck und Bestimmung der Harmonie. [Etc.]
N. p. (Harmonie, Ind.), n. d. (1824). Pagination in-

complete. Fifty separate numbers. Heading varies, or, in some cases, is lacking. Nos. 12-50 were printed Feb. 28-Apr. 15, 1824. IndStL.

Steines, Friedrich. Erstes Uebungsbuechlein fuer Kinder welche schnell und gruendlich lesen lernen wollen. Von Friedrich Steines, Lehrer an der deutschen Volksschule in St. Louis, Missouri. Gedruckt von Wilhelm Weber. 1837. From unverified copy transmitted by William Clark Breckenridge.

Wislizenus, Friedrich Adolf. Ein Ausflug nach den Fel-sen-Gebirgen im Jahre 1839, . . . 122, [4] pp. St. Louis, Wilh. Weber, 1840. ColU, LC, WisH.

C. *French and German Periodicals*

1. French

La gazette française. Detroit, Oct. 31, 1825-? See above, Chapter I, footnote 18.

2. German

(For a few other German newspapers, of which I have examined no copies, see above, Chapter I, footnote 40.)

Das Westland. Nordamerikanische Zeitschrift für Deutsche. Herausgegeben von Dr. G. Engelmann und Capt C. Neyfeld in St. Louis. Erster Band. Heidelberg, Ver-lagshandlung von Joseph Engelmann. 1837. 378, [2] pp. (Published quarterly.) Library of John H. Gund-lach, St. Louis; MoHist (has only Ersten Bandes zweiter Heft — pp. 113-256, [2]). Title and pagination of first volume from copy made by Miss Stella M. Drumm.

Deutscher Anzeiger des Westens. St. Louis, Oct. 31, 1835-1840 (and later). StLPL (excellent file).

II. Means of Communication

Commencement of the Ohio Canal, at the Licking Summit, July 4th, 1825. 22 pp. Lancaster, O., Printed by John Herman, n. d. WRHist.

Geddes, James. Canal Report, Made by James Geddes, Esq. the Engineer Employed by the State of Ohio. . . . 14 pp. Columbus, Printed at the Office of the Columbus Gazette by P. H. Olmsted, 1823. HistPSO.

Kilbourn, John. Public Documents, concerning the Ohio Canals, which are to Connect Lake Erie with the Ohio River, . . . [3], 403, [1] pp. Columbus, Compiled and Published by John Kilbourn, 1828. HistPSO.

Lapham, I. A. A Documentary History of the Milwaukee and Rock River Canal. Compiled and Published by Order of the Board of Directors of the Milwaukee and Rock River Canal Company. 151, [2] pp. Milwaukee, Printed at the Office of the Advertiser, 1840. WisH.

Minutes, of the Proceedings of a Convention, Holden at Warren, Ohio, on the 13th of November, 1833; on the Subject of Connecting the Pennsylvania and Ohio Canals. 40 pp. Warren, O., Printed by J. G. McLain, n. d. HistPSO.

Rail-road from the Banks of the Ohio River to the Tide Waters of the Carolinas and Georgia. 30 pp. Cincinnati, Printed by James and Gazlay, 1835. LC, WRHist.

Sketch of the Geographical Rout [sic] of a Great Railway, by which it is Proposed to Connect the Canals and Navigable Waters, of New-York, Pennsylvania, Ohio, Indiana, Illinois, Michigan, Missouri, and the Adjacent States and Territories; . . . 2d ed. 48 pp. New York, G. & C. & H. Carvill, 1830. LouPL, NewL, WRHist.

Williams, John S. Report of the Engineer to the Cincinnati, Columbus and Wooster Turnpike Company. 23 pp. Cincinnati, John H. Wood, Printer, 1831. HistPSO.

——, and John Hartman. Address to an Enterprising Public upon the Improvement of Roads, and the Introduction of Track Roads. 17 pp. Cincinnati, Printed by N. & G. Guilford & Co., 1833. HistPSO.

III. PRINCIPAL TOWNS

A. *Municipal Records*

1. Chicago

The Laws and Ordinances of the City of Chicago. Passed in Common Council. 46, [6] pp. Chicago, Printed by Edward H. Rudd, 1839. ChHist.

2. Cincinnati

Act Incorporating the City of Cincinnati, and the Ordinances of Said City now in Force. . . . 160, 69-76 pp. Cincinnati, Morgan, Fisher, & L'Hommedieu, Printers, January, 1828. CinPL.

An Act Incorporating the City of Cincinnati, and a Digest of the Ordinances of Said City, of a General Nature, now in Force. . . . 164 pp. Cincinnati, Lodge, L'Hommedieu and Co., Printers, 1835. CinPL, WRHist.

MS. Minutes City Council as follows: Vol. I (1813-1818), Vol. II (1818-1824), Vol. III (1824-1827), Vol. IV (1827-1829), Vol. V (1829-1831), Vol. VI (1831-1833), Vol. VII (1833-1835), Vol. VIII (1835-1838), Vol. IX (1838-1839), and Vol. X (1839-1841). In office of City Clerk, Cincinnati.

Ordinances of the City of Cincinnati, from April, 1828, to September, 1829. . . . 68 pp. Cincinnati, Looker & Reynolds, Printers, 1829. CinPL.

Proceedings of the Corporation of the Town of Cincinnati, with the Act of Incorporation. 48 pp. Cincinnati, Printed by J. Carpenter & Co., 1814. CinPL.

3.   Detroit

By-laws and Ordinances of the City of Detroit, as Revised
by the Recorder,   . . .   viii, 100 pp.   Detroit, Printed
at the Franklin Job Office, 1836.   BurColl.

By-laws and Ordinances of the City of Detroit, Made since
the Organization of the First Common Council, of the
City, September 21, 1824.   . . .   62, [2] pp.   Detroit, Printed by Chipman and Seymour, 1825.   BurColl.

By-laws and Ordinances of the City of Detroit, to which
is Prefixed the Revised Charter of Said City, Approved,
April 4, 1827.   88, [2] pp.   Detroit, Printed by Geo. L.
Whitney, 1831.   BurColl.

Journals and proceedings of the Board of Trustees and of
the Common Council recently printed under the following titles: *Corporation of the Town of Detroit Act of
Incorporation and Journal of the Board of Trustees
1802-1805*, ed. C. M. Burton, x, 86 pp., n. p., 1922
(BurColl) ; *Proceedings of the Board of the Trustees of
the City of Detroit from the Time of Organization October 24, 1815, to September 6, 1824*, 93 pp., n. p., n. d.
(BurColl) ; and *Journal of the Proceedings of the Common Council of the City of Detroit.   From the Time of
its First Organization.   September 21, A. D. 1824* [in-
cludes the period 1824-1843], 884 pp., n. p., n. d.
(BurColl).

4.   Lexington

MS. minutes of Trustees and Councilmen as follows: No.
1 (1782-1811), No. 2 (1811-1817), No. 3 (1818-1830),
No. 4 (1830-1836), No. 6 (1840-1843).   In office of the
City Clerk, Lexington (No. 5 missing).

5.   Louisville

A Collection of the Acts of Virginia and Kentucky, Relative to Louisville and Portland: with the Charter of the

City of Louisville and the Amendments thereto. Made under the Direction of the Mayor and Council. 211 pp. Louisville, Prentice and Weissinger, 1839. LouPL.

MS. Records of the Board of Trustees and City Council as follows: town Records for 1781-1825 and 1825-1828; city Records and Journals, No. 1 (1828-1829), No. 2 (1829-1831), No. 3 (1831-1832), No. 4 (1832-1834), No. 5 (1834-1835), No. 6 (1835-1836), No. 7 (1836-1838), No. 8 (1838-1840), and No. 9 (1840-1841). In office of the Clerks of the Boards of Aldermen and Councilmen, Louisville.

6. St. Louis

MS. town ordinances for the years 1809-1823; and city ordinances (printed, bound in improvised volume) for 1823-1839. In Municipal Reference Library, St. Louis.

The Revised Ordinances of the City of Saint Louis; Revised and Digested by the Board of Aldermen, during the Years 1835 and 1836. . . . [2], 261 pp. St. Louis, Printed at the Office of the Missouri Argus, 1836. MoHist.

7. Vincennes

Ordinances of the Borough of Vincennes, with the Act of Incorporation and Supplement thereto Prefixed. 64 pp. Vincennes, Printed by Stout & Osborn, 1820. IndStL (title-page and other pages restored by photostat).

B. *Directories*

1. Chicago

The Laws and Ordinances of the City of Chicago. Passed in Common Council. 46, [6] pp. Chicago, Printed by Edward H. Rudd, 1839. (Pp. 41-46 contain Chicago business directory.) ChHist.

2.   Cincinnati

The Cincinnati Directory, . . . By a Citizen. 155, [1] pp. N. p. (Cincinnati), Oliver Farnsworth, October, 1819. ChU, CinPL, HistPSO, LC, WRHist, WisH, YMML.

The Cincinnati Directory, for 1825, . . . By Harvey Hall. 137, [5] pp. Cincinnati, Printed by Samuel J. Browne, 1825. CinPL, LC, WRHist, WisH, YMML.

The Cincinnati Directory, for the Year 1829: . . . 201, [33] pp. Cincinnati, Robinson and Fairbank, 1829. CinPL, LC, LouPL, WRHist, WisH, YMML.

The Cincinnati Directory, for the Year 1831: . . . [19], 213, [1] pp. Cincinnati, Robinson & Fairbank, 1831. CinPL, HistPSO, LC, WRHist.

The Cincinnati Directory, for the Year 1834; . . . To which is Appended a Statistical Account of the Towns of Covington and Newport, Ky. [20], 266, [2] pp. Cincinnati, E. Deming, 1834. CinPL, LC, WRHist.

The Cincinnati Directory, for the Years 1836-7: . . . [24], 252 pp. Cincinnati, J. H. Woodruff, 1836. CinPL, LC, WRHist, WisH, YMML.

The Cincinnati, Covington, Newport and Fulton Directory, for 1840: . . . By David Henry Shaffer. 520 pp. Cincinnati, Printed by J. B. & R. P. Donogh, n. d. (1839). CinPL, LC, WRHist, WisH, YMML.

3.   Cleveland

A Directory of the Cities of Cleveland & Ohio, for the Years 1837-38: Comprising Historical and Descriptive Sketches of Each Place— . . . By Julius P. Bolivar MacCabe. [38], 144 pp. Cleveland, Sanford & Lott, 1837. LC, WRHist, WisH.

4. Detroit

Directory of the City of Detroit, with its Environs, and Register of Michigan, for the Year 1837. . . . By Julius P. Bolivar MacCabe. [40], 114, [1] pp. Detroit, Printed by William Harsha, 1837. BurColl.

5. Lexington

"Lexington Directory, Taken for Charless' Almanack, for 1806." No Pagination. In *Charless' Kentucky, Tennessee, and Ohio Almanac for the Year 1806*, Lexington, Printed by Joseph Charless, n. d. LouPL, WisH.

"Directory of the Town of Lexington, for 1818." Pp. 37-47 in an almanac for 1819 (title-page lacking) published by Worsley & Smith, Lexington. LexPL. *Cf. Worsley & Smith's Kentucky Almanac and Farmer's Calendar, for . . . 1819*, Lexington, n. d.

Directory of the City of Lexington and County of Fayette, for 1838 & '39; . . . Also — a List of the Landholders in the County of Fayette, . . . By Julius P. Bolivar MacCabe. [32], 136 pp. Lexington, Printed by J. C. Noble, 1838. ChU, LexPL, WisH.

6. Louisville

The Louisville Directory, for the Year 1832: to which is Annexed, Lists of the Municipal, County and State Officers; with a List of Various Societies, and their Officers. Also, an Advertiser. 198 pp. Louisville, Richard W. Otis, 1832. HistPSO, WisH.

The Louisville Directory, for the Year 1836: . . . By G. Collins. [34], xiv, 95, [1] pp. Louisville, Prentice & Weissinger, 1836. LouPL.

The Louisville Directory, for the Year 1838-9: . . . By G. Collins. [8], 154, [16], 10 pp. Louisville, J. B. Marshall, Printer, 1838. LouPL.

7. St. Louis

The St. Louis Directory and Register, . . . By John
A. Paxton, . . . No pagination. St. Louis, Printed
for the Publisher, 1821. MoHist.

The St. Louis Directory, for the Years 1836-7: . . . By
Charles Keemle. viii, 46, [1] pp. MercLStL.

The St. Louis Directory, for the Years 1838-9: . . . By
Charles Keemle. [21], x, [3], 67, [2] pp. St. Louis,
Printed by C. Keemle, 1838. MoHist.

The St. Louis Directory, for the Years 1840-1: . . . By
Charles Keemle. xii, 84 pp. St. Louis, C. Keemle, 1840.
MoHist.

C. *Local Guidebooks and Registers*

Drake, Benjamin, and Edward Deering Mansfield. Cincinnati in 1826. 100 pp. Cincinnati, Printed by Morgan, Lodge, and Fisher, February, 1827. ChU, CinPL,
HistPSO, WRHist, WisH, YMML.

Drake, Daniel. Notices concerning Cincinnati. 60, [iv]
pp. Cincinnati, Printed for the Author, at the Press of
John W. Browne & Co., 1810. CinPL, HistPSO, LC,
NYPL, WRHist.

M'Murtrie, Henry. Sketches of Louisville and its Environs; Including, among a Great Variety of Miscellaneous Matter, a Florula Louisvillensis; . . . viii, 255
pp. Louisville, Printed by S. Penn, 1819. ChU, CinPL,
LC, LouPL, NYPL, WRHist, WisH.

Martin, William T. Franklin County Register, Comprising Regular Lists of All Civil Officers that have Served
in the County since its Organization, until 1834, . . .
To which is Prefixed, a Brief History of the Settlement
of the County. . . . 52 pp. Columbus, Scott and
Wright, 1834. WRHist, WisH.

Picture of Cincinnati. The Cincinnati Almanac, for 1839.

To be Continued annually. 88, [1] pp. Cincinnati, Glezen & Shepard, n. d. (1839). CinPL, HistPSO, WRHist.

Picture of Cincinnati. The Cincinnati Almanac, for 1840. To be Continued annually. 82, [1] pp. Cincinnati, Glezen & Shepard, n. d. ChU, HistPSO, LC.

IV. CHURCHES

A. *Associate Methodist Church, Zanesville, O.*

An Appeal to the Public. 10 pp. N. p., n. d. (1829). WRHist.

B. *Associate Reformed Church*

Extracts from the Minutes of the Proceedings of the Associate Reformed Synod of the West, . . . 1835, . . . 34 pp. Hamilton, O., Printed at the Hamilton Intelligencer Office, by Leonard Gibbon, 1835. WRHist. For the years 1833, and 1836-1839. WRHist.

A Warning against Hopkinsian, and Other Allied Errors, Addressed by the Associate Reformed Synod of the West, to the Churches under their Care. . . . 37, 6 pp. Hamilton, O., Printed by James B. Camron, n. d. (1825 ?). WRHist.

C. *Baptist Church*

1. West

Proceedings of the General Meeting of Western Baptists, at Cincinnati, . . . 1833. 80 pp. Cincinnati, N. S. Johnson, 1834. WRHist. For the years 1834-1837. WRHist.

2. Illinois Local Associations

Minutes as follows: Bloomfield, 1839 (IllStHist); Little Wabash, 1829 (IndStL); Union, 1829 (IndStL).

3. Indiana

a. General Associations

Minutes of the First Session of the General Association of
Baptists of Indiana, . . . Held near Shelbyville,
. . . April, 1833. 6, [1] pp. N. p., n. d. IndStL.
For 2d-3d, and 5th-7th sessions, Oct., 1833-Oct., 1839
(IndStL); and for 8th session, Oct., 1840 (IndStL,
WRHist).

b. Local Associations

Minutes as follows: Salem, 1828-1829 (IndStL); Union,
1825 and 1827 (IndStL); and Wabash District, 1822-
1829 (IndStL).

4. Kentucky

a. General Associations

Minutes of the General Association of Baptists in Kentucky, which Met for Organization in Louisville, on
Friday, October 20, 1837. . . . 19 pp. Louisville,
1837. ChU.

b. Local Associations

Minutes as follows: Baptist Association [of Woodford
County and probably the neighboring district], for 1828-
1829, 1831, and 1838-1840 (ChU); Elkhorn Association,
for 1821 (library of Samuel M. Wilson, Lexington, Ky.);
Highland . . . Union County, for 1829 (IndStL).

5. Michigan

Constitution of the Baptist Convention of the State of
Michigan, . . . Detroit, . . . 1836. Together
with their Address to the Baptist Churches of the State;
. . . 14, [1] pp. Detroit, Printed at the Franklin
Job Office, 1836. BurColl.

The Fifth Annual Report of the Baptist Convention, of
the State of Michigan, Held at Troy, . . . 1840.
. . . 12 pp. Detroit, Asahel S. Bagg, Printer, 1840.
BurColl.

6. Missouri

Minutes of local associations as follows: Mount Pleasant,
1826; Salem, 1827 and 1829-1839. MoStHistS.

7. Ohio

a. State Conventions

Ohio Baptist Convention. Proceedings of the Ninth Anniversary Held in Cleveland, . . . 1835. 20 pp. N.
p., n. d. WRHist. For the years 1836-1840. WRHist.

b. Local Associations

Minutes as follows: Bethel, 1832 (WRHist); Columbus,
1819, 1822-1829, and 1831-1840 (WRHist); Eagle Creek,
1827 and 1830-1831 (WRHist); East Fork of the Little
Miami, 1825 and 1827-1839 (WRHist); Geauga, 1836-
1840 (WRHist); Grand River, 1820-1821, 1823, 1828,
and 1830-1840 (WRHist); Harmony, 1840 (WRHist);
Huron, 1822 and 1824-1840 (WRHist); Little Miami
Union Regular, 1831-1835 and 1837 (WRHist); Lorain,
1838-1840 (WRHist); Mad-River, 1831 and 1833-1840
(WRHist); Maumee River, 1838-1839, and MS. for 1840
(WRHist); Miami, 1810-1811 and 1813-1840 (WRHist);
Miami — Old School, 1836-1840 (WRHist); Mohecan,
1825, 1828, and 1834-1840 (WRHist); Mohican Regular,
1837-1838 (WRHist); Muskingum, 1822, 1828, 1830,
1834, 1837, and 1840 (WRHist); Ohio, 1830-1831 and
1833-1840 (WRHist); Portage Regular, 1833-1840
(WRHist); Rocky River, 1832-1840 (WRHist); Salem,
1832-1840 (WRHist); Sandusky, 1836-1840 (WRHist);

Scioto, 1809-1810, 1812-1820, 1831, 1833-1837, and 1839-1840 (WRHist) ; Scioto Predestinarian, 1840 (WRHist); Trumbull, 1840 (WRHist) ; Wills Creek, 1840 (WRHist) ; Wooster Regular, 1840 (WRHist) ; and Zoar Regular, 1835-1840 (WRHist).

c. Individual Congregation

Declaration of Faith of the Regular Baptist Church of Christ, in Marietta, Ohio, Adopted March, 1823. Also, the Church Discipline. 8 pp. Marietta, O., E. Prentiss, Printer, 1823. WRHist.

D. *Congregational Church*

The Articles of Faith, and Covenant, of the Congregational Church, in Harmar, Ohio. Adopted at the Organization of the Church, January 1, 1840. . . . 20, [1] pp. Marietta, O., G. W. Tyler & Co., Printers, 1840. WRHist.

The Articles of Faith, Constitution and History of the Congregational Church, of Whitewater, . . . Butler County, Ohio. 8 pp. N. p. (Hamilton, O., W. C. Howells, Printer), n. d. (1840). LaneTS.

The Confession of Faith and Covenant Adopted by the First Congregational Church of Michigan City, April, 1839. 7 pp. Michigan City, Ind., Printed by L. C. M'Kenney & Co., 1839. IndStL.

The Confession of Faith, and Covenant of the Congregational Church of Christ, in Marietta, Ohio. . . . 16 pp. Cincinnati, Printed by J. A. James, 1834. WRHist.

E. *Disciples of Christ*

Circular Letter. The Elders and Brethren of the Wabash Christi[an Confer]ence, Assembled at Union Meeting House, in P[osey Coun]ty, Indiana, October 8th, 1830, . . . 4 pp. N. p., n. d. WisH.

F. *Evangelical Lutheran Church*

1. West

Journal of the Fifth Annual Session of the Evangelical Lutheran Synod of the West, Convened at Hillsboro, Illinois, October . . . 1839. 35 pp. Louisville, Printed by Penn & Eliot, 1839. LaneTS.

2. Ohio

Minutes of the First Session of the Eastern District of the Synod and Ministerium of the Evangelical Lutheran Church in the State of Ohio. Convened at Greensburgh, Pa., . . . 1834. 16 pp. Pittsburg, Printed by D. and M. Maclean, 1835. WRHist.

G. *Friends*

1. West

Declarations . . . respecting a Publication Entitled "A Beacon to the Society of Friends." . . . 8 pp. London, Edmund Fry & Son, etc., 1836. NewL.

Memorial of the Representatives of the Religious Society of Friends, in the States of Ohio, Indiana, and Illinois, Praying Adoption of Measures for the Civilization and Improvement of the Indians. December 23, 1818. . . . 4 pp. Washington, Printed by E. De Krafft, 1818. WRHist.

2. Indiana

Address to the People of the United States, . . . On the Civilization and Christian Instruction of the Aborigines of our Country. By Indiana Yearly Meeting of Friends, Held at Whitewater, . . . 1838. 16 pp. Cincinnati, A. Pugh, Printer, 1838. ChU, IndStL, LC, WisH.

At Indiana Yearly Meeting of Friends, Held at White

Water, . . . 1837. 29, 7, 8 pp. N. p., n. d. ChU.
For the years 1838-1840. ChU.

The Discipline of the Society of Friends, of Indiana Yearly
Meeting, Revised by the Meeting Held at White Water,
in the Year 1838, and Printed by Direction of the Same.
97 pp. Cincinnati, A. Pugh, Printer, 1839. ChU,
IndStL, WRHist.

Minutes as follows: 1821-1827 (but probably a reprint)
and 1830-1840. IndStL.

A Testimony, and Epistle of Advice, Issued by Indiana
Yearly Meeting; and Approved by the Meeting for Suf-
ferings of Ohio. 10 pp. Mountpleasant, O., Elisha
Bates, 1827. WRHist.

3. Ohio

a. Yearly Meeting

Advice as follows: for 1824, 1826, and 1832. WRHist.

A Declaration of Ohio Yearly Meeting, . . . 1828. 16
pp. N. p. (Mountpleasant, O.?), n. d. WRHist.

The Discipline of the Society of Friends, of Ohio Yearly
Meeting; Held at Mountpleasant, in the Year 1819. 102
pp. Mountpleasant, O., Printed by Elisha Bates, n. d.
WRHist.

An Epistle from Ohio Yearly Meeting, . . . 1820.
. . . Broadside. LC, WRHist.

Extracts from the Minutes of Ohio Yearly Meeting of
Women Friends, . . . 1825. Broadside. WRHist.

Extracts of Ohio Yearly Meeting, . . . 1820. [2] pp.
N. p., n. d. WRHist.

The Following Pages Contain All that could be Procured
. . . in Relation to the Petition of that Part of the
Society of Friends Called Orthodox, to the Legislature
of this State, for an Act to Incorporate the "Ohio Yearly
Meeting." 32 pp. (incomplete?). N. p., n. d. WRHist.

Minutes as follows: for the years 1828-1829 and 1832-1838. WRHist.

Report to the Yearly Meeting of Friends for the State of Ohio, in North America, from its Committee on Indian Concerns, Dated the 8th of 9th Mo. 1819. 4 pp. London, W. Phillips, Printer, n. d. WRHist.

b. Cincinnati Monthly Meeting

Memorial. A Testimony of Cincinnati Monthly Meeting of Friends, Held 19th of Seventh Month, 1838, concerning our Esteemed Friend Mary Anthony, . . . 7 pp. N. p., n. d. ChU.

H. *Harmony Society in Indiana*

Thoughts on the Destiny of Man, particularly with Reference to the Present Times; by the Harmony Society in Indiana. 96 pp. N. p. (Harmonie, Ind.?), 1824. IndStL, WRHist, WisH.

I. *Latter Day Saints*

Doctrine and Covenants of the Church of the Latter Day Saints: carefully Selected from the Revelations of God, and Compiled by Joseph Smith Junior, Oliver Cowdery, Sidney Rigdon, Frederick G. Williams, . . . 257, xxv pp. Kirtland, O., Printed by F. G. Williams & Co., for the Proprietors, 1835. WRHist, WisH.

J. *Methodist Episcopal Church*

Minutes of the Fourteenth Illinois Annual Conference of the Methodist Episcopal Church, Held in Jacksonville, Illinois, Sept. 27, 1837. 8 pp. Jacksonville, Ill., Printed by Brooks, Curran and Day, n. d.? (title-page slightly mutilated). IllStHist.

Minutes Taken at the Several Annual Conferences of the
Methodist Episcopal Church, Commencing in December,
1821, and Ending in November, 1822. 60 pp. Cincinnati, M. Ruter, for the Methodist Episcopal Church, 1822.
WRHist.

Minutes Taken at the Several Annual Conferences of the
Methodist Episcopal Church. For the Year 1826. 64
pp. Cincinnati, Martin Ruter, for the Methodist Episcopal Church, 1826. WRHist.

K.   *New Jerusalem Church*

Documents for the Consideration of the Members of the
Western Convention, in Coming to its Next Annual Meeting . . . June, 1839. 4 pp. N. p., n. d. CinPL.

L.   *Presbyterian Church*

1.   West

Proceedings of the Convention of Ministers and Elders. 8
pp. N. p. (Cincinnati?), n. d. (1838?). LaneTS.

2.   Indiana

An Address of the Synod of Indiana, to the Churches
under their Care, . . . 17 pp. N. p., n. d. LaneTS.

3.   Kentucky

a.   Synod

Address on Slavery. 24 pp. N. p. (Newburyport, Mass.?),
n. d. (1836?). From LC card.

An Address to the Presbyterians of Kentucky, Proposing a
Plan for the Instruction and Emancipation of their
Slaves, by a Committee of the Synod of Kentucky. 64
pp. Cincinnati, Taylor & Tracy, 1835. LaneTS, LC.

36 pp. Newburyport, Mass., Charles Whipple, 1836.
LouPL, WRHist, WisH.

A Brief History of the Rise, Progress, and Termination of
the Proceedings of the Synod of Kentucky, Relative to
the Late Cumberland Presbytery: . . . Published by
Order of Synod at their Sessions Held at Harrodsburgh,
Oct. 1822. 29 pp. Lexington, Printed by Thomas T.
Skillman, 1823. ChU, LaneTS.

A Serious Address from the Synod of Kentucky, to the
Churches under their Care. From *Ky. Gaz.*, Nov. 20,
1804.

b. Presbyteries

An Apology for Renouncing the Jurisdiction of the Synod
of Kentucky. To which is Added, a Compendious View
of the Gospel, and a Few Remarks on the Confession of
Faith. 116 pp. Lexington, Printed, 1804; Carlisle, Pa.,
Reprinted by George Kline, March, 1805. ChU.

Extracts from the Minutes and Papers of the Transylvania
Presbytery; and Other Documents Relative to James
Moore's Trials for the Gospel Ministry in the Presby-
terian Church. (Lexington, Office of Stewart's Ken-
tucky Herald, 1796.) From *Stewart's Kentucky Herald,*
Oct. 18, 1796.

The Presbytery of Transylvania, to the Churches under
their Care. 2 pp. N. p., n. d. (1802). ChU.

c. Individual Congregations

A Manual for the Members of the Second Presbyterian
Church in the City of Louisville, Kentucky. Compiled
by Rev. E. N. Sawtell, Pastor. Published by Order of
the Session. 52 pp. Louisville, M'Ginnis & Settle,
Printers, 1833. LouPL, WRHist.

4. Ohio

a. Synod

A Memorial on the Present State of the Presbyterian
Church. To be Presented to the General Assembly, to
Meet in Philadelphia, in May, 1834. 23 pp. Cincinnati,
Printed by James M'Millan, 1833. IU.

Extracts from the Minutes of the Synod of Cincinnati, at
its Late Meeting in Dayton, Ohio, 1840. 8 pp. N. p.,
n. d. ChU.

b. Presbyteries

The Confession of Faith, and Covenant, of Portage Presbytery. Adopted, April, 1835. 11 pp. Cleveland, Rice
& Penniman's Press, 1835. WRHist.

The Confession of Faith, and Covenant, of the Presbytery
of Grand River. Adopted, February 5, 1840. 8 pp.
Painesville, O., Philander Winchester, Printer, 1840.
WRHist.

Declaration of the Presbytery of Cincinnati Relative to the
Present State of the Presbyterian Church. 8 pp. N. p.,
n. d. (1838?). LaneTS.

A Summary Confession of Faith, Covenant, and Articles
of Practice, Recommended by the Presbytery of Cleveland to the Churches under their Care, to be Used in the
Admission of Members. 12 pp. New York, Sleight and
Robinson, Printers, 1832. WRHist.

Two Letters, on the Subject of Slavery, from the Presbytery of Chillicothe, to the Churches under their Care.
50 pp. Hillsborough: Printed by Whetstone & Buxton,
Cincinnati, 1830. LaneTS.

c. Individual Congregations

Catalogue of the Members of the Second Presbyterian
Church, in Cincinnati. [24] pp. Cincinnati, Printed
by F. S. Benton, 1835. WRHist.

M. *Protestant Episcopal Church*

1. Illinois

Journal of the Fourth Annual Convention of the Protestant Episcopal Church, of the Diocese of Illinois, Held in Rushville, on the 4th and 5th June, 1838. 31, [1] pp. N. p. (Quincy, Ill.), Printed at the Quincy Whig Office, 1838. BurColl.

Journal of the Primary Convention of the Clergy and Laity of the Protestant Episcopal Church, in the Diocese of Illinois, Held in Peoria, on Monday, March 9, 1835. 16 pp. Peoria, Printed at the Champion Office, 1835. BurColl.

2. Michigan

Journal of the First Annual Convention of the Protestant Episcopal Church of the Diocese of Michigan, Held at Monroe, M. T. May 3d, 1834. 22, [2] pp. Detroit, Printed by George L. Whitney, 1834. BurColl.

Journal of the Second Annual Convention . . . June 13th, 1835. 14 pp. Detroit, Printed by George L. Whitney, 1835. BurColl.

Journal of the Special Conventions of the Diocese of Michigan, Held at Detroit, in the Years 1835 and 1836. 35, [1] pp. Detroit, Printed by George L. Whitney, 1836. BurColl.

3. Ohio

a. Diocese

Journals of state conventions as follows: for the years 1818, 1821, 1823-1824, 1826, 1828-1829, and 1831-1840. BurColl (has 1835 only), WRHist.

b. Individual Congregations

A Declaration and Protest of the Wardens and Vestry of Christ Church, Cincinnati, against the Proceedings of

Bishop Hobart, and the Trustees of the General Theological Seminary of the Episcopal Church, in Relation to the Mission of Bishop Chase to England. 14 pp. Cincinnati, Looker and Reynolds, Printers, 1823. From Thomson.

A Letter from the Wardens and Vestry of Christ Church, Cincinnati, to the Rev. Henry U. Onderdonk, on the Conduct of Bishop Hobart towards Bishop Chase. 17 pp. Cincinnati, Looker & Reynolds, Printers, 1824. BurColl, WRHist.

N. *Shakers (United Society of Believers)*

1. Indiana

MS. account book of Shaker settlement at Busseron Creek, Knox County (later Sullivan County), Indiana (Feb. 23, 1815-Apr. 8, 1822). Leaves numbered, 123 (= 246 pp.). Title supplied. IndStL.

2. Kentucky

A Memorial, Remonstrating against a Certain Act of the Legislature of Kentucky, Entitled "An Act to Regulate Civil Proceedings against Certain Communities Having Property in Common" — . . . Approved Feb. 11, 1828. 8 pp. N. p. (Harrodsburg, Ky., Printed at the Union Office), n. d. JCrerar, LC, WRHist.

A Revision and Confirmation of the Social Compact of the United Society Called Shakers, at Pleasant Hill, Kentucky. . . . 12 pp. Harrodsburg, Ky., Printed by Randall and Jones, 1830. HistPSO, WRHist.

3. Ohio

The Constitution of the United Societies, of Believers (Called Shakers) . . . Pagination irregular. Watervliet, O., 1833. HistPSO, WRHist.

An Improved Edition of the Church Covenant, or Constitution of the United Societies, Called Shakers. . . . Pagination irregular. Dayton, O., 1833. HistPSO, WRHist.

V. AUXILIARY RELIGIOUS SOCIETIES

Algic Society. Constitution of the Algic Society, Instituted March 28, 1832. For Encouraging Missionary Effort in Evangelizing the North Western Tribes, and Promoting Education, Agriculture, Industry, Peace & Temperance, among them. . . . 23 pp. Detroit, Cleland & Sawyer, 1833. BurColl.

Associate Reformed Society. Constitution of the Associate Reformed Society of ———— for the Promotion of Christian Knowledge. 16 pp. Lexington, Printed by T. T. Skillman, 1812. ChU, HistPSO.

Bible Society of Lexington. Constitution of the Bible Society of Lexington and Vicinity, Auxiliary to the American Bible Society. Formed November 24th, 1836. [5] pp. Lexington, N. L. Finnell, Printer, Observer and Reporter Office, 1836. LexPL.

Chillicothe Association for Promoting Morality. Addresses of the Chillicothe Association, for Promoting Morality and Good Order, to their Fellow Citizens, on Profane Swearing, the Violation of the Sabbath, and the Intemperate Use of Ardent Spirits. 18 pp. Chillicothe, Printed by J. Andrews, 1815. From LC card.

Connecticut Reserve Bible Society. Eleventh Report . . . Presented May 4, 1825. 24 pp. Warren, O., Printed by Hapgood & Quinby, 1825. WRHist.

Detroit Young Men's Temperance Society. Constitution and By Laws of the Detroit Young Men's Temperance Society; also, a List of Officers and Members and the Address of the Executive Committee to the Young Men of the Territory.   15 pp.   Detroit, S. M'Knight, Printer, 1835.   BurColl.

Female Auxiliary Bible Society of Cincinnati.   Sixth Annual Report of the Female Auxiliary Bible Society of Cincinnati, for the Year Ending on the Last Thursday of July, 1822.   12 pp.   N. p., n. d.   LaneTS.

Female Bible Society of Lexington.   Second Report of the Female Bible Society of Lexington, Kentucky,   . . . 1825.   12 pp.   Lexington, Printed for the Society, by Thomas T Skillman, 1825.   TransylvaniaU.

Foreign Missionary Society of the Valley of the Mississippi. First Annual Report of the Foreign Missionary Society of the Valley of the Mississippi.   Auxiliary to the American Board of Commissioners for Foreign Missions.   Presented October 30, 1833.   [1], 40, [2] pp.   Cincinnati, Published for the Society by Truman, Smith & Co., 1834. IllStHist.   Third, presented 1835.   IllStHist, LaneTS. Eighth, presented 1840.   IllStHist.

Green Bay Mission.   Green Bay Mission School (no caption or title).   44 pp.   N. p., n. d. (1834?).   BurColl.

Illinois Sunday School Union.   Illinois Sunday School Union.   Proceedings of the Second Annual Meeting . . . Vandalia, December 7, 1831.   15 pp.   Rock-Spring, Ill., Printed at the "Pioneer Office," 1831. BurColl.   For fourth annual meeting (1833) and fifth (1834).   BurColl.

Indiana Branch of the Presbyterian Society.   Second Annual Report of the Directors of the Indiana Branch of the Presbyterian Society, Presented at the Annual Meeting, Held in Crawfordsville, October 17, 1832.   19, [3] pp.   Crawfordsville, Ind., Printed by I. F. Wade, 1832. IndStL.

Indiana Sabbath School Union.   First Annual Report of the Indiana Sabbath School Union, Containing its Constitution; . . . 26 pp. Indianapolis, Printed by John Douglass, 1827. IndStL.

Kentucky Bible Society. The Fifth Annual Report of the Board of Managers of the Kentucky Bible Society, . . . April 19, 1821. 24 pp. Lexington, Printed for the Society, by Thomas T. Skillman, 1821. ChU. Sixth, for 1822 (TransylvaniaU); and Eighth, for 1824 (ChU).

Michigan Temperance Society. First Annual Report of the Michigan Temperance Society. 16 pp. N. p. (Detroit, Geo. L. Whitney, Printer), n. d. (1834?). BurColl.

Minutes of the Convention of Delegates, Met to Consult on Missions, in the City of Cincinnati, A. D. 1831. . . . 22 pp. Lexington, Printed by Thomas T. Skillman, 1831. ChU, LaneTS, WRHist.

New Jerusalem Western Missionary Society. Proceedings of the First Annual Meeting of the New Jerusalem Western Missionary Society, Held in the Temple, Cincinnati, October 2, 1831: . . . 16 pp. Cincinnati, John H. Wood, Printer, 1831. WRHist.

A Report of the Minority in the Convention on Domestic Missions, Held in Cincinnati, November, 1831. 48 pp. Cincinnati, Printed at the Cincinnati Journal Office, 1831. ChU.

Western Agency of the Presbyterian Education Society. Annual Report of the Directors of the Western Agency of the Presbyterian Education Society, . . . Cincinnati, October 30, 1834. 17, [3] pp. Cincinnati, Printed by F. S. Benton, 1834. WRHist.

Western Board of Agency of the American Sunday School Union. Second Annual Report of the Western Board of Agency of the American Sunday School Union. Cincinnati, Nov. 8, 1837. 12 pp. Cincinnati, Printed by L'Hommedieu & Co., n. d. LaneTS.

Western Reserve Foreign Missionary Society. First An-

nual Report of the Directors of the Western Reserve
Foreign Missionary Society, Auxiliary to the American
Board of Commissioners for Foreign Missions: Presented
October 8, 1834. 20 pp. Hudson, O., Printed at the
Office of the Ohio Observer, 1835. WRHist. Second
(1835), Third (1836), and Sixth (1839). WRHist.

Wyandotte Mission. The Report of the Wyandotte Mission, at Upper Sandusky, Instituted and Conducted by
the Methodist Ohio Annual Conference: . . . 17 pp.
Dayton, O., G. [?] S. Houston & A. T. Hays, Printers,
1823. BurColl, WRHist.

Young Men's Bible Society of Cincinnati. Annual reports (First to Fifth), 1836-1840. HistPSO.

Young Men's State Temperance Convention [Michigan].
The Proceedings of the Young Men's State Temperance
Convention, Held at Ann Arbor, January 20, 1836. 14
pp. Detroit, Printed by Morse and Bagg, 1836. BurColl.

VI.   PUBLIC SCHOOLS

A.   *Kentucky*

An Account of the Louisville City School, together with the
Ordinances of the City Council, and the Regulations of
the Board of Trustees for the Government of the Institution. 24 pp. Louisville, Printed by Norwood & Palmer, 1830. LouPL, USBurEd.

B.   *Michigan*

Report of the Superintendent of Public Instruction of the
State of Michigan; . . . January 5, 1837. 60 pp.
Detroit, John S. Bagg, Printer, 1837. BurColl.

State of Michigan. No. 10. In Senate January 11, 1839.
Report of the Superintendent of Public Instruction.
. . . December 31, 1838. . . . 40 pp. N. p., n. d.
BurColl.

State of Michigan. No. 2. In Senate. January 7, 1840.
Report of the Superintendent of Public Instruction.
. . . December 31, 1839. . . . 24, 85 pp. N. p.,
n. d. BurColl.

C. *Ohio*

1. State Superintendent's Reports

First Annual Report of the Superintendent of Common
Schools, Made to the Thirty-sixth General Assembly of
the State of Ohio, January, 1838. 65 pp. Columbus,
Samuel Medary, Printer, 1838. CinPL, LaneTS, WRHist.
Second, for Dec., 1838 (CinPL); Third, for Dec., 1839
(LC, WRHist).

2. Local School Reports

Fourth Annual Report of the Trustees and Visitors of
Common Schools, to the City Council of Cincinnati, for
the School Year Ending June 30, 1833: . . . Reprinted by Order of the School Board. 14 pp. Cincinnati, Printed at the Daily Times Office, 1833. HistPSO,
WRHist. For the year ending June 30, 1834 (HistPSO,
WRHist); rendered Mar. 23, 1836 (LaneTS); for
year ending June 30, 1836 (HistPSO, WRHist); for
year ending June 30, 1838 (HistPSO, WRHist — and,
with different title, LaneTS); for year ending June 30,
1839 (various imprints — HistPSO, WRHist); for the
year ending June 30, 1840 (various imprints — HistPSO,
WRHist).

VII. PRIVATE ACADEMIES

Chillicothe Female Seminary. Catalogue of the Officers
and Members of the Chillicothe Female Seminary, for the
Year Ending June 27th, 1834. 6 pp. Chillicothe,
Printed by William C. Jones and Co., 1834. WRHist.
Eclectic Institute. Prospectus of the Rev. Mr. Peers's

School, to be Known hereafter by the Name of the
Eclectic Institute, and Conducted by Rev. Benjamin O.
Peers, Mr. H. Hulbert Eaton, and Mr. Henry A. Griswold. 20 pp. Lexington, Printed by Joseph G. Norwood, 1830. ChU.

Lafayette Female Academy. School Exercises of the Lafayette Female Academy; . . . 75 pp. Lexington, T.
Smith, Printer, n. d. (1826). ChU.

—— Visit of General Lafayette to the Lafayette Female
Academy, in Lexington, Kentucky, May 16, 1825, and the
Exercises in Honour of the Nation's Guest: together
with a Catalogue of the Instructers, Visiters, and Pupils,
of the Academy. 32 pp. Lexington, Printed by John
Bradford, May, 1825. ChU, LexPL, LC.

Monticello Female Seminary. First and Second Catalogues
of the Teachers and Members of Monticello Female
Seminary. For the Years Ending 1839-40. 21 pp.
Alton, Ill., Printed at Parks' Book and Job Office, 1840.
IllStHist.

VIII.　Colleges and Universities

A.　*Augusta College*

Catalogue of the Officers and Students, and of the Graduates, both Honorary and Regular, of Augusta College.
16 pp. Augusta, Ky., June, 1836. LexPL.

Catalogue of the Officers and Students of Augusta College,
for the Year Commencing October 1, 1838. July, 1839.
16 pp. Cincinnati, Printed at the Methodist Book Room,
R. P. Thompson, Printer, 1839. LexPL.

B.　*Bacon College*

Catalogue of the Officers and Students, of Bacon College,
for the Academical Year, 1836-7. 15 pp. Georgetown,
Ky., College Press, 1837. LexPL.

Catalogue of the Officers and Students of Bacon College,
. . . for the Year 1837-8. 23 (should be 24) pp.
Lexington, Printed by J. C. Noble, n. d. TransylvaniaU.

C. *Cincinnati College*

A Catalogue of the Officers and Students in the Medical
and Law Departments of Cincinnati College; First Session: 1835-6. To which are Appended, a List of the
Graduates at the First Medical Commencement, and a
Report from the Trustees to the Corporators. Published
under the Direction of the Board. 22 pp. Cincinnati,
Printed by N. S. Johnson, 1836. HistPSO, WRHist.

Supplement to the Western Journal. A Catalogue of the
Officers and Students in the Medical and Law Departments of Cincinnati College; First Session: 1835-6. To
which is Appended a List of the Graduates at the First
Medical Commencement. Published under the Direction
of the Board of Trustees. 12 pp. Cincinnati, Printed
by N. S. Johnson, 1836. IU.

D. *Hanover College*

1. Catalogues

South Hanover College and Indiana Theological Seminary.
Catalogue of the Corporation, Faculty, and Students.
January, 1833. 16 pp. Cincinnati, M'Millan and Clop-
per, Printers, 1833. IndStL.

Catalogue of the Officers and Students of South Hanover
College, and Indiana Theological Seminary. February,
1834. 16 pp. South Hanover, Ind., Morrow and Bayless, Printers, 1834. IndStL.

Catalogue of the Officers and Students of Indiana Theological Seminary and Hanover College. 1834-5. 16 pp.
Hanover, Ind., Printed at the College Press, 1835. (Top
of title-page mutilated.) IndStL.

A Catalogue of the Officers and Students of Indiana Theological Seminary and Hanover College. 1835-6. 12 pp. South Hanover, Ind., Printed at the College Press, 1836. IndStL.

A Catalogue of the Officers and Students of Indiana Theological Seminary and Hanover College, 1836-7. 16 pp. South Hanover, Ind., 1837. IndStL.

Catalogue of the Officers and Students of Hanover College and Indiana Theological Seminary. 1837-8. 15 pp. South Hanover, Ind., Printed by James Morrow (1838? Date of printing mutilated.) IndStL.

Catalogue of the Officers and Students of Hanover College. 1838-9. 13 pp. South Hanover, Ind., Printed by James Morrow, 1839. IndStL.

2. Trustees' Reports

H. R. Report of the Trustees of Hanover College. December 16, 1835. 3 pp. N. p., n. d. IndStL.

H. R. Tuesday, January 3, 1837, Report of the Board of Trustees of Hanover College. 2 pp. N. p., n. d. IndStL.

3. Laws

Hanover College. The Laws of South Hanover College. 12 pp. Cincinnati, M'Millan and Clopper, Printers, 1833. IndStL.

E. *Illinois College*

1. Catalogues

Catalogue of the Officers and Students in Illinois College, 1833-34. 8 pp. N. p., n. d. IllStHist.

Catalogue of the Officers and Students in Illinois College: 1835-6. 20 pp. Jacksonville, Ill., Printed by E. T. & C. Goudy, 1836. IllStHist.

Catalogue of the Officers and Students of Illinois College:

1836-7. 24 pp. Jacksonville, Ill., Printed by E. T. & C. Goudy, 1837. IllStHist.

Catalogue of the Officers and Students of Illinois College: 1837-8. 17 pp. Jacksonville, Ill., Printed by C. & R. Goudy, 1838. ChHist, IllStHist.

Catalogue of the Officers and Students of Illinois College. 1838-9. 14 pp. Jacksonville, Ill., Printed by C. & R. Goudy, 1839. IllStHist.

Catalogue of the Officers and Students of Illinois College. 1839-40. 15, [1] pp. Jacksonville, Ill., Printed at Goudy's Job Office, 1840. IllStHist.

2. Miscellaneous Publications

An Appeal in Behalf of the Illinois College, recently Founded at Jacksonville, Illinois. 16 pp. New York, Printed by D. Fanshaw, 1831. IllStHist.

Description of Jacksonville and of the Plot of Lands hereto Annexed, and now Offered for Sale in Behalf of Illinois College. 12 pp. New York? 1836?. From LC card.

Historical Sketch of the Origin, Progress, and Wants, of Illinois College. May, 1832. [By Theron Baldwin.] 16 pp. New York, John T. West, Printer, 1832. ChPL, IllStHist.

Laws of Illinois College in Jacksonville, Illinois, Enacted by the Trustees. 22 pp. Jacksonville, Ill., Printed by E. T. & C. Goudy, 1837. IllStHist.

F. *Indiana Asbury University*

First Annual Catalogue of the Officers and Students of Indiana Asbury University. August 1839. 12 pp. Greencastle, Ind., Printed by W. J. Burns, 1839. IndStL.

Second Annual Catalogue of the Officers and Students of Indiana Asbury University, August, 1840. 16 pp. Indianapolis, Printed by Stacy & Williams, 1840. IndStL.

G.   *Indiana University*

1.   Catalogues

Indiana College.   7 pp.   N. p. (Bloomington, Ind.?), n. d. (1831).   IU.

Annual Catalogue of the Officers and Students of Indiana College. September, 1835.   8 pp.   N. p. (Jesse Brandon, Printer), n. d.   IU.

A Catalogue of the Officers and Students of Indiana College, Bloomington, 1836-7.   12 pp.   Bloomington, Ind., Printed by M. L. Deal, 1837.   IU.

A Catalogue, of the Officers and Students of Indiana College, Bloomington.   1837-8.   12 pp.   N. p. (Bloomington, Ind., M. L. Deal, Printer), n. d.   IU.

Catalogue of the Officers and Students of Indiana University, Bloomington, 1839.   8 pp.   Bloomington, Ind., J. Dale, Printer, n. d.   IU.

A Catalogue of the Officers and Students of Indiana University.   14 pp.   Bloomington, Ind., Printed by A. E. Drapier, 1840.   IU.

2.   Trustees' Proceedings

In Senate.   Report of the Trustees of Indiana College. December 4, 1834.   5 pp.   N. p., n. d.   IndStL.

Address by a Committee of the Trustees of Indiana University, to the People of Indiana.   15 pp.   Indianapolis, Printed by Stacy & Williams, 1840.   IndStL, IU.

H.   *Kenyon College*

Catalogue.   Theological Seminary of the Diocese of Ohio. Kenyon College.   Kenyon Preparatory Schools.   24 pp. Gambier, O., George W. Myers, Printer, 1836.   WRHist.

Interesting Report of the Rise and Progress of the

Protestant Episcopal Church, Kenyon College, and the New Town of Gambier, in the Diocese of Ohio, &c. &c. &c. 1827. 64 pp. N. p. (London, W. H. Birchall, Printer), n. d. HistPSO.

I. *Lane Theological Seminary*

1. Announcement

The Cincinnati Lane Seminary and Walnut Hill School. Its Character, Advantages and Present Prospects, January, 1832. 7 pp. Cincinnati, Robinson and Fairbank, 1832. From Thomson.

2. Trustees' Reports and Catalogues

Fourth Annual Report of the Trustees of the Cincinnati Lane Seminary: together with a Catalogue of the Officers and Students. January, 1834. 28 pp. Lane Seminary, Printed by the Students' Typographical Association, 1834. BurColl.

Fifth Annual Report of the Trustees . . . and a Catalogue . . . November, 1834. 47 pp. Cincinnati, Corey & Fairbank, 1834. BurColl, WRHist.

Sixth Annual Report of the Trustees . . . and a Catalogue . . . December, 1835. 24 pp. Cincinnati, Corey and Webster, 1835. BurColl, WRHist.

J. *Marietta College*

1. Catalogues

Catalogue of the Officers and Students of Marietta College. 1837-8. 24 pp. Marietta, O., I. Maxon, Printer, 1838. WRHist. 1838-9, 22 pp. Cincinnati, Isaac Hefley & Co., Printers, 1838. WRHist. 1839-40, 16, [1] pp. Marietta, O., G. W. Tyler & Co., Printers, 1840. WRHist.

2.   Trustees' Reports

First Annual Report of the Trustees of the Marietta Collegiate Institute, and Western Teachers' Seminary. August, 1834. 14 pp. Cincinnati, Gregory & Smith, Printers, 1834. HistPSO, WRHist.

Second Annual Report of the Trustees of Marietta College. September, 1835. 18 pp. Cincinnati, F. Stanley Benton, 1835. HistPSO, WRHist.

3.   Miscellaneous Publications

Annual Circular of Marietta College, with the Inaugural Address of the President, Delivered July 25, 1838. . . . 14 pp. Cincinnati, Isaac Hefley & Co., Printers, 1839. (Inaugural address not included in the 14 pp.) WRHist.

Laws of Marietta College, and a Catalogue of the Library. 56 pp. Marietta, O., G. W. Tyler & Co., Printers, 1840. From LC card.

K.   *Medical Institute of the City of Louisville*

Catalogue of the Officers and Students of the Medical Institute of the City of Louisville, January 1st, 1839. 12 pp. Louisville, Prentice & Weissinger, 1839. HistPSO.

Catalogue of the Officers and Students of the Medical Institute of the City of Louisville. January 1, 1840. 12 pp. Louisville, Prentice and Weissinger, 1840. LouPL.

L.   *Miami University*

1.   Catalogues

Catalogue of the Officers and Students of the Miami University. Oxford, Ohio. July, 1826. 11 pp. Hamilton, O., Printed by James B. Camron, n. d. ChU.

Catalogue of the Officers and Students of Miami University, . . . July, 1829. 15 pp. Oxford, O., Printed at the Societies' Press, 1829. ChU, MiamiU.

Catalogue of the Officers and Students of Miami University, . . . July, 1830. 16 pp. N. p. (Oxford, O.), W. W. Bishop, n. d. (1830). MiamiU.

A Catalogue of [the] Officers and Students of Miami University, Oxford, Ohio. July, 1833. 15 pp. Oxford, O., W. W. Bishop, 1833. Title-page slightly mutilated. Library of Samuel M. Wilson, Lexington, Ky.

The Ninth Annual Catalogue of the Officers and Students of Miami University. July, 1834. 16 pp. Oxford, O., W. W. Bishop, 1834. MiamiU.

[The Tenth Annual Catalogue . . . 1835]. 16 pp. (Title-page lacking.) MiamiU.

Second Triennial Catalogue of the Officers and Graduates of Miami University, A. D. 1836. 21 pp. Cincinnati, A. Pugh, Printer, 1836. ChU, MiamiU, WRHist.

The Twelfth Annual Catalogue of the Officers and Students of Miami University. July, 1837. 12 pp. Oxford, O., Printed by R. H. Bishop, Jun., 1837. ChU, MiamiU.

Catalogue of the Officers and Students of Miami University, for the Winter Session of 1837 and 1838. 13 pp. Oxford, O., Printed by R. H. Bishop, Jun., 1837. ChU, WRHist.

The Thirteenth Annual Catalogue of the Officers and Students of Miami University, July, 1838. 16 pp. Oxford, O., Printed by R. H. Bishop, Jun., 1838. ChU, WRHist.

The Fourteenth Annual Catalogue of the Officers and Students of Miami University, July, 1839. 16 pp. Oxford, O., Printed by W. W. Bishop, 1839. ChU.

Third Triennial Catalogue of the Officers and Graduates of Miami University, March A.D. 1840. 42 pp. Oxford, O., Printed by W. W. Bishop, 1840. ChU, MiamiU, WRHist.

2. Trustees' Reports

Report of the President & Trustees of the Miami University, Made in Conformity to an Act of the Legislature. 29 pp. Hamilton, O., Printed by Keen, Colby, & Company, 1815. WRHist.

Report. To the Honorable the Senate and House of Representatives, of the State of Ohio. 4 pp. N. p., n. d. (1822). WRHist.

3. Laws

Laws Passed by the Ohio Legislature, Establishing the Miami University, and the Ordinances, Passed by the President & Trustees of the Miami University. To which is Added, an Address to the Inhabitants of the Miami College Lands, Containing Brief Remarks and Observations. 68, [2] pp. Hamilton, O., Printed by Keen & Stewart, for James M'Bride, 1814. WRHist.

Ordinances, of 'the Miami University'. 9 pp. N. p., n. d. (1819?). WRHist.

Laws Relating to the Miami University, together with the Ordinances of the President and Trustees, and Extracts from the Journal of Proceedings. To which is Added a Table of the Lots and Lands Belonging to the University. . . . 148 pp. Cincinnati, Printed by F. S. Benton, 1833. HistPSO, LC, WRHist.

Ordinances Passed by the President and Trustees of the Miami University, in Addition to those Published in 1833, with Extracts from the Journal of Proceedings. . . . 11 pp. Oxford, O., 1836. WRHist.

4. Miscellaneous Publications

Communication, Made to the Committee Appointed to Inspect the Books and Accounts of the Miami University. 5 pp. N. p., n. d. (1819). WRHist.

Miami University and Cincinnati College; by the Oxford
Committee. 20 pp. Hamilton, O., Printed by James
B. Camron, 1822. HistPSO, WRHist.
Miami University, October, 1837. Broadside. WRHist.

M. *Oberlin Collegiate Institute*

Laws and Regulations of the Oberlin Collegiate Institute.
15 pp. Oberlin, Printed by James Steele, 1840. WRHist.

N. *Ohio University*

Addresses Delivered at the Inauguration of the Rev. Robert
G. Wilson, D.D., President of the Ohio University, Aug
11, 1824. Together with a Short Account of that Institution. 27 pp. Zanesville, Printed by Ezekiel T. Cox
& Co., 1824. From Thomson.
Catalogue of the Officers and Students in the Ohio University, 1831-32. [8] pp. Athens, O., Maxon, Printer,
n. d. BurColl.

O. *Transylvania University*

1. Catalogues

Catalogus senatus academici, eorum qui munera et officia
gesserunt, eorum quique alicujus gradus laurea donati
sunt in Universitate Transylvaniensi, Lexingtoniae in
Republica Kentuckiensi. 16 pp. Lexingtoniae, Gulielmo
Gibbes Hunt, typographo, MDCCCXXIII. Transyl-
vaniaU.
A Catalogue of the Officers and Students of Transylvania
University, Lexington, Kentucky, January, 1824. 20 pp.
N. p., n. d. ChU.
Catalogus senatus academici, eorum qui munera et officia
gesserunt, eorum quique alicujus gradus laurea donati
sunt in Universitate Transylvaniensi, Lexingtoniæ in

Republica Kentuckiensi. 20 pp. Lexingtoniæ, Gulielmo Tanner, typographo, MDCCCXXIV. ChU, TransylvaniaU.

A Catalogue of the Officers and Students of Transylvania University, Lexington, Kentucky, January, 1826. 19 pp. N. p., n. d. TransylvaniaU.

A Catalogue of the Officers, Teachers, and Graduates of [Transylva]nia University, ———— [Mutilated; for 1826.] 16 pp. TransylvaniaU.

Transylvania Journal of Medicine, Extra. Catalogue of the Officers of the Medical Department of Transylvania University, and of the Graduates of 1828. [8] pp. Lexington, Printed by Albert G. Meriwether, 1828. TransylvaniaU.

A Catalogue of the Trustees and Faculty of Transylvania University; together with the Course of Studies in the Institution. 4 pp. N. p., n. d. LaneTS.

Transylvania Journal of Medicine. . . . Extra. A Catalogue of the Officers and Students in the Medical and Law Departments of Transylvania University. Lexington, Kentucky, January, 1833. 15, [1] pp. Lexington, Printed by H. Savary & Co., 1833. LexPL.

Transylvania Journal of Medicine. . . . Extra. A Catalogue of the Officers and Students of Transylvania University. Lexington, . . . January, 1834. 14, 1 pp. Lexington, Printed by J. Clarke & Co., 1833. TransylvaniaU.

Catalogue for 1837-1838. Mutilated; title entirely lacking. 14, 1 pp. TransylvaniaU.

Transylvania Medical Journal . . . Extra. Transylvania Catalogue of Medical Graduates, with an Appendix, Containing a Concise History of the School from its Rise to the Present Time. 35 pp. Lexington, Intelligencer Print, 1838. ChU.

Catalogue of the Transylvania Law Class; Session of 1839-
40. 3pp. N. p., n. d. MoStHistS.

2. Official Reports and Miscellaneous Publications

Report of the Committee of the House of Representatives,
on the Subject of the Transylvania University together
with the Response of its Trustees. 21 pp. N. p., n. d.
(1816). WisH.

By-laws of the Transylvania University. 21 pp. Lexington, Printed by Worsley & Smith, 1818. TransylvaniaU.

Clarissimo Johanni Adair, Armigero, Gubernatori; . . .
aulæ academicæ Lexingtoniæ, in Republica Kentuckiensi,
sexto Idus Julii, anno salutis MDCCCXII [sic], Rerum-
que Publicarum Fœderatarum Americæ summæ potestatis
XLVII. 19 pp. Lexington, e typis Gulielmi Gibbes
Hunt, n. d. (1822?). WisH.

Clarissimo Johanni Adair, Armigero, Gubernatori; . . .
Lexingtoniæ . . . MDCCCXXIV . . . e typis
Gulielmi Tanner. 10 pp. (incomplete?). ChU.

The Order of Exercises in the Chapel of Transylvania Uni-
versity, a Collection of Original Pieces in Honour of the
Arrival of General La Fayette, the Hero, Patriot, and
Philanthropist, . . . 16 pp. Lexington, May, 1825.
ChU, LC, TransylvaniaU.

Laws of Transylvania University. August, 1829. 12 pp.
N. p., n. d. TransylvaniaU.

P. *University of Michigan*

Code of Laws for the Government of the Branches of the
University of Michigan, . . . 16 pp. Detroit, Harsha & Bates, Printers, 1839. From LC card.

Q. *Wabash College*

A Catalogue of the Officers and Students of Wabash College and Teachers' Seminary. July 1836. 12 pp. Crawfordsville, Ind., n. d. IndStL.

A Catalogue of the [Of]ficers and Students of Wabash College and Teachers' Seminary. 12 pp. Crawfordsville, Ind., Snyder & Holmes, Printers, July, 1837. IndStL.

A Catalogue of the Officers and Students of Wabash College. 14 pp. Indianapolis, Printed by Stacy & Williams, 1840. BurColl, IndStL.

R. *Woodward College*

Catalogue, By-laws, and Course of Study of the Woodward College, and of the High School, with an Address, by the President. . . . 47 pp. Cincinnati (Printed by L'Hommedieu & Co.), 1836. WRHist.

Catalogue of the Woodward College, and of the High School, with an Address, by the President. . . . 23 pp. Cincinnati, Kendall and Henry, Printers, 1837. WRHist.

Annual Circular and Catalogue of the Woodward College, and of the High School: with an Address, by the President. . . . 33 pp. Cincinnati, Pugh & Dodd, Printers, 1838. WRHist.

Annual Circular and Catalogue of the Woodward College, and of the High School: with an Address, by the President. . . . 29 pp. Cincinnati, A. Pugh, Printer, 1839. LaneTS.

IX. EDUCATIONAL ASSOCIATIONS

Common School Convention. [Of Cleveland and adjacent towns.] 24 pp. N. p., n. d. LaneTS.

Muskingum County Lyceum of Practical Teachers. The Annual Report of the Proceedings . . . 1837, . . . Zanesville (1837). From *The Western Academician and Journal of Education and Science*, I, 335 (Aug., 1837).

Professional Teachers. Proceedings of a Convention of Professional Teachers, and Others, Friends of Education; Held at Columbus, Ohio, in January, 1836. 39 pp. Columbus, James B. Gardiner, Printer, n. d. CinPL.

—— Proceedings of the Annual Convention of Professional Teachers and Other Friends of Education; Held in the City of Columbus, Ohio; on the 19th, 20th, 21st and 22nd, December, 1837. 24 pp. Columbus, Printed by Cutler and Pilsbury, 1838. LaneTS.

—— Proceedings of the Second Annual Convention of Professional Teachers, . . . Columbus, Dec., 1838. 35 pp. Columbus, Printed by Cutler and Pilsbury, 1839. LaneTS.

Western Education Society. First Annual Report of the Directors of the Western Education Society, Presented at the Annual Meeting, Held in the City of Cincinnati, November, 1835. 27 pp. Cincinnati, Printed at the Cincinnati Journal Office, 1835. IU, LaneTS.

—— Second Annual Report of the Directors of the Western Education Society, . . . 1836. 16, [2] pp. Cincinnati, Printed by A. Pugh, 1836. WRHist.

Western Literary Institute and College of Professional Teachers. The Annual Register of the Proceedings of the Western Literary Institute and College of Professional Teachers. 1833. 12 pp. N. p. (Cincinnati?), n. d. (1833?). IU.

—— Transactions of the Fourth Annual Meeting of the Western Literary Institute, and College of Professional Teachers, Held in Cincinnati, October, 1834. 324 pp.

Cincinnati, Josiah Drake, 1835. ChU, IU, LC, WisH.
Fifth to Tenth annual meetings, 1835-1840; published
1836-1841 (Ninth and Tenth meetings in same volume,
1841). ChU, IU, LC, WisH (lacks Eighth annual meeting).

X. SOCIETIES FOR PROMOTING HISTORY, SCIENCE, AND ART

Cincinnati Academy of Fine Arts. The Act of Incorpora-
tion of the Cincinnati Academy of Fine Arts. With an
Address to the Members . . . 12 pp. Cincinnati,
Printed by G. T. Williamson, 1828. WRHist.

Historical and Philosophical Society of Ohio. Journal of
the Historical and Philosophical Society of Ohio. 111
pp. Columbus, Printed for the Society, by Cutler and
Pilsbury, 1838. HistPSO, LC, WRHist.

—— Transactions of the Historical and Philosophical Society of Ohio. Part Second. Vol. I. Published by Order of the Society. 334 pp. Cincinnati, Geo. W. Bradbury & Co., Printers, 1839. HistPSO, WRHist, WisH.

Historical Society of Indiana. MS. minutes, Dec. 11, 1830-
July 8, 1879. 48 pp. IndStL.

Historical Society of Michigan. Constitution and By-laws
of the Historical Society of Michigan, Incorporated June
23d, 1828. 8 pp. Detroit, Printed at the Gazette Office,
1829. BurColl.

—— Historical and Scientific Sketches of Michigan. Com-
prising a Series of Discourses Delivered before the His-
torical Society of Michigan, and Other Interesting Papers
Relative to the Territory. 215 pp. Detroit, Stephen
Wells and George L. Whitney, 1834. BurColl, ColU,
LC, NewL, WRHist, WisH.

Illinois State Lyceum. Circular. Bluffdale, Greene Co.,
Illinois, . . . [with MS. date June 7, 1832]. [2]
pp. N. p., n. d. (1832). IllStHist.

Kentucky Historical Society. Act of Incorporation, and Constitution and By-laws of the Kentucky Historical Society, Organized March, 1838, at Louisville, Kentucky. 12 pp. Louisville, Prentice and Weissinger, Printers, 1838. LC, WisH.

Medical Convention of Ohio. Journal of the Medical Convention of Ohio, Held in Columbus, January 5, 1835. Cincinnati, Printed by A. Pugh (1835). From *The Western Monthly Magazine*, III, 171 (Mar., 1835).

Transylvania Botanic-garden Company. First Catalogues and Circulars of the Botanical Garden of Transylvania University at Lexington in Kentucky, for the Year 1824. Premiers catalogues et circulaires du Jardin Botanique de l'Université Transylvane a Lexington en Kentucky pour l'annee 1824. 24 pp. Lexington, Printed for the Botanical Garden Company, by John M. M'Calla, 1824. WisH.

——— Prospectus, By-laws & Charter, of the Transylvania Botanic-garden Company. Lexington, 1824. 16 pp. N., p., n. d. Library of Samuel M. Wilson, Lexington, Ky.

Western Methodist Historical Society. Proceedings of the Board of Managers of the Western Methodist Historical Society in the Mississippi Valley; Containing an Account of the Origin of the Society, its Organization, Constitution, Address, Circular, &c. 16 pp. Cincinnati, Printed at the Methodist Book Room, 1839. LexPL, WRHist, WisH.

XI. LIBRARIES AND BOOKSTORES

Circulating Library Society of Cincinnati. A Systematic Catalogue of Books Belonging to the Circulating Library Society of Cincinnati. To which are Prefixed an Historical Preface, the Act of Incorporation, and By-laws, of the Society. 36 pp. Cincinnati, Printed by Looker, Palmer and Reynolds, 1816. HistPSO.

Kenyon College. A Catalogue of Books Belonging to the Library of the Philomathesian Society of Kenyon College, July, 1834. 16, [1] pp. Gambier, O., G. W. Myers, Printer, 1834. WRHist.

—— Catalogue of Books Belonging to the Library of the Theological Seminary of the Diocese of Ohio, Kenyon College and the Preparatory Schools. MDCCCXXXVII. 76 pp. Gambier, O., G. W. Myers, Printer, 1837. From LC card.

—— Catalogue of the Library, and Names of Members, of the Philomathesian Society of Kenyon College, from its Formation in 1827 to 1840. 44 pp. Gambier, O., Printed by Thomas R. Raymond, 1840. LC, WRHist.

Lexington Library Company. Addition to the Catalogue of the Lexington Library. 26 pp. Lexington, Printed by F. Bradford Jr., 1817. ChU.

—— A Catalogue of the Books, Belonging to the Lexington Library Company; to which is Prefixed, a Concise Narrative of the Origin and Progress of the Institution; with its Charter, Laws & Regulations. xiv, [2], 172, [2] pp. Lexington, Printed by Thomas Smith, 1821. ChU, LexPL.

—— Catalogue of the Books in the Lexington Library. 72 pp. Lexington, Printed by F. Bradford, 1815. ChU, LexPL.

Louisville Book-store. Western Farmers' Almanac for 1822, . . . with a Catalogue of Books, for Sale at the Louisville Book-store. . . . From *Lou. Pub. Adv.*, Nov. 14, 1821.

Marietta College. Laws of Marietta College, and a Catalogue of the Library. 56 pp. Marietta, O., G. W. Tyler & Co., Printers, 1840. From LC card.

Miami University. A Catalogue of the Books Contained in the Library of Miami University, Arranged According to Subjects. A. D. 1833. 24 pp. Oxford, O., W. W. Bishop, 1833. WRHist.

—— A Catalogue of the Honorary and Ordinary Members of the Erodelphian Society of Miami University, with a List of the Books Belonging to the Society's Library: (Arranged According to Subjects.) 17 pp. Cincinnati, Corey & Webster, 1835. WRHist.

Ohio State Library. Catalog of Books in the Ohio State Library, December 1, 1826, with Additions to December 1, 1827. 25 pp. Columbus, 1828. From Smith catalogue (title evidently inaccurate). Now in WRHist.

—— Catalogue of the Ohio State Library. December, 1840. . . . Zechariah Mills, Librarian. 60 pp. Columbus, Samuel Medary, Printer, 1840. LC.

—— Catalogue of the State Library of Ohio. December, 1832. Published by Authority. 30 pp. Columbus, Printed by Zechariah Mills, Librarian, Office of the State Journal, n. d. HistPSO.

—— Catalogue of the State Library of Ohio. December, 1837. Published by Authority Zechariah Mills, Librarian. 42, 5 pp. Columbus, Samuel Medary, Printer, 1837. NYPL.

Transylvania University. [Catalogue of Books in the Library of Transylvania University.] 8 pp. (incomplete?). Lexington, John Bradford, 18-. Title improvised from fragmentary title-page. LexPL.

Whiting, Isaac N. A Catalogue of Valuable Books, for Sale by Isaac N. Whiting, at his New Book Store, High-Street, . . . 40, [2] pp. Columbus, E. Glover, Printer, 1831. WRHist.

—— Isaac N. Whiting's General Catalogue of Books, in the Various Departments of Literature and Science, for

Sale at his Book Store, High Street, Columbus. . . .
70 pp. Columbus, 1833. WRHist.

—— A Supplement to Isaac N. Whiting's Catalogue of
Valuable Books. 21 pp. Columbus, Printed by Jenkins
and Glover, 1832. WRHist.

—— A Supplement to Isaac N. Whiting's Catalogue of
Valuable Books, for Sale at his Book Store, High-Street,
Columbus. . . . 36 pp. Columbus, 1835. WRHist.

Worsley & Collins, Louisville. The Western Farmers'
Almanac, for the Year of our Lord, 1823, . . . Containing, . . . a Catalogue of Books, for Sale by Worsley & Collins . . . From *Lou. Pub. Adv.*, Nov. 27,
1822.

Young Men's Mercantile Library Association of Cincinnati.
A Catalogue of Books Belonging to the Young Mens'
[*sic*] Mercantile Library Association of Cincinnati; to
which is Prefixed the Constitution, By-laws, and Regulations of the Same. Library and Reading Room on East
Fourth Street. 40 pp. Cincinnati, Daily Express Office,
n. d. (1838?). WRHist.

XII. POLITICAL PARTIES

A. *Administration (Adams) Party, 1827-1828*

Address to the Freemen of Kentucky, from a Convention of
Delegates Friendly to the Re-election of John Quincy
Adams, as President of the United States, Held in the
Town of Frankfort, the 17th, 18th and 19th Days of
December, 1827. 16 pp. Maysville, "office of the
Eagle," n. d. ChU.

Administration Meeting in Cooper County [Missouri].
Feb. 22, 1828. 2 pp. N. p., n. d. Title transmitted
by William Clark Breckenridge.

Proceedings and Address of the Anti-Jackson Convention
of Missouri. 42 pp. N. p., n. d. (1828). MercLStL.

Proceedings of the Administration Convention, Held at Frankfort, Kentucky, on Monday, December 17, 1827. 23 pp. N. p. (Frankfort, Printed by J. H. Holeman), n. d. ChU.

Proceedings of the Administration Convention of Indiana, Held at Indianapolis, January 12, 1828. 24 pp. N. p. (Indianapolis, Indiana Journal Office), n. d. (1828). HistPSO, IndStL.

Supplement to the Kentucky Reporter. Address, of the Fayette County Corresponding Committee, on the Proceedings of the Senate of Kentucky, against the President, Secretary of State and Members of Congress; . . . 48 pp. Lexington, Thomas Smith, Printer, n. d. (1828). ChU.

Warren County [Ohio] Administration Meeting. 8 pp. Lebanon, O., Office of the Western Star, 1827. WRHist.

B. *Democratic Party*

Address and Proceedings of the Ohio State Convention which Met at Columbus, O. January 9, 1832, . . . 24 pp. Columbus, Printed at the Office of the "Sentinel," 1832. WRHist.

Address of the Jackson Committee of Jefferson County, Ohio. 8 pp. N. p. (Steubenville, O.?), n. d. (1827?). WRHist.

An Address to the Friends of Andrew Jackson, in the First Congressional District of Indiana. To the Democratic Republicans of the First Congressional District of Indiana. 7 pp. N. p. (Vincennes?), n. d. (1828). IndStL.

An Address to the People of Ohio, on the Important Subject of the Next Presidency; by the Committee Appointed . . . at a Convention . . . at Columbus, . . . July, 1824. 16 pp. Cincinnati, Looker & Reynolds, Printers, n. d. WRHist.

Democratic Free Press, Extra. Address of the Committee Appointed by the Territorial Democratic Republican Convention, Held at Ann Arbor the 12th February, 1833. 14 pp. N. p., n. d. BurColl.

New Albany Argus — Extra. Address of the Democratic Congressional Convention, Held at Lexington, Scott County, Ia. on the Eighth of January, 1839. . . . 16 pp. N. p., n. d. IndStL.

The Proceedings and Address of the Ohio Jackson Convention, Assembled at Columbus, on the Eighth of January, 1828, . . . 15 pp. N. p., Printed by David Smith, 1828. WRHist.

Proceedings of the Democratic Republican Convention of the State of Indiana, Friendly to the Nomination of Martin Van Buren and Richard M. Johnson, . . . 24 pp. N. p., n. d. (1836?). IndStL.

The Proceedings of the Democratic State Convention, Begun and Holden at Columbus on the 8th of Jan. 1834, . . . 24 pp. Columbus, John Gilbert & Co., Printers, 1834. WRHist.

Proceedings of the Democratic State Convention, Held in Columbus on the Eighth of January, 1838; with an Address to the People of Ohio. . . . 16 pp. Columbus, Printed at the Office of the Ohio Statesman, 1838. WRHist.

Proceedings of the Democratic Territorial Convention, Held at Ann Arbor, on the 29th and 30th January 1835. 16 pp. Detroit, Printed at the Free Press Office, 1835. BurColl.

Proceedings of the Friends of Gen. Jackson, at Louisville & Frankfort, Ky. 12 pp. N. p. (Louisville, S. Penn, Jr., Printer), n. d. (1827?). ChU.

Proceedings Resolutions and Address of the Jackson Convention, Held in Frankfort, 13th, Dec. 1830. 22 pp. N. p., n. d. ChU.

C. *Whig Party*

Address of the Central Committee, to the People of the State of Missouri. 46 pp. N. p., n. d. (1840?). MercLStL.

Proceedings of the Convention of the Friends of Gen. Wm. H. Harrison. 16 pp. N. p. (Indianapolis?), n. d. (1835?). HistPSO, IndStL, WisH.

XIII. ANTISLAVERY SOCIETIES

Anti-slavery Society of Hanover College. Preamble and Constitution of the Anti-slavery Society of Hanover College and Indiana Theological Seminary. With Miscellaneous Articles on the Subject of Slavery. 16 pp. Hanover, Ind., the Society, Printed by James Morrow, 1836. LaneTS, WisH.

Cincinnati Colonization Society. Proceedings of the Cincinnati Colonization Society, at the Annual Meeting, January 14, 1833. . . . 17 pp. Cincinnati, Printed by F. S. Benton, 1833. From LC card.

Illinois Anti-slavery Convention. Alton Observer. — Extra. Proceedings of the Ill. Anti-slavery Convention. Held at Upper Alton on the Twenty-sixth, Twenty-seventh, and Twenty-eighth October, 1837. 36 pp. Alton, Parks and Breath, 1838. LC, WisH.

Indiana Anti-slavery Society. Proceedings of the Indiana Convention, Assembled to Organize a State Anti-slavery Society, Held in Milton, Wayne Co., September 12th, 1838. 28 pp. Cincinnati, Samuel A. Alley, Printer, 1838. IndStL.

Kentucky Colonization Society. The Proceedings of the Colonization Society of Kentucky, with the Address of the Hon. Daniel Mayes, at the Annual Meeting, at Frankfort, December 1st, 1831. 24 pp. Frankfort, Printed at the Commentator Office, n. d. (1831). LaneTS, LC.

—— The Fourth Annual Report of the Kentucky Colonization Society, with an Address, . . . by Rev. John C. Young. 32 pp. Frankfort, Printed by Albert G. Hodges, 1833. LaneTS.

—— The Fifth Annual Report of the Kentucky Colonization Society, with an Address, . . . by the Hon. James T. Morehead. 32 pp. Frankfort, Printed at the Office of the Cross, 1834. LaneTS.

Lexington and Fayette County Auxiliary Colonization Society. Second Annual Report . . . July 8, 1828. . . . 15, [1] pp. Lexington, Smith & Palmer, Printers, 1828. Library of Samuel M. Wilson, Lexington, Ky.

Ohio Anti-slavery Society. Condition of the People of Color in the State of Ohio. With Interesting Anecdotes. 48 pp. Boston, I. Knapp, 1839. From LC card.

—— The Declaration of Sentiments, and Constitution of the Ohio State Anti-slavery Society. . . . 12 pp. Cincinnati, the Ohio Anti-slavery Society, 1839. WRHist.

—— Memorial of the Ohio Anti Slavery Society, to the General Assembly of the State of Ohio. 34 pp. Cincinnati, Pugh & Dodd, Printers, 1838. From LC card.

—— Proceedings of the Ohio Anti-slavery Convention, Held at Putnam, . . . 1835. 54 pp. N. p., Beaumont and Wallace, Printers, n. d. LC, WRHist.

—— Report of the First Anniversary of the Ohio Anti-slavery Society, . . . April, 1836. 53 pp. Cincinnati, the Ohio Anti-slavery Society, 1836. WRHist, WisH.

—— Report of the Second Anniversary of the Ohio Anti Slavery Society, Held in Mount Pleasant, Jefferson County, . . . April, 1837. 67 pp. Cincinnati, the Anti-slavery Society, 1837. WRHist, WisH.

—— Report of the Third Anniversary of the Ohio Anti-slavery Society, Held in Granville, Licking County, Ohio, on the 30th of May, 1838. 38 pp. Cincinnati, the Ohio Anti-slavery Society, 1838. WRHist.

Ohio State Colonization Society. A Brief Exposition of the Views of the Society for the Colonization of Free Persons of Colour, in Africa; . . . 16 pp. Columbus, Printed by David Smith, 1827. HistPSO, TransylvaniaU, WRHist.

—— The First Annual Report of the Ohio State Society for Colonizing the Free People of Colour, of the United States. . . . 14 pp. Columbus, Printed by David Smith, n. d. HistPSO.

XIV. Miscellaneous Societies

Brady Guards of the City of Detroit. Constitution of the Brady Guards of the City of Detroit. 7, [1] pp. N. p. (Detroit, Morse & Bagg), n. d. (1836?). From transcript in BurColl. Original also in BurColl.

Caledonian Society of Cincinnati. Charter and Constitution of the Caledonian Society of Cincinnati. 17, [2] pp. Cincinnati, Reynolds, Allen & Disney, Printers, 1833. WRHist.

Detroit Young Men's Society. Act of Incorporation, By-laws and Standing Rules of the Detroit Young Men's Society; Officers, Regular and Honorary Members, and a List of Questions Debated and Lectures Delivered before the Society. 24 pp. Detroit, Printed by Geo. L. Whitney, 1836. BurColl.

Freemasons, Kentucky. Proceedings of the Grand Lodge of Kentucky, . . . in the Town of Lexington, . . . 1819. 96 pp. (incomplete?). Lexington, Printed by D. Bradford, 1819. KyStHist. For 1831. 40 pp. Lexington, Printed by N. L. Finnell & J. F. Herndon, 1831. LexPL. For 1832. 30, [1] pp. Lexington,

Printed by N. L. Finnell & J. F. Herndon, 1832. LexPL.
For 1833. 19, [1] pp. Lexington, Printed by N. L.
Finnell, 1833. LexPL.

—— Proceedings of the Grand Chapter and of the Grand
Council of the State of Kentucky, at a Grand Annual
Convocation, . . . in the City of Lexington. 24 pp.
Frankfort, A. G. Hodges, Printer, 1832. LexPL.

—— Proceedings of the Grand Chapter of the State of
Kentucky, at a Grand Annual Convocation, . . . in
the City of Lexington, Kentucky. 14 pp. Frankfort,
A. G. Hodges, Printer, 1833. LexPL.

Freemasons, Missouri. Constitution and By-laws of the
Grand Lodge of Missouri, . . . 9 pp. St. Louis,
Printed by Edward Charless, 1827. MoHist.

—— The By-laws of Palmyra Lodge. No. 18. of Free and
Accepted Ancient Masons. 14 pp. Palmyra, Mo., B. F.
Hayden, Printer, 1837. MoHist.

Freemasons, Ohio. Journal of the Proceedings of the
Grand Royal Arch Chapter of the State of Ohio, . . .
at Columbus, January, 1834. 8 pp. Columbus, Printed
by Companion John Bailhache, 1834. WRHist.

The French Moral and Benevolent Society of the City of
Detroit and its Vicinity. MS. minutes (Sept. 17, 1818).
BurColl.

——MS. The Constitution of the French Moral and Benevolent Society of the City of Detroit and its Vicinity.
As Adopted July 16th 1818. BurColl.

Lexington Association of Master Carpenters. Bill of Prices
. . . Adopted May 15th, 1832. . . . 35, 1 pp.
Lexington, H. Savary & Co., Printers, 1832. LexPL.

Mechanics' Society of Detroit. Constitution of the Mechanics' Society of Detroit. . . . 17 pp. Detroit,
Printed by Sheldon & Wells, November, 1825. BurColl.

Milwaukee Union. The Constitution of the Milwaukee

Union. 9 pp. N. p. (W. T., Printed by Jason Lathrop), n. d. (1836?). WisH.

Ohio Mechanics' Institute. Report of the First Annual Fair of the Ohio Mechanics' Institute, Held at Cincinnati, on the 30th and 31st May, and 1st June, with an Address Delivered by E. D. Mansfield, Esq. upon the Occasion. 51 pp. Cincinnati, 1838. CinPL, WRHist.

Saint Louis Grays. By-laws of the Saint Louis Grays. Adopted 1832, Revised 1839. 11 pp. St. Louis, Chambers & Knapp, Printers, 1839. MercLStL.

CHAPTER II

TRAVEL AND OBSERVATION

I. Accounts of Captivity among the Indians

Biggs, William. Narrative of William Biggs, while he was a Prisoner with the Kickepoo Indians, then Living opposite the Old Weawes Town on the West Bank of the Wabash River. . . . 22 pp. N. p., Printed for the Author, June, 1826. WisH.

Brown, Thomas. A Plain Narrative of the Uncommon Sufferings, and Remarkable Deliverance of Thomas Brown, of Charlestown, in New-England; . . . How he was Taken Captive by the Indians, . . . to the Missisippi; . . . 3d ed. 24 pp. Boston, Printed and Sold by Fowle and Draper, 1760. NewL.

Bunn, Matthew. A Journal of the Adventures of Matthew Bunn, a Native of Brookfield, Massachusetts, who Enlisted with Ensign John Tillinghast, of Providence, in the Year 1791, on an Expedition into the Western Country; — was Taken by the Savages, and Made his Escape into Detroit the 30th of April, 1792. . . . 24 pp. Providence, Printed, Litchfield, Reprinted by Thomas Collier, 1796. BurColl. 7th ed. 59 pp. (Narrative of the Life and Adventures of Matthew Bunn . . .) Batavia, Printed for the Author, 1828. BurColl, WRHist, WisH.

D'Eres, Charles Dennis Rusoe. Memoirs of Charles Dennis Rusoe D'Eres, a Native of Canada; who was with the Scanyawtauragahrooote Indians Eleven Years, . . .

176 pp. Exeter, Henry Ranlet, 1800. BurColl, LC, NewL.

Horn, Mrs. A Narrative of the Captivity of Mrs. Horn, and her Two Children, with Mrs. Harris, by the Camanche Indians, after they had Murdered their Husbands and Travelling Companions; . . . 60 pp. St. Louis, C. Keemle, Printer, 1839. NewL.

Hunter, John Dunn. Manners and Customs of Several Indian Tribes Located West of the Mississippi; . . . to which is Prefixed the History of the Author's Life during a Residence of Several Years among them. 402 pp. Philadelphia, Printed by J. Maxwell, for the Author, 1823. LC, WisH. New ed. ix, 447 pp. (Memoirs of a Captivity among the Indians . . .) London, Longman, Hurst, Rees, Orme, Brown, and Green, 1823. ChU, LC, NYPL, WRHist.

Jeffries, Ewel. A Short Biography of John Leeth, Giving a Brief Account of his Travels and Sufferings among the Indians for Eighteen Years, . . . from his Own Relation, . . . 33 pp. Lancaster, O., Printed at the Gazette Office, 1831. WRHist, WisH.

Johnston, Charles. A Narrative of the Incidents Attending the Capture, Detention, and Ransom of Charles Johnston, of Botetourt County, Virginia, who was Made Prisoner by the Indians, on the River Ohio, in the Year 1790; . . . 264 pp. New York, Printed by J. & J. Harper, 1827. HistPSO, NewL, WRHist.

Johonnot, Jackson. The Remarkable Adventures of Jackson Johonnet [sic], of Massachusetts; who Served as a Soldier in the Western Army, in the Massachusetts Line, in the Expedition under General Harmar, and the Unfortunate General St. Clair. Containing an Account of his Captivity, Sufferings, and Escape from the Kickapoo Indians. Written by himself, . . . 16 pp. Boston, for Samuel Hall, 1793. NewL. 15 pp. Lexington, Printed, 1791, Providence, Reprinted, 1793. From LC card.

Kinnan, Mary. A True Narrative of the Sufferings of Mary Kinnan, who was Taken Prisoner by the Shawanee Nation of Indians on the Thirteenth Day of May, 1791, . . . 15 pp. Elizabethtown, printed by Shepard Kollock, 1795. NewL.

Lewis, Mrs. Hannah. Narrative of the Captivity and Sufferings of Mrs. Hannah Lewis, and her Three Children, who were Taken Prisoners by the Indians, near St. Louis, on the 25th May, 1815, . . . 24 pp. Boston, Printed by Henry Trumbull, 1817. NewL.

M'Donald, Philip, and Alexander M'Leod. A Surprising Account of the Captivity and Escape of Philip M'Donald & Alexander M'Leod, of Virginia, from the Chickkemogga Indians. And of their Great Discoveries in the Western World, from June 1779, to January 1786, . . . 11 pp. Keene, N. H., Printed by Henry Blake, & Co., 1794. NewL.

Narrative of the Captivity and Providential Escape of Mrs. Jane Lewis, (Wife of James Lewis,) who, with a Son and Daughter, . . . and an Infant Babe, were Made Prisoners within a Few Miles of Indian Creek, by a Party of Indians of the Tribes of Sacs and Foxes, Commanded by Black Hawk. . . . 24 pp. N. p., 1833. HistPSO, WisH.

Narrative of the Captivity and Sufferings of Mrs. Harriot Lewis and her Three Children, who were Taken Prisoners by the Indians near St. Louis, on the 25th May, 1815, . . . 24 pp. Boston, George Billings, 1818. CinPL.

Narrative of the Capture and Providential Escape of Misses Frances and Almira Hall, . . . who were Taken Prisoners by the Savages, at a Frontier Settlement, near Indian Creek, in May Last, . . . Likewise is Added, the Interesting Narrative of the Captivity and Sufferings of Philip Brigdon, a Kentuckian, . . . Communicated by Persons of Respectability Living in the Neighborhood of the Captives. 24 pp. N. p., 1832. CinPL, LC, NewL, WRHist.

A Narrative of the Horrid Massacre by the Indians, of the Wife and Children of the Christian Hermit, a Resident of Missouri, with a Full Account of his Life and Sufferings, never before Published. 24 pp. St. Louis, Leander W. Whiting & Co., 1840. LC, MercLStL, NewL.

Narrative of the Massacre, by the Savages, of the Wife & Children of Thomas Baldwin, who, since the Melancholy Period of the Destruction of his Unfortunate Family, has Dwelt entirely Alone, in a Hut of his Own Construction, Secluded from Human Society, in the Extreme Western Part of the State of Kentucky. . . . 24 pp. New York, Martin & Perry, 1836. NewL, WisH.

Narratives of a Late Expedition against the Indians: with an Account of the Barbarous Execution of Col. Crawford, and the Wonderful Escape of Dr. Knight and John Slover from Captivity in 1782. 38 pp. Philadelphia, Printed by Francis Bailey, 1773 [1783]. From Thomson.

Pattie, James O. The Personal Narrative of James O. Pattie, of Kentucky, during an Expedition from St. Louis, through the Vast Regions between that Place and the Pacific Ocean, and thence back through the City of Mexico to Vera Cruz, during Journeyings of Six Years; . . . Edited by Timothy Flint. 300 pp. Cincinnati, John H. Wood, 1831. ChU, CinPL, LC, NYPL, WisH.

Seaver, James E. A Narrative of the Life of Mrs. Mary Jemison, who was Taken by the Indians, in the Year 1755, when only about Twelve Years of Age, and has Continued to Reside amongst them to the Present Time. . . . Carefully Taken from her Own Words, Nov.

29th, 1823. . . . 189 pp. Canandaigua, N. Y., J.
D. Bemis and Co., 1824. LC, NewL, WisH.

Smith, James. An Account of the Remarkable Occurrences
in the Life and Travels of Col. James Smith, (now a
Citizen of Bourbon County, Kentucky) during his Captivity with the Indians, in the Years 1755, '56, '57, '58,
& '59, . . . To which is Added, a Brief Account of
Some very Uncommon Occurrences, which Transpired
after his Return from Captivity; as well as of the Different Campaigns Carried on against the Indians to the
Westward of Fort Pitt, since the Year 1755, to the
Present Date. Written by himself. 88 pp. Lexington,
Printed by John Bradford, 1799. NewL.

Spencer, O. M. Indian Captivity: a True Narrative of the
Capture of the Rev. O. M. Spencer by the Indians, in
the Neighbourhood of Cincinnati. Written by himself.
157 pp. New York, B. Waugh and T. Mason, for the
Sunday School Union of the Methodist Episcopal Church,
1835. CinPL, WRHist. 56 pp. Washington, Pa., G.
W. Brice, Printer, 1835. WisH.

Swan, Eliza. An Affecting Account of the Tragical Death
of Major Swan, and of the Captivity of Mrs. Swan and
Infant Child, by the Savages, in April Last — (1815.)
. . . Taken Prisoners by the Indians, at a Small Village near St. Louis, and Conveyed near 700 Miles
. . . 24 pp. Boston, Printed by H. Trumbull, n. d.
(1815). LC, NewL.

Tanner, John. A Narrative of the Captivity and Adven-
tures of John Tanner, (U. S. Interpreter at the Saut de
Ste. Marie,) during Thirty Years Residence among the
Indians in the Interior of North America. Prepared for
the Press by Edwin James, M.D. 426 pp. New York, G.
& C. & H. Carvill, 1830. ColU, NYPL, WisH.

II. Narratives of Adventurers and Travellers from the Eastern States and from Europe

Abdy, Edward Strutt. Journal of a Residence and Tour in the United States of North America, from April, 1833, to October, 1834. 3 vols. London, John Murray, 1835. CinPL, ColU, NewL, WRHist, WisH.

An Account of Louisiana, being an Abstract of Documents, in the Offices of the Department of State, and of the Treasury: Presented to Both Houses of Congress, in a Message from the President, on the 16th of November, 1803. 48 pp. Albany, Printed by John Barber, 1803. BurColl, WisH.

An Account of Monsieur de la Salle's Last Expedition and Discoveries in North America. Presented to the French King, and Published by the Chevalier Tonti, Governour of Fort St. Louis, in the Province of the Islinois. Made English from the Paris Original. . . . 211, 44 pp. London, J. Tonson, S. Buckley, and R. Knaplock, 1698. WisH.

Alexander, J. E. Transatlantic Sketches, Comprising Visits to the most Interesting Scenes in North and South America, . . . 2 vols. London, Richard Bentley, 1833. WisH.

Arfwedson, C. D. The United States and Canada, in 1832, 1833, and 1834. 2 vols. London, Richard Bentley, 1834. BurColl, WRHist, WisH.

Aristocracy in America. From the Sketch-book of a German Nobleman. Edited by Francis J. Grund. . . . 2 vols. London, Richard Bentley, 1839. ChU, LC, WisH.

Asbury, Francis. The Journal of the Rev. Francis Asbury, Bishop of the Methodist Episcopal Church, from August 7, 1771, to December 7, 1815. 3 vols. New

York, N. Bangs and T. Mason, for the Methodist Episcopal Church, 1821. IU, WRHist.

Ashe, Thomas. Memoirs and Confessions of Captain Ashe,
. . . 3 vols. London, Henry Colburn, 1815. CinPL.

—— Memoirs of Mammoth, and Various Other Extraordinary and Stupendous Bones, of Incognita, or Non-
descript Animals, Found in the Vicinity of the Ohio,
Wabash, Illinois, Mississippi, Missouri, Osage, and Red
Rivers, &c. &c. . . . 12, 60 pp. Liverpool, Printed
by G. F. Harris, 1806. LC, WRHist, WisH.

—— Travels in America, Performed in 1806, for the Purpose of Exploring the Rivers Alleghany, Monongahela,
Ohio, and Mississippi, and Ascertaining the Produce and
Condition of their Banks and Vicinity. 3 vols. London, Richard Phillips, 1808. CinPL (lacks Vol. III),
WRHist. 366 pp. Newburyport, Wm. Sawyer & Co.,
1808. IU, WRHist.

Audubon, John James. Ornithological Biography, or an
Account of the Habits of the Birds of the United States
of America; . . . Interspersed with Delineations of
American Scenery and Manners. 5 vols. Edinburgh,
Adam Black, etc. (Vol. I), and Adam & Charles Black,
etc. (Vols. II-V), 1831-1839. CinPL.

Barbé-Marbois, François. The History of Louisiana, particularly of the Cession of that Colony to the United
States of America; . . . Translated from the French
by an American Citizen. 455, [1] pp. Philadelphia,
Carey & Lea, 1830. ChU, WRHist.

Beatty, Charles. The Journal of a Two Months Tour; with
a View of Promoting Religion among the Frontier Inhabitants of Pennsylvania, and of Introducing Christianity among the Indians to the Westward of the Alegh-
geny Mountains. . . . 110, [1] pp. London, Wil-

liam Davehill, and George Pearch, 1768. BurColl, WRHist, WisH.

Beltrami, J. Constantino. La découverte des sources du Mississippi et de la Riviere Sanglante. Description du cours entier du Mississippi, . . . v, [1], 327, [1] pp. Nouvelle-Orleans, Imprimé par Benj. Levy, 1824. BurColl, WRHist.

—— A Pilgrimage in Europe and America, Leading to the Discovery of the Sources of the Mississippi and Bloody River; with a Description of the Whole Course of the Former, and of the Ohio. 2 vols. London, Hunt and Clarke, 1828. ColU, MoHist, WRHist, WisH.

Bernhard, Duke of Saxe-Weimar Eisenach. Travels through North America, during the Years 1825 and 1826. 2 vols. Philadelphia, Carey, Lea & Carey, 1828. CinPL, NYPL, WRHist, WisH.

Berquin-Duvallon. Travels in Louisiana and the Floridas, in the Year, 1802, Giving a Correct Picture of those Countries. Translated from the French, with Notes, &c. by John Davis. viii, 181 pp. New York, I. Riley & Co., 1806. LC, NYPL, WisH.

Bird, Robert Montgomery. Peter Pilgrim: or a Rambler's Recollections. By the Author of "Calavar," "Nick of the Woods," &c. . . . 2 vols. Philadelphia, Lea & Blanchard, 1838. LC.

Blane, William Newham. An Excursion through the United States and Canada during the Years 1822-23. By an English Gentleman. . . . [2], 511 pp. London, Baldwin, Cradock, and Joy, 1824. WisH.

Bossu, Jean Bernard. Travels through that Part of North America formerly Called Louisiana. . . . Translated from the French by John Reinhold Forster, F. A. S. 2 vols. London, T. Davies, 1771. ColU, LC, WRHist, WisH.

Brackenridge, Henry Marie.   Recollections of Persons and Places in the West.   244 pp.   Philadelphia, James Kay, Jun. and Brother, etc., n. d. (1834).   ChU, CinPL, IU, OhioStL, WRHist, WisH.

Bradbury, John.   Travels in the Interior of America, in the Years 1809, 1810, and 1811; Including a Description of Upper Louisiana, together with the States of Ohio, Kentucky, Indiana, and Tennessee, with the Illinois and Western Territories, and Containing Remarks and Observations Useful to Persons Emigrating to those Countries.   364 pp.   Liverpool, Printed for the Author, by Smith and Galway, and Published by Sherwood, Neely, and Jones, London, 1817.   ChU, CinPL, LC, WRHist, WisH.

Bristed, John.   The Resources of the United States of America; or, a View of the Agricultural, Commercial, Manufacturing, Financial, Political, Literary, Moral and Religious Capacity and Character of the American People.   xvi, 505, [1] pp.   New York, James Eastburn & Co., 1818.   IU, LC, WisH.

Brown, Samuel R.   Views of the Campaigns of the Northwestern Army, &c.   Comprising, . . .   View of the Lake Coast from Sandusky to Detroit.   156 pp.   Troy, N. Y., Printed by Francis Adancourt, 1814.   BurColl, WRHist.   156 pp.   Philadelphia, William G. Murphey, 1815.   LC, WRHist, WisH.

—— Views on Lake Erie, Comprising. [*sic*] a Minute and Interesting Account of the Conflict on Lake Erie — . . .   View of the Lake Coast from Buffalo to Detroit.   96 pp.   Troy, N. Y., Printed by Francis Adancourt, 1814.   NYPL, WRHist.

Bullock, William.   Sketch of a Journey through the Western States of North America, from New Orleans, by the Mississippi, Ohio, City of Cincinnati and Falls of Niagara, to New York, in 1827. . . . With a Description of the New and Flourishing City of Cincinnati, by Messrs. B. Drake and E. D. Mansfield. . . . xxxi, viii, 135 pp. London, John Miller, 1827. ChU, HistPSO, LC, WRHist, WisH.

Buttrick, Tilly, Jr. Voyages, Travels and Discoveries of Tilly Buttrick, Jr. 58 pp. Boston, Printed for the Author, John Putnam, Printer, 1831. LC, WRHist.

Carver, Jonathan. Travels through the Interior Parts of North-America, in the Years 1766, 1767, and 1768. [20], 543, [1] pp. London, Printed for the Author, and Sold by J. Walter, and S. Crowder, 1778. CinPL, ColU, WisH.

Charlevoix, Pierre François Xavier de. Histoire et description generale de la Nouvelle France, avec le journal historique d'un voyage fait par ordre du Roi dans l'Amérique Septentrionnale. 3 vols. Paris, Nyon Fils, 1744. WisH.

—— Journal of a Voyage to North-America. Undertaken by Order of the French King. . . . In a Series of Letters to the Duchess of Lesdiguieres. Translated from the French . . . 2 vols. London, R. and J. Dodsley, 1761. LC, WRHist, WisH.

Chevalier, Michel. Society, Manners and Politics in the United States: being a Series of Letters on North America. . . . Translated from the Third Paris Edition. iv, 467, [1] pp. Boston, Weeks, Jordan and Company, 1839. CinPL, HistPSO, LC, WisH.

Cobbett, William. A Year's Residence, in the United States of America. . . . In Three Parts. 2d ed. 610 pp. London, Sherwood, Neely, and Jones, 1819. (Part III contains Thomas Hulme's "Introduction to the Journal" and "The Journal".) IU, NYPL.

Colby, John. The Life, Experience, and Travels of John

Colby, Preacher of the Gospel. Written by himself. 3d ed., revised and corrected. 2 vols. in one. 381 pp. Cornish, Me., S. W. and C. C. Cole, 1829. LC.

Collot, Victor. A Journey in North America, Containing a Survey of the Countries Watered by the Mississipi, Ohio, Missouri, and Other Affluing Rivers; . . . [3], iv, v, [1], 272 pp. Paris, Arthus Bertrand, 1826. LC, WisH.

Colton, Calvin. Tour of the American Lakes, and among the Indians of the North-West Territory, in 1830: . . . 2 vols. London, Frederick Westley and A. H. Davis, 1833. ColU, LC, WRHist, WisH.

Cowan, William Bowie. A Description of Grand Tower, on the Mississippi, . . . 42, [1] pp. New York, Alexander S. Gould, Printer, 1839. ChPL.

Cox, F. A., and J. Hoby. The Baptists in America; a Narrative of the Deputation from the Baptist Union in England, . . . 476, 4 pp. New York, Leavitt, Lord & Co., etc., 1836. WRHist.

Cox, Ross. Adventures on the Columbia River, . . . together with a Journey across the American Continent. 2 vols. London, H. Colburn and R. Bentley, 1831. From LC card. 335 pp. New York, J. & J. Harper, 1832. ChU, LC, WisH.

Coxe, Daniel. A Description of the English Province of Carolana, by the Spaniards Call'd Florida, and by the French La Louisiane. As also of the Great and Famous River Meschacebe or Missisipi, the Five Vast Navigable Lakes of Fresh Water, and the Parts Adjacent. . . . [52], 122 pp. London, Printed for B. Cowse, 1722. LC, NewL.

Crèvecœur, St. Jean de. Lettres d'un cultivateur américain addressées à Wm. S . . . on Esqr. depuis l'année 1770 jusqu'en 1786. . . . traduites de l'anglois.

. . . 3 vols. Paris, Cuchet Libraire, 1787. LC, WRHist.

Cuming, Fortescue. Sketches of a Tour to the Western Country, through the States of Ohio and Kentucky; a Voyage down the Ohio and Mississippi Rivers, and a Trip through the Mississippi Territory, and Part of West Florida. Commenced at Philadelphia in the Winter of 1807, and Concluded in 1809. 504 pp. Pittsburg, Cramer, Spear & Richbaum, 1810. LC, WRHist, WisH.

Cutler, Jervis. A Topographical Description of the State of Ohio, Indiana Territory, and Louisiana. . . . By a Late Officer in the U. S. Army. 219 pp. Boston, Charles Williams, 1812. BurColl, LC, WRHist, WisH.

Cutler, Manasseh. An Explanation of the Map which Delineates that Part of the Federal Lands, Comprehended between Pennsylvania West Line, the Rivers Ohio and Scioto, and Lake Erie; Confirmed to the United States by Sundry Tribes of Indians, in the Treaties of 1784 and 1786, and now Ready for Settlement. 24 pp. Salem, Printed by Dabney and Cushing, 1787. BurColl, LC, WRHist, WisH.

—— Description du sol, des productions, &c. &c. de cette portion des États-Unis, située entre la Pensylvanie, les rivières de l'Ohio & du Scioto, & le lac Erié. Traduite d'une brochure imprimée à Salem, en Amérique, en 1787. 30 pp. Paris, 1789. LC, WRHist.

Darby, William. A Tour from the City of New-York, to Detroit, in the Michigan Territory, Made between the 2d of May and the 22d of September, 1818. . . . 228, lxiii, [7] pp. New York, Kirk & Mercein, for the Author, 1819. ChU, ColU, LC, WRHist, WisH.

Davidson, Robert. An Excursion to the Mammoth Cave, and the Barrens of Kentucky. With Some Notices of the Early Settlement of the State. 148 pp. Philadelphia, Thomas Cowperthwait, and Co., 1840. ChU, KyStL, LC, WisH.

Decalves, Don Alonzo. New Travels to the Westward, or, Unknown Parts of America. Being a Tour of almost Fourteen Months Containing, an Account of the Country, upwards of Two Thousand Miles West of the Christian Parts of North-America; with an Account of White Indians, their Manners, Habits, and Many Other Particulars. . . . Confirmed by Three Other Persons. 4th ed. 35, [1] pp. New London, Printed and Sold by James Springer, 1796. LC. 7th ed. 46 pp. Greenwich, Mass., Printed by John Howe, 1805. HistPSO.

Dodge, John. An Entertaining Narrative of the Cruel and Barbarous Treatment and Extreme Sufferings of Mr. John Dodge during his Captivity of Many Months among the British, at Detroit . . . 2d ed. 32 pp. Danvers, Printed and Sold by E. Russell, 1780. NewL.

Ellicott, Andrew. The Journal of Andrew Ellicott, Late Commissioner on Behalf of the United States during Part of the Year 1796, the Years 1797, 1798, 1799, and Part of the Year 1800: for Determining the Boundary between the United States and the Possessions of His Catholic Majesty in America, . . . vii, 299, 151, [1] pp. Philadelphia, Thomas Dobson, 1803. Harvard, LC, NewL, NYPL, WRHist, WisH.

Elliot, James. The Poetical and Miscellaneous Works of James Elliot, Citizen of Guilford, Vermont, and late a Noncommissioned Officer in the Legion of the United States. In Four Books. 271, [5] pp. Greenfield, Mass., Printed by Thomas Dickman for the Author, 1798. WRHist.

Evans, Estwick. A Pedestrious Tour, of Four Thousand Miles, through the Western States and Territories, during the Winter and Spring of 1818. . . . 256 pp.

Concord, N. H., Joseph C. Spear, 1819. HistPSO, IllHist, LC, MoHist, NYPL, WRHist, WisH.

Eyre, John. The Christian Spectator: being a Journey from England to Ohio, Two Years in that State, Travels in America, &c. 72 pp. Albany, N. Y., Printed by J. Munsell, 1838. CinPL, IU, LC, NewL, NYPL, WRHist, WisH.

—— The European Stranger in America. 84 pp. New York, Sold at Folsom's Book Store, 1839. IU, LC, NewL, NYPL, WRHist, WisH.

Faux, William. Memorable Days in America: being a Journal of a Tour to the United States, principally Undertaken to Ascertain, by Positive Evidence, the Condition and Probable Prospects of British Emigrants; Including Accounts of Mr. Birkbeck's Settlement in the Illinois: and Intended to Shew Men and Things as they are in America. xvi, 488 pp. London, W. Simpkin and R. Marshall, 1823. ChU, IU, LC, NYPL, WisH.

Fearon, Henry Bradshaw. Sketches of America. A Narrative of a Journey of Five Thousand Miles through the Eastern and Western States of America; Contained in Eight Reports Addressed to the Thirty-nine English Families by whom the Author was Deputed, in June 1817, to Ascertain whether Any, and What Part of the United States would be Suitable for their Residence. With Remarks on Mr. Birkbeck's "Notes" and "Letters." vii, [1], 462 pp. London, Longman, Hurst, Rees, Orme, and Brown, 1818. CinPL. 2d ed. xi, 454 pp. London, Longman, Hurst, Rees, Orme, and Brown, 1818. IU, LC, NYPL, WRHist, WisH.

Featherstonhaugh, G. W. Geological Report of an Examination Made in 1834, of the Elevated Country between the Missouri and Red Rivers. 97 pp. Washington, Printed by Gales and Seaton, 1835. BurColl, ChU, LC, NYPL, WisH.

—— Report of a Geological Reconnoissance Made in 1835, from the Seat of Government, by the Way of Green Bay and the Wisconsin Territory, to the Coteau de Prairie, . . . 168 pp. Washington, Printed by Gales and Seaton, 1836. LC, WRHist, WisH.

Ferrall, Simon Ansley. A Ramble of Six Thousand Miles through the United States of America. xii, 360 pp. London, Effingham Wilson, 1832. ColU, LC, LouPL, NYPL, WRHist, WisH.

Flint, James. Letters from America, Containing Observations on the Climate and Agriculture of the Western States, the Manners of the People, the Prospects of Emigrants, &c. &c. viii, 330 pp. Edinburgh, W. & C. Tait, etc., 1822. CinPL, LC, NewL, NYPL, WRHist, WisH.

Garrett, L. Recollections of the West. 240 pp. Nashville, Tenn., W. Cameron, Printer, 1834. LC, WisH.

Gass, Patrick. A Journal of the Voyages and Travels of a Corps of Discovery, under the Command of Capt. Lewis and Capt. Clarke . . . during the Years 1804, 1805 & 1806. . . . 262 pp. Pittsburg, David M'Keehan, 1807. ChU, LC.

Gilman, Chandler Robbins. Life on the Lakes: being Tales and Sketches Collected during a Trip to the Pictured Rocks of Lake Superior. By the Author of "Legends of a Log Cabin." 2 vols. New York, George Dearborn, 1836. HistPSO, LC, WRHist, WisH.

Griffiths, D., Jr. Two Years' Residence in the New Settlements of Ohio, North America: with Directions to Emigrants. 197 pp. London, Westley and Davis, etc., 1835. LC, NYPL, WRHist, WisH.

Grund, Francis J. The Americans in their Moral, Social, and Political Relations. 2 vols. London, Longman, Rees, Orme, Brown, Green, & Longman, 1837. LC, WisH.

Hall, Basil. Forty Etchings, from Sketches Made with the Camera Lucida, in North America, in 1827 and 1828. No pagination. Edinburgh, Cadell & Co., etc., 1829. CinPL, ColU, LC, WisH.

—— Travels in North America, in the Years 1827 and 1828. 3 vols. Edinburgh, Cadell and Co., etc., 1829. LC, WisH. 2 vols. Philadelphia, Carey, Lea & Carey, 1829. LC, WRHist.

Hall, Frederick. Letters from the East and from the West. xi, 168 pp. Washington, F. Taylor and Wm. M. Morrison, etc., n. d. (1840). LC, LouPL, NYPL, WRHist.

Hamilton, Thomas. Men and Manners in America. By the Author of Cyril Thornton, etc. 410 pp. Philadelphia, Carey, Lea & Blanchard, 1833. LC, WisH.

Harding, Benjamin. A Tour through the Western Country, A.D. 1818 & 1819. By Benjamin Harding, Surveyor. Published for the Use of Emigrants. 17 pp. New London, Printed by Samuel Green, for the Author, 1819. MercLStL, WisH.

Harmon, Daniel Williams. A Journal of Voyages and Travels in the Interiour of North America, between the 47th and 58th Degrees of North Latitude, . . . 432 pp. Andover, Printed by Flagg and Gould, 1820. LC, WRHist, WisH.

Harris, Thaddeus Mason. The Journal of a Tour into the Territory Northwest of the Alleghany Mountains; Made in the Spring of the Year 1803. With a Geographical and Historical Account of the State of Ohio. . . . 271 pp. and maps. Boston, Printed by Manning & Loring, 1805. ChU, LC, WRHist, WisH.

Harris, William Tell. Remarks Made during a Tour through the United States of America, in the Years 1817, 1818, and 1819. . . . In a Series of Letters to Friends in England. 196 pp. London, Sherwood, Neely, & Jones, 1821. LC, NYPL, WRHist, WisH.

Hawley, Zerah. A Journal of a Tour through Connecticut, Massachusetts, New-York, the North Part of Pennsylvania and Ohio, Including a Year's Residence in that Part of the State of Ohio, Styled New Connecticut, or Western Reserve. . . . 158 pp. New Haven, Printed by S. Converse, 1822. LC, NewL, WRHist, WisH.

Hebert, William. A Visit to the Colony of Harmony, in Indiana, in the United States of America, recently Purchased by Mr. Owen for the Establishment of a Society of Mutual Co-operation and Community of Property, in a Letter to a Friend; to which are Added, Some Observations on that Mode of Society, and on Political Society at Large: also, a Sketch of the Formation of a Co-operative Society. . . . 35 pp. London, Printed for George Mann, 1825. LWI. Title supplied by Mrs. Nora C. Fretageot, New Harmony, Ind.

Heckewelder, John Gottlieb. A Narrative of the Mission of the United Brethren among the Delaware and Mohegan Indians, from its Commencement, in the Year 1740, to the Close of the Year 1808. . . . 429, [1] pp. Philadelphia, M'Carty & Davis, 1820. HistPSO, IU, LC, WRHist.

Hennepin, Louis. A New Discovery of a Vast Country in America, Extending above Four Thousand Miles, between New France and New Mexico. With a Description of the Great Lakes, Cataracts, Rivers, Plants, and Animals: . . . To which is Added, Several New Discoveries in North-America, not Publish'd in the French Edition. [20], 299, [31], 303-355 pp. London, M. Bentley, J. Tonson, H. Bonwick, T. Goodwin, and S. Manship, 1698. HistPSO, LC, NYPL, WisH. Title-page and pagination vary.

Henry, Alexander. Travels and Adventures in Canada and the Indian Territories, between the Years 1760 and

1776. In Two Parts. vi, 330, [1] pp. New York, I. Riley, 1809. BurColl, ColU, LC, WRHist, WisH.

Henshaw, David. Letters on the Internal Improvements and Commerce of the West, . . . 29 pp. Boston, Dutton and Wentworth, 1839. LC, WRHist.

Hibernicus; or Memoirs of an Irishman, now in America: . . . 251 pp. Pittsburg, Printed for the Author by Cramer & Spear, 1828. LC, MoHist.

Hildreth, James. Dragoon Campaigns to the Rocky Mountains; . . . By a Dragoon. . . . 288 pp. New York, Wiley & Long, 1836. LC, NewL, WisH.

Hodgson, Adam. Letters from North America, Written during a Tour in the United States and Canada. 2 vols. London, Hurst, Robinson, & Co., etc., 1824. ColU, LC, NYPL, WRHist, WisH.

—— Remarks during a Journey through North America in the Years 1819, 1820, and 1821, in a Series of Letters: . . . 335 pp. New York, Collected, Arranged, and Published by Samuel Whiting, 1823. LC, NYPL, WisH.

Hoffman, Charles Fenno. A Winter in the West. By a New-Yorker. . . . 2 vols. New York, Harper & Brothers, 1835. ChU, CinPL, IU, LexPL, LC, LouPL, NewL, WisH.

Holmes, Isaac. An Account of the United States of America, Derived from Actual Observation, during a Residence of Four Years . . . 476 pp. and map, etc. London, Printed by Henry Fisher, n. d. (1823?). LC, NYPL, WRHist, WisH.

Hoskins, Nathan, Jr. Notes upon the Western Country. Contained within the States of Ohio, Indiana, Illinois, and the Territory of Michigan: Taken on a Tour through that Country in the Summer of 1832. 108 pp. Greenfield, Mass., Printed by James P. Fogg, 1833. HistPSO, LC, WRHist.

Howitt, Emanuel. Selections from Letters Written during a Tour through the United States, in the Summer and Autumn of 1819; . . . xxi, [1] pp. Nottingham, Printed and Sold by J. Dunn, n. d. (1820). ChU, ColU, LC, WisH.

Hutchins, Thomas. A Topographical Description of Virginia, Pennsylvania, Maryland, and North Carolina, Comprehending the Rivers Ohio, Kenhawa, Sioto, Cherokee, Wabash, Illinois, Mississippi, &c. . . . And an Appendix, Containing Mr. Patrick Kennedy's Journal up the Illinois River, and a Correct List of the Different Nations and Tribes of Indians, . . . ii, 67, [1] pp. London, the Author, Printed and Sold by J. Almon, 1778. ChU, IndStL, LC, WRHist, WisH.

Imlay, Gilbert. A Topographical Description of the Western Territory of North America; . . . In a Series of Letters to a Friend in England. xv, 247, [1] pp. London, J. Debrett, 1792. ChU, CinPL, HistPSO, LC, NYPL, WRHist, WisH. 2d ed., with considerable additions. xvi, 433, [22] pp. London, J. Debrett, 1793. CinPL, HistPSO, IndStL, LC, WRHist. 2 vols. New York, Printed by Samuel Campbell, 1793. ColU, IU, LC, NYPL, WisH. 3d ed., with great additions. xii, 598, [30] pp. London, J. Debrett, 1797. HistPSO, IU, WRHist.

Irving, John T. Indian Sketches, Taken during an Expedition to the Pawnee Tribes. 2 vols. Philadelphia, Carey, Lea and Blanchard, 1835. ChU, CinPL, LC, NewL, WisH.

Irving, Washington. A Tour on the Prairies. By the Author of the Sketch Book. 274 pp. Philadelphia, Carey, Lea, & Blanchard, 1835. MoHist.

Jacobs, Bela. A Voice from the West. Rev. Bela Jacobs' Report of his Tour in the Western States, Performed in the Spring and Summer of 1833. Presented to the Executive Committee of the Western Baptist Educational Association, . . . 27 pp. Boston, J. Howe, Printer, 1833. LC, MercLStL.

James, Edwin. Account of an Expedition from Pittsburgh to the Rocky Mountains Performed in the Years 1819-20, by Order of the Honourable John C. Calhoun Secretary of War. Maps and Plates. 4, [14] pp., with maps and plates. Philadelphia, H. C. Carey and I. Lea, 1822. CinPL, HistPSO, LC, NewL, WisH.

—— Account of an Expedition from Pittsburgh to the Rocky Mountains, . . . under the Command of Major Stephen H. Long. From the Notes of Major Long, Mr. T. Say, and Other Gentlemen of the Exploring Party. 2 vols. Philadelphia, H. C. Carey and I. Lea, 1823. WRHist, WisH.

Jameson, Anna Brownell. Winter Studies and Summer Rambles in Canada. 2 vols. New York, Wiley and Putnam, 1839. BurColl, CinPL, IndStL, WRHist.

Janson, Charles William. The Stranger in America: Containing Observations Made during a Long Residence in that Country, on the Genius, Manners and Customs of the People of the United States; . . . 22, 499, [1] pp. London, James Cundee, 1807. LC, NYPL, WisH.

Jaquith, James. The History of James Jaquith, being his Travels through the United States and Upper and Lower Canada. Containing Great Geographical Information. Written by himself. 3d ed. 36 pp. N. p., the Author, 1830. WisH.

Jones, David. A Journal of Two Visits Made to Some Nations of Indians on the We-t Side of the River Ohio, in the Years 1772 and 1773. 95, [1] pp. Burlington, N. J., Printed and Sold by Isaac Collins, 1774. WisH.

Joutel, Henri. A Journal of the Last Voyage Perform'd

by Monsr. de la Sale, to the Gulph of Mexico, to Find out
the Mouth of the Missisipi River; Containing, an Account
of the Settlements he Endeavour'd to Make on the Coast
of the Aforesaid Bay, his Unfortunate Death, and the
Travels of his Companions for the Space of Eight Hundred Leagues across that Inland Country of America.
[sic] now Call'd Louisiana, . . . till they Came into
Canada. Written in French . . . and Translated
from the Edition just Publish'd at Paris. . . . xxi,
[9], 205, [5] pp. London, A. Bell, B. Lintott, and J.
Baker, 1714. ChU, LC, WRHist, WisH.

Keating, William H. Narrative of an Expedition to the
Source of St. Peter's River, Lake Winnepeek, Lake of
the Woods, &c. &c. Performed in the Year 1823, . . .
under the Command of Stephen H. Long, . . . Compiled from the Notes of Major Long, Messrs. Say, Keating, and Calhoun, . . . 2 vols. Philadelphia, H. C.
Carey & I. Lea, 1824. BurColl, NYPL, WisH.

Ker, Henry. Travels through the Western Interior of the
United States, from the Year 1808 up to the Year 1816:
with a Particular Description of a Great Part of Mexico,
or New-Spain. . . . 372 pp. Elizabethtown, N. J.,
the Author, 1816. ColU, LC, WRHist, WisH.

Knight, Henry Cogswell. Letters from the South and
West; by Arthur Singleton, Esq. 159 pp. Boston,
Richardson and Lord, 1824. CinPL, ColU, LC, NYPL,
WRHist, WisH.

Lahontan, Armand Louis. New Voyages to North-America. Containing an Account of the Several Nations of
that Vast Continent; their Customs, Commerce, and
Way of Navigation upon the Lakes and Rivers; . . .
Done into English. In Two Volumes. A Great Part of
which never Printed in the Original. 2 vols. London,

H. Bonwicke; T. Goodwin, M. Wotton, B. Tooke; and S. Manship, 1703. WisH.

Latrobe, Charles Joseph. The Rambler in North America: MDCCCXXXII-MDCCCXXXIII. 2 vols. London, R. B. Seeley and W. Burnside, 1835. LC, LouPL, NYPL, WRHist. 2 vols. New York, Harper & Brothers, 1835. LC, NYPL, WisH.

Leonard, Zenas. Narrative of the Adventures of Zenas Leonard, a Native of Clearfield County, Pa. who Spent Five Years in Trapping for Furs, Trading with the Indians, &c., &c., of the Rocky Mountains: Written by himself. 87 pp. Clearfield, Pa., D. W. Moore, 1839. NewL, WisH.

Le Page du Pratz. The History of Louisiana, or of the Western Parts of Virginia and Carolina: Containing a Description of the Countries that Lye on Both Sides of the River Missisipi: with an Account of the Settlements, Inhabitants, Soil, Climate, and Products. Translated from the French, . . . 2 vols. London, T. Becket and P. A. DeHondt, 1763. LC, NewL, NYPL, WRHist, WisH.

Levasseur, A. Lafayette in America in 1824 and 1825; or, Journal of a Voyage to the United States: . . . Translated by John D. Godman, M.D. 2 vols. Philadelphia, Carey and Lea, 1829. HistPSO, WisH. 2 vols. New York, White, Gallaher & White, etc., 1829. BurColl.

Logan, James. Notes of a Journey through Canada, the United States of America, and the West Indies. xii, 259 pp. Edinburgh, Fraser and Co., etc., 1838. LC, NewL, WisH.

Logan, John. The Western Woodpecker, being the Journal of a Journey, Performed in the Months of February, March and April, 1818. From Georgetown, in the District of Columbia, to the Miami, in the State of Ohio, and back again. 38 pp. Georgetown, D. C., the Author, 1818. LC, WRHist.

Long, John. Voyages and Travels of an Indian Interpreter and Trader, . . . x, [1], 295 pp. London, Printed for the Author, 1791. ColU, NYPL, WisH.

McKenney, Thomas L. Sketches of a Tour to the Lakes, of the Character and Customs of the Chippeway Indians, and of Incidents Connected with the Treaty of Fond du Lac. 493, [1] pp. Baltimore, Fielding Lucas, Jun'r., 1827. ChU, LexPL, LC, NYPL, WisH.

Mackenzie, Alexander. Voyages from Montreal, on the River St. Laurence, through the Continent of North America, . . . 1789 and 1793. . . . viii, cxxvi, 392 pp. Philadelphia, John Morgan, 1802. HistPSO.

Marryat, Frederick. A Diary in America, with Remarks on its Institutions. 2 vols. Philadelphia, Carey & Hart, 1839. ChU, WisH.

—— A Diary in America, with Remarks on its Institutions. Part Second. 3 vols. London, Longman, Orme, Brown, Green, & Longmans, 1839. ColU, WisH.

—— Second Series of a Diary in America, with Remarks on its Institutions. 300 pp. Philadelphia, T. K. & P. G. Collins, 1840. ChU.

Martineau, Harriet. Retrospect of Western Travel. 2 vols. London, Saunders and Otley, etc., 1838. ChU, ColU, LC, WRHist, WisH.

—— Society in America . . . 2 vols. New York and London, Saunders and Otley, 1837. ColU, IU, LC.

Mead, Charles. Mississippian Scenery; a Poem, Descriptive of the Interior of North America. 113 pp. Philadelphia, S. Potter and Co., 1819. HistPSO.

Melish, John. Travels in the United States of America, in the Years 1806 & 1807, and 1809, 1810, & 1811; . . .

2 vols. Philadelphia, the Author, 1812. IU, LexPL, LC, NewL, WRHist.

Michaux, François André. The North American Sylva, . . . Translated from the French of F. Andrew Michaux, . . . 3 vols. Paris, Printed by C. d'Hautel, 1819. NYPL, TransylvaniaU, WisH.

—— Travels to the Westward of the Allegany Mountains, in the States of the Ohio, Kentucky, and Tennessee, and Return to Charlestown, through the Upper Carolinas; . . . Undertaken in the Year X, 1802, under the Auspices of His Excellency M. Chaptal, Minister of the Interior. . . . Faithfully Translated from the Original French, by B. Lambert. xvi, 350, [2] pp. London, Printed by W. Flint, for J. Mawman, 1805. ChU, LouPL, WRHist.

Miller, Andrew. New States and Territories, or the Ohio, Indiana, Illinois, Michigan, North-Western, Missouri, Louisiana, Missisippi and Alabama in their Real Characters, in 1818; . . . Collected from the Accounts of Gentlemen . . . and Personal Observation. 32 pp. N. p. (Keene, N. H.?), n. d. (1819?). LC, WRHist, WisH.

Mills, Samuel J., and Daniel Smith. Report of a Missionary Tour through that Part of the United States which Lies West of the Allegany Mountains; Performed under the Direction of the Massachusetts Missionary Society. 64 pp. Andover, Mass., Printed by Flagg and Gould, 1815. ChU, ColU, LC, WRHist, WisH.

Montulé, Édouard de. A Voyage to North America, and the West Indies, in 1817. 102, 16 pp. London, Sir Richard Phillips and Co., 1821. ChU, LC, WRHist, WisH.

Morris, Thomas. Miscellanies in Prose and Verse. vi, 181 pp. London, James Ridgway, 1791. WisH.

Morse, Jedidiah. A Report to the Secretary of War of the United States, on Indian Affairs, Comprising a Narrative of a Tour Performed in the Summer of 1820, . . . 96, 400 pp. New Haven, Printed by S. Converse, etc., 1822. ChU, NewL, WRHist.

Murray, Charles Augustus. Travels in North America during the Years 1834, 1835, & 1836. Including a Summer Residence with the Pawnee Tribe of Indians, in the Remote Prairies of the Missouri, and a Visit to Cuba and the Azore Islands. 2 vols. New York, Harper & Brothers, 1839. ChU, ColU, HistPSO, WRHist, WisH.

Narrative of a Tour of Observation, Made during the Summer of 1817, by James Monroe, President of the United States, through the North-eastern and North-western Departments of the Union: . . . 228, xxxvi pp. Philadelphia, S. A. Mitchell & H. Ames, 1818. LC, WisH.

Nuttall, Thomas. A Journal of Travels into the Arkansa Territory, during the Year 1819. With Occasional Observations on the Manners of the Aborigines. Illustrated by a Map and Other Engravings. 296 pp. Philadelphia, Thos. H. Palmer, 1821. ChU, WRHist, WisH.

O'Bryan, William. A Narrative of Travels in the United States of America, with Some Account of American Manners and Polity, and Advice to Emigrants and Travellers Going to that Interesting Country. 419 pp. London, for the Author, 1836. LC, WisH.

Ogden, George W. Letters from the West, Comprising a Tour through the Western Country, and a Residence of Two Summers in the States of Ohio and Kentucky: originally Written in Letters to a Brother. 126 pp. New Bedford, Mass., Melcher & Rogers, 1823. ChHist, HistPSO, LC, NewL, WRHist, WisH.

Parker, Amos Andrew. Trip to the West and Texas. Comprising a Journey of Eight Thousand Miles, through

New-York, Michigan, Illinois, Missouri, Louisiana and Texas, in the Autumn and Winter of 1834-5. Interspersed with Anecdotes, Incidents and Observations. 276 pp. Concord, N. H., White & Fisher, 1835. LC, NewL, WRHist, WisH.

Parker, Samuel. Journal of an Exploring Tour beyond the Rocky Mountains, under the Direction of the A. B. C. F. M. Performed in the Years 1835, '36, and '37; . . . 371 pp. Ithaca, N. Y., the Author, 1838. LC, NYPL, WisH.

Perrin du Lac, François Marie. Travels through the Two Louisianas, and among the Savage Nations of the Missouri; also, in the United States, along the Ohio, and the Adjacent Provinces, in 1801, 1802, & 1803. . . . Translated from the French. 106, [2] pp. London, Richard Phillips, 1807. LC, NewL, WisH.

Pike, Zebulon Montgomery. An Account of a Voyage up the Mississippi River, from St. Louis to its Source; Made under the Orders of the War Department, by Lieut. Pike, of the United States Army, in the Years 1805 and 1806. Compiled from Mr. Pike's Journal. 68 pp. N. p. (Washington), n. d. (1807). WisH.

—— An Account of Expeditions to the Sources of the Mississippi, and through the Western Parts of Louisiana, . . . Performed by Order of the Government of the United States during the Years 1805, 1806, and 1807. And a Tour through the Interior Parts of New Spain . . . 5, [1], 277, [1], 65, [1], 53, 87 pp. Philadelphia, C. & A. Conrad, & Co., etc., 1810. ColU, NewL, WRHist, WisH.

—— Exploratory Travels through the Western Territories of North America: Comprising a Voyage from St. Louis, on the Mississippi, to the Source of that River, and a Journey through the Interior of Louisiana, and the

North-eastern Provinces of New Spain. Performed in the Years 1805, 1806, 1807, by Order of the Government of the United States. xx, 436 pp. London, Longman, Hurst, Rees, Orme, and Brown, 1811. HistPSO, NewL.

Pittman, Philip. The Present State of the European Settlements on the Missisippi; with a Geographical Description of that River. Illustrated by Plans and Draughts. viii, 99 pp., and charts. London, J. Nourse, 1770. ChU, WRHist, WisH.

Pope, John. A Tour through the Southern and Western Territories of the United States of North-America; the Spanish Dominions on the River Mississippi, and the Floridas; . . . 104 pp. Richmond (Va.?), Printed by John Dixon, for the Author and his Three Children, 1792. MercLStL.

Postl, Karl ("Charles Sealsfield"). The Americans as they are; Described in a Tour through the Valley of the Mississippi. By the Author of "Austria as it is." [1], vi, [4], 218, [3] pp. London, Hurst, Chance, and Co., 1828. ChU, HistPSO, LC, NewL, WisH.

—— The United States of North America as they are. xii, 242 pp. London, W. Simpkin and R. Marshall, 1828. HistPSO, NYPL, WisH.

Pownall, Thomas. A Topographical Description of Such Parts of North America as are Contained in the (Annexed) Map of the Middle British Colonies, &c. in North America. vi, 46, 16 pp. London, J. Almon, 1776. ChU, LC, WRHist, WisH.

The Present State of the Country and Inhabitants, Europeans and Indians, of Louisiana, on the North Continent of America. By an Officer at New Orleans to his Friend at Paris. Containing . . . also an Account of their Drunken Lewd Lives, . . . Translated from the

gether with a Comprehensive View of the Canadas and United States. As Adapted for Agricultural Emigration. v, 473 pp. Edinburgh, Oliver and Boyd, etc., 1835. ColU, LC, WRHist, WisH.

Short, Rich. Travels in the United States of America, . . . With Advice to Emigrants. 2d ed. 24 pp. London, Richard Lambert, n. d. LC, NewL.

Smyth, John F. D. A Tour in the United States of America: Containing an Account of the Present Situation of that Country; . . . 2 vols. London, G. Robinson; J. Robson; and J. Sewell, 1784. ChU, ColU, IU, LC, NYPL, WRHist, WisH.

Stoddard, Amos. Sketches, Historical and Descriptive, of Louisiana. viii, 488 pp. Philadelphia, Mathew Carey, 1812. ChU, ColU, LC, NewL, WRHist, WisH.

Stone, Alvan, and David Wright. Memoir of Alvan Stone, of Goshen Mass. By David Wright, . . . 256 pp. Boston, Gould, Kendall and Lincoln, etc., 1837. BurColl.

Storrow, Samuel A. Narrative of a Tour in the Summer of 1817 on the Shores of Lake Superior and Other Northern Lakes of the United States. . . . 39 pp. (1818?). Title from *The Cambridge History of American Literature*, 1917, I, 487. Pagination from the original (which lacks the title-page) in WisH.

Stuart, James. Three Years in North America. 2 vols. Edinburgh, Robert Cadell, etc., 1833. ChU, LC, WRHist. 2 vols. New York, J. & J. Harper, 1833. ColU, IU, LC, WRHist, WisH.

Taylor, G. A Voyage to North America, Perform'd by G. Taylor, of Sheffield, in the Years 1768, and 1769; . . . up the River Mississipi, to the Illinois, and down from Fort Chartres, over the Ohio River, . . . [6], 248 pp. Nottingham, Printed by S. Cresswell for the Author, 1771. LC, NewL.

Thomas, David. Travels through the Western Country in the Summer of 1816. . . . with a Map of the Wabash Country, now Settling. [2], 320 pp. Auburn, N. Y., Printed by David Rumsey, 1819. IndStL, IU, LC, WRHist, WisH.

Tocqueville, Alexis de. Democracy in America. . . . Translated by Henry Reeve, Esq. 2d ed. 2 vols. London, Saunders and Otley, 1836. ColU.

—— Democracy in America. Part the Second, the Social Influence of Democracy. . . . Translated by Henry Reeve, Esq. . . . xx, 355 pp. New York, J. & H. G. Langley, etc., 1840. IU.

A Topographical and Statistical Account of the Province of Louisiana, . . . to which is Annexed, a Copious Preface; and, the Recent Conventions, between the United States, and the French Republic. Compiled by Different Individuals, . . . from the Documents Communicated to Congress, by the President. . . . 80, [1] pp. Baltimore, John Rice, Samuel Butler, and Warner & Hanna, 1803. NewL, WisH.

" 'Tother Side of Ohio" or a Review of a "Poem in Three Cantos, by J. Oldfield. . . . 40 pp. Hartford, Conn., S. G. Goodrich, for the Author, 1818. WRHist.

Townsend, John K. Narrative of a Journey across the Rocky Mountains, to the Columbia River, and a Visit to the Sandwich Islands, Chili, &c. . . . 352 pp. Philadelphia, Henry Perkins, etc., 1839. WRHist, WisH.

Trollope, Frances. Domestic Manners of the Americans. 2 vols. London, Whittaker, Treacher, & Co., 1832. ChU, LC, WisH. ix, 325 pp. London, Printed for Whittaker, Treacher, & Co., New York, Reprinted for the Booksellers, 1832. HistPSO, LC, WRHist. 4th ed. 2 vols. London, Whittaker, Treacher, & Co., 1832. HistPSO.

Trumbull, H. Western Emigration. Journal of Doctor

Jeremiah Simpleton's Tour to Ohio Containing an Account of the Numerous Difficulties, Hair-breadth Escapes, Mortifications and Privations, which the Doctor and his Family Experienced on their Journey from Maine, to the '*Land of Promise*,' and during a Residence of Three Years in that highly Extolled Country. [1], 36 pp. Providence, R. I., for the Author, n. d. WisH. 36 pp. Boston, Printed by S. Sewall, n. d. LC, WRHist.

Tudor, Henry. Narrative of a Tour in North America; Comprising Mexico, the Mines of Real del Monte, the United States, and the British Colonies: with an Excursion to the Island of Cuba. In a Series of Letters, Written in the Years 1831-2. 2 vols. London, James Duncan, 1834. ChU, ColU, LC, WRHist, WisH.

Volney, Constantin François. View of the Climate and Soil of the United States of America: to which are Annexed Some Accounts of Florida, the French Colony on the Scioto, Certain Canadian Colonies, and the Savages or Natives: Translated from the French of C. F. Volney, . . . xxiv, v, [1], 503, [1] pp. London, J. Johnson, 1804. ColU, IU, JCrerar, LC, NYPL, WRHist.

Waldo, Samuel Putnam. The Tour of James Monroe, President of the United States, in the Year 1817; through the States of Maryland, Pennsylvania, New-Jersey, New York, Connecticut, Rhode-Island, Massachusetts, New-Hampshire, Vermont, and Ohio, . . . and Historical and Geographical Notices of the Principal Places through which he Passed. . . . xii, 300 pp. Hartford, Conn., Printed by F. D. Bolles & Co., 1818. ChU, LC, WRHist.

Walker, Adam. A Journal of Two Campaigns of the Fourth Regiment of U. S. Infantry, in the Michigan and Indiana Territories, . . . during the Years 1811, & 12. 143 pp. Keene, N. H., Printed by the Author, 1816. LC, WRHist.

Walker, George ?   A View of North America, in its Former
Happy, and its Present Belligerent State. . . . with
the Travels and Adventures of the Author, through
Great Part of that Continent, in the Years 1774, 75, 76,
77, and 78. . . . 247 pp. Glasgow, Printed by William Smith, for the Author, 1781. LC, WisH.

Ward, Nahum. A Brief Sketch of the State of Ohio, one
of the United States in North America: with a Map De-
lineating the Same into Counties. Giving the Opinion of
Thomas Hutchison, Esq. Geographer of the United States,
and British Travellers in 1787, . . . By a Resident
of Twelve Years at Marietta, in that State. 16 pp.
Glasgow, Printed by J. Niven, 1822. HistPSO, LC,
WRHist.

Welby, Adlard. A Visit to North America and the English
Settlements in Illinois, with a Winter Residence at Philadelphia; solely to Ascertain the Actual Prospects of
the Emigrating Agriculturist, Mechanic, and Commercial Speculator. xii, 224, [1] pp. London, J. Drury,
etc., 1821. IllHist, LC, NewL, WRHist, WisH.

Weld, Isaac, Jr. Travels through the States of North
America, and the Provinces of Upper and Lower Canada,
during the Years 1795, 1796, and 1797. 464 pp. London, Printed for John Stockdale, 1799. ColU, LC, WisH.

Western Emigration. Narrative of a Tour to, and One
Year's Residence in "Edensburgh," (Illinois,) by Major
Walter Wilkey, an Honest Yeoman of Mooseboro' State
of Maine. . . . Embellished with Appropriate Cuts.
. . . 24 pp. New York, Sackett & Sargent, 1839.
ChPL, IllStHist.

Weston, Richard. A Visit to the United States and Canada in 1833; with the View of Settling in America. Including a Voyage to and from New-York. ii, 312 pp.
Edinburgh, Richard Weston and Sons, etc., 1836. LC,
NYPL, WRHist, WisH.

Wheelock, Eleazar. A Continuation of the Narrative of
the Indian Charity-school, Begun in Lebanon, in Connecticut; now Incorporated with Dartmouth-College, . . .
68 pp. Hartford, Conn., 1773. USBurEd, WRHist.

Woods, John. Two Years' Residence in the Settlement on
the English Prairie, in the Illinois Country, United
States. . . . 310 pp. and maps. London, Printed
for Longman, Hurst, Rees, Orme, and Brown, 1822.
ChPL, CinPL, LC, NewL, WRHist, WisH.

Wright, John S. Letters from the West; or, a Caution to
Emigrants; . . . ix, [1], 72. pp. Salem, N. Y.,
Printed by Dodd & Stevenson, 1819. ChHist. From
copy of title supplied by ChHist.

Wyeth, John B. Oregon; or a Short History of a Long
Journey from the Atlantic Ocean to the Region of the
Pacific. By Land. Drawn up from the Notes and Oral
Information of John B. Wyeth . . . 87 pp. Cam-
bridge, Mass., Printed for John B. Wyeth, 1833. LC,
MercLStL.

III. Travel and Observation by Western Writers

Allen, J., and Henry Rowe Schoolcraft. . . . A Map
and Report of Lieut. Allen and H. B. [sic] Schoolcraft's
Visit to the Northwest Indians in 1832. 68 pp. In Doc.
323, 23d Congress, 1st Session. NYPL, WisH.

Atwater, Caleb. Remarks Made on a Tour to Prairie du
Chien; thence to Washington City, in 1829. vii, [2],
296 pp. Columbus, Isaac N. Whiting, 1831. CinPL,
ChHist, WRHist, WisH.

Birkbeck, Morris. An Address to the Farmers of Great
Britain; with an Essay on the Prairies of the Western
Country: . . . 52 pp. London, Printed for James
Ridgway, 1822. ChHist, NewL.

—— Extracts from a Supplementary Letter from the Illi-

nois, Dated January 31st, 1819. Address to British
Emigrants Arriving in the Eastern Ports. July 13th,
1819. Reply to William Cobbett, Esq. July 31st, 1819.
29 pp. New York, C. Wiley and Co., 1819. BurColl.

—— Letters from Illinois. 154 pp. Philadelphia, M.
Carey and Son, 1818. BurColl, ChU, LexPL, WRHist,
WisH. 2d ed. xv, 114 pp. London, Taylor and Hessey, 1818. NewL.

—— Notes on a Journey in America, from the Coast of
Virginia to the Territory of Illinois. With Proposals
for the Establishment of a Colony of English. 189 pp.
Philadelphia, Caleb Richardson, 1817. BurColl, WRHist.
iv, 144 pp. London, Ridgway and Sons, 1818. WisH.

Brackenridge, Henry Marie. Journal of a Voyage up the
River Missouri; Performed in Eighteen Hundred and
Eleven, . . . 2d ed., revised and enlarged. viii,
247 pp. Baltimore, Coale and Maxwell, 1815. LC.

—— Views of Louisiana; together with a Journal of a
Voyage up the Missouri River, in 1811. 304 pp. Pittsburg, Cramer, Spear and Richbaum, 1814. ChU,
CinPL, LC, WRHist, WisH.

Brown, Paul. Twelve Months in New-Harmony; Presenting a Faithful Account of the Principal Occurrences
which have Taken Place there within that Period; Interspersed with Remarks. 128 pp. Cincinnati, Wm.
Hill Woodward, 1827. CinPL, IndStL, WRHist, WisH.

The Capitulation; or, a History of the Expedition Conducted by William Hull, Brigadier-General of the Northwestern Army. By an Ohio Volunteer. 78, iv, [1] pp.
Chillicothe, Printed by James Barnes, 1812. Title from
printed title-page (clipped) in copyright book for the
District of Ohio, 1806-1828 (MS. entry dated Oct. 23,
37th Year of Independence); pagination, place, publisher, and date from Thomson.

Caswall, Henry. America, and the American Church. xviii, [1], 368 pp. London, J. G. & F. Rivington, 1839. HistPSO, WRHist, WisH.

Darnall, Elias. A Journal, Containing an Accurate and Interesting Account of the Hardships, Sufferings, Battles, Defeat and Captivity of those Heroic Kentucky Volunteers and Regulars, Commanded by General Winchester in the Year 1812-1813. Also, Two Narratives, by Men who were Wounded in the Battles on the River Raisin, and Taken Captive by the Indians. 57, 7, [1] pp. Paris, Ky., Printed by Joel R. Lyle, 1813. From Thomson. 87, [1] pp. Philadelphia, Grigg & Elliot, 1834. LC, HistPSO.

Delafield, John, Jr. A Brief Topographical Description of the County of Washington, in the State of Ohio, . . . 39 pp. New York, Printed by J. M. Elliott, 1834. LC, WRHist, WisH.

Drake, Daniel. Natural and Statistical View, or Picture of Cincinnati and the Miami Country, Illustrated by Maps. With an Appendix, Containing Observations on the Late Earthquakes, the Aurora Borealis, and Southwest Wind. 251, [4] pp. Cincinnati, Looker and Wallace, 1815. CinPL, HistPSO, LC, NYPL, WRHist.

—— Notices concerning Cincinnati. 60, [iv] pp. Cincinnati, Printed for the Author, at the Press of John W. Browne & Co., 1810. CinPL, HistPSO, LC, NYPL, WRHist.

Filson, John. The Discovery, Settlement and Present State of Kentucke: and an Essay towards the Topography, and Natural History of that Important Country: . . . 118 pp. Wilmington, Printed by James Adams, 1784. LC, NewL, WisH.

—— Histoire de Kentucke, nouvelle colonie a l'ouest de la Virginie: . . . Traduit de l'anglois, de M. John

Filson; par M. Parraud, . . . xvi, 234 pp. Paris, Buisson, 1785. BurColl, WRHist.

Flagg, Edmund. The Far West: or, a Tour beyond the Mountains. Embracing Outlines of Western Life and Scenery; Sketches of the Prairies, Rivers, Ancient Mounds, Early Settlements of the French, etc., etc. . . . 2 vols. New York, Harper & Brothers, 1838. HistPSO, LC, LouPL, NewL, WRHist, WisH.

Flint, Timothy. Recollections of the Last Ten Years, Passed in Occasional Residences and Journeyings in the Valley of the Mississippi, from Pittsburg and the Missouri to the Gulf of Mexico, and from Florida to the Spanish Frontier; in a Series of Letters to the Rev. James Flint, of Salem, Massachusetts. 395 pp. Boston, Cummings, Hilliard, and Company, 1826. BurColl, ChU, CinPL, ColU, HistPSO, LC, LouPL, NewL, NYPL, WRHist, WisH, YMML.

Flower, Richard. Letters from Lexington and the Illinois, Containing a Brief Account of the English Settlement in the Latter Territory, and a Refutation of the Misrepresentations of Mr. Cobbett. 32 pp. London, Printed by C. Teulon for J. Ridgway, 1819. LC, NewL, WRHist.

——, and Benjamin Flower, and Morris Birkbeck. Letters from the Illinois, 1820. 1821. Containing an Account of the English Settlement at Albion and its Vicinity, and a Refutation of Various Misrepresentations, those more particularly of Mr. Cobbett. By Richard Flower. With a Letter from M. Birkbeck; and a Preface and Notes by Benjamin Flower. 76 pp. (pagination incorrect). London, Printed for James Ridgway, by C. Teulon, 1822. LC, NewL, WisH.

Hall, James. Letters from the West; Containing Sketches of Scenery, Manners, and Customs; and Anecdotes Connected with the First Settlements of the Western Sections of the United States. vi, 385, [1] pp. London, Henry Colburn, 1828. BurColl, ChU, CinPL, HistPSO, LC, NewL, NYPL, OhioStL, WRHist, WisH, YMML.

—— Notes on the Western States; Containing Descriptive Sketches of their Soil, Climate, Resources and Scenery. xxiii, 304 pp. Philadelphia, Harrison Hall, 1838. BurColl, ChU, ColU, HistPSO, IndStL, LC, NewL, NYPL, WRHist, WisH.

—— Reply to Strictures on Sketches of the West, in the North American Review, No. 92; being the Preface to Notes on the Western States, just Published. xxiii pp. Philadelphia, Harrison Hall, 1838. WRHist, WisH.

—— Sketches of History, Life, and Manners in the West; Containing Accurate Descriptions of the Country and Modes of Life, in the Western States and Territories of North America. 2 vols. Cincinnati, Hubbard and Edmands, 1834. LC, WRHist, YMML (Vol. I). 2 vols. Philadelphia, Harrison Hall, 1835. ChU, IU, LC, NYPL, OhioStL, WRHist, WisH.

—— Statistics of the West, at the Close of the Year 1836. xviii, 284, [2] pp. Cincinnati, J. A. James & Co., 1836. ChU, LC, NYPL, WRHist, WisH.

A Journal, Containing an Interesting Account of the Hardships, Sufferings, Battles, and Defeat of the Kentucky Volunteers and Regulars, Commanded by Brigadier General James Winchester, in the Years 1812 & '13. To which is Added a Geographical Description of the Northwestern Section of the State of Ohio — . . . From *Ky. Gaz.*, Jan. 9, 1815. *Cf.* entry under Elias Darnall, above.

M'Murtrie, Henry. Sketches of Louisville and its Environs; Including, among a Great Variety of Miscella-

neous Matter, a Florula Louisvillensis; . . . viii, 255
pp. Louisville, Printed by S. Penn, 1819. ChU, CinPL,
LC, LouPL, NYPL, WRHist, WisH.

Madox, D. T. Late Account of the Missouri Territory,
Compiled from Notes Taken during a Tour through that
Country in 1815, and a Translation of Letters from a
Distinguished French Emigrant, Written in 1817. ix,
65, [1] pp. Paris, Ky., Printed for the Author, by John
Lyle, 1817. LexPL, WisH.

Notes on the Northern Part of Ohio. 22 pp. Cuyahoga
Falls, James Lowry, Printer, 1837. HistPSO, LC, WisH.

Schoolcraft, Henry Rowe. Henry R. Schoolcraft — Expedition into the Indian Country. 20 pp. N. p. (Washington?), n. d. (1831?). (Doc. No. 152, H. R., 22d Congress, First Session.) WisH.

—— Journal of a Tour into the Interior of Missouri and
Arkansaw, from Potosi, or Mine à Burton, in Missouri
Territory, in a South-west Direction, toward the Rocky
Mountains; Performed in the Years 1818 and 1819. 102
pp. London, Sir Richard Phillips and Co., 1821. BurColl,
ChU, LC, NewL, NYPL, WRHist, WisH.

—— Narrative Journal of Travels, through the North-
western Regions of the United States Extending from
Detroit through the Great Chain of American Lakes, to
the Sources of the Mississippi River. Performed as a
Member of the Expedition under Governor Cass. In the
Year 1820. 419, [4] pp. Albany, N. Y., E. & E. Hosford,
1821. BurColl, CinPL, ColU, LC, NewL, WRHist,
WisH, YMML.

—— Narrative of an Expedition through the Upper Mississippi to Itasca Lake, the Actual Source of this River;
Embracing the Exploratory Trip through the St. Croix
and Burntwood (or Broule) Rivers; in 1832. Under
the Direction of Henry R. Schoolcraft. 307, [1] pp.

New York, Harper & Brothers, 1834. BurColl, CinPL, LexPL, LC, NewL, NYPL, WRHist, WisH, YMML.

—— Northwestern Indians . . . 16 pp. N. p. (Washington?), n. d. (1833?). (Doc. No. 125, H. R., 22d Congress, Second Session.) WisH.

—— Travels in the Central Portions of the Mississippi Valley: Comprising Observations on its Mineral Geography, Internal Resources, and Aboriginal Population. . . . iv, 459 pp. New York, Collins and Hannay, 1825. CinPL, LC, NewL, NYPL, WRHist, WisH.

—— A View of the Lead Mines of Missouri; Including Some Observations on the Mineralogy, Geology, Geography, Antiquities, Soil, Climate, Population, and Productions of Missouri and Arkansaw, and Other Sections of the Western Country. . . . 299 pp. New York, Charles Wiley & Co., 1819. BurColl, CinPL, LC, NewL, WRHist, WisH, YMML.

Smith, Michael. A Complete History of the Late American War with Great-Britain and her Allies, . . . Sixth Edition Revised and Corrected by the Author. To which is Added, a Narrative of the Author's Sufferings in Canada with his Family, and Journey to Virginia and Kentucky. 287, [1] pp. Lexington, Printed for the Author, by F. Bradford, Jun., 1816. LC, NYPL, WisH.

—— A Narrative of the Sufferings in Upper Canada, with his Family, in the Late War, and Journey to Virginia and Kentucky, of M. Smith, Minister of the Gospel, Author of the "View of the British Possessions in North America," "History of the Late War," and "Beauties of Divine Poetry," &c. &c. . . . 3d ed., with alterations and additions. 161, [1] pp. Lexington, Printed for the Author by Worsley & Smith, 1817. LC, WisH.

Toulmin, Henry. Thoughts on Emigration. To which are Added, Miscellaneous Observations Relating to the Unit-

ed States of America: and a Short Account of the State
of Kentucky. . . . 24, 121, [3] pp. N. p., October,
1792. LC, NewL, WisH.

IV. GUIDEBOOKS AND GAZETTEERS

Amphlett, William. The Emigrant's Directory to the
Western States of North America; Including a Voyage
out from Liverpool; . . . By William Amphlett,
formerly of London, and late of the County of Salop,
now Resident on the Banks of the Ohio River. vii, 208
pp. London, Longman, Hurst, Rees, Orme, and Brown,
1819. LC, WRHist.

Beck, Lewis C. A Gazetteer of the States of Illinois and
Missouri; Containing a General View of Each State —
a General View of their Counties — and a Particular Description of their Towns, Villages, Rivers, &c. &c. With
a Map, and Other Engravings. 352 pp. Albany, Printed
by Charles R. and George Webster, 1823. LC, WRHist,
WisH.

Blois, John T. Gazetteer of the State of Michigan, in Three
Parts, Containing a General View of the State, a De-
scription of the Face of the Country, Soil, Productions,
Public Lands, Internal Improvements, Commerce, Gov-
ernment, Climate, Education, Religious Denominations,
Population, Antiquities, &c. &c. With a Succinct His-
tory of the State, . . . 418 pp. Detroit, Sydney L.
Rood & Co., etc., 1838. BurColl, CinPL, GrandRPL,
WRHist. 418, [1] pp. Detroit, Sydney L. Rood & Co.,
etc., 1839. BurColl, WisH.

Blunt, Edmund M. Traveller's Guide to and through the
State of Ohio, with Sailing Directions for Lake Erie.
28, [4] pp. New York, Sold by Betts & Anstice, etc.,
1833. WRHist.

Brown, Samuel R. The Western Gazetteer; or Emigrant's

Directory, Containing a Geographical Description of the Western States and Territories, . . . 360 pp. Auburn, N. Y., Printed by H. C. Southwick, 1817. ColU, IU, LC, NYPL, WRHist, WisH.

Bryan, John A. The Ohio Annual Register, Containing, a Condensed History of the State, with a Full and Complete Catalogue of All the Public Officers in the Several Counties of Ohio; Officers of State; Members of Congress, and the Legislature; . . . since the Adoption of the State Constitution; . . . For the Year 1835. 128 pp. Columbus, J. Gilbert & R. C. Bryan, n. d. (1834). CinPL, NYPL, WRHist, YMML.

Chapin, William. A Complete Reference Gazetteer of the United States . . . to which are Added a Number of Valuable Tables of the Population, Colleges, and Benevolent Institutions, . . . 347, [3] pp. New York, W. Chapin and J. B. Taylor, 1839. JCrerar, LC.

Collins, S. H. The Emigrant's Guide to the United States of America. . . . 2d ed. iv, 134 pp. Hull, Joseph Noble, 1829. NewL.

Colton, Calvin. Manual for Emigrants to America. x, 203, [1] pp. London, F. Westley and A. H. Davis, 1832. LC, NewL.

Colton, J. H.? The State of Indiana Delineated: . . . 92 pp. New York, J. H. Colton, 1838. ChU, IndStL, IU, LC, NYPL, WisH.

Cramer, Zadok. The Navigator: Containing Directions for Navigating the Monongahela, Alleghany, Ohio, and Mississippi Rivers; . . . and a Concise Description of their Towns, Villages, Harbours, Settlements, &c. . . . 6th ed., enlarged. 156 pp. Pittsburg, Zadok Cramer, 1808. ChU, WRHist.

Cumings, Samuel. The Western Navigator; Containing Directions for the Navigation of the Ohio and Mississippi, and Such Information concerning the Towns, &c. on their Banks, as will be most Useful to Travellers. . . . 2 vols. Philadelphia, E. Littell, 1822. ChU (lacks Vol. I), LC, WRHist.

—— The Western Pilot, Containing Charts of the Ohio River, and of the Mississippi . . . 143 pp. Cincinnati, Morgan, Lodge and Fisher, Printers, 1825. ChU, WRHist.

Dana, Edmund. A Description of the Bounty Lands in the State of Illinois: also, the Principal Roads and Routes, by Land and Water, through the Territory of the United States; . . . 108 pp. Cincinnati, Looker, Reynolds & Co., Printers, 1819. LC, WRHist, WisH.

—— Geographical Sketches on the Western Country: Designed for Emigrants and Settlers: . . . 312 pp. Cincinnati, Looker, Reynolds & Co., Printers, 1819. IndStL, LC, NYPL, WRHist, WisH.

Darby, William. The Emigrant's Guide to the Western and Southwestern States and Territories: . . . [3], 311, xiii pp. New York, Kirk & Mercein, 1818. ColU, IU, LexPL, LC, MoHist, WRHist, WisH.

——, and Theodore Dwight, Jr. A New Gazetteer of the United States of America; . . . 630 pp. Hartford, Conn., Edward Hopkins, 1833. ChU, IU, LC, WRHist, WisH.

Davison, G. M. The Traveller's Guide through the Middle and Northern States, . . . 6th ed. 452 pp. Saratoga Springs, N. Y., G. M. Davison, etc., 1834. BurColl, LC, NYPL.

The Emigrant's Guide, or Pocket Geography of the Western States and Territories, . . . Compiled from the Best and Latest Authorities. 266 pp. Cincinnati, Phillips & Speer, 1818. HistPSO, LC, WisH.

Galland, I. Galland's Iowa Emigrant: Containing a Map,

and General Descriptions of Iowa Territory: 32 pp. Chillicothe, Printed by Wm. C. Jones, 1840. LC, WisH.

A Geographical, Historical, Commercial, and Agricultural View of the United States of America; Forming a Complete Emigrant's Directory through Every Part of the Republic: Particularising the States of Kentucky, Tennessee, Ohio, Indiana, Mississippi, Louisiana, and Illinois; and the Territories of Alabama, Missouri, with a Description of the Newly-acquired Countries, East and West Florida, Michigan, and North-Western; . . . Compiled by Several Gentlemen, . . . 7, 746, xvi pp. London, Edwards & Knibb, etc., 1820. WisH.

Gilleland, J. C. The Ohio and Mississippi Pilot, . . . 274 pp. Pittsburg, R. Patterson & Lambdin, 1820. HistPSO, IndStL, LC.

Hewett, D. The American Traveller; or, National Directory, . . . 440 pp. Washington, Printed by Davis & Force, 1825. LC, WisH.

Holditch, Robert. The Emigrant's Guide to the United States of America; . . . iv, 123, [1] pp. London, William Hone, 1818. WRHist.

Illinois in 1837; a Sketch Descriptive of the Situation, Boundaries, Face of the Country, Prominent Districts, Prairies, Rivers, Minerals, Animals, Agricultural Productions, Public Lands, Plans of Internal Improvement, Manufactures, &c. . . . together with a Letter on the Cultivation of the Prairies, by the Hon. H. L. Ellsworth. To which are Annexed the Letters from a Rambler in the West. . . . 143, [1] pp. Philadelphia, S. Augustus Mitchell, and Grigg & Elliot, 1837. WRHist, WisH.

Jenkins, Warren. The Ohio Gazetteer, . . . 546 pp. Columbus, Isaac N. Whiting, n. d. (1837). ChU, WRHist. First revised ed. 546 pp. Columbus, Isaac N. Whiting, 1837. HistPSO.

Jones, Abner Dumont. Illinois and the West. With a Township Map, Containing the Latest Surveys and Improvements. 255, [1] pp. Boston, Weeks, Jordan and Company, etc., 1838. ChU, LC, NYPL, WisH.

Kilbourn, John. The Ohio Gazetteer: or Topographical Dictionary, . . . alphabetically Arranged. 166 pp. Columbus, P. H. Olmsted & Co., July, 1816. LC. 2d ed. 114 pp. Columbus, J. Kilbourn, Nov., 1816. WRHist, WisH.

Lea, Albert M. Notes on Wisconsin Territory, with a Map. 53 pp. Philadelphia, Henry S. Tanner, 1836. LC, WisH.

Lyford, William Gilman. The Western Address Directory: Containing the Cards of Merchants, Manufacturers, and Other Business Men, in Pittsburgh, (Pa.) Wheeling, (Va.) Zanesville, (O.) Portsmouth, (O.) Dayton, (O.) Cincinnati, (O.) Madison, (Ind.) Louisville, (K.) St. Louis, (Mo.) together with Historical, Topographical & Statistical Sketches, (for the Year 1837,) of those Cities, and Towns in the Mississippi Valley. Intended as a Guide to Travellers. To which is Added, alphabetically Arranged, a List of the Steam-boats on the Western Waters. 468 pp. Baltimore, Printed by Jos. Robinson, 1837. WRHist, WisH.

Melish, John. A Geographical Description of the United States; with Topographical Tables of the Counties, Towns, Population, &c. From the Census of 1810. 32 pp. Philadelphia, Printed for the Author by G. Palmer, 1815. WisH.

—— The Traveller's Directory through the United States: . . . Pagination irregular. Philadelphia, Printed for the Author, by G. Palmer, 1815. ChU.

—— The Traveller's Manual; and Description of the United States: . . . 497, [15] pp. New York, A. T. Goodrich, 1831. WisH.

Mitchell, Samuel Augustus. Mitchell's Traveller's Guide through the United States, . . . 78 pp. Philadelphia, Hinman & Dutton, 1838. WisH.

—— The Principal Stage, Steam-boat, and Canal Routes in the United States; . . . 96 pp. Philadelphia, Mitchell & Hinman, 1834. LC, WRHist.

Morse, Jedidiah, and Richard C. Morse. The Traveller's Guide: or Pocket Gazetteer of the United States; . . . 323, [1] pp. New Haven, Conn., Nathan Whiting, 1823. NYPL, WRHist.

Notes on the Navigation of the Mississippi; . . . Taken by a Gentleman of Talents and Observation; . . . (Lexington, James M. Bradford, 1804.) From *Ky. Gaz.*, May 31, 1803; and Mar. 20, 1804.

Peck, John Mason. A Gazetteer of Illinois, in Three Parts: Containing a General View of the State; a General View of Each County; and a Particular Description of Each Town, Settlement, Stream, Prairie, Bottom, Bluff, etc. — Alphabetically Arranged. viii, 376 pp. Jacksonville, Ill., R. Goudy, 1834. ChU, LC, NYPL, WisH. 2d ed. xi, 328 pp. Philadelphia, Grigg & Elliot, 1837. LC, WRHist.

—— A Guide for Emigrants, Containing Sketches of Illinois, Missouri, and the Adjacent Parts. 336 pp. Boston, Lincoln and Edmands, 1831. ChHist, LC, WRHist, WisH.

—— A New Guide for Emigrants to the West, . . . 374 pp. Boston, Gould, Kendall & Lincoln, 1836. IU, LC, WRHist.

—— The Traveller's Directory for Illinois; . . . 219 pp. New York, J. H. Colton, 1839. WisH.

Plumbe, John, Jr. Sketches of Iowa and Wisconsin, Taken during a Residence of Three Years in those Territories. 103 pp. St. Louis, Chambers, Harris & Knapp, 1839. LC, MercLStL, WRHist, WisH.

Remarks on the Western States of America or Valley of the Mississippi: with Suggestions to Agricultural Emigrants, Miners, &c. 45, [2] pp. London, R. J. Kennett, 1839. LC, WisH.

Rupp, Israel Daniel. The Geographical Catechism of Pennsylvania, and the Western States; . . . iv, 384 pp. Harrisburg, Pa., John Winebrenner, V. D. M., 1836. LC, WRHist. iv, 384 pp. Philadelphia, Bonsal & Desilver, etc., 1837. LC, WRHist, WisH.

Scott, John. The Indiana Gazetteer, or Topographical Dictionary, . . . alphabetically Arranged . . . 143 pp. Centreville, Ind., John Scott & William M. Doughty, 1826. IndStL, LC. 2d ed., corrected and enlarged. 200 pp. Indianapolis, Douglass and Maguire, 1833. IndStL, JCrerar, WRHist, WisH.

Sketches of Illinois; Descriptive of its Principal Geographical Features, . . . 32 pp. Philadelphia, S. Augustus Mitchell, and Grigg & Elliot, 1838. BurColl.

Smith, John Calvin. The Western Tourist and Emigrant's Guide, with a Compendious Gazetteer of the States of Ohio, Michigan, Indiana, Illinois, and Missouri, and the Territories of Wisconsin, and Iowa; . . . 180 pp. New York, J. H. Colton, 1839. BurColl, NewL, WRHist.

Smith, Thomas. The Emigrant's Guide to the United States of America; Including the Substance of the Journal of Thomas Hulme, Esq. 2d ed., enlarged and improved. 52 pp. London, etc., Sherwood, Neely, and Jones, 1818. From LC card.

Smith, William Rudolph. Observations on the Wisconsin Territory; chiefly on that Part Called the "Wisconsin Land District." With a Map, Exhibiting the Settled Parts of the Territory, as Laid off in Counties by Act of the Legislature in 1837. viii, 134 pp. Philadelphia, E. L. Carey & A. Hart, 1838. BurColl, LC, WisH.

Steele, Oliver G. Steele's Western Guide Book, and Emigrant's Directory, Containing Different Routes through the States of New-York, Ohio, Indiana, Illinois and Michigan, . . . 5th ed. 108 pp. Buffalo, N. Y., Oliver G. Steele, 1836. HistPSO.

Stranger, Traveller, and Merchant's Guide through the United States. 156 pp. Philadelphia, 1825. From LC card.

Tanner, Henry S. The American Traveller; or Guide through the United States. . . . 144 pp. Philadelphia, the Author, 1834. BurColl, LC.

Van Zandt, Nicholas Biddle. A Full Description of the Soil, Water, Timber, and Prairies of Each Lot, or Quarter Section of the Military Lands between the Mississippi and Illinois Rivers. iv, 127 pp. Washington, Printed by P. Force, 1818. ChHist, ChU, LC, WisH.

View of the Valley of the Mississippi: or the Emigrant's and Traveller's Guide to the West. Containing a General Description of that Entire Country; and also, Notices of the Soil, Productions, Rivers, and Other Channels of Intercourse and Trade: and likewise of the Cities and Towns, Progress of Education, &c. of Each State and Territory. . . . xii, 341, 10 pp. Philadelphia, H. S. Tanner, 1832. WRHist. 2d ed. 372 pp. Philadelphia, H. S. Tanner, 1834. LouPL, TerreHPL, WisH.

The Western Guide Book, and Emigrant's Directory; Containing General Descriptions of Different Routes through the States of New-York, Ohio, Indiana, Illinois, and the Territory of Michigan, . . . 90, [2] pp. Buffalo, Oliver G. Steele, 1834. WisH.

The Western Traveller's Pocket Directory and Stranger's Guide: . . . 93, [3] pp. Schenectady, N. Y., Printed at the Reflector Office, 1836. LC, MercLStL.

Wetmore, Alphonso. Gazetteer of the State of Missouri.

With a Map of the State, . . . to which is Added an Appendix, Containing Frontier Sketches, and Illustrations of Indian Character. . . . 382 pp. and map. St. Louis, C. Keemle, 1837. ChU, ColU, IU, LC, NYPL, WRHist, WisH.

Williams, Jesse. A Description of the United States Lands in Iowa: being a Minute Description of Every Section and Quarter Section, Quality of Soil, Groves of Timber, . . . etc., etc., etc. With an Appendix. 180, [1] pp. New York, J. H. Colton, 1840. LC, NYPL, WisH.

V. FOREIGN TRAVEL BY WESTERN WRITERS

Cass, Lewis. France, its King, Court, and Government, by an American. 191 pp. New York, Wiley & Putnam, 1840. ColU, NYPL, WRHist.

Paxton, J. D. Letters from Palestine: Written during a Residence there in the Years 1836, 7, and 8. 263, [9] pp. London, Charles Tilt, 1839. LC.

Thome, James A., and J. Horace Kimball. Emancipation in the West Indies. A Six Months' Tour in Antigua, Barbadoes, and Jamaica, in the Year 1837. 489 pp. New York, the American Anti-slavery Society, 1838. ChU, CinPL, LC, WRHist.

CHAPTER III

NEWSPAPERS AND MAGAZINES

I. Newspapers

(A representative selection including those used as sources in the various chapters of this book.)

The Beacon.
    St. Louis, Mar. 2, 1829-? With issue for Mar. 16, 1829, title changed to *St. Louis Beacon.* StLPL (has Mar. 2, 1829-Sept. 15, 1831; 11 issues missing and many mutilated).

The Centinel of the North-Western Territory.
    Cincinnati, Nov. 9, 1793-June 4 (or a short time later), 1796. HistPSO (lacks Nos. 1 and 2, 10, 34, 67, 71, 81, 82, 90, 93, 114, 122), OhioStL (lacks issues later than Nov. 8, 1794).

Cincinnati 'Commercial Register.'
    Cincinnati, 1825?-? Daily. From *Detroit Gaz.,* Jan. 31, 1826. YMML. Check list records issues for Dec., 1825, and later, but file is missing.

Commercial Bulletin and Missouri Literary Register.
    St. Louis, May 18, 1835-Dec. 31, 1836 (or later). With issue of July 17, 1835, the title became *St. Louis Commercial Bulletin and Missouri Literary Register*; and with number for Aug. 22, 1836, it was changed to *Daily Commercial Bulletin and Missouri Literary Register.* WisH.

The Daily Chronicle.
    Cincinnati, Nov. 28, 1839-1840 (and later). CinPL,

HistPSO, NYPL (lacks Nov. 28, 1839-May 30, 1840; and Dec., 1840), OhioStL (lacks Dec., 1840).

The Daily Cincinnati Gazette.

Cincinnati, June 25? (No. 2 is for Tuesday, June 26) 1827-1840 (and later). Name changed to *Cincinnati Daily Gazette* with issue for Sept. 27, 1830, and to *The Cincinnati Daily Gazette* with issue for May 14, 1832. CinPL (lacks June 26-end of Dec., 1831; and July-Dec., 1835), HistPSO (broken files), NYPL (fragmentary files for 1828, 1830, 1831, 1838, 1839, and 1840), OhioStL, YMML.

Detroit Courier.

Detroit, Dec., 1830? (No. 9 is for Feb. 17, 1831)-Jan. 14, 1835. BurColl.

Detroit Daily Advertiser.

Detroit, June 11, 1836-1840 (and later). DetroitPL, WisH (lacks June 11, 1836-Feb., 1840; and July-Dec., 1840).

Detroit Daily Free Press.

Detroit, Sept. 28, 1835-Jan. 3, 1837 (or later). DetroitPL.

Detroit Free Press. New Series. . . . Daily.

Detroit, June 5, 1837-1840 (and later). DetroitPL, LC (lacks Oct. 16, 1837-Dec., 1840).

Detroit Gazette.

Detroit, July 25, 1817-1830. BurColl (lacks July, 1827-Sept., 1828, and all but 14 issues for Oct. 2, 1828-Apr., 1830), DetroitPL (fragmentary file), LC (lacks 1817-1818 and 1827-1828), WisH (lacks 1817; Jan.-Mar., 1818; all but 9 issues for Apr., 1818-June, 1819; and Aug., 1828-1830).

Detroit Journal and Courier.

Detroit, Jan. 21, 1835-1839 (or later). Follows the *Detroit Journal and Michigan Advertiser*. BurColl, LC (lacks 1835-1837 and 1839).

Detroit Journal and Michigan Advertiser.

Detroit, Nov. 24, 1830-Jan. 14, 1835. Continuation of *North-Western Journal*; followed by *Detroit Journal and Courier*. BurColl, LC (lacks 1832 and 1834-1835).

Du Buque Visitor.

DuBuque, Wisconsin Territory, 1836 (and possibly later). Vol. I, No. 27 for Nov. 9, 1836. WisH.

The Farmer's Library, or, Ohio Intelligencer.

Louisville, 1801?-1810? Vol. II, No. 58 for Feb. 18, 1802. ChU (has scattering copies for Feb. 18, 1802-July 23, 1807). For one earlier copy (Dec. 7, 1801), see Brigham.

Freeman's Journal.

Cincinnati, June? (No. 4 of Vol. I is for July 9), 1796-1800. CinPL (Oct. 27, 1798, only — Vol. III, No. 19, whole No. 123). For issues in Harvard, HistPSO, and AmericanAS, see Brigham.

Green-Bay Intelligencer.

Navarino (Green Bay), Dec. 11, 1833-June 1, 1836 (or later). With issue of June 27, 1835, the title became *Green-Bay Intelligencer, and Wisconsin Democrat*. WisH.

The Illinois Herald.

Kaskaskia, 1814 (Vol. I, No. 30, is for Dec. 13)-1815. IllStHist (has Dec. 13, 1814). See also above, Chapter III, footnote 22. For reproduction of heading of the number for Dec. 13, 1814, see Franklin William Scott, *Newspapers and Periodicals of Illinois 1814-1879*, 1910, frontispiece.

The Illinois Intelligencer.

Kaskaskia, Ill. (at Vandalia, Ill., 1820-1832), May 27, 1818-1832. Successor to *The Western Intelligencer*. MercLStL (lacks June-Dec., 1819; 1820; 1821, except Feb. 20; 1822, except Oct. 12 — mutilated — and Dec. 7;

1823-1825; Jan.-Mar., 1826, except Mar. 30). Title changed to *Illinois Intelligencer* sometime between Feb. 20, 1821, and Dec. 7, 1822.

Independent Press.

Cincinnati, July 4, 1822-(continuously?) Dec. 16, 1826 (or later). With issue for Oct. 8, 1822, title changed to *Independent Press & Freedom's Advocate.* CinPL (1822-1823), HistPSO (broken files).

Indiana Gazette.

Vincennes, July 31? (No. 2 is for Aug. 7), 1804-1806? Latest number located is for Apr. 12, 1806. See above, Chapter III, footnote 13. For a number of issues for period Aug. 7, 1804, to Aug. 14, 1805, in AmericanAS and Harvard, see Brigham. Photostat copies for this period in IndStL.

The Kentucke Gazette.

Lexington, Aug. 11, 1787-1840 (and later). With issue of Mar. 14, 1789, the title was changed to *The Kentucky Gazette.* Later changes in the title were of slight importance. For a somewhat detailed account of this paper, see above, Chapter III, footnote 5. ChU (fragmentary files; for detailed check list, see Henry), CinPL (has 1814-1816 and 1831-1834), LexPL (by far the best file — lacks 1807-1808, 1821-1824, 1829, 1832 except one number, 1833-1834; a considerable part of 1817, 1818, 1827, 1828, 1830, and 1831; and a small number of issues from other years), LC (has only Jan. 1, 1819-Oct. 10, 1828; and Jan. 5, 1833-1840, and later), WisH (has 34 issues for 1787-1788 and 11 for 1812-1814); IndStL, LexPL, NewL, UMich, and several other libraries have copies of *The Kentucky Gazette Lexington, Kentucky Reproduced by the Photostat Process from the File Owned by the Public Library of Lexington, Ky.,* 1918,

published by the General Library of the University of
Michigan (includes file for 1787-1800).

The Lamp.

Lincoln County, Ky., 1807?-1808 (or later). Vol. I, No.
24 for Jan. 12, 1808. ChU.

Lexington Intelligencer. New Series.

Lexington, 1833? (Vol. I, No. 42, is for Jan. 7, 1834)-
1839 (or later). LexPL (has 1834-1839).

Lexington Observer.

Lexington, May 14 (Vol. I, No. 2, is for May 21), 1831-
Apr. 6, 1832. Succeeded by *Lexington Observer & Kentucky Reporter*. ChU, LexPL.

Lexington Observer & Kentucky Reporter.

Lexington, Apr. 13, 1832-1840 (and later). Title shortened in 1840 to *Lexington Observer & Reporter*. ChU
(for issues lacking see Henry), LexPL (lacks 1837). An
edition of the *Lexington Observer & Kentucky Reporter*
called *Observer & Reporter* was for a long time issued
simultaneously with the paper bearing the longer title.
I have not attempted here a complete record of such
minor alterations in the title as the change from *&* to *and*.

Liberty Hall and Cincinnati Mercury.

Cincinnati, Dec. 4, 1804-Nov. 23, 1837 (or later). With
issue of Apr. 13, 1809, this title changed to *Liberty Hall*;
and with issue of Dec. 11, 1815, the title changed to *Liberty Hall & Cincinnati Gazette*. CinPL (lacks 1804-
1810; 1813; 1825; 1826, except July 4; 1828-1834; and
1838-1840), HistPSO (has 3 vols. for years 1815-1824),
OhioStL (lacks 1804; Jan.-Nov., 1805; Dec., 1808;
1809-1815; Jan.-Feb., 1816; July-Dec., 1827; 1828-1829;
Jan.-May, 1830; 1833, except Jan. 3; 1834-1835; and
Jan.-May, 1836), YMML (lacks 1826-1828 and 1834-
1837).

The Logansport Herald.

Logansport, Ind., Aug.? (Vol. I, No. 9, is for Sept. 28), 1837-1840 (or later).   IU, LC (Mar. 18-Oct. 7, 1840).

The Louisville Daily Focus.

Louisville, Jan. 28, 1831-Jan. 30, 1832.   With issue of Apr. 20, 1831, the title was shortened to *Louisville Daily Focus*.   ChU, LouPL.

The Louisville Daily Journal.

Louisville, Nov. 24, 1830-1840 (and later).   Title from issue for Dec. 1, 1840 (LouPL); date of first issue from *Daily Lou. Pub. Adv.*, Nov. 25, 1830.

The Louisville Public Advertiser.

Louisville, June 30? (Vol. I, No. 5, is for July 28), 1818-1840 (and later).   Called *Public Advertiser* until issue of Jan. 27, 1819, when the longer title was first used. Name changed to *Daily Louisville Public Advertiser* with issue of June 14, 1830 (daily publication had begun with the issue of Jan. 1, 1830).   Called *Louisville Public Advertiser*, beginning with the issue for Dec. 19, 1831, but reverted to the longer title (*Daily* etc.) with issue of Jan. 16, 1832.   The shorter title was resumed after July 26, 1834; but the paper was, as always since 1830, continued as a daily.   ChU (nearly complete; for detailed check list see Henry), LC (has only Jan. 19, 1820-Sept. 19, 1821; Jan. 2-28, 1822; and 1823-1830).

Michigan Essay; or, the Impartial Observer.

Detroit, Aug. 31, 1809 (Vol. I, No. 1).   AmericanAS, BurColl.   There were probably two later issues.   See above, Chapter III, footnote 24.

Missouri Gazette.

St. Louis, July 12? (Vol. I, No. 3, is for July 26), 1808-1840 (and later).   Later called *Louisiana Gazette, Missouri Republican*, etc.   For changes in title, see above, Chapter III, footnote 20.   MercLStL (has 1827, except

15 issues; 1828, except 3 issues; 1830, Jan.-Oct. 5, except 9 issues — for detailed check list, see *St. Louis Mercantile Library Reference Lists I*, Feb., 1898, p. 3), MoHist (excellent but not complete file covering the whole period).

The National Republican and Ohio Political Register.

Cincinnati, Jan. 1, 1823-1830. Successor to the *Western Spy*. CinPL (has Mar. 12, 1824-Dec. 28, 1827), HistPSO (has three vols., commencing with Jan. 1, 1823), OhioStL (Jan. 1, 1823-Dec. 26, 1826), WRHist (has 1823-1826), YMML (has 1823-1830).

North-Western Journal.

Detroit, Nov. 20, 1829-Nov. 17, 1830. Continued as *Detroit Journal and Michigan Advertiser*. BurColl.

The Palladium: a Literary and Political Weekly Repository.

Frankfort, Aug. 9, 1798-1816 (or later — as late as 1826, according to Major, as cited by W. H. Perrin, *The Pioneer Press of Kentucky*, 1888, p. 24). ChU (has 1798-1808; Jan.-Apr. 20, 1809); KyStL (has 1798-1803), WisH (has 1798-Oct., 1803). For copies in Harvard, see Brigham.

The Reporter.

Lexington, Mar. 12, 1808-Apr. 4? 1832. With issue for Oct. 1, 1817, the title was changed to *Kentucky Reporter*. In 1832, this paper was merged with *Lexington Observer* to form the *Lexington Observer & Kentucky Reporter*, the first issue of which appeared on Apr. 13 of that year. ChU (has 1812-1832, except Sept.-Dec., 1814, and several scattering issues for each year thereafter to and including 1826; lacks one issue for 1832), CinPL (has Mar. 12, 1808-Dec. 30, 1809, and 1815-1817), LexPL (excellent but not complete file, covering the whole period), LC (has Jan. 3-Oct. 20, 1819; Apr. 4, 1825-Dec. 24, 1828).

Sangamon Journal.
> Springfield, Ill., Nov. 10, 1831-1840 (and later). With
> issue of Jan. 19, 1832, the title was changed to *Sangamo
> Journal*. IllStHist.

Spirit of the West.
> Cincinnati, July 26, 1814-1815. CinPL (has July 26,
> 1814-Apr. 29, 1815).

Stewart's Kentucky Herald.
> Lexington (later Paris, Ky.), Feb., 1795?-1806? Pub-
> lished at Paris 1805 and later. ChU (has 18 issues for
> period Nov. 17, 1795-May 25, 1802. For the few issues to
> be found in other libraries, see Brigham.

The Supporter.
> Chillicothe, Oct.? (Vol. I, No. 10, is for Dec. 8), 1808-
> 1820 (or later). OhioStL (has Dec. 8, 1808-Sept. 26,
> 1815; and Oct. 29, 1816-Nov. 22, 1820). The numbers of
> volume and issue cited above are from Brigham.

The Western Courier.
> Louisville, Nov., 1811?-1817 (or later). WisH (has Nov.
> 30, 1813-Sept. 26, 1816, except one whole issue and parts
> of several others).

The Western Intelligencer.
> Kaskaskia, Apr.? (No. 4 is for May 15), 1816-May 20,
> 1818. With issue of May 27, 1818, this paper became
> *The Illinois Intelligencer*. MercLStL.

The Western Spy, and Hamilton Gazette.
> Cincinnati, May 28, 1799-Dec. 28, 1822 (except for a
> short period). Followed by *The National Republican
> and Ohio Political Register*. With issue of Sept. 4, 1805,
> the title became *The Western Spy, and Miami Gazette*;
> sometime between July 2, 1808, and Sept. 15, 1810, the
> shorter title *The Western Spy* came into use (see Brigham
> for history of the paper during this period); with issue
> of Jan. 16, 1819, this was changed to *Western Spy, and*

Cincinnati General Advertiser; with issue of Apr. 29, 1820, it became *Western Spy, and Literary Cadet.* Later changes were inconsiderable. CinPL (has July 25, 1817-Mar. 9, 1822), HistPSO (has broken files for 1805-1806; 1812-1816; and 1820-1822), OhioStL (has May 24, 1816-Dec. 28, 1822), YMML (has May, 1799-Jan., 1804; Aug. 26, 1806-July 2, 1808; and Sept. 9, 1810-Oct. 17, 1812).

The Western Sun.

Vincennes, July 4? (Vol. I, No. 2, is for July 11), 1807-1840 (and later). Successor to *Indiana Gazette.* For changes of title, etc., see above, Chapter III, footnote 13. IndStL (has excellent file for whole period), LC (has 1819-1823, 1826, and 1837, with some omissions).

II. Weekly Publications Other than Newspapers
(A selection.)

The Buckeye and Cincinnati Mirror. A Western Gazette of Literature and Science.

Cincinnati, J. B. Marshall, 1835-1836. Edited by James B. Marshall. Vol. V (follows Vol. IV of *The Cincinnati Mirror, and Chronicle*), Oct. 31, 1835-Jan. 23, 1836, Nos. 1-13, 104 pp. CinPL.

The Calvinistic Family Library, Devoted to the Republication of Standard Calvinistic Works. . . .

Cadiz, O., David Christy, 1835-1837 (or later). Vol. I, June 1, 1835-Feb. 15, 1837, Nos. 1-26, [1], 411 pp. WRHist.

The Campaign.

Frankfort, Brown & Hodges, 1840-1841. Nos. 1-26, Apr. 23, 1840-May, 1841 (none published between Oct. 8, 1840, and May, 1841), 436 pp. HistPSO.

The Catholic Telegraph.

Cincinnati, 1831-1832 (or later). Vol. I, Oct. 22, 1831-Oct. 13, 1832, Nos. 1-52, 416 pp. HistPSO.

The Cincinnati Literary Gazette.

Cincinnati, John P. Foote, 1824-1825. Vol. I, Jan. 1-
June 26, 1824, Nos. 1-26, 208 pp. HistPSO, IU, WRHist,
WisH. Vol. II, July 3-Dec. 25, 1824, Nos. 1-26, 208 pp.
HistPSO (lacks Nos. 19-26), IU, LouPL, WisH (lacks
No. 23). Vols. III and IV, two vols. in one, Jan. 1-Oct.
29, 1825, Nos. 1-35, 280 pp. HistPSO (lacks Nos. 9, 19-21,
and 23-27), LouPL (lacks Vol. IV), WisH (lacks No. 8).

The Cincinnati Mirror, and Western Gazette of Literature
and Science.

Cincinnati, 1833-1836 (follows *The Cincinnati Mirror
and Ladies' Parterre*, Vol. II). Vol. III (Shreve and
Gallagher; Edited by William D. Gallagher and Thomas
H. Shreve), Oct. 5, 1833-Oct. 11, 1834, Nos. 1-52, iv, 412
pp. CinPL (lacks No. 4), WRHist. Vol. IV (title
changes, with No. 25, to *The Cincinnati Mirror, and
Chronicle; Devoted to Literature and Science*; T. H.
Shreve & Co.; Edited by William D. Gallagher, Thomas
H. Shreve, and J. H. Perkins), Oct. 18, 1834-Oct. 24,
1835, Nos. 1-52, 416 (incomplete?) pp. CinPL. Vol.
V (*The Cincinnati Mirror, and Western Gazette of Lit-
erature, Science, and the Arts*; Flash, Ryder, and Com-
pany; Edited partly by William D. Gallagher and Thomas
H. Shreve, and partly by Joseph Reese Fry), Nos. 3-34
for Feb. 13-Sept. 17, 1836, pp. 17-272. CinPL (lacks
Nos. 6-31 and 33).

Cleveland Liberalist.

Cleveland, S. Underhill & Son, etc., 1836-1838. Edited
by Samuel Underhill. Vol. I, Sept. 10, 1836-Sept. 16,
1837, Nos. 1-52, 416 pp. WRHist. Vol. II, Sept. 23,
1837-Sept. 29, 1838, Nos. 1-52, 416 pp. WRHist (lacks
Nos. 2-15). Vol. III, Oct. 6-27, 1838, Nos. 1-4, 32 pp.
WRHist.

The Eclectic Journal of Science.

Columbus, 1832?-1834 (or later). Edited by William Hance. Weekly. Vol. II, No. 26 for Jan. 8, 1834, pp. 17-32. WRHist.

The Gambier Observer: Devoted to the Interests of Religion in the Protestant Episcopal Church.

Gambier, O., 1830-1835 (or later). Title-page from Vol. II. Vol. I, May 28, 1830-Aug. 5, 1831, Nos. 1-52, 416 pp. CinPL (lacks Nos. 1-20), WRHist. Vol. II (George W. Myers, Printer; Edited by M. T. C. Wing), Aug. 12, 1831-Aug. 31, 1832, Nos. 1-52, [2], 412 pp. CinPL, WRHist. Vol. III (George W. Myers, Printer; Edited by M. T. C. Wing), Sept. 7, 1832-Sept. 6, 1833, Nos. 1-52, [2], 416 pp. CinPL, WRHist. Vol. IV (George W. Myers, Printer; Edited by M. T. C. Wing), Sept. 13, 1833-Sept. 12, 1834, Nos. 1-52, [3], 416 pp. CinPL, WRHist. Vol. V (George W. Myers, Printer; Edited by Wm. Sparrow and M. T. C. Wing), Nos. 5-52 for Nov. 7, 1834-Oct. 2, 1835, pp. 33-412. CinPL, WRHist.

The Gridiron.

Dayton, O., John Anderson, 1822-1823 (or later). Vol. I, Nos. 3-25 for Sept. 11, 1822-Apr. 24, 1823, 196 pp. DaytonPL (lacks Nos. 6, 11, and 22), WRHist (lacks Nos. 1-4, 8, and 22-25).

The Indiana Religious Intelligencer.

Madison, Ind., 1828-1830. Edited by James H. Johnson. Vol. I (Printed by C. P. J. Arion), June 27, 1828-June 26, 1829, Nos. 1-41, 330 pp. IndStL. Vol. II (Arion & Lodge, for the Indiana Missionary Society), July 3, 1829-Jan. 29, 1830, Nos. 1-30, 240 pp. IndStL.

The Literary Register a Weekly Paper.

Oxford, O., Printed at the Societies' Press, 1828. Edited by the Professors of the Miami University. Vol. I, June

2-Dec. 8, 1828, Nos. 1-26, 416 pp. Smith (lacks No. 1),
WRHist, WisH (has only Nos. 24 and 26).

Louisville Literary News-letter. Devoted to News, Science, Literature and the Arts.

Louisville, Prentice & Weissinger, 1838-1840. Vol. I
(Edited by Edmund Flagg), Dec. 1, 1838-Nov. 23, 1839,
Nos. 1-52, 416 pp. ChU, WisH (lacks Nos. 2-6, 8-11,
13-16, 20-21, 24-25, and 27-40). Vol. II (Edited by
Leonard Bliss), Nov. 30, 1839-Nov. 21, 1840, Nos. 1-52,
426 pp. ChU, WisH (lacks No. 26). Vol. III, Nov.
28, 1840, No. 1, 8 pp. ChU, WisH.

The Microscope.

Louisville (later New Albany), T. H. Roberts, 1824-1825
(or later). Vol. I, Apr. 17, 1824-Apr. 23, 1825, Nos.
1-52, no pagination. No. 22 (Sept. 22, 1824) and later
issues published at New Albany. ChU (lacks Nos. 8 and
9, 16, and 49-51). Vol. II (*The Microscope and General Advertiser*; title had been enlarged with Vol. I, No.
27, Oct. 30, 1824), Nos. 1-20 for Apr. 30-Sept. 10, 1825,
no pagination. ChU.

Missouri Saturday News.

St. Louis, C. Keemle & Co., 1838-1839. Edited by A. Wetmore and C. Keemle. Vol. I, Jan. 6, 1838-Jan. 19, 1839,
Nos. 1-52, no pagination. WisH.

The New-Harmony and Nashoba Gazette, or the Free Enquirer.

New Harmony, Ind., 1828-1829 (the successor to *The
New-Harmony Gazette*; removed to New York after
eighteen issues, appearing there under the title *The
Free Enquirer* from Mar. 4, 1829). Printed by William
Phiquepal and his Pupils; Edited by Frances Wright,
Robert Dale Owen, and Robert L. Jennings. Vol. I
(Second Series; Vol. IV, Whole Series), Oct. 29, 1828-
Feb. 25, 1829, Nos. 1-18, 144 pp. IndStL.

The New-Harmony Gazette.

New Harmony, Ind., 1825-1828. Vol. I (Edited by Robert L. Jennings and William Owen, Nos. 1-12; Robert L. Jennings, Nos. 13-22; William Pelham, Nos. 23-40 or 45; Thomas Palmer and others, Nos. 41 or 46-52), Oct. 1, 1825-Sept. 20, 1826, Nos. 1-52, iv, 416 pp. See above, Chapter III. HistPSO, IndStL, WRHist, WisH. Vol. II (Edited by Robert Dale Owen, Nos. 3-32; and William Owen, Nos. 33-52), Oct. 4, 1826-Oct. 3, 1827, Nos. 1-52, iv, 416 pp. HistPSO, IndStL. Vol. III (Edited by William Owen, Nos. 1-20; Robert Dale Owen and William Owen, Nos. 21-33; Frances Wright and William Owen, Nos. 34-38; Frances Wright and Robert Dale Owen, Nos. 39-52), Oct. 10, 1827-Oct. 22, 1828, Nos. 1-52, [4], 416 pp. HistPSO, IndStL.

The Patriot.

Frankfort, William Tanner, 1826. Twenty-two issues, Feb. 22-July 31, 1826 (no more published?), 352 pp. TransylvaniaU.

The Philanthropist, a Weekly Journal, Containing Essays, on Moral and Religious Subjects, Domestic Economy, Agriculture, and the Mechanic Arts; together with a Brief Notice of the Events of the Times.

Mountpleasant, O., Elisha Bates, 1818-1822. Edited by Elisha Bates. Vol. I, 12th Month, 11, 1818-4th Month, 10, 1819, Nos. 1-18, 288 pp. WRHist. Vol. II, 4th Month, 17-10th Month, 23, 1819, Nos. 1-26, 416 pp. WRHist. Vol. III, 10th Month, 30, 1819-4th Month, 22, 1820, 419, [2] pp. WRHist. Vol. IV, 4th Month, 29-10th Month, 28, 1820, Nos. 1-26, 413, [3] pp. WRHist. Vol. V, Nos. 1-25 for 11th Month, 4, 1820-4th Month, 21, 1821, 396 pp. WRHist. Vol. VI, 5th Month, 5-10th Month, 27, 1821, Nos. 1-26, 408 pp. WRHist. Vol. VII, Nos. 1-24 for 11th Month, 10, 1821-4th Month, 27, 1822, 384 pp. WRHist.

The Sentinel, and Star in the West.

Cincinnati (later Philomath, Ind., and, simultaneously, Cincinnati and Madisonville, O.,), 1829-1837 (or later). Vol. I (Cincinnati), Oct. 3, 1829-Oct. 2, 1830, Nos. 1-52, 416 pp. WRHist. Vol. II (Cincinnati, Samuel Tizzard; Edited by J. Kidwell, J. C. Waldo, and S. Tizzard), Nos. 2-52 for Oct. 30, 1830-Oct. 22, 1831, pp. 9-414, [2]. CinPL, WRHist. Vol. III (Cincinnati, Samuel Tizzard; Edited by J. Kidwell and S. Tizzard), Nov. 19, 1831-Nov. 10, 1832, Nos. 1-52, 413, [3] pp. CinPL, IndStL (has No. 7 only). Vol. IV (Philomath, Union County, Ind., Samuel Tizzard; Edited by J. Kidwell and S. Tizzard), Jan. 12, 1833-Feb. 15, 1834, Nos. 1-52, 414, [2] pp. CinPL, IndStL (has No. 27 only). Vol. V (Philomath, Ind., Samuel Tizzard; Edited by J. Kidwell, S. Tizzard, and A. A. Davis), Nos. 25-48 for Aug. 30, 1834-Apr. 11, 1835. IndStL (has Nos. 25, 45, and 48). Vol. VI (Philomath, Ind., Samuel Tizzard; Edited by Samuel Tizzard, J. Kidwell, and A. A. Davis — later, Cincinnati and Madisonville, O., Samuel Tizzard; Edited by Samuel Tizzard and Asher A. Davis), Nos. 1-37 for May 16, 1835-Mar. 12, 1836. IndStL (has Nos. 1, 32, and 37). Vol. VIII (Cincinnati and Madisonville, O., S. & W. B. Tizzard; Edited by S. Tizzard and G. Rogers), No. 7 for Nov. 11, 1837. IndStL (has No. 7 only).

The Spirit of '76.

Frankfort, J. H. Holeman, 1826 (and possibly later). Vol. I, Nos. 1-22 for Mar. 10-Aug. 4, 1826. 352 pp. WisH.

Western Christian Advocate.

Cincinnati, 1834-1840 (and later). Weekly. Vol. I, No. 1 for May 2, 1834. DePauwU (has nearly complete file 1834-1837).

The Western Luminary.

> Lexington, Thomas T. Skillman, 1824-1835 (possibly published at Cincinnati or elsewhere after 1835). Vols. I-V, whole Nos. 1-259 for July 14, 1824-June 34 [24], 1829. ChU (has Vol. I, except No. 45), CinPL (has Vols. I and III-V), WRHist (has Vol. I, Nos. 25-27; and Vol. II, Nos. 45-48). For cessation of publication in Lexington on Oct. 21, 1835, and transfer of its entire establishment to Eli Taylor, of Cincinnati, see *Ky. Gaz.*, Oct. 24, 1835.

III. SEMIMONTHLIES, MONTHLIES, AND QUARTERLIES

(Including periodicals of all kinds appearing either fortnightly or at longer intervals.)

Abolition Intelligencer, and Missionary Magazine.

> Shelbyville, Ky., John Finley Crow, 1822-1823. Edited by John Finley Crow. Vol. I, Nos. 1-11 for May 7, 1822-Mar., 1823, 176 pp. WRHist (has Nos. 3 and 6-10), WisH (has Nos. 1-7 and 11).

The Academic Pioneer, and Guardian of Education.

> Cincinnati, an Association of Teachers, 1831?-? Vol. I, No. 2 for Dec., 1832, pp. 27-66. LexPL, WRHist.

Alethian Critic; or Error Exposed.

> Lexington? Apr. or May, 1804-? Quarterly. From *Ky. Gaz.*, May 1, 1804.

The Almoner, a Periodical Religious Publication: . . .

> Lexington, Thomas T. Skillman, 1814-1815. Vol. I, Apr., 1814-May, 1815, Nos. 1-6, 304 pp. LexPL, LC, WRHist.

Analysis of Prophetic Times; in which is Interpreted the Apocalypse of John, the Apostle, together with Several of the more Difficult Places of Other Sacred Prophecies. In Two Volumes. Published in Monthly Numbers. 12 or More Nos. in Each Vol.

> Xenia, O., Printed by J. H. Purdy, 1835. Edited by

James Adams. Vol. I (no division into monthly numbers indicated, but title-page dated 1835), 488 pp. Smith,
WRHist.

The Anti-conspirator, or, Infidelity Unmasked; being a
   Development of the Principles of Free Masonry; to
   which is Added, Strictures on Slavery, as Existing in
   the Church.
   Cincinnati, Dyer Burgess, 1831-1832 (Vol. II was announced conditionally to appear at West Union, O.).
   Edited by Dyer Burgess. Vol. I, June 5, 1831-Apr. 22,
   1832, Nos. 1-24, 384 pp. WRHist.

The Baptist Advocate.
   Cincinnati, 1835-1836 (or later). Vol. I, Jan.-Dec.,
   1835, Nos. 1-12, 312 pp. Smith, WRHist. Vol. II,
   Jan.-Nov. and Dec., 1836, Nos. 1-11 and 12, with documentary supplement, 296 pp.   TransylvaniaU, WRHist.

The Boatman's Magazine.
   Cleveland, 1834. Vol. I, No. 1 for Oct., 1834, 48 pp.
   (was to have been continued quarterly). WRHist.

Botanical Luminary.
   Saline, Mich., 1836?-? Published monthly by Dr. H.
   Wright. From *Detroit Daily Advertiser*, July 30, 1836.

The Botanico-medical Recorder, or Impartial Advocate of
   Botanic Medicine, and the Principles which Govern
   the Botanico-medical Practice.
   Columbus, A. Curtis, 1837-1840 (and later). Follows
   Vol. V of *The Thomsonian Recorder*. Edited by A.
   Curtis. Vol. VI, Oct. 7, 1837-Sept. 22, 1838, Nos. 1-26,
   xv, 416 pp. HistPSO. Vol. VIII, Oct. 5, 1839-Sept.
   19, 1840, Nos. 1-26, 13, 416 pp. HistPSO. Vol. IX,
   Oct. 3, 1840-Sept. 18, 1841, Nos. 1-26, 16, 416 pp.
   WRHist.

Both Sides of Religious Ceremonies: a Monthly Periodical,

Devoted to the Investigation of Every Variety of
Rituals in Religion.

Cincinnati, Looker & Graham, Printers, 1839-1840 (or
later). Edited by Robert Smith. Vol. I, Nov. 1, 1839-
Oct. 1, 1840, Nos. 1-12, iv, 284 pp. CinPL, TransylvaniaU.

The Child's Newspaper.

Cincinnati, Corey and Fairbank, 1834 (and possibly
later). Edited by Thomas Brainerd, assisted by B. P.
Aydelott, under supervision of a committee of the Cin-
cinnati Sunday School Union. Semimonthly. From
The Western Monthly Magazine, II, 107 (Feb., 1834).
WRHist (has Jan. 7-Sept. 2, 1834) file not collated.

The Christian Examiner, Published monthly.

Lexington (later, Louisville), 1829-1830 (or later). Vol.
I (Lexington, J. G. Norwood), Nov., 1829-Oct. 25, 1830,
Nos. 1-12, 292 pp. ChU (has Nos. 1-4), TransylvaniaU
(lacks Nos. 1-2). Vol. II (Louisville, Jos. G. Norwood),
Nos. 1-10 for Jan. 3-Oct. 3, 1831, 240 pp. Transyl-
vaniaU.

The Christian Intelligencer, and Evangelical Guardian.

Hamilton, Rossville, Oxford (and possibly other towns),
O., 1829-1831 and 1833-1840 (and later). Until the beginning of Vol. II the title was *The Christian Intelligencer*. Vol. I, Nos. 1-11 for Jan.-Nov., 1829, 352 pp.
LaneTS (lacks Nos. 4-6). Vol. II, Jan.-Dec., 1830, Nos.
1-12, 384 pp. LaneTS (lacks No. 5), WRHist (lacks
Nos. 1 and 5-6). Vol. III, Jan.-Dec., 1831, Nos. 1-12,
383, [1] pp. LaneTS (lacks No. 7). Vol. IV, Mar.,
1833-Feb., 1834, Nos. 1-12, 384 pp. LaneTS, WRHist.
Vol. V (Hamilton, O., Printed by Lewis D. Campbell;
Edited by David Macdill), Mar., 1834-Feb., 1835, Nos.
1-12, 432 pp. LaneTS, WRHist (lacks No. 11). Vol.

VI (Hamilton, O., Printed by L. Gibbon & D. B. Gardner; Edited by David Macdill), Mar., 1835-Feb., 1836,
Nos. 1-12, 432 pp. LaneTS (lacks Nos. 5 and 9-10),
WRHist (lacks No. 2). Vol. VII (Rossville, O., Edited
and Published by David Macdill), Apr., 1836-Mar., 1837,
Nos. 1-12, [1], 382 pp. LaneTS, WRHist. Vol. VIII (Oxford, O., R. H. Bishop, Jun.; Edited by David Macdill),
Apr., 1837-Apr., 1838 (no issue in May, 1837), twelve
issues, 580 pp. LaneTS, WRHist (lacks issue for Apr.,
1837). Vol. IX (Oxford, O., R. H. Bishop, Jun.;
Edited by David Macdill), May, 1838-Apr., 1839, twelve
issues, 582 pp. LaneTS, WRHist, WisH (lacks issue
for July). Vol. X (Oxford, O., John Christy; Edited
by David Macdill), May, 1839-Apr., 1840, twelve issues,
576 pp. LaneTS. Vol. XI (Oxford, O., John Christy;
Edited by David Macdill), May, 1840-May, 1841 (no
issue in Feb., 1841), twelve issues, 576 pp. LaneTS,
WRHist.

The Christian Messenger.

Georgetown, Ky. (1826-1834), and Jacksonville, Ill.
(1835-1840 and later). Edited by Barton Warren Stone
(assisted by John T. Johnson, 1832-1834; and by Tho's
M. Allen and Jacob Creath, Jr., 1840). Vol. I, Nov. 25,
1826-Oct.. 25, 1827, Nos. 1-12, 287, [1] pp. TransylvaniaU. Vol. III, Nos. 5-12 for Mar.-Oct., 1829, pp. 97-
288. KyStHist (has No. 5), TransylvaniaU (has No.
12). Vol. IV, Dec., 1829-Dec., 1830, Nos. 1-12 (no issue
for Nov., 1830), 288 pp. TransylvaniaU. Vol. V, Jan.-
Dec., 1831, Nos. 1-12, 288 pp. TransylvaniaU. Vol. VI,
Nos. 2-11 for Feb.-Nov., 1832, pp. 33-352. TransylvaniaU
(lacks Nos. 4-8). Vol. VII, Jan.-Dec., 1833, Nos. 1-12,
381, iii pp. TransylvaniaU. Vol. VIII, Jan.-Dec., 1834,
Nos. 1-12, 381, iii pp. TransylvaniaU. Vol. IX, Jan.-

Dec., 1835, Nos. 1-12, 288 pp. TransylvaniaU (lacks
Nos. 5-7 and 9). Vol. XI, Sept., 1840-Aug., 1841, Nos.
1-12, 432 pp. TransylvaniaU.

The Christian Panoplist.

Versailles (later Lexington), Ky., Jan.-Dec., 1837. Pub-
lished by James Virden (Nos. 1-9 or 10) and J. C. Noble
(Nos. 10 or 11-12). Edited by B. F. Hall and W. Hunt-
er (Nos. 1 and 2); by W. Hunter (Nos. 3-12). Vol. I,
Jan.-Dec., 1837, Nos. 1-12, 191, [1] pp. LouPL (lacks
No. 10).

The Christian Preacher, Consisting of Monthly Discourses
and Essays, by Living Writers. . . .

Cincinnati, Printed by James and Gazlay, 1836 (and
possibly later). Edited by D. S. Burnet. Vol. I, Jan.-
Dec., 1836, Nos. 1-12, 288 pp. TransylvaniaU.

The Christian Register.

Lexington, Thomas T. Skillman, 1822-1823. Edited by
James Blythe. Vol. I, June, 1822-May, 1823, Nos. 1-12,
764, [4] pp. ChU.

Chronicles of the North American Savages; Containing
Sketches of their Ancient and Modern History, Religion, Traditions, Customs, and Manners, Laws and
Regulations, Language and Dialects, Medicine, Biography, &c., together with Topographical Sketches of
the Country West of the Mississippi, and North of the
Missouri Rivers.

Carthage, Ill., 1835 (and possibly later). Edited by J.
Galland. Full title for No. 1, as given in *The Western
Monthly Magazine*, IV, 64 (July, 1835). Title in issues
I have examined is *Chronicles of the North-American
Savages*. Vol. I, Nos. 1-5 for May 1-Sept., 1835, 80 pp.
From *The Western Monthly Magazine, loc. cit.* (mentions
only No. 1), LC (lacks No. 1).

The Cincinnati Mirror and Ladies' Parterre. Devoted to
Polite Literature.

Cincinnati, 1831-1833 (followed by *The Cincinnati Mirror, and Western Gazette of Literature and Science*, Vol.
III). Edited by William D. Gallagher. Vol. I (John
H. Wood), Oct. 1, 1831-Sept. 15, 1832, Nos. 1-26, [2],
208 pp. CinPL, OhioStL, WRHist. Vol. II (Wood and
Stratton), Sept. 29, 1832-Sept. 13, 1833, Nos. 1-26, [1],
208 pp. CinPL (lacks Nos. 13-14, 17 and 26), OhioStL,
WRHist.

The College Mirror.

Cincinnati, John C. Schooley, 1839. Edited by John C.
Schooley. Vol. I, July 13-Sept. 28, 1839, Nos. 1-6, [24]
pp. HistPSO.

Common School Advocate. A Monthly Paper, for the Promotion and Improvement of Common School Education.

Madison, Ind. (later Cincinnati), 1837-1840 (or later).
Vol. I (Edited by William Twining, assisted part of the
time by John H. Harney), Jan.-Dec., 1837, Nos. 1-12, 96
pp. IndStL. Vol. IV? No. 43 for July, 1840. WRHist.

The Common School Journal.

Cincinnati, 1838 (and probably later). Monthly. Vol.
I, No. 2. From *The Western Messenger*, VI, 212 (Jan.,
1839).

The Disseminator of Useful Knowledge; Containing Hints
to the Youth of the United States — from the "School
of Industry."

New Harmony, Ind., Edited and Published by the Pupils
of the School of Industry, 1828-1830. Vol. I, Jan. 16-
Dec. 31, 1828, Nos. 1-26, 416 pp. CinPL. Vol. II, Jan.
14-Dec. 30, 1829, Nos. 1-26, 416 pp. CinPL. Vol. III,
Jan. 16-May 12, 1830, Nos. 1-9, 144 pp. CinPL.

Elders' Journal of the Church of Jesus Christ of Latter
Day Saints.

Kirtland, O., and Far West, Mo., 1837-1838. Title given
above is from third issue. Vol. I, Oct., 1837-July, 1838
(no issues between Nov., 1837, and July, 1838), Nos. 1-3,
48 pp. WRHist (lacks Nos. 2 and 3), WisH.

The Errand Boy: or, New Church Messenger. Intended to
Illustrate and Defend the Doctrines of the New
Church, as Taught by Emanuel Swedenborg.

Chillicothe, 1839-1840 (and later). Vol. I, Nos. 1 and
2 for Apr. 15 and Sept. 16, 1839, 48 pp. (Vol. I, No.
7, is for July, 1841). WRHist.

The Evangelical Record, and Western Review, . . .

Lexington, Printed by Thomas T. Skillman, 1812 (and
probably later; for mention of this periodical in 1813,
showing that it was probably still being published at that
time, see *Ky. Gaz.*, May 25, 1813). Vol. I, Jan.-Dec.,
1812, Nos. 1-12, [2], 396 pp. HistPSO.

The Evangelist.

Cincinnati, the Editor, 1832-1840? (and later). Edited
by Walter Scott. Vol. I, Jan. 2-Dec. 3, 1832, Nos. 1-12,
iv, 284 pp. HistPSO, TransylvaniaU. Vol. II (Cincinnati, Nos. 1-10; Carthage, O., Nos. 11-12), Jan. 7-Dec.
2, 1833, Nos. 1-12, 288 pp. TransylvaniaU. Vol. III
(Carthage, O.), Jan. 6-Dec. 3, 1834, Nos. 1-12, 288, iv pp.
TransylvaniaU. Vol. IV (Carthage, O., Nos. 1-7; Cincinnati, Printed by O. Donogh, Nos. 8-12), Jan. 5-Dec. 7,
1835, Nos. 1-12, [3], 284 pp. TransylvaniaU. Vol. VI
(Carthage, O.), Nos. 1-11 for Jan.-Nov. 1, 1838, 264 pp.
TransylvaniaU. Vol. VII (Carthage, O., Nos. 1-10; Cincinnati, Nos. 11-12), Jan. 1-Dec. 1, 1839, Nos. 1-12, 287,
[1] pp. TransylvaniaU. See also above, Chapter III,
footnote 179, and below, bibliography for Chapter IV,
under Walter Scott.

Evening and Morning Star.

Independence, Mo., and Kirtland, O., 1832-1834. Reprinted, Kirtland, O., Jan., 1835-Oct., 1836. Vol. I (first published at Independence), June, 1832-May, 1833, Nos. 1-12, 192 pp. LC (has Kirtland reprint), WRHist (Kirtland reprint), WisH (Kirtland reprint). Vol. II (Nos. 13 and 14 first published at Independence; Nos. 15-24 first published at Kirtland; entire volume reprinted at Kirtland), June, 1833-Sept., 1834, Nos. 13-24 (no issue between July and Dec., 1833). LC (Kirtland reprint), WRHist (Kirtland reprint), WisH (Kirtland reprint).

The Extra Equator: Devoted to the Interests of Science and Literature in the West.

Bloomington, Ind., 1840 (and later). Published by the Editor; Edited by A. E. Drapier. Vol. I, No. 1 for Nov., 1840, [2], iv, 84, [2] pp. IndStL, IU. No more published till Mar., 1841.

The Family Magazine; or, Monthly Abstract of General Knowledge.

Cincinnati (at least part of the same contents was published in an Eastern edition of this work), 1836-1840 (and later). Vol. I (Eli Taylor), Jan.-Dec.? 1836, viii, 472 pp. IU, WisH. Vol. II (Eli Taylor), Jan. ?-Dec. ? 1837, viii, 472 pp. WisH. Vol. III (Eli Taylor), Jan.?-Dec.? 1838, 7, 560 pp. WisH. Vol. IV (Eli Taylor), Jan. ?-Dec.? 1839, vii, 560 pp. WisH. Vol. V (J. A. James & Co., new edition, revised and corrected), Jan. ?-Dec. ? 1840, viii, 560 pp. WisH.

Farmer's Reporter, and United States Agriculturalist. Containing Original and Selected Essays on Agriculture, Horticulture, Culinary Art, Farriery, Live Stock, Valuable Receipts, and Every Branch of Husbandry. Illustrated with Engravings. . . . New Series.

Cincinnati, H. L. Barnum, 1831-1833 (or later). First

volume, not numbered, eleven issues, numbered irregularly, for Oct., 1831-Aug., 1832, pagination irregular. CinPL (lacks issues for May and July), WRHist (Feb. issue only). Vol. II, Nos. 1-5 for Oct., 1832-Feb., 1833, 128 pp. CinPL (lacks issue for Jan., except cover), WRHist (Feb. issue only).

Florula Lexingtoniensis.

Lexington? 1828? (and possibly later). Fasciculus I, for Feb., Mar., and part of Apr. From *The Western Monthly Review*, II, 51 (June, 1828). For notices of later numbers, with mention of pp. 43-63, see *ibid.*, II, 289-290 (Oct., 1828) and 403-404 (Dec., 1828).

Genius of Universal Emancipation.

Mountpleasant, O., 1821-1822 (removed to Greenville, Tenn., after eight or nine issues). Edited by Benjamin Lundy. Vol. I, Nos. 1-11 for 7th Month, 1821-5th Month, 1822, 180 pp. WRHist (lacks No. 2).

Gospel Advocate.

Georgetown, Ky. (later, Lexington, and Versailles, Ky.), 1835-1836 (or later). Vol. I (Georgetown, Ky., Edited by J. T. Johnson and B. F. Hall), Jan.-Dec., 1835, Nos. 1-12, 192, [1] pp. TransylvaniaU. Vol. II (Lexington, Edited by J. T. Johnson and B. F. Hall, Nos. 1-9; Versailles, Ky., Edited by B. F. Hall and W. Hunter, Nos. 10-12), Jan.-Dec., 1836, Nos. 1-12, 192 pp. TransylvaniaU.

The Gospel Herald, . . .

Lexington, the Kentucky Annual Conference of the Methodist Episcopal Church, 1829-1830 (or later). Printed by Thomas Smith at the Reporter Office. Edited by O. B. Ross. Vol. I, Aug., 1829-July, 1830, Nos. 1-12, 192 pp. KyStHist.

The Herald of Literature and Science.

Detroit, 1831 (and possibly later). Conducted by the

Detroit Debating Society (later, beginning with No. 5,
by McKinstry, Rowland, Roby & Williams). Vol. I,
Nos. 1-5 for May?-Sept. 17, 1831, 40 pp. BurColl (has
No. 5 only). For notice of first issue, see *Detroit Journal
and Michigan Advertiser*, May 18, 1831.

The Heretic Detector, a Monthly Publication, Devoted to
Primitive Christianity, and to the Destruction of Sectarianism.

Middleburg, Logan Co., O., ?-1840. Printed by S. M.
Scott; Edited by Arthur Crihfield. A continuation of
*The Northern Reformer, Heretic Detector, and Evan-
gelical Review*. Vol. IV, Jan.-Dec., 1840, Nos. 1-12, 382,
ii pp. LouPL (lacks No. 7), TransylvaniaU .

The Hesperian; or, Western Monthly Magazine.

Columbus (later Cincinnati), 1838-1839. Vol. I (Columbus, John D. Nichols; Edited by William D. Gallagher
and Otway Curry), May-Oct., 1838, Nos. 1-6, 500, ii pp.
CinPL, HistPSO, LC, WRHist, WisH. Vol. II (*The
Hesperian; a Monthly Miscellany of General Literature,
Original and Select*; Columbus, John D. Nichols; Edited
by William D. Gallagher), Nov., 1838-Apr., 1839, Nos.
1-6, 500 pp. CinPL, HistPSO, LC, WRHist, WisH.
Vol. III (Cincinnati, John D. Nichols; Edited by William D. Gallagher), June-Nov., 1839, Nos. 1-6, 500 pp.
CinPL, HistPSO, LC, WRHist, WisH.

Illinois Monthly Magazine.

Vandalia (and, at times, St. Louis and Cincinnati), 1830-
1832. Edited by James Hall. Vol. I (Vandalia, Robert
Blackwell, printer, according to title-page; Blackwell &
Hall, according to a statement on the covers of at least
three copies, were the publishers at Vandalia, and C. D.
Bradford & Co. were the Cincinnati agents), Oct., 1830-
Sept., 1831, twelve issues, ii, 576 pp. CinPL, LC,
WRHist, WisH. Vol. II (Cincinnati, Corey and Fair-

bank, according to title-page; but the cover of No. 19, for Apr., 1832, has "St. Louis. Published by Charles Keemle. C. Keemle, Printer, Olive-st.''), Oct., 1831-Sept., 1832, Nos. 13-24, iv, 572 pp. CinPL, LC, WRHist (lacks Nov. and Dec., 1831; and July, 1832), WisH.

The Independent Botanic Register, Comprising Essays, Intelligence on Botanic Medicine, General Literature, Interesting Cases, Current Events, and Useful Improvements in Medical Practice.

Columbus, Thomas Hersey, 1835-1836 (after discontinuance at Columbus in 1836, the periodical was to have resumed publication at Baltimore). Edited by Thomas Hersey. Vol. I, May, 1835-Apr., 1836, Nos. 1-12, 192 pp. WRHist.

Investigator and Expositor.

Troy, O., 1839?-1840 (or possibly later). Vol. I, Nos. 13-16 for July-Oct., 1840, pp. 177-240. WRHist (lacks No. 14).

Jewett's Advertiser. Published quarterly.

Columbus, 1835-1836 (or later). Vol. I, Jan. 1-Oct. 1, 1835, Nos. 1-4, 64 pp. WRHist. Vol. II, Jan. 1-Oct., 1836, Nos. 1-4, pp. 65-128 (pagination continued from Vol. I), with extra issue for Jan. 1, 1836, 15, [1] pp. WRHist.

The Juvenile Museum, a Miscellaneous Journal, Devoted to the Improvement and Moral Amusement of the Junior Class of Society. . . .

Mountpleasant, O., Ezekiel Harris & Co., 1822-1823. Edited by Horton J. Howard. Vol. I, 9th Month, 16, 1822-9th Month, 27, 1823, Nos. 1-17, 190 pp. CinPL.

Latter Day Saints' Messenger and Advocate.

Kirtland, O., 1834-1837. Vol. I (Edited by Oliver Cowdery, Nos. 1-8, and John Whitmer, Nos. 9-12), Oct., 1834-Sept., 1835, Nos. 1-12, 192 pp. WRHist, WisH.

Vol. II (Edited by John Whitmer, Nos. 1-6, and Oliver
Cowdery, Nos. 7-12), Oct., 1835-Sept., 1836, Nos. 1-12,
pp. 193-384. WRHist (lacks Nos. 5-11), WisH. Vol.
III (Edited by Oliver Cowdery), Nos. 3-12 for Dec.,
1836-Sept., 1837, pp. 417-576. HistPSO (has Nos. 3-12),
WRHist (has No. 3).

The Literary Cabinet.

St. Clairsville, O., 1833. Edited by Thomas Gregg.
Monthly, twelve issues. From W. H. Venable, *Beginnings of Literary Culture in the Ohio Valley*, 1891, p.
125.

The Literary Focus, a Monthly Periodical.

Oxford, O., the Erodelphian and Union Literary Societies of the Miami University, 1827-1828. Edited by the
Erodelphian and Union Literary Societies. Vol. I, June,
1827-May, 1828, Nos. 1-12, [2], 240 pp. OhioStL,
WRHist, WisH.

Louisville Journal of Medicine and Surgery.

Louisville, 1838. Edited by Professors Miller and Yandell, and Dr. Thomas H. Bell. From *The Western Journal of Medicine and Surgery*, I, publishers' notice (Jan.,
1840) ; and E. D. Mansfield, *Memoirs of the Life and Services of Daniel Drake*, 1855, p. 185. *Cf.* above, Chapter
III, footnote 193.

The Masonic Miscellany and Ladies' Literary Magazine, a
Periodical Publication, Devoted to Masonic and General Literature.

Lexington, William Gibbes Hunt, 1821?-1823. Vol. II,
July, 1822-June, 1823, Nos. 1-12, 480 pp. ChU (has
only No. 6), WRHist.

The Masonic Register.

Vevay, Ind., William C. Keen, 1824?-1825 (or later).
Vol. I, Nos. 2-12 for Jan. 11-July 4, 5825, no pagination.
IndStL (lacks Nos. 3-11).

Medical Friend of the People.

Harrodsburg (later Danville), Ky., Anthony Hunn, 1829-1830. Vol. I, Nos. 1-15 for June 3, 1829-May, 1830, 383 pp. ChU (has only Nos. 4, 9, and 14), LouPL.

The Medley, or Monthly Miscellany. For the Year 1803. Containing Essays, on a Variety of Subjects, Sketches of Public Characters, Moral Tales, Poetry, &c. &c. Intended to Combine Amusement with Useful Information. . . .

Lexington, Daniel Bradford, 1803. Vol. I, Jan.-Dec., 1803, Nos. 1-12, 287, [1] pp. The twelve numbers of the magazine proper cover 240 pp. The remaining pages are occupied by a variety of selected and original verse. LexPL, WisH.

Michigan Temperance Herald.

Jackson, Mich., 1839 (and possibly later). Vol. I, No. 9 for Nov., 1839, four pages. Edited by G. W. Clark. BurColl.

The Miscellaneous Repository.

Mountpleasant (later St. Clairsville), O., and Kendal, England, Elisha Bates, 1828?-1836 (or later). Edited by Elisha Bates. Vol. II, Nos. 1-8 for 1st Month, 1-2d Month, 20, 1829, 128 pp. WRHist (has Nos. 1 and 5-8). Vol. III, Nos. 1-17 for 7th Month, 2, 1829-2d Month, 20, 1830, 272 pp. WRHist (has Nos. 14-17; for OhioStL file, beginning with No. 1, see below). Vol. IV, Nos. 7-26 for 11th Month, 27, 1830-1st Month, 27, 1832, pp. 97-416. WRHist (has Nos. 7-10 and 26). Vol. V, No. 13 for 1st Month, 10, 1833, pp. 191-206. WRHist. English edition, Nos. 19-28 for 1st Month, 9-9th Month, 1, 1836, pp. 288-460. NewL. File in OhioStL, Vols. III-V, not collated.

The Monthly Chronicle of Interesting and Useful Knowledge, Embracing Education, Internal Improvements,

and the Arts.   With Notices of General Literature and
Passing Events.

Cincinnati, A. Pugh, 1838-1839.   Vol. I, Dec., 1838-Nov.,
1839, twelve issues, iv, 568 pp.   HistPSO, LC, WRHist,
WisH.

The Moral Advocate, a Monthly Publication, on War,
Duelling, Capital Punishments, and Prison Discipline.
Mountpleasant, O., Printed by the Editor, 1821-1824
(or later).   Edited by Elisha Bates.   Vol. I, 3d Month,
1821-6th Month, 1822, Nos. 1-12, iv, 204 pp.   WRHist.
Vol. II, 7th Month, 1822-6th Month, 1823, Nos. 1-12, with
Nos. 1 and 2 Supplementary to No. 12, 207, [1] pp.
WRHist.   Vol. III, 7th Month, 1823-unnumbered Month,
1824, Nos. 1-12, with Supplementary to No. 12, 200 pp.
WRHist.

The Mothers' and Young Ladies' Guide.
Ohio City, O., T. H. Smead, 1837?-1840.   Edited by
Mrs. Maria Herrick.   Vol. III, June, 1839-May, 1840,
twelve issues, 383, [1] pp.   WRHist.

The Northern Reformer, Heretic Detector, and Evangelical
Review.   Continued quarterly.
Middleburg, O., Arthur Crihfield, Printer, 1837 (and
later).   Continued till after 1840, with change of title
(see *The Heretic Detector*).   Vol. I, Jan., Feb., Mar.-
Apr., May, June (became monthly with issue for July)
and July-Dec., 1837, Nos. 1-2 and 7-12, 382, [2] pp.
WRHist.

The Oberlin Evangelist.   A Semi-monthly Periodical, Devoted to the Promotion of Religion.   Conducted by
an Association.
Oberlin, O., 1838-1840 (and later).   Vol. I (Printed
by James Steele), Nov. 1, 1838-Dec. 18, 1839, Nos. 1-26,
with Extra No. 1 for Nov. 20, 1839, [1], 208, 8 pp.   LC,

WRHist. Vol. II (R. E. Gillett), Jan. 1-Dec. 16, 1840, Nos. 1-26, [1], 208 pp. LC, WRHist.

Ohio and Michigan Register, and Emigrants Guide.

Florence, O., 1832 (and possibly later). Edited by J. W. Scott. Vol. I, No. 12 for Dec., 1832, pp. 177-192. WRHist.

The Ohio Medical Repository.

Cincinnati? 1826-1827? Semimonthly. Edited by Guy W. Wright and James M. Mason. From E. D. Mansfield, *Memoirs of the Life and Services of Daniel Drake*, 1855, p. 185. *Cf.* above, Chapter III, footnote 190.

The Ohio Miscellaneous Museum.

Lebanon, O., 1822. Vol. I, Jan.-May, 1822, Nos. 1-5, 232 pp. WRHist, WisH.

The Olio.

Cincinnati, John H. Wood and Samuel S. Brooks, 1821-1822. Edited by John H. Wood and Samuel S. Brooks. Semimonthly. From W. H. Venable, *Beginnings of Literary Culture in the Ohio Valley*, 1891, pp. 66 and 124.

The Olive Branch.

Circleville, O., 1832. Bimonthly. Edited by a Number of Gentlemen. From W. H. Venable, *Beginnings of Literary Culture in the Ohio Valley*, 1891, p. 125.

The Pedobaptist.

Danville, Ky., Printed by J. J. Polk and W. G. Johnson, 1829 (and possibly later). Vol. I, Jan.-Dec., 1829, Nos. 1-12, 192 pp. ChU.

The Precursor.

Cincinnati, 1836-1839 (or later). Vol. I, Nos. 1-23, Sept. 15, 1836-Mar. 25, 1839, 396 pp. CinPL.

The Rational Bible-reformer, and Unitarian Monitor.

Near West Union, O., 1825? (and possibly later).

Monthly. From *The North American Review*, XXII, 250 (Jan., 1826).

The Regular Baptist.

Indianapolis, Printed by J. S. Willets, 1839 (and possibly later). Edited by T. W. Haynes. Vol. I, No. 7 for July, 1839, pp. [1], 97-112, [2]. IndStL.

The Religious Examiner.

Cadiz, etc., O., 1827-1834. Edited by Samuel Findley. Vol. I (Cadiz, O., Printed by D. Christy), Sept., 1827-Aug., 1828, Nos. 1-12, 580 pp. Smith. Vol. II (Cadiz, O., Printed by D. Christy), Sept., 1828-Oct., 1829, Nos. 1-12, 384, [1] pp. Smith, WRHist. Vol. III (Washington, O., Printed by Hamilton Robb), Nov., 1829-Oct., 1830, Nos. 1-12, 348 pp. Smith, WRHist. Vol. IV (Washington, O., Printed by Hamilton Robb), Jan.-Dec., 1831, Nos. 1-12, 384, [2] pp. Smith, WRHist. Vol. V (Washington? O., Printed by Henry Kennon), Jan.-Dec., 1832, twelve issues, 383, [1] pp. WRHist. Vol. VI (St. Clairsville, O., Printed by Horton J. Howard), Jan.-Dec., 1833, twelve issues, 383, [1] pp. WRHist. Vol. VII, Jan.-Dec., 1834, Nos. 1-12, 392 pp. WRHist (lacks Nos. 7, 8, and 11).

The Rose of the Valley: a Flower of the West, that Blooms to Enrich the Mind. Devoted to Literature, Instruction, Amusement, and Interesting Biography.

Cincinnati, G. G. Moore, 1839 (and possibly later). Vol. I, separate issues not dated, Nos. 1-12, [4], 280 pp. CinPL, OhioStL, WRHist.

The Schoolmaster, and Academic Journal.

Oxford, O., 1834 (and possibly later). Edited by B. F. Morris. Semimonthly. From *The Western Monthly Magazine*, II, 334 (June, 1834).

The Thomsonian Recorder, or Impartial Advocate of Botanic Medicine, and the Principles which Govern the Thomsonian Practice.

Columbus, 1832-1837 (followed by *The Botanico-medical Recorder,* Vol. VI). In Vols. I, II, III, and V only the punctuation of the title undergoes any change. Vol. I (Pike, Platt & Co., Nos. 1-11, and Jarvis Pike & Co., Nos. 12-32; Thomas Hersey, Senior Editor), Sept. 15, 1832-Sept. 28, 1833, Nos. 1-32, xv, 608 pp. WRHist. Vol. II (Jarvis Pike & Co.; Thomas Hersey, Senior Editor), Oct. 12, 1833-Sept. 27, 1834, Nos. 1-26, 15, 416 pp. IU, WRHist. Vol. III (Jarvis Pike & Co.; Edited by Thomas Hersey, Nos. 1-22? and A. Curtis, Nos. 23-26), Oct. 11, 1834-Sept. 26, 1835, Nos. 1-26, xiv, 516 pp. WRHist. Vol. V (Dr. A. Curtis; Edited by A. Curtis), Oct. 8, 1836-Sept. 23, 1837, Nos. 1-26, xvi, 416 pp. WRHist.

Times and Seasons.

Commerce (later Nauvoo), Ill., E. Robinson and D. C. Smith, 1839-1840 (and later). Edited by E. Robinson and D. C. Smith (Smith became sole editor and proprietor with issue for Dec. 15, 1840). Vol. I, Nov., 1839-Oct., 1840, Nos. 1-12, 192 pp. LC, WisH. Vol. II, Nos. 1-4 for Nov. 1-Dec. 15, 1840, pp. 193-256. LC, WisH.

The Transylvania Journal of Medicine and the Associate Sciences.

Lexington, 1828-1839 (or later). Vol. I (Printed by Joseph G. Norwood; Edited by John Esten Cooke and Charles Wilkins Short), 1828, Nos. 1-4, 600, iv (vi), [1] pp. TransylvaniaU. Vol. II (Printed by J. G. Norwood; Published by James W. Palmer; Edited by John Esten Cooke and Charles Wilkins Short), 1829, Nos. 1-4, viii, 594, [1] pp. TransylvaniaU. Vol. III (Printed by Joseph G. Norwood; Edited by John Esten Cooke and Charles Wilkins Short), 1830, four issues, 596 pp. TransylvaniaU. Vol. IV (Printed by John F.

Herndon & Co.; Edited by John Esten Cooke and Charles Wilkins Short), 1831, four issues, 600 pp. ChU, TransylvaniaU. Vol V (Printed by H. Savary & Co.; Edited by Lunsford P. Yandell), 1832, four issues, [1], iv, 600 pp. TransylvaniaU. Vol. VI (Printed by J. Clarke & Co.; Edited by Lunsford P. Yandell), 1833, four issues, 600 pp. TransylvaniaU. Vol. VII (J. Clarke & Co.; Edited by Lunsford P. Yandell), 1834, four issues, 600 pp. TransylvaniaU. Vol. VIII (J. Clarke & Co.; Edited by Lunsford P. Yandell), 1835, four issues, 607 pp. ChU, TransylvaniaU. Vol. IX, New Series I (J. Clarke & Co.; Edited by Lunsford P. Yandell), 1836, four issues, 808 pp. ChU, TransylvaniaU. Vol. X (J. Clarke & Co.; Edited by Robert Peter), 1837, four issues, 800, ix pp. ChU, TransylvaniaU. Vol. XI (Edwin Bryant; Edited by the Medical Faculty of Transylvania University), 1838, two issues, 498, vi pp. ChU (lacks second issue), TransylvaniaU. Vol. XII, issue for Jan., Feb., and Mar., 1839, 248 pp. TransylvaniaU.

The Transylvanian or Lexington Literary Journal.
Lexington, 1829 (and possibly later). Vol. I, Jan.-Sept., 1829, Nos. 1-9, 360 pp. ChU, OhioStL (lacks Nos. 8 and 9), TransylvaniaU (lacks No. 6), WisH.

Truth's Advocate and Monthly Anti-Jackson Expositor.
Cincinnati, Lodge, L'Hommedieu, and Hammond, Printers, 1828. Edited by an Association of Individuals, Jan.-Oct., 1828, ten issues, [2], 400 pp. See above, Chapter III, footnote 186. LC, WRHist, WisH.

Universal Educator.
Cincinnati, Kendall & Henry, Printers, 1837 (and possibly later). Edited by N. Holley. Monthly. From *The Western Monthly Magazine, and Literary Journal*, I, 143 (Mar., 1837).

The Western Academician and Journal of Education and
Science.

Cincinnati, James R. Allbach, 1837-1838. Edited by
John W. Picket. Vol. I, Mar., 1837-Feb., 1838, Nos. 1-12,
iv, 704 pp. CinPL, HistPSO, IU, JCrerar, LC, NYPL,
WRHist.

The Western Baptist.

Rock Spring, Ill., J. M. Peck, Editor & Publisher, 1830-
1831 (or later). Vol. I, Nos. 1-9 for Aug., 1830-May,
1831, 72 pp. IllStHist.

The Western Christian Monitor.

Chillicothe, Printed at the Fredonian Press, by J. Bailhache, 1816 (and possibly later). Edited by William
Beauchamp. Vol. I, Jan.-Dec., 1816, Nos. 1-12, 576 pp.
LexPL, Smith, WRHist, WisH (has issue for Nov., 1816,
only).

The Western Emigrants' Magazine, and Historian of
Times in the West.

Carthage, Ill., Th. Gregg, 1837. Vol. I, No. 1 for May,
1837, 16 pp. WisH.

The Western Farmer, Devoted to Agriculture, Horticulture, and Rural Economy.

Cincinnati, 1839-1840 (and later). Vol. I (E. J. Hooper;
Edited by G. G. Moore, Nos. 1-8, and by E. J. Hooper,
Nos. 9-12), Sept., 1839- Aug., 1840, Nos. 1-12, viii, 344
pp. CinPL, HistPSO, OhioStL, WRHist. Vol. II (*The
Western Farmer and Gardener, . . .* ; Charles
Foster; Edited by E. J. Hooper and Thomas Affleck),
Oct., 1840-Sept., 1841, Nos. 1-12, vi, 288 pp. CinPL,
HistPSO, OhioStL, WRHist.

The Western Gem and Cabinet of Literature, Science, and
News.

St. Clairsville, O., Gregg and Duffey, 1834. Semimonthly, later weekly. From W. H. Venable, *Beginnings of Literary Culture in the Ohio Valley*, 1891, p. 125.

The Western Journal of Medicine and Surgery. . . . Louisville, Prentice & Weissinger, 1840 (and later). Edited by Daniel Drake and Lunsford P. Yandell. Vol. I, Jan.-June (issued irregularly), Nos. 1-6 (numbered irregularly), 488 pp. (with additional pages irregularly inserted). CinPL, JCrerar, LouPL. Vol. II, July-Dec., Nos. 7-12 (with supplementary issues for Aug. and Oct.), iv, 488 pp. (with additional pages irregularly inserted). CinPL, JCrerar, LouPL.

The Western Journal of the Medical and Physical Sciences. Cincinnati, 1828-1839 (follows Vol. I of *The Western Medical and Physical Journal*). For Vols. XI-XII, see above, Chapter III, footnote 191. Vol. II (Printed by Whetstone and Buxton, for the Editor; Edited by Daniel Drake),Apr., 1828-Mar., 1829, twelve issues, 658 pp. IU (lacks issues for Apr. and Aug.), JCrerar, TransylvaniaU, WRHist. Vol. III (Printed by Whetstone and Buxton, for the Editor; Edited by Daniel Drake), 1829-1830, four issues, 616 pp. IU, JCrerar (lacks first to third issues), TransylvaniaU, WRHist. Vol. IV (E. Deming; Edited by Daniel Drake and James C. Finley), 1830-1831, four issues, 621, [1] pp. IU, TransylvaniaU. Vol. V (E. Deming; Edited by Daniel Drake and James C. Finley), 1831-1832, four issues, 567, [2] pp. IU, JCrerar (lacks first issue), TransylvaniaU. Vol. VI (E. Deming; Edited by Daniel Drake and James C. Finley), 1832-1833, four issues, 640 pp. CinPL, IU, WRHist. Vol. VII (E. Deming; Edited by Daniel Drake), 1833-1834, four issues, 660 pp. IU, JCrerar (lacks fourth issue), TransylvaniaU, WRHist. Vol. VIII (at the Chronicle Office; Edited by Daniel

Drake), 1834-1835, four issues, 648 pp. IU (lacks second issue), JCrerar (lacks second issue), TransylvaniaU.
Vol. IX (Printed by N. S. Johnson; Edited by Daniel
Drake and Wm. Wood), 1835-1836, four issues, 697 pp.
IU, JCrerar, TransylvaniaU. Vol. X (Printed by N.
S. Johnson; Edited by Daniel Drake and Wm. Wood),
1836-1837, four issues, 644, [3] pp. JCrerar, Transylvaniau. Vol. XI, 1837-1838, four issues. JCrerar
(lacks third issue).

The Western Lady's Book.
Cincinnati, Printed by H. P. Brooks, 1840 (and possibly
later). Edited by an Association of Ladies and Gentlemen. Vol. I, No. 1 for Aug., 1840, 28 pp. From W.
H. Venable, *Beginnings of Literary Culture in the Ohio
Valley,* 1891, pp. 82 and 126.

The Western Literary Journal, and Monthly Review.
Cincinnati, Smith and Day, 1836. Edited by William
D. Gallagher. Vol. I, June-Nov., 1836, Nos. 1-6, iv, 440
pp. CinPL, LC, WisH.

The Western Medical and Physical Journal, Original and
    Eclectic.
Cincinnati, Hatch & Nichols, 1827-1828 (followed by *The
Western Journal of the Medical and Physical Sciences,*
Vol. II). Edited by Daniel Drake and Guy W. Wright.
Vol. I, Apr., 1827-Mar., 1828, twelve issues, 720 pp. IU,
TransylvaniaU, WRHist.

The Western Medical Gazette.
Cincinnati, 1832-1835 (or later). Vol. I (John Stapleton, Nos. 1-18, and Silas Reed, Nos. 19-24; Edited irregularly by Doctors Eberle, Mitchell, Staughton, Bailey,
Smith, and Gross), Dec. 15, 1832-Apr. 1, 1834 (suspended Oct., 1833-Jan., 1834), Nos. 1-24, 383 pp. CinPL,
WRHist (has No. 1 only). Vol. II (Silas Reed; Edited
partly by Drs. Eberle, Mitchell, Smith, and Gross — by

Feb., 1835, Reed was the sole editor), May 1, 1834-Feb. (or later), 1835, Nos. 1-10, 480 pp. *Cf. The Western Monthly Magazine*, II, 445 (Aug., 1834); and III, 172 (Mar., 1835). CinPL.

The Western Medical Reformer: a Monthly Journal of Medical and Chirurgical Science.

Worthington, O., 1836-1838. Suspended in 1838, but revived in 1844, at Cincinnati (see above, Chapter III, footnote 197). Vol. I (Worthington, O.), Jan.-Dec., 1836. WRHist (not collated). Vol. II (Worthington, O., at least No. 12), No. 12 for Dec., 1837, pp. 369-384. HistPSO (has No. 12 only), WRHist (has all except July and Oct.; but I have not collated this volume). Vol. III (Worthington, O., Published and Edited by the Medical Professors of Worthington College), Nos. 1-11 for Jan.-Nov., 1838, iv, 176 pp. HistPSO (has Nos. 1-11).

The Western Messenger; Devoted to Religion and Literature.

Cincinnati (and, for a time, Louisville), 1835-1840 (and later). Vol. I, June, 1835-July, 1836, Nos. 1-12 (no issue in Mar.), xii, 864 pp. For additional information regarding this and later volumes of the magazine, see above, Chapter III, footnote 162. CinPL, HistPSO (lacks No. 1), IU (lacks Nos. 1-2), LC, WRHist, WisH. Vols. II and III (2 vols. in 1), Aug., 1836-July, 1837, Nos. 1-6 and 1-6, viii, 854 pp. CinPL, IU, LC, LouPL (lacks Vol. III), WRHist, WisH. Vol. IV, Sept., 1837-Feb., 1838, Nos. 1-6, vii (viii), 432 pp. CinPL, IU, LC, LouPL, WRHist, WisH. Vol. V, Apr.-Sept., 1838, Nos. 1-6, 424 pp. CinPL, IU, LC, LouPL, WRHist, WisH. Vol. VI, Nov., 1838-Apr., 1839, Nos. 1-6, 432 pp. CinPL, IU (lacks No. 5), LC, WRHist, WisH. Vol. VII, May-Oct., 1839, Nos. 1-6, 436 pp. CinPL, IU (lacks No. 4),

LC, WRHist, WisH. Vol. VIII, May, 1840-Apr., 1841, Nos. 1-12, [2], 572 pp. CinPL, LC, WRHist, WisH (lacks Nos. 1-5 and 7-12).

Western Minerva, or American Annals of Knowledge and Literature.

Lexington, Thomas Smith, 1821. Edited by Constantine S. Rafinesque. Vol. I, Jan., 1821, No. 1, 80 pp. See above, Chapter III, footnotes 104-107.

Western Mirror, and Ladies' Literary Gazette.

St. Louis, 1837. J. Ruggles. Edited by Mrs. H. A. Ruggles. Vol. I, Jan.-Oct. 11, 1837, Nos. 1-12, 96 pp. ChU.

The Western Miscellany.

Zanesville, O., George C. Sedwick, 1829-1831. With Vol. I, No. 11, the title changes to *The Regular Baptist Miscellany.* Vol. I, Oct., 1829-Sept., 1830, Nos. 1-12, 196 pp. WRHist. Vol. II, Oct., 1830-June, 1831, Nos. 1-9, 144 pp. WRHist.

The Western Monthly Magazine, a Continuation of the Illinois Monthly Magazine, . . .

Cincinnati, 1833-1836 (followed by *The Western Monthly Magazine, and Literary Journal. New Series*). Vol. I (Corey & Fairbank; Edited by James Hall), Jan.-Dec., 1833, twelve issues, vi, 600 pp. IU, LC, OhioStL, WRHist, WisH. Vol. II (Corey & Fairbank, and later Eli Taylor, and finally Taylor & Tracy; Edited by James Hall), Jan.-Dec., 1834, twelve issues, 670 pp. IU, LC, OhioStL, WRHist, WisH, YMML. Vol. IV [III] (Taylor & Tracy; Edited by James Hall), Jan.-June, 1835, six issues, 399, [1] pp. IU, LC, OhioStL, WRHist, WisH, YMML. Vol. III [IV] (Taylor & Tracy; Edited by James Hall), July-Dec., 1835, six issues, 425, [1] pp. IU, LC, OhioStL, WRHist, WisH, YMML. Vol. V (Flash, Ryder, & Co., etc.; Edited by James Hall, Nos. 1-6, and

Joseph Reese Fry, Nos. 7-12), Jan.-Dec., 1836, Nos. 1-12,
[2], 760 pp.   IU, LC, OhioStL, WRHist, WisH, YMML.
The Western Monthly Magazine, and Literary Journal.
New Series.
Louisville and Cincinnati (printed in Louisville), Mar-
shall & Gallagher, 1837.   Edited by James B. Marshall
and William D. Gallagher.   Vol. I, Feb.-June, 1837, Nos.
1-5, 364 pp.   CinPL (lacks Nos. 2 and 5), LC (lacks
Nos. 4 and 5), WRHist, WisH.
The Western Monthly Review.
Cincinnati, E. H. Flint, 1827-1830.   Edited by Timothy
Flint.   Vol. I (title of first three issues: *The Western
Magazine and Review*), May, 1827-Apr., 1828, twelve
issues, 756 pp.   CinPL, HistPSO, IU, LC, LouPL,
WRHist, WisH.   Vol. II, June, 1828-May, 1829, twelve
issues, 704 pp.   HistPSO, LC, LouPL, WRHist, WisH.
Vol. III, July, 1829-June, 1830, twelve issues, [2], 668
pp.   CinPL, HistPSO, IU, LC, LouPL, WRHist, WisH.
The Western Peace-maker, and Monthly Religious Journal.
Oxford, O., Printed by W. W. Bishop, 1839-1840 (or
later).   Edited by R. H. Bishop, C. E. Stowe, and J.
W. Scott.   Vol. I, Nos. 1-9 for May, 1839-Sept., 1840,
425 pp. (incomplete number of pages?).   Smith, WRHist
(lacks No. 9).
Western People's Magazine.
Cincinnati, H. S. Barnum (Nos. 5-13 bear additional
imprint "J. D. Weston, & Co., Alexandria, La.," which
is replaced in Nos. 14-23 by "Sanford & Page, Alexan-
dria, La."), 1834-1835 (or later).   Vol. I, Nos. 1-23 for
Mar. 1, 1834-Jan. 3, 1835, 184 pp. (the volume was to contain 208 pp. when completed).   WRHist.
The Western Quarterly Journal of Practical Medicine,
. . .
Cincinnati, J. A. James & Co., 1837.   Edited by John

Eberle, A. G. Smith, J. Moorhead, J. Locke, I. Cobb, and J. T. Shotwell. No. 1 for June, 1837, vi, 163 pp. JCrerar.

The Western Quarterly Reporter of Medical, Surgical, and Natural Science.

Cincinnati, 1822-1823. Vol. I (J. P. Foote; Edited by John D. Godman), 1822, Nos. 1-4, 414, [2] pp. CinPL, HistPSO, TransylvaniaU, WRHist (lacks No. 4). Vol. II (J. P. Foote; Edited by John D. Godman), 1823, Nos. 1-2, 212 pp. CinPL, TransylvaniaU.

The Western Religious Magazine.

Cincinnati (later Zanesville, O.), 1826-1829 (or later). Vol. I (Cincinnati, Printed by Morgan, Lodge and Fisher, No. 1; Zanesville, O., George C. Sedwick, Nos. 2-12), June 20, 1826-May, 1828, Nos. 1-12, 192 pp. WRHist (lacks Nos. 2-5 and 7). Vol. II (Zanesville, O., Geo: C. Sedwick, under the Patronage of the Ohio Baptist Convention), Nos. 1-10 for June, 1828-Mar., 1829, 160 pp. WRHist (lacks Nos. 6 and 8).

The Western Review and Miscellaneous Magazine, a Monthly Publication, Devoted to Literature and Science.

Lexington, William Gibbes Hunt, 1819-1821. Edited by William Gibbes Hunt? Vol. I, Aug., 1819-Jan., 1820, Nos. 1-6, [2], 384 pp. ChU, HistPSO, KyStL, LexPL, OhioStL (lacks No. 1), TransylvaniaU, WRHist, WisH. Vol. II, Feb.-July, 1820, Nos. 1-6, [2], 384 pp. ChU, HistPSO, KyStL, LexPL, OhioStL, TransylvaniaU, WRHist, WisH. Vol. III, Aug., 1820-Jan., 1821, Nos. 1-6, [2], 384 pp. ChU, HistPSO, KyStL, OhioStL, TransylvaniaU, WRHist, WisH. Vol. IV, Feb.-July, 1821, Nos. 1-6, [2], 384 pp. ChU, HistPSO, KyStL, LexPL, OhioStL, TransylvaniaU, WRHist, WisH.

Youth's Magazine.

Cincinnati, 1834-1836 (or later). Vol. I, No. 27 for Sept. 29, 1835. HistPSO (has only No. 27). Vol II, Nos. 2-26 for Oct. 13, 1835-Oct. 14, 1836, pp. 17-416. HistPSO (lacks No. 14).

IV. PERIODICALS NOT DEFINITELY ASSIGNED TO ANY OF THE THREE PRECEDING GROUPS

Buckeye Blossom.

Xenia, O., P. Lapham and W. B. Fairchild, 1839 (and possibly later). Vol. I? No. 1? 16 pp. From *The Hesperian*, III, 91 (June, 1839).

The Common School Advocate, and Journal of Education.

Jacksonville, Ill., E. T. & C. Goudy, 1837? (and possibly later). From *The Western Emigrants' Magazine*, I, 15 (May, 1837).

The Family Schoolmaster.

Richmond, Ind., Halloway and Davis, 1839. From W. H. Venable, *Beginnings of Literary Culture in the Ohio Valley*, 1891, p. 126.

The Ladies' Museum and Western Repository of Belles Lettres.

Cincinnati, Printed by John Whetstone, 1830-1831? Edited by Joel T. Case. From W. H. Venable, *Beginnings of Literary Culture in the Ohio Valley*, 1891, pp. 124-125.

Self Instructor.

Berea, O.? 1840? Edited by Josiah Holbrook, of Berea, O. From *The Extra Equator*, I, 82 (Nov., 1840).

The Western Minerva.

Cincinnati, Francis and Wm. D. Gallagher, 1826. From W. H. Venable, *Beginnings of Literary Culture in the Ohio Valley*, 1891, pp. 124 and 439.

Western Review: . . .

N. p. (Watervliet, O. ?), n. d. (1837?). Edited by Richard McNemar. No. 7, 10, [4] pp. WRHist.

CHAPTER IV

CONTROVERSIAL WRITINGS

I. POLITICAL PAMPHLETS AND SPEECHES

Adair, John. Letters of Gen. Adair & Gen. Jackson, Relative to the Charge of Cowardice, Made by the Latter against the Kentucky Troops at New Orleans. 63, [1] pp. N. p. (Lexington, Printed by Thomas Smith), n. d. (1827). ChU.

Allan, Chilton. Circular Letter of Chilton Allan, to his Constituents, in the Congressional District Composed of the Counties of Franklin, Woodford, Fayette, & Clarke [sic], in the State of Kentucky. 16 pp. Washington, Printed by Jonathan Elliot, 1835. ChU.

—— Circular, to the People of the Congressional District . . . 12 pp. N. p. (Lexington?), n. d. (1833?). ChU.

—— Speech of Chilton Allan, on the Subject of the Removal of the Deposites. Delivered in the House of Representatives of the United States, March 27 and 28, 1834. 30 pp. Washington, Printed by Gales and Seaton, 1834. From LC card.

—— Speech of Mr. Allan, of Kentucky, on the Division of the Proceeds of the Public Lands among the States. Delivered in the House of Representatives of the United States, March, 1836. 29 pp. Washington, Jacob Gideon, Jr., Printer, 1836. WRHist.

Allen, William. Speech of Mr. Allen, of Ohio, on the Bill to Separate the Government from the Banks. Delivered in the Senate of the United States, Feb. 20, 1838. 20 pp. Philadelphia, John Ferral, 1838. WRHist, WisH.

—— Speech of the Honorable William Allen, Delivered at the Great Democratic Festival, Held at Lancaster, Ohio, on the 19th Day of August, 1837. 16 pp. Lancaster, O., Printed by J. and C. H. Brough, 1837. WRHist.

An Appeal to the People of Kentucky; on the Relief System, &c. By one of the Minority. 24 pp. N. p., n. d. (1824). WisH.

An Argument in Favor of Establishing the State Bank of Ohio; Contained in a Series of Five Numbers, that Appeared, editorially, in the Cincinnati Republican. Together with a Draft of a Charter for that Projected Institution; . . . 66 pp. Cincinnati, Reynolds, Allen & Disney, Printers, 1833. WRHist.

Aydelott, Benjamin P. The Duties of American Citizens. An Address . . . 16 pp. Cincinnati, A. Pugh, Printer, 1840. WRHist, WisH.

Barrow, David. Involuntary, Unmerited, Perpetual, Absolute, Hereditary, Slavery, Examined on the Principles of Nature, Reason, Justice, Policy, and Scripture. From R. H. Bishop, *An Outline of the History of the Church in the State of Kentucky,* 1824, p. 298.

Barry, Wm. T. Address of William T. Barry, Postmaster General, to the People of the United States. 24 pp. Washington, Printed by Francis Preston Blair, 1834. WRHist.

—— Letter of William T. Barry, Postmaster General, to the House of Representatives of the United States; Reviewing the Report of the Select Committee of that House, Appointed to Investigate the Affairs of the Post Office Department. March 2, 1835. 30 pp. Washington, Printed by Blair and Rives, 1835. WRHist.

·—— Remarks of William T. Barry, Esq. L. L. D. Lieutenant Governor of Kentucky . . . in Opposition

to Mr. Flournoy's Motion, to Strike out the First Section
of the Bill Establishing the Bank of the Commonwealth,
at the Session of 1820. 28 pp. N. p. (Lexington),
Printed at the Office of the Kentucky Gazette, 1822.
TransylvaniaU.

—— Speech of W. T. Barry, Esq. at the Great Dinner
Given by the Citizens of Fayette County, in Honor of
Gen. Jackson and the People's Rights, July 21st, 1827.
12 pp. N. p. (Louisville, S. Penn, Jr.), n. d. ChU.

Barton, David. In Senate United States — March 6, 1830.
Mr. Barton's Speech, in Reply to Mr. White, of Tennessee. Upon the Appropriation Bill. 4 pp. N. p., n. d.
(1830). WisH.

—— In the Senate of the United States. — March 17, 1830.
Executive Session. Speech of Mr. Barton, of Missouri,
upon the Power of the President to Remove Federal Officers; . . . 28 pp. Washington, Office of the National Journal, 1830. WisH.

—— Speech of Mr. Barton, of Missouri. In Senate United
States. — Feb. 9, 1830. 42 pp. N. p., n. d. WRHist,
WisH.

Bates, Edward. Edward Bates against Thomas H. Benton.
12 pp. St. Louis, Charless and Paschall, Printers, 1828.
BurColl.

Beecher, Catharine E. An Essay on Slavery and Aboli-
tionism, with Reference to the Duty of American Fe-
males. 152 pp. Philadelphia, Henry Perkins, etc.,
1837. HistPSO, LC, WRHist.

Beecher, Edward. Narrative of Riots at Alton: in Connection with the Death of Rev. Elijah P. Lovejoy. 159
pp. Alton, Ill., George Holton, 1838. CinPL, ColU,
NYPL, WRHist, WisH.

Bell, Daniel S. American Speeches, or, Some Valuable
Specimens of Congressional Eloquence; together, with

Several Presidential Messages, a Biography of Henry
Clay, and Some Other Pieces of Interest. 239 pp.
Xenia, O., Printed for the Compiler, 1825. WRHist.

Benton, Thomas Hart. Mr. Benton's Letter to Maj. Gen.
Davis, of the State of Mississippi, Declining the Nomination of the Convention of that State; Defending the Nomination of Mr. Van Buren . . . 16 pp. Washington, Printed by Blair & Rives, 1835. LC, MoHist.

—— Remarks of Mr. Benton, of Missouri, on his Motion
for Leave to Introduce a Bill for the Repeal of the Salt
Duties and Fishing Bounties; . . . in the Senate
. . . January 1839. 16 pp. (incomplete). Washington, Printed by Blair and Rives, 1839. WRHist.

—— Remarks of Mr. Benton of Missouri, on the Annual
Expenditures of the Government. In Senate, Thursday,
May 7, 1840. 8 pp. N. p., n. d. LC, WRHist, WisH.

—— Report of the Secretary of the Treasury, on the Resolution of the Senate, Calling for Information in Relation to the State of the Revenue: to which is Added the
Speech of Mr. Benton, on Said Report. 8 pp. N. p.,
n. d. (1834). WisH.

—— Speeches of Messrs. Buchanan and Benton, on the
Bill to Admit the State of Michigan into the Union. Delivered in the Senate, January 3, 1837. 14 pp. N. p.,
n. d. WRHist, WisH.

—— Speech of Mr. Benton, in the Senate of the United
States, January 6, 1829, on his Resolution in Relation to
the Public Debt, . . . 14 pp. Washington, Printed
by Gales and Seaton, 1829. NewL.

—— Speech of Mr. Benton, of Missouri, Delivered in the
Senate of the United States, on the Mission to Panama.
March 13, 1826. 59 pp. N. p., n. d. LC, WisH.

—— Speech of Mr. Benton, of Missouri, in Reply to Mr.

Calhoun's Report upon the Subject of Executive Patronage. Delivered in the Senate of the United States, February 9, 1835. 16 pp. Washington, Printed by Blair & Rives, 1835. WisH.

—— Speech of Mr. Benton, of Missouri. In Senate, January 6, 1840 — on Mr. Benton's Resolutions against the Constitutionality and Expediency of Assuming, or Providing for the Payment of the State Debts, . . . 16 pp. N. p., n. d. WRHist.

—— Speech of Mr. Benton of Missouri. In Senate, Tuesday, May 27, 1840. Bankrupt Bill — Inclusion of Corporations. 16 pp. N. p., n. d. ChU.

—— Speech of Mr. Benton, of Missouri, in the Senate of the United States, February 27, 1835, on his Resolution to Expunge from the Senate Journal the Resolution Condemnatory of the President, Adopted by the Senate, March 28, 1834. 20 pp. Washington, Printed by Blair and Rives, 1835. WisH.

—— Speech of Mr. Benton, of Missouri, on his Motion to Expunge from the Journal the Sentence Pronounced against President Jackson for Violating the Laws and Constitution. Delivered in Senate . . . 18th and 21st March, 1836. 34 pp. Washington, Blair & Rives, Printers, 1836. WisH.

—— Speech of Mr. Benton, of Missouri, on his Motion to Expunge from the Journal the Sentence Pronounced against President Jackson for Violating the Laws and Constitution. In Senate, March 18, 1836.— . . . 32 pp. N. p., n. d. WRHist.

—— Speech of Mr. Benton, of Missouri, on his Motion to Strike out from the 19th and 20th Sections of the Independent Treasury Bill, the Clauses which Permitted the Reception and Disbursement of Bills, Notes, or Paper

Issued under the Authority of the United States; . . .
Senate U. S. January 16, 1840. 16 pp. Washington,
Printed at the Globe Office, 1840. WRHist.

—— Speech of Mr. Benton, of Missouri, on Mr. Calhoun's
Amendment to the Bill to Provide for the Collection,
Keeping and Disbursement of the Public Moneys, without
the Agency of the Banks. Delivered in Senate U. S.
September 22, 1837. 15 pp. Washington, Printed at
the Globe Office, 1837. WisH.

—— Speech of Mr. Benton, of Missouri, on the Bill to
Graduate the Price of the Public Lands. Delivered in
the Senate of the U. States. May 16, 1826. 36 pp. (incomplete). N. p., n. d. WRHist.

—— Speech of Mr. Benton, of Missouri, on the Bill to
Provide for the Abolition of Unnecessary Duties, . . .
Delivered in the Senate of the United States, February
23, 1830. 12 pp. Washington, Printed by D. Green,
1830. WisH.

—— Speech of Mr. Benton, of Missouri, on the Expunging
Resolution. Delivered in the Senate, January 12, 1837.
7 pp. N. p., n. d. LC, WisH.

—— Speech of Mr. Benton, of Missouri, on the Graduation
Bill, and in Reply to Mr. Clay's Attacks upon Gen.
Jackson. Delivered in the Senate of the United States,
January 4, 1839. 8 pp. Washington, Blair and Rives,
Printers, 1839. NewL, WisH.

—— Speech of Mr. Benton, of Missouri, on the Resolutions
Offered by Mr. Clay, on 26th December, Relative to the
Removal of the Public Deposites from the Bank of the
United States. Delivered in the Senate, January 2d,
3d, 6th and 7th, 1834. 47 pp. Washington, Printed
by Francis Preston Blair, 1834. JCrerar, WisH.

—— Speech of Mr. Benton, of Missouri, on the Subject

of the Fortifications. In Senate, February 23, 1836.
12 pp. N. p., n. d. BurColl.

—— Speech of Thomas H. Benton, of Missouri. Delivered,
March 14th, 1838. In the United States Senate on the
Bill to Separate the Government from the Banks. 42
pp. Philadelphia, Printed by John Wilbank, 1838. LC,
WisH.

—— Speech . . . on the Resolution of Mr. Ewing,
for Rescinding the Treasury Order . . . Delivered
in the Senate, Dec., 1836. 28 pp. Washington, 1837.
Title supplied from Sabin. From LC card.

—— Substance of Mr. Benton's Speech, on the Motion for
a Reduction of the Duty on Salt. Delivered in the
Senate of the United States, May 1830. 8 pp. Washington, Printed by Duff Green, 1830. WisH.

Birkbeck, Morris. An Appeal to the People of Illinois on
the Question of a Convention. 25 pp. Shawneetown,
Printed by C. Jones, July, 1823. From reprint, by C.
W. Smith (1905), of copy in the Boston Athenaeum.

Birney, James Gillespie. Addresses and Speeches. 1835.
From William Birney, *James G. Birney and his Times,*
1890, p. 436.

—— Address to Slave-holders, October, 1836. From W.
Birney, *loc. cit.*

—— American Churches the Bulwarks of American Slavery. 1840. From W. Birney, *loc. cit.*

—— Argument of Fugitive Slave Case. 1837. From W.
Birney, *loc. cit.*

—— A Collection of Valuable Documents, being Birney's
Vindication of Abolitionists — . . . 80 pp. Boston,
Isaac Knapp, 1836. WRHist.

—— Letter on Colonization, Addressed to the Rev. Thornton J. Mills, Corresponding Secretary of the Kentucky

Colonization Society. 46 pp. New York, Office of the Anti-slavery Reporter, 1834. BurColl, LaneTS, WRHist.

—— Letters to Presbyterian Church. 1834. From W. Birney, *loc. cit.*

—— Letter to Colonel Stone. May, 1836. From W. Birney, *loc. cit.*

—— Mr. Birney's Second Letter. To the Ministers and Elders of the Presbyterian Church in Kentucky: . . . 16 pp. N. p., n. d. (1834?). WRHist.

—— No. 8. The Anti-slavery Examiner. Correspondence, between the Hon. F. H. Elmore, . . . and James G. Birney, . . . 68 pp. New York, the American Anti-slavery Society, 1838. TransylvaniaU, WRHist.

—— Political Obligations of Abolitionists. 1839. From W. Birney, *loc. cit.*

—— Report on the Duty of Political Action. May, 1839. From W. Birney, *loc. cit.*

—— Speeches in England. 1840. From W. Birney, *loc. cit.*

—— Ten Letters on Slavery and Colonization. [1833?] From W. Birney, *loc. cit.*

—— Vindication of the Abolitionists. 1835. From W. Birney, *loc. cit.*

Blackford, Isaac. An Address, at the First Stated Meeting of the Indiana Colonization Society Delivered at Indianapolis, in the Hall of Representatives, . . . December, 1829. 14 pp. Indianapolis, Printed at the State Gazette Office, 1829. IndStL.

Bledsoe, Jesse. The Speech of Jesse Bledsoe, Esq. on the Resolutions Proposed by him, concerning Banks. Delivered in the Senate of Kentucky, . . . 1818. 45 pp. Lexington, Printed by J. Norvell & Co., 1819. ColU, NewL.

Blythe, James. A Speech Delivered at the Anniversary of the Indiana Colonization Society, on December 23, A. D. 1833. 13 pp. Indianapolis, N. Bolton & Co., Printers, 1834. IndStL, LC.

Bodley, Thomas. To the People of Kentucky. viii, 27 pp. N. p. (Lexington?), n. d (1808?). ChU.

Bond, William Key. Speech of Mr. Bond, of Ohio, on the Treasury Note Bill. Delivered in the House of Representatives, March 18, 1840. 31 pp. N. p., n. d. WRHist.

Bonsall, J. The War Exterminated. 8 pp. N. p.(Cincinnati?), n. d. (1839?). WRHist.

Bowmar, Herman. Argus Extra. To the People of Kentucky. 40 pp. N. p. (Frankfort?), n. d. (1828?). ChU.

Boyle, John, and William Owsley, and B. Mills. The Response of the Judges of the Court of Appeals, to the Preamble, Resolutions and Address, Proposed by a Joint Committee of the Senate and House of Representatives, for the Purpose of Removing them from Office. House of Representatives, December 9, 1824. 38 pp. N. p. (Frankfort?), n. d. (1824?). WisH.

Breckinridge, Robert J. An Address Delivered before the Colonization Society of Kentucky, at Frankfort, on the 6th Day of January, 1831. 24 pp. Frankfort, A. G. Hodges, Printer, 1831. ChU, LaneTS, LC, WRHist.

Brown, Paul. A Dialogue, on Commonwealths. 16 pp. Cincinnati, Printed by S. J. Browne, 1828. LC.

Brunt, Jonathan. Extracts, from Locke's Essay on the Human Understanding; and Other Writers; . . . Together with a Short Account of the Publisher's Difficulties, Intermixed with Some Political Remarks. . . . 36 pp. Frankfort, Printed and Sold by J. Brunt, 1804. From LC card.

Bryan, John A. Address Delivered at Columbus, Ohio, on the Anniversary of the Victory of N. Orleans, . . . January 9, 1832. 8 pp. N. p., n. d. WRHist.

Buckner, Alex. Speech of Mr. Buckner, of Missouri, on the Resolution Proposing to Purchase Sixty Copies of the History of the Bank of the United States, March 1832. 8 pp. Washington, Printed by Gales and Seaton, 1832. WisH.

Burnet, Jacob. Speech of Judge Burnett [sic], of Ohio, in the Whig National Convention, Giving a Brief History of the Life of Gen. William Henry Harrison. 8 pp. Washington, Printed at the Madisonian Office, 1839. LC, WRHist.

Caldwell, Charles. A Discourse on the First Centennial Celebration of the Birth-day of Washington, . . . to the Citizens of Lexington, on the 22nd of February, 1832. 56 pp. Lexington, Printed by N. L. Finnell & J. F. Herndon, 1832. ChU, LC.

The Captive, or "the Great Western" Dialogians, Telling about Private Jails, Factories, the Slave-trade, and the "Curiosities" of N. O. In Dialogues, between Henry and Plain John. No. I. 40 pp. Cincinnati, Samuel A. Alley, 1839. WRHist.

Cass, Lewis. Considerations on the Present State of the Indians, and their Removal to the West of the Mississippi. From the North American Review, No. LXVI, for January 1830 [sic]. 61 pp. Boston, Gray and Bowen, 1828 [sic]. WisH.

—— Remarks on the Policy and Practice of the United States and Great Britain in their Treatment of the Indians . . . From the North American Review, No. LV, for April, 1827. 78 pp. Boston, F. T. Gray, 1827. From LC card.

—— To the Public. 8 pp. N. p. (Washington?), n. d. (1837). From LC card.

Chase, Philander. Bishop Chase's Address to the Legislature of Ohio. 3 pp. N. p. (Columbus?), n. d. (1827 or 1828?). WRHist.

Chase, Salmon Portland. Speech of Salmon P. Chase, in the Case of the Colored Woman, Matilda, who was Brought before the Court of Common Pleas of Hamilton County, Ohio, by Writ of habeas corpus; March 11, 1837. 40 pp. Cincinnati, Pugh & Dodd, Printers, 1837. LC, WRHist.

Chilton, Thomas. The Circular Address of Thomas Chilton, of Kentucky, to his Constituents. Washington City, February 27, 1831. . . . 20 pp. Washington, Printed by Stephen C. Ustick, 1831. WRHist.

—— Speech of Mr. Chilton, of Kentucky, on the Proposed Alteration of the Tariff: Delivered in the House of Representatives of the United States, April, 1828. 7 pp. Washington, Printed by Green & Jarvis, 1828. LouPL.

—— To the Voters of the Eleventh Congressional District. Washington City, February 8th, 1828. 8 pp. N. p., n. d. LouPL.

Clark, James. Circular Address of James Clark, to his Constituents. To the Voters of the Third Congressional District of Kentucky, Consisting of the Counties of Fayette, Woodford, and Clark. 42 pp. N. p. (Washington?), n. d. (1831). ChU.

Clark, John S. Twelve Months in Alton, Including a Brief History of the City; the Establishment of the Alton Observer; the First, Second, Third and Fourth Destruction of the Press by a Mob, and the Death of the Rev'd. E. P. Lovejoy; . . . From MS. copyright record for District of Illinois, 1821-1848; MS. entry dated Feb. 3, 1838.

For evidence tending to show that this book was published, see advertisement of it in William S. Lincoln, *Alton Trials*, 1838. Both books were entered in the record of the District Court on the same day.

Clarke, George Rogers. An Address to the People of the Western States, on the Subject of the Next Presidency: . . . 15 pp. Louisville, S. Penn, Jr., Printer, n. d. (1824 ?). ChU.

Clarke, James. Speech of Almon H. Read, Esq. of Susquehanna, . . . also the Speech of James Clarke, Esq. of Indiana, Delivered in the Convention, to Amend the Consti[tution] of Pennsylvania, . . . December 1, 1837. 29 pp. Harrisburg, Pa., Printed at the Office of the Reporter, 1838. BurColl.

Clay, Henry. An Address, Delivered to the Colonization Society of Kentucky, at Frankfort, December 17, 1829, . . . 26 pp. Lexington, Thomas Smith, Printer, 1829. HistPSO, WRHist. 24 pp. Frankfort, Printed by J. H. Holeman, 1830. LaneTS.

—— The Addresses of Henry Clay to his Constituents, and his Speech at the Dinner Given him at Lewisburg, Va. 32 pp. Louisville, Printed by W. W. Worsley, 1827. HistPSO.

—— An Address of Henry Clay, to the Public; Containing Certain Testimony in Refutation of the Charges against him, Made by Gen. Andrew Jackson, Touching the Last Presidential Election. 61 pp. Washington, Printed by Peter Force, 1827. BurColl, IU, NYPL, WRHist, WisH. 52 pp. Supplement to the Kentucky Reporter, Lexington, Jan. 23, 1828. Library of Samuel M. Wilson, Lexington, Ky.

—— The Beauties of the Hon. Henry Clay. To which is Added, a Biographical and Critical Essay. . . . 235

pp. New York, Edward Walker, 1839. DetroitPL, LexPL, LC.

—— Gen. Jackson's Letter to Carter Beverley, and Mr. Clay's Reply. Mr. Clay's Speech at the Lexington Dinner. Gen. Jackson's Reply to Mr. Clay, . . . Mr. Buchanan's Reply, . . . 16 pp. Portsmouth, Printed by Miller and Brewster, Portsmouth Journal Office, Aug. 21, 1827. HistPSO, NewL.

—— Mr. Clay's Speech. At the Dinner at Noble's Inn, near Lexington, July 12, 1827. 14 pp. N. p., n. d. LC, WRHist, WisH.

—— Mr. Clay's Speech upon the Tariff: or the "American System," so Called; or the Anglican System, in Fact, . . . 188 pp. Richmond, Va., Printed by Thomas W. White, 1827. WisH.

—— A Speech Delivered by the Hon. H. Clay, on the Doctrines, and on the Question of Recording the Protest of the President of the United States against a Resolution of the Senate, which had been Proposed by Mr. Clay. Delivered in the Senate of the United States, on the 30th Day of April, 1834. 20 pp. Washington, Printed by Gales and Seaton, 1834. BurColl, WRHist, WisH.

—— Speech Delivered by the Hon. Henry Clay, in the House of Representatives of the United States, on Friday, the Eighth Day of January, 1813, on the Bill for Raising an Additional Military Force of Twenty Thousand Men for One Year. 20 pp. Washington, Office of the National Intelligencer, 1813. From LC card.

—— Speeches of Henry Clay & Daniel Webster, in Senate of the United States, Sept. 25, 1837, on the Sub-treasury Bill. 48 pp. Norwich, J. Dunham, n. d. NYPL. Copy of title supplied by Miss Winifred Cody.

—— The Speeches of Henry Clay, Delivered in the Congress of the United States; to which is Prefixed a Biographical Memoir; with an Appendix Containing his Speeches at Lexington and Lewisburgh, and before the Colonization Society at Washington; together with his Address to his Constituents, on the Subject of the Late Presidential Election; . . . xx, 381 pp. Philadelphia, H. C. Carey & I. Lea; New York, G. & C. Carvill, etc., 1827. LC.

—— Speech in Support of an American System for the Protection of American Industry; Delivered in the House of Representatives, on the 30th and 31st of March, 1824. 39 pp. Washington, Printed at the Columbian Office, 1824. NewL, WRHist. 34 pp. Philadelphia, Joseph R. A. Skerrett, 1824. HistPSO.

—— Speech of Henry Clay, Delivered at the Mechanics' Collation, in the Apollonian Garden, in Cincinnati, (Ohio,) on the 3d of August, 1830. 24 pp. N. p., n. d. LC, WisH.

—— Speech of Henry Clay, in Defence of the American System, against the British Colonial System: . . . Delivered in the Senate of the United States, February 2d, 3d, and 6th, 1832. 43 pp. Washington, Printed by Gales and Seaton, 1832. BurColl, HistPSO, JCrerar, LC, WRHist.

—— Speech of Henry Clay, in the Senate of the United States, February 25, 1833, in Vindication of his Bill, Entitled "An Act to Modify the Act of the 14th July, 1832, and All Other Acts Imposing Duties on Imports." 8 pp. N. p., n. d. WisH.

—— Speech of Henry Clay, of Kentucky, on Certain Resolutions Offered to the Senate of the United States, in December, 1837, by Mr. Calhoun, . . . Delivered in the Senate U. S., January 9, 1838. 13 pp. Washington, Printed by Gales and Seaton, 1838. WRHist.

—— Speech of Henry Clay, of Kentucky, on the Bill Imposing Additional Duties, as Depositaries, in Certain Cases, on Public Officers. In Senate of the United States, Sept. 25, 1837. 19 pp. Boston, Benjamin H. Greene, 1837. HistPSO, IllU, WisH.

—— Speech of Mr. Clay, of Kentucky, on the Resolution to Expunge a Part of the Journal for the Session of 1833-1834. Delivered in the Senate of the United States, January, 1837. 14 pp. Washington, Printed by William W. Moore, 1837. NewL.

—— Speech of Mr. Clay, of Kentucky, on the Specie Circular. Delivered in the Senate of the United States, January 11, 1837. 13 pp. Washington, Printed by Duff Green, 1837. HistPSO, WisH.

—— Speech of the Hon. Henry Clay, before the American Colonization Society, in the Hall of the House of Representatives, January 20, 1827. 15 pp. Washington, Printed at the Columbian Office, 1827. LexPL, WRHist.

—— Speech of the Hon. Henry Clay, in the Senate of the United States, on the Subject of Abolition Petitions, February 7, 1839. 42 pp. Boston, James Munroe & Company, 1839. WRHist, WisH.

—— Speech of the Hon. Henry Clay, of Kentucky, Establishing a Deliberate Design, on the Part of the Late and Present Executive of the United States, to Break down the Whole Banking System of the United States, . . . and in Reply to the Speech of the Hon. J. C. Calhoun, of South Carolina, . . . Delivered in the Senate of the United States, February 19, 1838. 32 pp. Washington, Printed by Gales and Seaton, 1838. BurColl, IU, LC, NewL, NYPL, WRHist, WisH.

—— Speech of the Hon. Henry Clay, of Kentucky, in the House of Representatives of the United States, on the 8th Day of January, 1813, on the Bill for Raising an

Additional Military Force of Twenty Thousand Men, for One Year. 17 pp. Baltimore, from the Patriot Press, E. French & Co., Printers, n. d. BurColl.

—— Speech of the Hon. Henry Clay, on the Subject of the Removal of the Deposites; Delivered in the Senate of the United States, December 26, 30, 1833. 31 pp. Washington, Printed by Duff Green, 1834. IU, JCrerar, LC, NewL, NYPL, WRHist, WisH.

—— Speech of the Hon. Henry Clay, on the Sub-treasury Bill, Delivered in the Senate of the United States, January 20, 1840. 23 pp. Boston, George Oscar Bartlett, 1840. BurColl, WisH.

—— Speech of the Hon. Henry Clay, on the Sub-treasury Scheme, Delivered in the Senate of the United States, February 19, 1838. 48 pp. Troy, N. Y., Tuttle, Belcher & Burton, Printers, 1838. NYPL. Copy of title supplied by Miss Winifred Cody.

—— A Supplement to the Address of Henry Clay to the Public, which was Published in December, 1827. Exhibiting Further Evidence in Refutation of the Charges against him, . . . Made by Gen. Andrew Jackson. 22 pp. Washington, Printed by P. Force, 1828. From LC card.

—— To the People of the Congressional District Composed of the Counties of Fayette, Woodford, and Clarke, in Kentucky. 33 pp. N. p. (Washington?), n. d. (1825). ChU, LC, NYPL, WRHist.

Considerations, on Some of the Matters to be Acted on, at the Next Session of the General Assembly of Kentucky. . . . 39 pp. Louisville, Printed by A. G. Hodges and Co., 1824. From copy supplied by William Clark Breckenridge.

The Constitutionalist, Addressed to the People of Kentucky, by a Kentuckian. 34 pp. N. p., n. d. ChU.

Cooke, Eleutheros. Speech of Mr. Cooke, of Ohio, in the Case of Samuel Houston, . . . Delivered in the House of Representatives, on the 8th Day of May, 1832. 19 pp. Washington, Printed by Gales and Seaton, 1832. WRHist.

Corwin, Thomas. Speech of Mr. Corwin, of Ohio, in Reply to General Crary's Attack on General Harrison. Delivered in the House of Representatives February 15, 1840. 16 pp. Washington, Printed by Gales and Seaton, 1840. LC, NewL, WRHist.

—— Speech of Mr. Corwin, of Ohio, on the Bill . . . to Reduce the Revenue of the United States to the Wants of the Government. Delivered in the House of Representatives of the United States, January 12, 1837. 15 pp. Washington, Gales & Seaton, 1837. WRHist, WisH.

—— Speech of Mr. Corwin, of Ohio, on the Subject of the Removal of the Deposites. Delivered in the House of Representatives, April, 1834. 42 pp. Washington, Jacob Gideon, Jr., Printer, 1834. WRHist.

Crane, Joseph H. Speech of Mr Crane, of Ohio, in the Case of Samuel Huston, Tried for a Breach of the Privileges of the House of Representatives of the United States. Delivered May 9th, 1832. 12 pp. Washington, Printed at the Office of Jonathan Elliot, 1832. LaneTS, WRHist.

Daniel, Henry. Circular. Washington City, April 21, 1828. To the People of the First Congressional District in the State of Kentucky. 24 pp. N. p., n. d. LouPL.

—— Speech of Mr. Daniel, of Kentucky, on the Bill Authorizing the President to Use Force against South Carolina. Delivered in the House of Representatives, February 28, 1833. 27 pp. Washington, Printed by D. Green, 1833. From LC card.

—— Substance of a Speech of Mr. Daniel, on the Tariff;

and in Reply to Mr. Burges's Slander of Kentucky; Delivered in the House of Representatives of the U. States, April, 1828. Second Speech. 18 pp. Washington, Printed by Green and Jarvis, 1828. LouPL.

Daveiss, Joseph Hamilton. An Essay on Federalism. 64 pp. N. p., n. d. ChU.

—— The Sketch of a Bill for an Uniform Militia . . . with Reflections on the State of the Nation: . . . 183, 64 pp. (includes *An Essay on Federalism*). Frankfort, Printed by Henry Gore, 1810. Library of Samuel M. Wilson, Lexington, Ky.

—— A View of the President's Conduct, concerning the Conspiracy of 1806. 64 pp. Frankfort, Printed by Joseph M. Street, 1807. ChU, Harvard, HistPSO, NYPL.

Daveiss, Samuel. The Speech of Samuel Daveiss, Esq. Delivered in the Senate of Kentucky, on the 6th Day of February, 1828, . . . 16 pp. N. p., n. d. ChU.

Davis, Amos. Remarks of the Hon. Amos Davis, of Kentucky, on the Contested Election of Moore and Letcher, Delivered in the House of Representatives, May 28, 1834. 16 pp. Washington, 1834. WisH.

Davis, John W. Speech of Mr. Davis of Indiana, on an Appropriation for the Cumberland Road. In the House of Representatives, April 30, 1840. 7 pp. N. p., n. d. WRHist, WisH.

Deming, E. An Oration, Delivered at Oldtown, Ross County, Ohio, on the Fifty-first Anniversary of American Independence. From *The Western Monthly Review*, I, 239 (Aug., 1827).

Doty, James Duane. To the People of Wiskonsin. 4 pp. N. p., n. d. (1840?). BurColl.

Douglas, Richard. Speech of Richard Douglas, Esq., of Chillicothe, Delivered before the Whig Convention, Held in Columbus, February 22d & 23d; A.D. 1836. 15 pp. Columbus, Scott & Wright, Printers, 1836. WRHist.

Drake, Charles D. The Duties of American Citizens. An Address Delivered before the Franklin Society of St. Louis, on the Occasion of its Second Anniversary, January 7th, 1837, . . . 28 pp. St. Louis, Printed by Charles Keemle, 1837. MoStHistS.

Duncan, Alexander. Remarks of Mr. Duncan, of Ohio, on the Resolution Offered by Mr. Haynes. Delivered in the House of Representatives, December 18, 1837. 8 pp. Washington, Printed at the Globe Office, 1837. WRHist, WisH.

—— Speech of Mr. Duncan, of Ohio. In House of Representatives, January 17, 1839— . . . 16 pp. N. p., n. d. WRHist.

—— Speech of Mr. Duncan, of Ohio, on the Bill Making Appropriations for Harbors, and in Reply to Mr. Bond, of Ohio, Delivered in the House of Representatives, . . . July 7, 1838. 20 pp. Washington, Printed at the Globe Office, 1838. LC, WRHist.

—— Speech of Mr. Duncan, of Ohio, on the Bill to Authorize the Issue of Treasury Notes; Delivered in . . . House of Representatives, March 26, 1840. 16 pp. Washington, Printed at the Globe Office, 1840. BurColl, WRHist.

—— Speech of Mr. Duncan, of Ohio, on the Subject of the New Jersey Election . . . Delivered in the House of Representatives, January 9, 1840. 24 pp. Washington, Printed at the Globe Office, 1840. WRHist.

Duncan, James. A Treatise on Slavery; in which is Shewn forth the Evil of Slave Holding, . . . 88 pp. Vevay, Ind., Printed at the 'Indiana Register' Office, 1824. IndStL. 136 pp. Cincinnati, Republished by the Cincinnati Anti-slavery Society, 1840. LaneTS, WRHist.

Dunn, George H. Speech of Mr. Dunn, of Indiana, on the Treasury Note Bill. Delivered in the House of Representatives, May 14, 1838. 15 pp. N. p., n. d. IndStL.

Easton, Rufus. Judge Easton's opinion of the appointment of J. L. Donaldson, by Gov. James Wilkinson, as District Attorney in and for the District of St. Louis, dated October 28th, 1805; and his letter in self defence, dated St. Louis, November 23d, 1805. 4, 14 pp. Titlepage lacking. N. p., n. d. (1805?). From LC card.

Edwards, Ninian. Speech of Mr. Edwards, in the Senate — January 11, 1821. On the Bill for the Relief of the Purchasers of the Public Lands. 20 pp. N. p. (Washington?), n. d. ChHist.

Eells, James H. The American Revolution, Compared with the Present Struggle for the Abolition of Slavery in the United States. An Oration . . . Delivered at Elyria, July 4, 1836. 20 pp. Elyria, O., Lorain County Anti-slavery Society, A. Burrell, Printer, n. d. WRHist.

Ewing, John. A Refutation of Certain Calumnies, Published in John Laws [sic] Hand-bill, Addressed to the Citizens of Knox, Daviess and Martin Counties. 12 pp. Vincennes, 1827. IndStL.

—— To my Fellow-citizens, of Knox, Daviess and Martin Counties. 17 pp. N. p. (Vincennes), n. d. (1829?). IndStL.

Ewing, Thomas. Speech of Mr. Ewing, of Ohio, in Favor of the Protecting System. Delivered in the Senate of the United States, February 17 and 20, 1832. 22 pp. Washington, Printed by Gales and Seaton, 1832. BurColl, ChU, WRHist, WisH.

—— Speech of Mr. Ewing, of Ohio, on Introducing the Bill to Settle and Determine the Northern Boundary

Line of the State of Ohio. Delivered in the Senate of the United States, December 21, 1835. 13 pp. Washington, Printed by Gales and Seaton, 1835. WRHist.

—— Speech of Mr. Ewing, of Ohio, on the Bill Providing for the Distribution of the Proceeds of the Sales of the Public Lands, for a Limited Time. Delivered in the Senate of the United States, June 28, 1832. 14 pp. Washington, Printed by Gales & Seaton, 1832. WRHist.

—— Speech of Mr. Ewing, of Ohio, on the Bill to Appropriate for a Limited Time the Proceeds of the Sales of the Public Lands. Delivered in the Senate of the United States, on the 15th and 16th of March, 1836. 24 pp. Washington, National Intelligencer Office, 1836. WRHist.

—— Speech of Mr. Ewing, of Ohio, on the Land Bill. Delivered in the Senate of the United States, on the 21st and 23d January, 1833. 16 pp. Washington, Printed by Gales and Seaton, 1833. WRHist.

—— Speech of Mr. Ewing, of Ohio, on the Removal of the Deposites; Delivered in the Senate of the United States, January, 1834. 32 pp. Washington, Printed by Gales & Seaton, 1834. WRHist, WisH.

—— Speech of Mr. Ewing, of Ohio, on the Resolution of Mr. Benton, to Expunge a Part of the Senate Journal of 1833-1834. Delivered in the Senate of the United States, January 16, 1837. 7 pp. N. p., n. d. WisH.

—— Speech of Mr. Ewing, of Ohio, on the Subject of the Removal of the Deposites; Delivered in the Senate of the United States, January, 1834. 32 pp. Washington, Printed by Gales and Seaton, 1834. WRHist, WisH.

—— Speech of the Hon. Thomas Ewing, Delivered at a Public Festival, Given him by the Whigs of Ross County, O., June 10, 1837. 18 pp. Chillicothe, S. W. Ely, Printer, n. d. (1837). From LC card.

Facts concisely Stated for the Information of the Legislature of Ohio. 8 pp. Cincinnati, the Faculty of the Medical College of Ohio, Printed by F. S. Benton, 1835. LaneTS.

Farnham, John H.   Oration Delivered at Salem, Indiana. On the Fiftieth Anniversary of American Independence. . . . 18 pp.   New Albany, Ind., Printed by Roberts & Campbell, 1826.   IndStL.

French, Richard.   Speech of Mr. French, of Kentucky, upon the Fortification Bill and the Amendment Proposed by Mr. Cambreleng, . . . House of Representatives, May 12, 1836.   11 pp.   Washington, Blair and Rives, Printers, 1836.   BurColl.

Garrard, Daniel.   An Address to the Young Men of Kentucky, Comprising a Brief Review of the Military Services of General William Henry Harrison, during the Late War between Great Britain and the United States. 29 pp.   Frankfort, Printed by Robinson & Adams, 1840. ChU.

Genin, Thomas H.   Oration, Delivered at the Court House in St. Clairsville, on Washington's Birth Day, . . . 16 pp.   N. p., n. d. (1823?).   WisH.

Giddings, Joshua R.   Speech of Joshua R. Giddings, of Ohio.   In Answer to Mr. Duncan, on the Bill Providing for the Civil and Diplomatic Expenses of Government for the Year 1840.— Delivered in the House of Representatives, April 11, 1840.   16 pp.   N. p., n. d.   WRHist.

Glover, Elias.   An Oration Delivered at the Court-house in Cincinnati, on the Fourth of July, 1806, . . . 24 pp.   Cincinnati, Press of J. W. Browne, n. d. (1806?). From LC card.

Goodenow, John M.   Letter of the Hon. John M. Goodenow, on the Subject of the Northern Boundary of Ohio. 15 pp.   St. Clairsville, O., Printed by J. Y. & J. Glessner, 1835.   WRHist, WisH.

Graves, William Jordan. Concluding Portion of the Speech of Mr. Graves, of Kentucky, on the Treasury Note Bill. Delivered in the House of Representatives, on the 26th March, 1840. 8 pp. N. p., n. d. ChU.

Griswold, Henry A. An Address, Delivered in the Second Presbyterian Church, on the 22nd February, 1830, in Behalf of Transylvania Whig Society. 15 pp. Lexington, Printed at the Office of the Kentucky Gazette, 1830. LexPL.

Hall, James. An Oration, Delivered at Vandalia, July 4, 1830, by James Hall. 15 pp. Vandalia, Ill., Printed by Blackwell & Hall, 1830. Harvard. From copy made by William C. Lane.

Hamer, Thomas Lyon. Speech of Mr. Hamer, of Ohio. 16 pp. N. p., n. d. (1836?). From LC card.

—— Speech of Mr. Hamer, of Ohio. 8 pp. N. p., n. d. (1837?). WRHist.

—— Speech of Mr. Hamer, of Ohio, on the Bill Authorizing Appropriations for a Survey and Exploring Expedition to the South Sea. House of Representatives, May, 1836. 16 pp. Washington, 1836. LC, WisH.

—— Speech of Mr. Hamer, of Ohio, on the Kentucky Contested Election: Delivered in the House of Representatives, May 22, 1834. 21 pp. Washington, Printed by Francis Preston Blair, 1834. WRHist, WisH.

—— Speech of Mr. Hamer, of Ohio, on the Resolution of Mr. Wise, Proposing an Inquiry into the Condition of the Executive Departments. Delivered in the House of Representatives, Jan. 5, 1837. 15 pp. Washington, Printed at the Globe Office, 1837. WRHist, WisH.

Hance, William. An Appeal to the Citizens of Ohio; Showing the Unconstitutionality, Injustice, and Impolicy of the Medical Law, . . . 20 pp. Columbus, Printed by Charles Scott, 1830. From Thomson.

Hannegan, Edward A. Speech of Mr. Hannegan, of Indiana, on the Resolution of Mr. Wise, Proposing an Inquiry into the Condition of the Executive Departments. Delivered in the House of Representatives, Jan. 5, 1837. 6 pp. Washington, Printed at the Globe Office, 1837. WisH.

Hardin, Benjamin. Speech of Ben. Hardin, on the Bill to Reorganize the Court of Appeals. Delivered in the House of Representatives December 23, 1824.— . . . 29 pp. N. p. (Frankfort, J. H. Holeman, Printer), n. d. WisH.

—— Speech of Mr. Hardin, of Kentucky . . . Delivered in the House of Representatives of the United States, February 4, 1820. 27 pp. N. p. (Washington?), n. d. (1820). From LC card.

—— Speech of Mr. Hardin, of Kentucky, on Mr. Adams's Resolutions concerning the Loss of the Fortification Bill of the Last Session: Delivered in the House of Representatives, January 28, 1836. 28 pp. Washington, National Intelligencer Office, 1836. BurColl, WisH.

—— Speech of the Hon. Ben Hardin, on the Subject of the Removal of the Deposites. Delivered in the House of Representatives, April 1 and 3, 1834. 52 pp. Washington, Printed by Gales and Seaton, 1834. BurColl, LC.

Harrison, Micajah. To the Good People of Montgomery Cty. and the Public generally. 34 pp. N. p., n. d. (1824?). ChU.

Harrison, William Henry. Address by General Harrison; Delivered on the Fourth of July, 1833, at Cheviot, Greene Township, Hamilton County, Ohio. Published by the Committee of Arrangements. 22 pp. Cincinnati, Reynolds, Allen & Disney, Printers, 1833. Harvard. From copy made by William C. Lane.

—— An Address, Delivered before the Hamilton County Agricultural Society, at their Annual Exhibition, . . . 1831. 26 pp. Cincinnati, the Hamilton County Agricultural Society, 1831. HistPSO.

—— Address, Delivered by Gen. William H. Harrison, on Friday Evening, January 23, 1824, at the Request of the Euterpeian [sic] Society of Cincinnati, at their Concert Given for the Benefit of the Grecian Fund. 16 pp. N. p. (Cincinnati, Printed by Looker & Reynolds), n. d. (1824). HistPSO, WRHist.

—— Gen. Harrison's Address. . . . at the Circus in the City of Cincinnati, in September Last. . . . 7 pp. N. p., n. d. HistPSO.

—— Gen. Harrison's Speech at Fort Meigs. Reported for the Detroit Advertiser. 8 pp. N. p., n. d. (1840?). HistPSO, WRHist.

—— Gen. Harrison's Speech at the Dayton Convention, September 10, 1840. Published by the Whig Republican Association, Boston. 8 pp. N. p., n. d. BurColl, LC, HistPSO, WRHist.

—— Remarks of General Harrison, Late Envoy Extraordinary and Minister Plenipotentiary of the United States to the Republic of Colombia, on Certain Charges Made against him by that Government. To which is Added, an Unofficial Letter, from General Harrison to General Bolivar, on the Affairs of Colombia; with Notes, Explanatory of his Views of the Present State of that Country. 69 pp. Washington, Printed by Gales & Seaton, 1830. HistPSO, LC, WRHist, WisH.

—— Speech of Mr. Harrison, on the Bill for the Relief of the Surviving Officers of the Revolution. Delivered in the Senate of the United States, January 28, 1828. 12 pp. N. p., n. d. HistPSO.

Hart, Cyrus W. Political Dissertations and Essays, and a

Third and Concluding Epistle to a Departed Spirit;
. . . 24 pp. Newlisbon, O., the Author; William D.
Lepper, Printer, 1819. WRHist.

Hart, William. An Appeal to the People: or, an Exposi-
tion of the Official Conduct of Return Jonathan Meigs,
Governor of the State of Ohio; Relative to the Disband-
ing of a Light Infantry Company in the County of
Washington, . . . 94 pp. N. p., Printed for the
People, 1812. WRHist.

Hastings, John. Speech of Mr. John Hastings, of Ohio, in
Committee of the Whole, on the Independent Treasury
Bill, Delivered in the House of Representatives, Thurs-
day, June 25, 1840. 24 pp. Washington, Printed by
Blair and Rives, 1840. WRHist, WisH.

A History of the Federal and Democratic Parties in the
United States, from their Origin to the Present Time.
. . . By a Citizen of Wayne County, Ind. 56 pp.
Richmond, Ind., Published for the Richmond Democratic
Association, 1837. IndStL.

Howard, Tilghman A. Outline of the Remarks of Mr.
Howard, of Indiana. In the House of Representatives,
February 12, 1840 — On . . . a Bill Appropriating
$150,000 to Each of the States of Ohio, Indiana, and Il-
linois, for the Continuation of the Cumberland Road.
8 pp. N. p., n. d. BurColl.

Jameson, John. Speech of Mr. Jameson of Missouri, on
the General Appropriation Bill. Delivered in Committee of the Whole. In the House of Representatives,
April 21, 1840. 15 pp. Washington, Printed at the
Globe Office, 1840. WRHist, WisH.

Jewett, M. Augustus. An Oration, Delivered before the
Citizens of Vigo County, Indiana, in the Court-house in
Terre-Haute, July 4, 1840. 12 pp. Terre Haute, Print-
ed by J. and T. Dowling, 1840. IndStL.

Johnson, Richard M. Senate of the United States, January 14, 1822. Speech of Col. Richard M. Johnson, of Kentucky, on his Proposition so to Amend the Constitution of the United States as to Give to the Senate Appellate Jurisdiction over the Decisions of the Supreme Court in Cases Involving State Sovereignty. 28 pp. N. p., n. d. TransylvaniaU.

—— Speech of Col. Richard M. Johnson, of Kentucky, on a Proposition to Abolish Imprisonment for Debt, Submitted by him to the Senate of the United States, January 14, 1823. 23, [1] pp. Boston, Printed for the Society for the Relief of the Distressed, by E. G. House, 1823. BurColl, WisH.

Jones, George W. To the People of Wisconsin. 8 pp. N. p. (Washington?), n. d. (1838). WisH.

Jones, Joseph. Letters on the Colonization Society; . . . By M. Carey. . . . To which is Prefixed the Important Information Collected by Joseph Jones, a Coloured Man, lately Sent to Liberia, by the Kentucky Colonization Society, to Ascertain the True State of the Country— . . . 4, 32 pp. Philadelphia, for Sale by Carey & Hart, Sept. 17, 1834. WRHist.

Jones, William T. T. Oration Delivered on the Fourth Day of July, A.D. 1840, at the Episcopal Church in Evansville, Ind. on the Occasion of the Celebration of that Anniversary by the Independent Order of Odd-Fellows. 8 pp. Evansville, Ind., Printed by Order of the Morning Star Lodge, No. 7, 1840. IndStL.

Kane, Elias K. Speech of Mr. Kane, of Illinois, on the Motion of Mr. Poindexter that the Protest of the President of the United States, against the Resolutions of Censure Passed by the Senate, be not Received. In Senate, Thursday, April 24—. 8 pp. N. p., n. d. WisH.

Kendall, Amos. Letters to John Quincy Adams, [?] Relative

to the Fisheries and the Mississippi. First Published in the Argus of Western America. Revised and Enlarged. 102 pp. Lexington, Printed by William Tanner, 1823. LC, Smith.

—— Mr. Kendall's Address to the People of the United States. 7 pp. N. p., n. d. (1840?). LC, WRHist.

—— Organization of the Post Office Department. 7 pp. N. p., 1835. From LC card.

Kinkead, George Blackburn. An Oration Delivered in Behalf of Transylvania Whig Society, on the 22d February, 1831. 8 pp. N. p. (Lexington, Herndon & Savary, Printers), n. d. LexPL.

Leonard, Benjamin G. An Oration, Delivered at Chillicothe on the Fourth Day of July, 1831. 19, [1] pp. Chillicothe, 1831. WRHist.

Letters of Decius, to the Members of the Legislature of the Indiana Territory, to B. Park, Delegate to Congress for Indiana, and to William Henry Harrison, Governor; . . . 44 pp. Louisville, Printed for the Author, December 10th, 1805. From LC card.

Littell, William. An Epistle from William, Surnamed Littell, to the People of the Realm of Kentucky. 40 pp. Frankfort, Printed by William Hunter, 1806. ChU, WisH.

—— Political Transactions in and concerning Kentucky, from the First Settlement thereof, until it Became an Independent State, in June, 1792. 81, 66 pp. Frankfort, William Hunter, 1806. ChU, CinPL, KyStL, NYPL, WisH.

Loomis, Andrew W. Speech of Mr. Loomis, of Ohio, on the Bill to Postpone the Payment to the States of the Fourth Instalment of the Surplus Revenue. Delivered in the House of Representatives, September 21, 1837. 4 pp. N. p., n. d. WRHist.

Lucas, Charles. To the People of Missouri Territory. Charles Lucas' Exposition of a Late Difference between John Scott and himself. 24 pp. (incomplete?). St. Louis, Printed at the Missouri Gazette Office, 1816. MercLStL, MoHist.

Lucas, Robert. Inaugural Address of Robert Lucas, on being Inducted into the Office of Governor of the State of Ohio, Delivered in the Representatives' Hall, December 8th, 1832. 7 pp. Columbus, David Smith, Printer, n. d. BurColl.

Lyon, Chittenden. Circular Letter of Chittenden Lyon, to his Constituents, . . . In the State of Kentucky. 15 pp. Washington, Printed at J. Elliot's Office, 1835. From LC card.

—— Circular. To the People of the Twelfth Congressional District of Kentucky. 16 pp. N. p. (Washington?), n. d. (1828). LouPL.

—— Mr. Lyon's Circular to his Constituents, of the Counties . . . Composing the Twelfth Congressional District of Kentucky. 12 pp. N. p. (Washington?), n. d. (1830). LouPL.

M'Afee, Robert B. American — Extra. Speech of Gen. Robert B. M'Afee, in the Legislature of Kentucky, Shewing his Views of the Policy the State should Pursue, in Making Internal Improvements. January 14th, 1831. 15 pp. Harrodsburg, Ky., Printed at the American Office, 1831. LouPL.

—— To the Citizens of Mercer County. 16 pp. N. p., n. d. (1820?). ChU.

M'Coy, Isaac. Remarks on the Practicability of Indian Reform, Embracing their Colonization. 47 pp. Boston, Printed by Lincoln & Edmands, December, 1827. IndStL.

M'Dougall, George. Petition of George M'Dougall, to Congress. 17 pp. Detroit, Printed by Sheldon & Reed, November, 1824. BurColl.

McLean, John. The Following Letter on the Compensation Bill, was Addressed by Mr. McLean, a Member of Congress, to a Friend. . . . 12 pp. N. p., n. d. (1816?). ChU, WRHist.

Magruder, Allan B. The Political Characters of John Adams and Thomas Jefferson. From *The Lamp*, Lincoln County, Ky., Jan. 12, 1808.

—— Political, Commercial and Moral Reflections, on the Late Cession of Louisiana, to the United States. 150 pp. Lexington, Printed by D. Bradford, 1803. ChU, WisH.

Marshall, Humphrey. An Address to the Independent Electors of Franklin County. By Humphrey Marshall. Relative to the Charges Exhibited against him, by the Select Committee of the House of Representatives, upon the Letter of Thomas Bodley. 15 pp. Frankfort, from the Press of Joseph M. Street (1808?). Title-page clipped at bottom; date probably printed on original. TransylvaniaU.

—— An Address to the People of Kentucky. 48 pp. Philadelphia, Printed by Ormrod & Conrad, 1796. WisH.

—— The Question Examined, &c. . . . 15 pp. N. p., n. d. TransylvaniaU.

Mason, Samson. Charge against General Harrison for Voting to Sell White Men for Debt. Speech of Mr. Mason, of Ohio, on the General Appropriation Bill. Delivered in . . . the House of Representatives, April 24, 1840. 8 pp. N. p., n. d. WRHist.

May, William L. Speech of William L. May, of Illinois, upon the Bill to Grant Pre-emption Rights to Settlers on Public Lands. Delivered in the House of Representatives, June 7, 1838. 13 pp. Washington, Printed at the Madisonian Office, 1838. ChHist.

Memorial of the Citizens and Inhabitants of the Indiana Territory, Praying for the Interposition of Congress, to Relieve them from Certain Oppressions and Embarrassments. 6 pp. Washington, Printed by William Duane & Son, 1804. BurColl.

Merrill, Samuel. To the Public. 24 pp. N. p. (Indianapolis?), n. d. (1827?). IndStL.

Metcalfe, Thomas. Address of General Metcalfe, to the People of Kentucky. 8 pp. N. p. (Louisville, W. W. Worsley, Printer), n. d. (1828?). LouPL.

Michigan — Inhabitants North of Missouri. Memorial of the Inhabitants of the Country North of the State of Missouri on the West Bank of the Mississippi River, Praying that the Protection of the Government of the United States may be Extended to them, either by Attaching them to the Territory of Michigan, or by the Organization of a Separate Territorial Government West of the Mississippi, and North of the State of Missouri. March 25, 1834. . . . 3 pp. N. p. (Washington), Gales & Seaton, Printers, n. d. (1834). (H. R. Doc. 245, 23d Congress, First Session.) GrandRPL.

Miller, John G. The Great Convention. Description of the Convention of the People of Ohio, Held at Columbus, on the 21st and 22d February, 1840. . . . Embracing the Speeches of the Hon. J. C. Wright, Charles Anthony, Esq., and Others. 40 pp. Columbus, Cutler & Wright, n. d. CinPL, HistPSO, WRHist.

The Missouri Delegation to their Constituents. 14 pp. N. p. (Washington), n. d. (1840). MercLStL, WRHist.

Mr. Buchanan's Statement, &c. From the Cincinnati Advertiser, Aug. 29, 1827. General Jackson and Mr. Buchanan. 16 pp. N. p., n. d. ChU.

Moore, Thomas Patrick. Address of Thomas P. Moore, to his Constituents. 28 pp. N. p., n. d. (1828). ChU, LouPL.

—— Speech of Mr. Thomas P. Moore, of Kentucky, on the Kentucky Contested Election. At the Bar of the House of Representatives, May 31, 1834 ——. 16 pp. N. p., n. d. WisH.

—— Speech of Thomas P. Moore, Esq. Delivered in the Court House in Harrodsburg, June 3d, 1827. 36 pp. Harrodsburg, Ky., Printed at the Watchtower Office, 1827. ChU, LouPL.

—— To the Citizens of Lincoln, Jessamine, Mercer, and Washington Counties. 7 pp. N. p. (Washington?), n. d. (1829?). ChU.

—— To the Citizens of the Seventh Congressional District. 14 pp. N. p. (Lexington?), n. d. (1825?). From LC card.

Moorhead, Thomas. A Letter to George W. Jones, Esq. in Reply to his Slanders. 20 pp. Cincinnati, 1838. WRHist.

Morris, Thomas. No. 10. The Anti-slavery Examiner. Speech of Hon. Thomas Morris, of Ohio, in Reply to the Speech of the Hon. Henry Clay. In Senate, February 9, 1839. 40 pp. New York, the American Anti-slavery Society, 1839. LexPL, NYPL, WRHist.

—— Speech of Mr. Morris, of Ohio, on the Bill Imposing Additional Duties as Depositaries in Certain Cases, . . . Delivered in the Senate of the United States, March, 1838. 13 pp. Washington, Printed at the Globe Office, 1838. NYPL. Copy of title supplied by Miss Winifred Cody.

—— Speech of Mr. Morris, of Ohio, on the Bill to Appropriate the Proceeds of the Sale of the Public Lands among the States and to Grant Lands to Certain States. In Senate, April, 1836. 16 pp. Washington, Blair and Rives, Printers, 1836. NYPL, WRHist.

Narrative of the Late Riotous Proceedings against the Liberty of the Press, in Cincinnati. With Remarks and Historical Notices, Relating to Emancipation. . . . 48, [2] pp. Cincinnati, 1836. CinPL, HistPSO, LC, WRHist, WisH.

Nicholas, George. Correspondence between George Nicholas, of Kentucky, and Robert G. Harper, Member of Congress, from the District of 96, South-Carolina. (Lexington, Office of the Kentucky Gazette, 1799.) From *Ky. Gaz.*, Sept. 26, 1799.

—— A Letter from George Nicholas, of Kentucky, to his Friend, in Virginia. Justifying the Conduct of the Citizens of Kentucky, as to Some of the Late Measures of the General Government; and Correcting Certain False Statements, which have been Made in the Different States, of the Views and Actions of the People of Kentucky. 42 pp. Lexington, John Bradford, 1798. LC, NewL, NYPL. 39 pp. Lexington, Printed, Philadelphia, Reprinted by James Carey, 1799. ColU, LC, NewL, TransylvaniaU, WRHist, WisH.

Norvell, John. Speech of Mr. Norvell, of Michigan, on the Bill Imposing Additional Duties as Depositaries in Certain Cases, on Public Officers, &c. Delivered in the Senate of the United States, March 6, 1838. 14 pp. Washington, Printed at the Globe Office, 1838. WisH.

Observations, on a Letter from George Nicholas; of Kentucky; to his Friend in Virginia. [?] In which, Some of the Errors, Mistatements [*sic*], and False Conclusions in that Letter are Corrected, and the Late Measures of the Government, which have been Complained of in Kentucky, are Justified. By an Inhabitant of the North-Western Territory. 46 pp. Cincinnati, Printed and Sold by Edmund Freeman, Feb. 14, 1799. HistPSO.

Olcott, Charles. Two Lectures on the Subjects of Slavery and Abolition. Compiled for the Special Use of Anti-slavery Lecturers and Debaters. . . . 128 pp. Massillon, O., the Author, 1838. LC, WRHist.

Orations on the Anniversary of American Independence, &c. Delivered in the State House in Frankfort on the Fourth Day of July Last, by Four Students. (Frankfort? 1801.) From *Ky. Gaz.*, Aug. 31, 1801.

Owen, Robert Dale. Democratic Address. . . . Address to the People of Indiana. 8 pp. Indianapolis (Printed by Bolton & Livingston), 1838. NYPL.

——Popular Tracts. No. 1. Containing a Tale of Old England by Robert Dale Owen. Pagination irregular (fourteen tracts, separately paged). New York, Office of the Free Enquirer, 1830. IndStL.

Peck, John Mason. The Principles and Tendencies of Democracy; an Address, Made in Belleville, St. Clair County, Illinois, July 4th, 1839. 11 pp. Belleville, Ill., J. R. Cannon, 1839. From *The North American Review*, L, 296 (Jan., 1840).

Petition of Sundry Citizens, Inhabitants of the County of Wayne, in the Territory of the United States North-west of the River Ohio. 2d January, 1801. . . . 7 pp. N. p., n. d. BurColl.

Petition of Sundry Inhabitants of the Territory of Louisiana. March 22, 1806. Referred to the Committee on the Public Lands. 10 pp. Washington, A. and G. Way, Printers, 1806. MoHist.

Pettis, Spencer. Speech of Mr. Pettis, of Missouri, on the Proposition to Distribute the Proceeds of the Public Lands. House of Representatives, January 13, 1830. 10 pp. N. p., n. d. WisH.

A Plain Tale, Supported by Authentic Documents, Justifying the Character of General Wilkinson, . . . By a Kentuckian. 24 pp. New York, 1807. LC, WisH.

Pope, John. Mr. Pope's Speech. 16 pp. N. p. (Lexington?), n. d. (1812?). ChU.

—— Speech of Mr. John Pope, Delivered in the House of Representatives of the Legislature of Kentucky, at the November Session, in the Year 1823, on . . . the Court of Appeals of Kentucky, . . . 29 pp. Louisville, S. Penn, Jr., Printer, 1824. BurColl.

The Presidential Election. Written by a Private Man and a Volunteer, for the Benefit of the People of the United States; but particularly for those of the State of Kentucky. By Philo-Jackson. 35 pp. Frankfort, Printed for the Author, 1823. TransylvaniaU. Second Series. vii, 28 pp. Louisville, Printed for the Author, 1823. ChU, TransylvaniaU. Third Series. 48 pp. Frankfort, Printed for the Author, May, 1824. TransylvaniaU. Fourth Series. vii, 54 pp. Frankfort, Printed for the Author, 1824. TransylvaniaU. Fifth Series. vii, 24 pp. Frankfort, Printed for the Author, 1824. TransylvaniaU, WisH. Sixth Series. 47 pp. Frankfort, Printed for the Author, 1824. TransylvaniaU, WisH. Seventh Series. 47 pp. Frankfort, Printed for the Author, 1824. TransylvaniaU.

Proceedings of the Friends of Mr. Richard, Relative to the Contested Election. 20 pp. N. p. (Detroit?), n. d. (1825?). BurColl.

Rankin, John. Letters on Slavery, Addressed to Mr. Thomas Rankin, Merchant at Middlebrook, Augusta County, Virginia. 214 pp. Ripley, O., D. Ammen, Printer, 1826. ChU, WRHist.

A Refutation of the Charges Made against John Pope, Esq. by a "Citizen of Washington." 16 pp. N. p., n. d. (1824?). ChU.

A Reply to the Statement of John Cleves Symmes, Addressed to a Committee of Congress, January 30th, 1802; and Published in the Western Spy, October 19th, 1803; Respecting the Reserved Township. 67 pp. Cincinnati, Printed by Joseph Carpenter, n. d. HistPSO.

A Report of the Proceedings in Relation to the Contested Election for Delegate to the Nineteenth Congress, from the Territory of Michigan, between Austin E. Wing, Gabriel Richard, and John Biddle; . . . 58, [1] pp. Detroit, Printed by Chipman & Seymour, 1825. BurColl.

The Report of the Select Committee, to whom was Referred the Information Communicated to the House of Representatives, Charging Benjamin Sebastian, one of the Judges of the Court of Appeals of Kentucky, with having Received a Pension from the Spanish Government. 27 pp. Frankfort, from the Press of J. M. Street, 1806. WisH.

Representation and Petition of the Representatives Elected by the Freemen of the Territory of Louisiana. 4th January, 1805. . . . 30 pp. Washington, Printed by William Duane & Son, 1805. MoHist.

The Republican Bank: being an Essay on the Present System of Banking: Showing its Evil Tendency and Developing an entirely New Method of Establishing a Currency, . . . By a Citizen of Indiana. 24 pp. Madison, Ind., Printed by W. H. Webb, Banner Office, 1839. IndStL.

[Resolutions adopted at a meeting of the citizens of the Territory of Michigan, Oct. 16, 1809, after hearing the report of "the Committee Charged to Enquire into the Different Forms of Territorial Governments in the United States."] Broadside. Title improvised. French and English text. N. p. (Detroit), James M. Miller, Printer, n. d. (1809). BurColl.

Reynolds, John. Letter of the Hon. J. Reynolds of Illinois, to his Constituents. 8 pp. Washington, Printed at the Globe Office, 1840. WRHist.

Rice, David. Slavery Inconsistent with Justice and Good Policy; Proved by a Speech Delivered in the Convention, Held at Danville, Kentucky. 24 pp. Philadelphia Printed, 1792; London Reprinted, M. Gurney, 1793. LC.

Ridgely, G. W. An Oration Delivered in the Chapel of Transylvania University, at Lexington, Kentucky, on the Fourth Day of July, 1822. 14 pp. Lexington, Printed by William Gibbes Hunt, 1822. ChU.

Ridgely, Richard H. An Oration Delivered on the 4th of July, 1837, at Lewis's Ferry, . . . 14 pp. Lexington, Intelligencer Print., 1837. Library of Samuel M. Wilson, Lexington, Ky.

The Rights of the Judiciary: in a Series of Letters, Addressed to John Sloan, Esq. late a Member of the House of Representatives of Ohio. 40 pp. N. p., n. d. HistPSO, WRHist.

Robertson, George. Speech of Mr. Robertson, on the Bill to Reorganize the Court of Appeals. Delivered in the House of Representatives of Kentucky, Dec. 23d, 1824. 28 pp. N. p. (Frankfort, Robinson, Printer), n. d. WisH.

—— Speech of the Hon: George Robertson, Delivered in Committee of the Whole in the Legislature of Kentucky . . . 1823, on . . . the Court of Appeals, . . . 59 pp. N. p., n. d. TransylvaniaU.

Rowan, John. Speech of Mr. Rowan, of Kentucky, in the Senate . . . on the Bill for the Abolition of Imprisonment for Debt. 22 pp. N. p., n. d. WisH.

—— Speech of Mr. Rowan, of Kentucky, on Mr. Foot's Resolution, Proposing an Inquiry into the Expediency of Abolishing the Office of Surveyor General of Public

Lands, . . . Delivered in the Senate . . . February 29, 1830. 24 pp. Washington, Printed by Duff Green, 1830. LC.

—— Speech of Mr. Rowan, of Kentucky, on Mr. Foot's Resolution, Relating to the Public Lands, in Reply to Mr. Webster, of Massachusetts. Delivered in the Senate United States, February 4th, 1830. 41 pp. Washington, Printed by Way and Gideon, 1830. LC, WisH.

Ruggles, Benjamin. An Oration, Delivered at the New Meeting House, in Marietta, . . . on the Fourth of July, 1809. 16 pp. Marietta, Printed by Samuel Fairlamb, 1809. BurColl.

St. Clair, Arthur. Letter from Arthur St. Clair, Governor of the North-Western Territory, on the Subject of a Division of the Said Territory; . . . Read the 14th. March 1800. . . . Printed by Order of the House of Representatives of the United States. 8 pp. Philadelphia, Printed by Zachariah Poulson, Junior, 1800. BurColl, WRHist, WisH.

Shannon, George. Speech of George Shannon, Esq. On the Resolution for the Removal of Judge Clark from Office on Account of his Decision in the Bourbon Circuit Court against the Constitutionality of the Endorsement and Replevin Laws. 19 pp. N. p. (Frankfort? Printed by Kendall & Russell), n. d. (1822?). TransylvaniaU.

Shannon, James. Kentucky Gazette — Extra. Letters of Miltiades to the People of Kentucky, on the Subject of the Gubernatorial Election. 35 pp. Lexington, Printed by J. G. Norwood, 1828. ChU.

Shelby, Isaac. Battle of King's Mountain. To the Public. 24 pp. N. p., n. d. (1823?). LC, WisH.

Shelby, James. Kentucky Reporter Extra. Chickasaw Treaty. An Attempt to Obtain the Testimony of James Jackson Esq. to Prove the Connexion of Gen. Andrew

Jackson with a Company of Land Speculators, whileActing as United States' Commissioner; . . . October, 1828. 8 pp. N. p. (Lexington, Kentucky Reporter), n. d. (1828). ChU, LC.

Short, J. C. An Oration, Delivered the 4th July, Instant. From *Liberty Hall*, July 24, 1815.

Smith, Henry Pendleton. Extracts from Letters Written by the Late Henry Pendleton Smith, [to] his Friends and Correspondents. 32 pp. Frankfort, Printed by Kendall and Russells, 1820. ChU (imperfect copy).

Smith, Oliver Hampton. Speech of Mr. Smith, of Indiana, on the Amendment of Mr. Buchanan to the Cumberland Road Bill. Delivered in Committee of the Whole, on the Floor of Congress. Wednesday, January 28, 1829. 22 pp. Washington, P. Force, 1829. From LC card.

—— Speech of Mr. Smith, of Indiana, on the Report and Resolutions Relative to the Non-assumption of State Debts. Delivered in the Senate of the United States, February 12, 1840. 16 pp. N. p., n. d. WRHist.

—— Speech of Mr. Smith, of Indiana, on the Sub-treasury System. Delivered in the Senate of the United States, September 21, 1837. 13 pp. Washington, Printed by Gales and Seaton, 1837. IndStL.

Snyder, Adam Wilson. Speech of Mr. Snyder, of Illinois, on the Bill Granting Pre-emption Rights to Settlers on the Public Lands, Delivered in the House of Representatives, June 14, 1838. 8 pp. Washington, Printed by Blair and Rives, 1838. ChHist.

. . . Southern Boundary of Michigan. Proceedings of a Meeting of the Citizens of Detroit, . . . 6 pp. N. p. (Washington), Blair & Rives, Printers, n. d. (1836). From LC card.

Southgate, William Wright. Speech of Mr. Southgate, of Kentucky, upon the Bill Providing for the Re-issue of

Ten Millions of Treasury Notes; and in Reply to Mr. Rhett, of South Carolina, and Mr. Cambreleng, of New York. Delivered in the House of Representatives, May 12, 1838. 15 pp. Washington, National Intelligencer Office, 1838. ChU.

Speed, John. Fellow Citizens of Jefferson and Oldham Counties. 8 pp. N. p. (Louisville?), n. d. (1827?). LouPL.

Storer, Bellamy. Speech of Mr. Storer, in Defence of Gen. William Henry Harrison. To which is Annexed, a Short Sketch of the Principal Events of his Life. 32 pp. Baltimore, Printed by Sands & Neilson, 1836. LC, WRHist.

—— Speech of Mr. Storer, of Ohio, Delivered in the House of Representatives, April 6, 1836, . . . on the Appropriation Bill for the Naval Service. 23 pp. Washington, Printed by Gales and Seaton, 1836. BurColl, WRHist.

Strictures, upon the Constitutional Powers of the Congress and Courts of the United States, . . . By a Citizen of Ohio. 17 pp. Cincinnati, Morgan, Lodge and Fisher, Printers, 1825. WRHist.

Symmes, John Cleves. [A True Copy] of Judge Symme's [sic] Pamphlet. On the First Settlement of this Country. (Cincinnati, Office of the Centinel of the North-Western Territory, 1796.) First square brackets are in the original. From Cent. N.-W. Ter., Mar. 12 and 26, 1796.

Tappan, Benjamin. Remarks of Mr. Tappan, of Ohio, on Abolition Petitions, Delivered in Senate, February 4, 1840. 4 pp. N. p., n. d. ChU, NYPL.

—— A Review of the Question whether the Common Law of England, respecting Crimes and Punishments, is in Force in the State of Ohio, in a Letter Addressed by a

Citizen, to a Member of the Legislature. 44 pp. Pittsburg, Printed at Butler & Lambdin's Office, 1817. WRHist.

Test, John. Speech of Mr. Test, of Indiana, on the Bill from the Senate for the Removal of the Indians, West of the Mississippi River. Delivered in the House of Representatives of the United States, May 21, 1830. 18 pp. Washington, Printed by Way and Gideon, 1830. From LC card.

Thome, James A. Debate at the Lane Seminary, Cincinnati. Speech of James A. Thome, of Kentucky, Delivered at the Annual Meeting of the American Anti-slavery Society, May 6, 1834. . . . 16, [1] pp. Boston, Garrison & Knapp, 1834. WRHist.

——, and J. Horace Kimball. Emancipation in the West Indies. A Six Months' Tour in Antigua, Barbadoes, and Jamaica, in the Year 1837. 489 pp. New York, the American Anti-slavery Society, 1838. ChU, CinPL, LC, WRHist.

Tipton, John. Speech of the Hon. John Tipton, of Indiana, on the Bill for the Protection of the Aborigines. Delivered in the Senate of the United States, April 18, 1838. 14 pp. Washington, Printed at the Globe Office, 1838. IndStL.

To my Fellow Citizens of Kentucky and the West. 8 pp. N. p., n. d. (1820?). ChU.

Torch Light. An Examination of the Origin, Policy and Principles of the Opposition to the Administration, and an Exposition of the Official Conduct of Thomas H. Benton, one of the Senators from Missouri; . . . 88 pp. St. Louis, Printed at the Missouri Republican Office, 1826. MoHist, WRHist.

Toulmin, Harry. An Oration Delivered at the Celebration of American Independence at Frankfort, (K.) on the 4th

of July, 1804. 8 pp. N. p. (Lexington, Printed by
Thomas Anderson), n. d. (1804). From LC card.

Translation of a Memorial in the French Language, of
Sundry Citizens of the County of Wayne, in the Indiana
Territory. 17th of January, 1805. Referred to the
Committee . . . 15 pp. Washington, William
Duane & Son, 1805. BurColl, HistPSO.

Trimble, David. The Address of David Trimble, . . .
in Relation to the Charges against the President of the
United States, and Mr. Henry Clay. 40 pp. Frankfort,
Printed by J. H. Holeman, 1828. ChU, WisH.

—— Circular. [?] Washington, May 20, 1824. Fellow-
citizens: . . . 27 pp. N. p., n. d. (Top of title-
page mutilated.) ChU.

—— Reply of Mr. Trimble, of Kentucky, to Mr. McDuffie,
of S. Carolina, on the Amendment of the Constitution.
House of Representatives, April 1, 1826. 19 pp. N. p.,
n. d. BurColl, ChU, LC, WRHist.

Triplett, Philip. To the People of Daviess County. 7 pp.
N. p. (Frankfort?), n. d. (1824). WisH.

Trotter, George, Sr., and George Trotter, Jr. To the Public. 33, vi pp. N. p., n. d. (1814?). ChU.

Trotter, J. Pope. A Plain Statement. 28 pp. N. p. (Lexington?), n. d. (1824). ChU.

Underwood, Joseph R. Address Delivered before the Colonization Society of Bowlinggreen, on the 4th July,
1832. 24 pp. N. p., n. d. HistPSO, WRHist.

—— An Address Delivered to the Colonization Society of
Kentucky, at Frankfort, Jan. 15, 1835. 24 pp. Frank-
fort, Printed by Albert G. Hodges, 1835. LaneTS,
LexPL.

Vance, Joseph. Reply of Mr. Vance, of Ohio, to Mr. Mc-
Duffie, of S. Carolina, on the Amendment of the Consti-

tution. House of Representatives, April, 1826. 12 pp.
N. p., n. d. WRHist.

Varnum, James M., Arthur St. Clair, and others. An Oration, Delivered at Marietta, July 4, 1788, by the Hon.
James M. Varnum, Esq. one of the Judges of the Western
Territory; the Speech of His Excellency Arthur St. Clair,
Esquire, upon the Proclamation of the Commission Ap-
pointing him Governor of Said Territory; and the Proceedings of the Inhabitants of the City of Marietta. 14
pp. Newport, R. I., Printed by Peter Edes, 1788. WisH.

A View of the Administration of the Federal Government.
Containing an Address Delivered at a Public Meeting of
the Citizens of Mason and the Adjacent Counties. — By
a Citizen of Kentucky. (Frankfort, Hunter & Beaumont, 1798.) From *The Palladium*, Sept. 18, 1798.

Wallace, Cadwallader. To the Hon, [*sic*] Lyttleton W.
Tazewell of the Senate, . . . Hon. John Randolph of
the House of Representatives . . . of the United
States. 14 pp. N. p. (Chillicothe?), n. d. (1827?).
WRHist.

Wallace, David. H. R. Governor Wallaces, [*sic*] Inaugural
Address. December 6, 1837. 7 pp. N. p. (Indianapolis?), n. d. IndStL.

White, John. Speech of Mr. White, of Kentucky, Delivered in the House of Representatives, on Friday, June
5, 1840, . . . in Opposition to the Sub-treasury Bill.
48 pp. N. p., n. d. BurColl, ChU, LC, WRHist.

Whittlesey, Elisha. An Address, Delivered before the Tall-
madge Colonization Society, on the Fourth of July, 1833;
by Hon. Elisha Whittlesey . . . 27 pp. Ravenna, O.,
Printed at the Office of the Ohio Star, 1833. From LC
card. Also in WRHist.

Wickliffe, Charles A. Mr. Wickliffe's Letter Relative to

the Expenditures of the Government, Addressed to the Editors of the National Intelligencer, . . . 8 pp. N. p., n. d. (1830?). ChU.

—— Speech of C. A. Wickliffe, Esq. upon the Memorial of the Legislature of Kentucky; Delivered in the House of Representatives of the United States, May 3, 1824. 12 pp. Smith.

—— Speech of Mr. Wickliffe in the House of Representatives, on the 30th of January, 1828, . . . 20 pp. Washington, Printed by F. S. Myer, 1828. LouPL.

—— Speech of Mr. Wickliffe, of Ky. Delivered in the House of Representatives, on the Mission to Panama. April 5, 1826. 32 pp. N. p., n. d. WisH.

—— Speech of the Hon. C. A. Wickliffe, Delivered at the Court House in Louisville, on the 14th October, 1826. 16 pp. N. p. (Louisville), Printed by S. Penn, Jr., n. d. LouPL.

—— To the Citizens of Jefferson, Oldham, Nelson & Bullitt Counties. 8 pp. N. p., n. d. (1827). Smith.

—— To the Citizens of Jefferson, Oldham, Nelson & Bullitt Counties. 4 pp. N. p., n. d. (1827). Smith.

—— To the Citizens of the Ninth Congressional District. 11 pp. N. p., n. d. LouPL.

Wickliffe, Robert. Address of Robert Wickliffe, Esq. to his Constituents. 16 pp. N. p. (Lexington?), n. d. (1827?). ChU.

—— An Address to the People of Kentucky, on the Subject of the Charleston & Ohio Rail-road. 40 pp. Lexington, N. L. Finnell, Printer, 1838. From LC card.

—— Important to the People of Washington County. 8 pp. N. p., n.d. (1816?). Smith.

—— Letter from Robert Wickliffe, to his Constituents. Frankfort, Jan. 12, 1825. 19 pp. N. p., n. d. (1825?). ChU.

—— A Letter from Robert Wickliffe. To his Constituents, Occasioned by the Attack upon him, first Published in the Washington City Gazette, under the Signature of "Kentucky," . . . 31 pp. N. p. (Frankfort?), n. d. (1825?). Smith.

—— The Shakers. Speech of Robert Wickliffe. In the Senate of Kentucky — Jan. 1831. . . . 32 pp. N. p. (Frankfort, A. G. Hodges, Printer), n. d. (1832). WRHist, WisH.

—— Speech of Robert Wickliffe, Delivered in the Court House, in Lexington, on Monday, the 10th Day of August, 1840, upon Resigning his Seat as Senator from the County of Fayette, more especially in Reference to the "Negro Law." 36 pp. Lexington, Observer & Reporter Print., 1840. ChU.

—— Speech of Robert Wickliffe, in Reply to the Rev. R. J. Breckenridge, Delivered in the Court House, in Lexington, on Monday, the 9th November, 1840. 55 pp. Lexington, Observer & Reporter Print., 1840. ChU.

—— Speech of Robert Wickliffe, in the Senate of Kentucky, on a Bill to Repeal . . . "An Act to Regulate Civil Proceedings against Certain Communities Having Property in Common." 16 pp. N. p. (Lebanon, O., Star Office), n. d. (1831). WRHist.

—— Speech of Robert Wickliffe in the Senate of Kentucky, upon the Preamble and Resolutions in Relation to the Tariff and Internal Improvements; and in Response to Certain Resolutions from South Carolina. 59 pp. Frankfort, Printed by J. H. Holeman, 1830. LC, ChU.

—— Wickliffe's Speech, against the Bill to Repeal the Law Organizing a Court of Appeals, and to Re-organize a Court of Appeals. 52 pp. N. p., n. d. WisH.

Wickliffe, Robert, Jr. An Oration Delivered before the Transylvania Whig Society, February 22d, 1835. 28 pp.

Lexington, N. L. Finnell, Printer, 1835.   From LC card.

Wilmot, Robert.   A New Work, in Favor of the Whig Cause, and the Election of General Harrison to the Presidential Chair. . . . 36, [2] pp.   Cincinnati, 1840. IndStL, LC, WRHist.

Woodbridge, William.   A Letter to the Hon. Abraham Edwards, President of the Legislative Council of the Territory of Michigan.   16 pp.   N. p. (Detroit?), n. d. (1827?).   WRHist.

Woodward, Augustus Brevoort.   The Presidency of the United States.   88 pp.   New York, D. Van Veghten, 1825.   From LC card.

Worthington, Thomas.   Communication of those Citizens of the North-Western Territory, Opposed to an Alteration of the Boundaries of the States as Established by Congress, . . . 16 pp.   Chillicothe, Printed by N. Willis, 1802.   From Thomson.

Wright, John C.   Speech of Mr. John C. Wright, on the Subject of Retrenchment.   Delivered in the House of Reps., Feb. 6, 1828.   44 pp.   Washington, Printed by Gales & Seaton, 1828.   BurColl.

Wright, Joseph Albert.   Speeches of Mr. Wright, of Ohio, on the Resolution Calling on the Secretary of State for Information Relative to the Selection of Newspapers for the Publication of the Laws.   36 pp.   Washington, 1827. BurColl,WRHist, WisH.

Wylie, Andrew.   An Eulogy on Lafayette, Delivered in Bloomington, Indiana, on the Ninth of May, 1835, at the Request of the Citizens and Students.   32 pp.   Cincinnati, Taylor and Tracy, 1835.   LC, WisH.

Yancey, Joel.   Circular.   To the Citizens of the Tenth Congressional District of Kentucky.   Washington City, May 22, 1828.   15, [1] pp.   N. p. (Washington?), n. d. LouPL.

II. Religious Polemics and Sermons

An Account of an Extraordinary Revival of Religion in Kentucky. Extract of a Letter from Lexington, Kentucky, Dated August 16, 1801. 7 pp. N. p. ("To be sold at no. 189, Pearl-street, New-York."), n. d. ChU.

Allen, Ethan. Christ and the Church. A Sermon Preached during the Meeting of the Miami Clerical Association, at St. James Church, Piqua, Ohio. 19, [1] pp. Dayton, O., R. N. & W. F. Comly, Printers, 1834. WRHist.

Allen, William. Brief Remarks upon the Carnal and Spiritual State of Man, . . . 23 pp. Mountpleasant, O., 1831. WRHist.

Aydelott, Benjamin P. Rev. B. P. Aydelott, in Answer to the Rt. Rev. P. Chase. 45, viii pp. Cincinnati, Printed by Lodge & L'Hommedieu, n. d. (1832). From Thomson.

Badin, Stephen Theodore. The Real Principles of Roman Catholics, in Reference to God and the Country. A New Edition, carefully Revised . . . By a French Clergyman. . . . 95, [1] pp. Bardstown, Ky., Printed by F. Peniston, 1805. LexPL. For attribution to Badin, see above, Chapter IV, footnote 37.

Bailey, John. Fanaticism Exposed: or the Scheme of Shakerism Compared with Scripture, Reason and Religion, and Found to be Contrary to them All. By the Rev. John Bailey, of Kentucky. From *Ky. Gaz.*, Dec. 3, 1811.

Baker, Bartholomew. A Looking-glass, for every one to See their Face in: or, a Treatise, on the Revelations of St. John. 93 pp. Chillicothe, Printed for the Author, 1818. WRHist.

Bates, Elisha. An Address to the Members of the Society

of Friends. 15, [1] pp. London, Whittaker & Co., etc., 1836. ColU, NewL.

—— An Appeal to the Society of Friends. vi, 28 pp. London, Hamilton, Adams, & Co., etc., 1836. NewL.

—— Correspondence between Elisha Bates and Others, on the Subject of his having been Baptized. iv, 12 pp. London, Hamilton, Adams, & Co., etc., 1836. NewL.

—— The Doctrines of Friends: or Principles of the Christian Religion, as Held by the Society of Friends, commonly Called Quakers. 8, 320 pp. Mountpleasant, O., the Author, 1825. ChU, LC, NYPL, WRHist.

—— A Document of the Meeting for Sufferings of Ohio Yearly Meeting, with a Refutation of the Same, by Elisha Bates, together with his Resignation of his Right of Membership in the Society of Friends. . . . 55, [1] pp. London, Hamilton, Adams, & Co., etc., 1837. NewL.

—— An Examination of Certain Proceedings and Principles of the Society of Friends, Called Quakers. 309, [2] pp. St. Clairsville, O., Printed for the Author by Horton J. Howard, 1837. LexPL, NYPL, WRHist.

—— Extracts from the Writings of the Early Members of the Society of Friends, . . . Together with Some Additional Observations . . . 56 pp. Mountpleasant, O., the Author, 1825. WRHist.

—— The Incorporation of Ohio Yearly Meeting, for the Purpose of Establishing a Boarding School, Defended: . . . 23 pp. Mountpleasant, O., 1833. WRHist.

—— Letter of Resignation of the Right of Membership in the Society of Friends. Addressed to Short Creek Monthly Meeting. 8 pp. London, Hamilton, Adams, & Co., etc., 1837. NewL.

—— Reasons for Receiving the Ordinance of Christian Baptism; to which are Added Some Observations on the Lord's Supper; in a Letter Addressed to the Society of

Friends. 2d ed. 20 pp. London, Whittaker & Co., etc., 1836. NewL. 23 pp. St. Clairsville, O., Printed by Horton J. Howard, from the First London Edition, 1837. LexPL.

—— Sermons, Preached by Mr. Elisha Bates . . . iv, 104 pp. London, Hamilton, Adams & Co., 1836. From LC card.

Baxter, George A. Sermon Preached before the Presbytery of Lexington . . . April 30, 1825. 32 pp. Lexington, 1825. From Smith catalogue.

Beauchamp, William. Essays on the Truth of the Christian Religion: . . . 223, iii pp. Marietta, Printed for the Author, by Joseph Israel, 1811. WRHist.

Beecher, Catharine. Letters on the Difficulties of Religion. 350 pp. Hartford, Conn., Belknap & Hammersley, 1836. LaneTS.

Beecher, Lyman. Lectures on Scepticism, Delivered in Park Street Church, Boston, and in the Second Presbyterian Church, Cincinnati. 160, [6] pp. Cincinnati, Corey and Fairbank, 1835. ChU, NYPL, TransylvaniaU, WRHist.

—— Views in Theology. . . . Published by Request of the Synod of Cincinnati. 240, [4] pp. Cincinnati, Truman and Smith, etc., 1836. LaneTS, NYPL, WRHist, WisH.

The Belief of the Rational Brethren of the West, . . . Cincinnati, 1819. From Richard McNemar? *The Other Side of the Question*, 1819, p. 160.

Birch, Thomas Ledlie. Seemingly Experimental Religion, Instructors Unexperienced — Converters Unconverted — Revivals Killing Religion — Missionaries in Need of Teaching — or, War against the Gospel by its Friends. Being the Examination and Rejection of Thomas Ledlie Birch, a Foreign Ordained Minister, by the Rev. Presbytery of Ohio, . . . 144 pp. Washington, Printed for the Author, 1806. HistPSO, WRHist.

Bishop, Robert Hamilton. Another Voice from the Tomb; being a Funeral Sermon, Occasioned by the Death of Joseph Cabell Breckinridge, Esq. . . . Delivered . . . February 8th, 1824. 28 pp. Lexington, Printed by Thomas T. Skillman, 1824. LaneTS.

—— An Apology for Calvinism. 40 pp. Lexington, Printed by Daniel Bradford, 1804. CinPL.

—— A Discourse Occasioned by the Death of Rev'd. James M'Chord; Delivered in Market-street Church, Lexington, Ky. Sabbath, 13th August, 1820. To which is Added the Address Delivered at his Interment. 20 pp. Lexington, Printed by Thomas T. Skillman, 1821. ChU, LouPL, NYPL, TransylvaniaU, WRHist.

—— The God of Israel the Protector of the Fatherless and the Widow. A Sermon Occasioned by the Death of James R. Hughs, M.D., of Oxford, Ohio; . . . 12 pp. Oxford, O., Printed by W. W. Bishop, 1839.

—— A Letter Addressed to Rev. J. L. Wilson, D. D. 14 pp. N. p., n. d. (1835). LaneTS.

—— An Outline of the Political Economy of the Bible. A Sermon, Delivered in the First Presbyterian Church of Oxford, on the Annual Thanksgiving Day of the State of Ohio, December 14th, 1837, . . . 16 pp. Oxford, O., Printed by R. H. Bishop, Jun., 1838. ChU, LaneTS, WRHist.

—— A Plea for United Christian Action, Addressed particularly to Presbyterians. A Sermon . . . Cincinnati, April 23, 1833. 2d ed. 19 pp. Cincinnati, Corey & Fairbank, 1833. LaneTS, WRHist.

—— Sermons on Plain and Practical Subjects. viii, 276 pp. Lexington, Printed by D. and C. Bradford, at the

Office of the Kentucky Gazette, 1809. LexPL, Transylvaniau, WRHist.

—— A Tribe Lacking in Israel, a Sermon . . . Oxford, 1838. From Smith Catalogue.

—— A Tribute of Respect to Departed Friends, and a Word of Encouragement to their Sons. . . . 17 pp. Oxford, O., R. H. Bishop, Jun., 1837. ChU, WRHist.

Blanchard, Amos. Original Sin and the Atonement. A Trial Sermon, Preached before the Cincinnati Presbytery, July 20, 1831. 23 pp. Cincinnati, Printed by Robinson and Fairbank, 1831. WRHist.

Blythe, James. A Discourse on the Present State and Duty of the Church; Delivered at the Opening of the Synod of Kentucky, Oct: 1824. 32 pp. Lexington, Printed by Thomas T. Skillman, 1824. LaneTS.

—— A Portrait of the Times; being a Sermon, Delivered at the Opening of the Synod of Kentucky, which Met at Lexington, Sept. 7th, 1814. 47 pp. Lexington, Printed by Thomas T. Skillman, 1814. WisH.

—— A Summary of Gospel Doctrine and Christian Duty, being a Sermon Delivered to the Church and Congregation of Pisgah, on the Resignation of the Pastoral Charge, after a Connection of Forty Years. 16 pp. Lexington, Printed by Thomas T. Skillman, 1832. IU.

Bond, Thomas E. An Appeal to the Methodists, in Opposition to the Changes Proposed in their Church Government. 52 pp. Cincinnati, Printed by Morgan, Fisher, and L'Hommedieu, 1827. LexPL.

Brisbane, William Henry. A Letter from William Henry Brisbane to the Baptist Denomination in South Carolina. 29, 8 pp. Cincinnati, Samuel A. Alley, Printer, 1840. IU.

Britton, James B. The Practice of Duelling in View of

Human and Divine Law. A Sermon Preached before the Congregation of Christ Church, in Indianapolis, on Lord's Day, March 25, 1838, . . . 9 pp. Indianapolis, Printed by Livingston and Comingore, 1838. IndStL.

Brooke, John T. The Doctrine of a Special Providence: briefly Tested by Scripture and Reason. A Discourse, . . . 15 pp. Cincinnati, A Pugh, Printer, 1840. ChU.

Brown, Samuel. A Countercheck to Shakerism. 76 pp. Cincinnati, Looker & Reynolds, Printers, 1824. HistPSO, WRHist.

Brownlee, George, and John Murphy. A Defence of the Late Lexington Society of Methodists, against the Charges of the Rev. William Burke. (Lexington ? 1802.) From *Ky. Gaz.*, July 16 and 23, 1802.

Burke, William. The Methodist Episcopal Church, their Doctrines and Discipline, together with the Characters of Certain Individuals, Vindicated from the Unjust Representations of Joshua L. Wilson. 94 pp. Cincinnati, Printed for E. Hall & O. M. Spencer, by John W. Browne & Co., 1812. HistPSO, WRHist.

Bush, George. Ezekiel's Vision. An Attempted Explication . . . 70 pp. Cincinnati, Printed by M'Calla and Davis, 1829. LaneTS.

—— "Lack of Vision the Ruin of the People." A Sermon Preached at Indianapolis, Indiana. Dec. 25th, 1825. 24 pp. Indianapolis, Printed at the Gazette Office, 1826. From copy supplied by William Clark Breckenridge.

Caldwell, Charles. Correspondence between Dr. Charles Caldwell, of the Medical School of Transylvania University, and Dr. James Fishback, Pastor of the First Baptist Church of Lexington. 40 pp. Lexington, Printed by Thomas T. Skillman, 1826. ChU; Library of Samuel M. Wilson, Lexington, Ky.

—— Thoughts on the True Connexion of Phrenology and Religion, in a Letter to the Editor of the American Phrenological Journal and Miscellany, in Philadelphia. 24 pp. Louisville, J. Maxwell, Jr., 1839. ChU.

Cameron, Archibald. The Monitor, . . . (Lexington? Office of the Kentucky Gazette? 1806.) From *Ky. Gaz.*, Sept. 18, 1806.

Campbell, John P. The Pelagian Detected; or, a Review of Mr. Craighead's Letters, Addressed to the Public and the Author. 80 pp. Lexington, Printed for the Author, by Thomas T. Skillman, 1811. ChU.

—— A Portrait of the Times; or, the Church's Duty. In a Discourse, Delivered at the Opening of the Synod of Kentucky, . . . Lexington, October 14, 1812. 40 pp. Lexington, Printed by Thomas T. Skillman, n. d. HistPSO.

—— Remarks on a Letter of Mr. David Jones Addressed to the Author on Occasion of his Sermon on Christian Baptism. . . . 152 pp. Philadelphia, Printed by Dennis Heartt, 1812. TransylvaniaU.

—— A Sermon, Preached in Stoner-mouth Meeting House, October 28, 1810. . . . in which Christian Baptism, . . . is largely Treated, . . . 132 pp. Lexington, Printed by Thomas Smith, for the Author, 1811. ChU, HistPSO.

—— Several Letters, Addressed to the Rev. T. B. Craighead, in Answer to a Pamphlet Published by him, Containing a Sermon on Regeneration, an Address to the Synod of Kentucky, and an Appendix. 193, [1] pp. Lexington, Printed by Thomas Smith, for the Author, 1810. ChU, TransylvaniaU.

—— Strictures on Two Letters Published by Barton W. Stone, Entitled Atonement, . . . (Lexington? Office of the Kentucky Gazette? 1805.) From *Ky. Gaz.*, July 23, 1805.

—— Vindex: or the Doctrines of the Strictures Vindicated, against the Reply of Mr. Stone. 154 pp. Lexington, Printed by Daniel Bradford, 1806. NYPL.

Carpenter, Benjamin Owen. Adventures of a Copy of
Swedenborg's Treatise, concerning Heaven & Hell, ''by
itself.'' . . . Arranged for the Press by Benjamin
Owen Carpenter. 41, [1] pp. Chillicothe, for the
Author, 1839. WRHist.

Carpenter, Samuel. The Reply of Samuel Carpenter to
Doctor James Wilson, Editor of the Baptist Banner. 16
pp. N. p. (Bardstown, Ky., D. D. Jones, Printer), n. d.
(1835?). WisH.

Chandler, Elizabeth Margaret. Essays, Philanthropic and
Moral, . . . principally Relating to the Abolition of
Slavery in America. . . . 120 pp. Philadelphia,
Lemuel Howell, 1836. ChU, NYPL, WRHist.

Chapman, George T. A Discourse on Religious Liberty,
Delivered in the Unitarian Church, in Louisville, July
4th, 1832. 19 pp. Louisville, Printed at J. G. Dana's
Office, 1832. ChU, WisH.

—— Sermons, upon the Ministry, Worship, and Doctrines
of the Protestant Episcopal Church, and Other Subjects.
viii, 399 pp. Lexington, Printed by Smith and Palmer,
1828. ChU, CinPL, LexPL, LC.

Chase, Philander. Advice from the Grave of Amelia:
Addressed to the Youth of Cincinnati, . . . Being a
Sermon, Preached in the Protestant Episcopal Church,
March 16th, 1823. 23 pp. Cincinnati, Looker & Reyn-
olds, Printers, n. d. WRHist.

—— Bishop Chase's Defence against the Slanders of the
Rev. G. M. West. 72 pp. N. p., n. d. (1831?). WRHist,
WisH.

—— Bishop Chase's Pastoral Letter to his Diocese of Illinois: Read in Springfield, Sangamon County, . . .

May 14, A.D. 1837.   25 pp.   Peoria, Ill., Printed at the Register Office, 1837.   WRHist.

—— A Correspondence between Bishops Chase and M'Ilvaine.   32 pp.   Detroit, Printed by Geo. L. Whitney, 1834.   NYPL, WRHist.

—— A Letter from Bishop Chase, on the Subject of his Going to England, for the Relief of the Protestant Episcopal Church in the State of Ohio.   Addressed to the Right Reverend Bishop White.   40 pp.   New York, Printed by J. Seymour, 1823.   BurColl.

—— A Sermon on the Christian Ministry, Preached in Christ Church, Cincinnati, Ohio, June 29, A. D. 1823, at the Ordination of Mr. James A. Fox to the Holy Order of Deacons.   20 pp.   N. p. (Cincinnati), Looker & Reynolds, Printers, n. d.   WRHist.

—— Supplement to "The Western Herald and Steubenville Gazette."   Bishop Chase's Defence of himself, against the Late Conspiracy at Gambier, Ohio.   In a Series of Letters to his Friends.   60 pp.   N. p. (Steubenville), n. d. (1832 ?).   WRHist.

Chase, Samuel.   Remarks upon Recent Publications against the Rt. Rev. Philander Chase, D. D.   28 pp.   Steubenville, Printed by James Wilson, 1832.   WRHist.

Clark, Christopher.   A Shock to Shakerism; or, a Serious Refutation of the Idolatrous Divinity of Anne Lee, of Manchester, (England.)   106 pp.   (incomplete).   Russellville, Ky., Printed for Robert Paisley, 1816.   WRHist.

Claybaugh, Joseph.   The Genius of the Gospel, the Genius of Universal Freedom;   . . .   A Discourse Delivered on Sabbath, the Fourth of July, 1830, in the Associate Reformed Church, Chillicothe: . . .   16, iv pp. Chillicothe, Printed by Robert Kercheval, 1830.   WisH.

Cleland, Thomas.   The Destructive Influence of Sinners; a Sermon, Delivered in Harrodsburgh [sic], Ky. June

8th, 1823. 30 pp. Lexington, Printed by Thomas T. Skillman, 1823. LaneTS.

——Letters to Barton W. Stone, Containing a Vindication principally of the Doctrines of the Trinity, the Divinity and Atonement of the Saviour, against his Recent Attack, in a Second Edition of his "Address." 172 pp. Lexington, Printed for the Author, by Thomas T. Skillman, 1822. KyStL, LaneTS.

—— The Socini-Arian Detected: a Series of Letters to Barton W. Stone, on Some Important Subjects . . . Referred to in his "Address" to the Christian Churches in Kentucky, Tennessee, and Ohio. 101 pp. Lexington, Printed by Thomas T. Skillman, 1815. CinPL, WRHist, WisH.

—— Unitarianism Unmasked; . . . in a Reply to Mr. Barton W. Stone's Letters to the Rev. Dr. Blythe. 184 pp. Lexington, Printed by T. T. Skillman, 1825. From LC card. (For list of publications — sermons and controversial works — not given here, see *Memoirs of the Rev. Thomas Cleland*, ed. Edward P. Humphrey and Thomas H. Cleland, 1859, pp. 131-132.)

Cook, Valentine. A Treatise on the Subject of Baptism, principally Dedicated to the Clergy of the Methodist & Presbyterian Churches; . . . 74, [1] pp. Russellville, Ky., Printed by Charles Rhea, 1821. WisH.

Cooke, John Esten. Answer to the Review of An Essay on the Invalidity of Presbyterian Ordination . . . 136, [1] pp. Lexington, Printed at the Reporter Office, 1830. ChU.

—— An Essay on the Invalidity of Presbyterian Ordination. 216, xxiv pp. Lexington, Printed at the Reporter Office, 1829. ChU, TransylvaniaU.

Corrill, John. A Brief History of the Church of Christ

of Latter Day Saints, . . . with the Reasons of the Author for Leaving the Church. 50 pp. St. Louis, Printed for the Author, 1839. WisH.

Craig, James. The Reign of the Messiah, or the Grace of God Exemplified . . . 24 pp. Lexington, Printed by T. T. Skillman, 1816. From LC card.

Craighead, T. B. A Sermon on Regeneration, with an Apology and an Address to the Synod of Kentucky: . . . 93 pp. Lexington, Printed by William W. Worsley, for the Author, 1809. ChU.

Crothers, Samuel, James Dickey, and William Graham. An Address to the Churches on the Subject of Slavery. 24 pp. Georgetown, O., D. Ammen & Co., Printers, August 5, 1831. WRHist, WisH.

—— The Gospel of the Jubilee. . . . 84 pp. Hamilton, O., Printed by I. M. Walters, 1837. WRHist, WisH.

—— The Gospel of the Typical Servitude: the Substance of a Sermon Preached in Greenfield, Jan. 1, 1834. 22 pp. Hamilton, O., Printed at the Office of the Intelligencer, by Gardner & Gibbon, 1835. LaneTS, LC, WRHist, WisH.

—— Strictures on African Slavery. 46 pp. Rossville, O., the Abolition Society of Paint Valley, Printed by Taylor Webster, 1833. LaneTS, LC, WRHist, WisH.

—— The Use of Strong Drink, Contrary to the Scriptures, &c. The Substance of a Sermon Delivered in Greenfield, January 22, 1829. 27 pp. Chillicothe, Printed by Robert Kercheval, 1829. LaneTS, WRHist.

Crowe, John Finley? Conversations on Infant Baptism, Proving Infant Membership in the Gospel Church. In a Dialogue . . . Mainly Abridged from a Work of Charles Jerram, A.M. of England. . . . By a Member of the Salem Presbytery, Indiana. To which is

Added, by Another Hand, a Conversation on the Mode of Baptism. 52 pp. N. p. (Lexington), Printed for the Salem Presbytery, by T. T. Skillman, 1825. IndStL.

Cushman, Ralph. An Appeal to the Christian Public, against the Allegations Contained in a Pamphlet Written by J. L. Wilson, Entitled "Four Propositions Sustained against the Claims of the American Home Missionary Society." 20 pp. Cincinnati, Robinson & Fairbank, Printers, 1831. WRHist.

Davidge, Henry. Reflections, Moral and Theological. . . . Part II. 147 pp. Frankfort, Gerard & Kendall, Printers, 1816. TransylvaniaU.

Davidson, Robert. The Bible, the Young Man's Guide; a Discourse . . . Delivered in the McChord Church, Lexington, Nov. 24, 1833, . . . 10, [1] pp. Lexington, Printed by J. Clarke & Co., 1833. LaneTS.

Dickey, James H. A Review of a Summary of Biblical Antiquities, Compiled . . . by John W. Nevin, . . . 36 pp. Ripley, O., the Abolition Society of Paint Valley, Printed by Campbell & Palmer, 1834. LaneTS.

Dillard, Ryland T. Funeral Oration on the Death of President Giddings; Delivered . . . in Georgetown, on the Fifth Day of January, 1840. 16 pp. Louisville, Printed at the Office of the Baptist Banner, 1840. LexPL.

Drown, William. An Appeal in Favor of Sunday Schools; with Directions for their Management, &c. Principally Compiled . . . 65, [1] pp. Cincinnati, Printed at Harrison's Press, 1822. LaneTS.

Duffield, George. A Sermon on American Slavery: . . . 32 pp. Detroit, J. S. and S. A. Bagg, 1840. BurColl, NewL.

—— A Thanksgiving Sermon. The Religious Character

of a People the True Element of their Prosperity. . . . 20 pp. Detroit, Dawson & Bates, Printers, 1839. BurColl, NewL.

Duncan, James. Polemic Disquisitions on Four General Subjects: viz. I. On the Unity of the Church . . . II. . . . Church Government. III. . . . Covenanting, . . . IV. . . . Creeds . . . 215 pp. Indianapolis, Printed by John Douglass, 1828. IndStL.

Dunlavy, John. The Manifesto, or a Declaration of the Doctrines and Practice of the Church of Christ. [vi], 520 pp. Pleasant Hill, Ky., P. Bertrand, Printer, 1818. TransylvaniaU, WRHist.

—— Plain Evidences, by which the Nature and Character of the True Church of Christ may be Known and Distinguished from All Others. Taken from a Work Entitled "The Manifesto, or a Declaration of the Doctrines and Practice of the Church of Christ;" Published at Pleasant Hill, Kentucky, 1818. 120 pp. Albany, N. Y., Printed by Hoffman and White, 1834. WRHist, WisH.

Eastin, Augustine. Letters on the Divine Unity. Addressed to Mr. David Barrow, in Answer to his Letter to a Friend. 75 pp. Lexington, Printed by D. Bradford, 1804. CinPL.

Eastman, Samuel. Four Discourses, Delivered at Bloomfield, Ky. on Four of the most Important Subjects in the Bible. 140 pp. N. p., J. H. Darlington, Printer, 1824. ChU.

Edgerton, Joseph. An Address to Friends of Ohio Yearly Meeting, . . . 10 pp. Mountpleasant, O., Printed by E. Harris, 1834. WRHist.

Eliot, William Greenleaf, Jr. Discourse, Preached at the Dedication of the First Congregational Church; St. Louis, Mo. October 29th, 1837, . . . 14, [1] pp. N. p.

(St. Louis), Printed by Chambers, Harris & Knapp, 1837. BurColl.

Emmons, Francis W. The Voice of one Crying in the Wilderness: being an Essay to Extend the Reformation, . . . 252 pp. Noblesville, Ind., L. H. Emmons, Printer, 1837. ChU, IndStL, TransylvaniaU.

Espy, Josiah M. The Contrast; or, Certain Doctrines of the Protestant Churches, Compared with the Doctrines of the New Jerusalem Church. . . . 268, [6] pp. Columbus, the Society of the New Church, 1835. CinPL.

Este, David K. Anniversary Address of the Cincinnati Miami Bible Society. Cincinnati, Looker & Reynolds. From *The Western Monthly Review*, III, 102 (Aug., 1829).

An Exposition of Facts Connected with the Late Prosecutions in the Methodist Episcopal Church of Cincinnati. . . . 60 pp. Cincinnati, Looker & Reynolds, Printers, 1828. WRHist.

Farley, Charles A. What is Unitarianism? A Sermon Delivered in the Protestant Episcopal Methodist Church of Alton, Illinois. From *The Western Messenger*, III, 641 (Apr., 1837).

Fishback, James. A Defence of the Elkhorn Association; in Sixteen Letters, Addressed to Elder Henry Toler, . . . 185, [2] pp. Lexington, Printed for the Author by Thomas T. Skillman, 1822. ChU, LexPL, TransylvaniaU.

—— Essays and Dialogues, on the Powers and Susceptibilities of the Human Mind for Religion; . . . iv, 293 pp. Lexington, J. Clarke & Co., 1834. ChU, LexPL, TransylvaniaU.

—— A New and Candid Investigation of the Question Is Revelation True? 30 pp. Lexington, Printed by D. & C. Bradford, 1809. ChU.

—— The Philosophy of the Human Mind, in Respect to Religion; or, a Demonstration, from the Necessity of Things, that Religion Entered the World by Revelation. . . . [2], 306, [2] pp. Lexington, Printed by Thomas T. Skillman, 1813. ChU, HistPSO, KyStL, TransylvaniaU.

—— The Substance of a Discourse, in Two Parts; Delivered in the Meeting House of the First Baptist Church in Lexington, February 3, 1822; to the Class of the Medical School of Transylvania University, . . . 22 pp. Lexington, Joseph Ficklin, Printer, n. d. TransylvaniaU. Part II. 23 pp. Lexington, Printed by Thomas T. Skillman, 1822. TransylvaniaU?

Fisher, Charles. A Serious Expostulation with the Followers of Elias Hicks, . . . 23 pp. Cincinnati, Printed by M'Calla and Davis, 1829. WRHist.

Fitch, Charles. Lunatics Special Objects of Benevolent Attention and Effort. A Sermon Delivered at the Opening of the Ohio Lunatic Asylum, November 25, 1838. 16 pp. Columbus, Printed by Cutler and Pilsbury, 1838. LaneTS.

Fry, Joseph Reese. Oration: Delivered before the Members of the St. Peters Benevolent Society of Cincinnati, at the Anniversary Meeting, January 1st, 1836. From *The Western Monthly Magazine*, V, 62 (Jan., 1836).

Galloway, Samuel. Address . . . before the Society of Inquiry on Missions of Miami University, December 19th, 1836. 32 pp. Oxford, O., R. H. Bishop, Jun., 1837. ChU, LaneTS. Title-pages vary.

Giddings, Salmon. A Sermon Delivered at St. Louis, August 17, 1817, on Account of the Death of Edward Hempstead, Esq., late of St. Louis, M. T. 20 pp. St. Louis, Printed by Sergeant Hall, 1818. MercLStL.

Gilruth, James. The Fair Reasoner, or, a Lecture on Baptism: Delivered before the Local Conference of Lancaster District, August 28, 1822. 64 pp. Steubenville, Printed by James Wilson, 1824. WRHist.

Green, Beriah. Four Sermons, Preached in the Chapel of the Western Reserve College, . . . 1832. 52 pp. Cleveland, Printed at the Office of the Herald, 1833. WRHist.

Greene, John P. Facts Relative to the Expulsion of the Mormons or Latter Day Saints, from the State of Missouri, under the "Exterminating Order." 43 pp. Cincinnati, Printed by R. P. Brooks, 1839. LC, NYPL, WisH.

Hall, Baynard Rush. Righteousness the Safe-guard and Glory of a Nation. A Sermon Preached in the Representative Hall, at Indianapolis, Indiana; December 31st, 1826, . . . 23 pp. N. p. (Indianapolis), Smith & Bolton, Printers, n. d. IndStL.

Hall, Richard D. A Sermon against Conformity to this World. . . . Preached in Lexington, Kentucky, 14th Dec. 1822. . . . 12 pp. Lexington, Printed and Sold by Thomas T. Skiillman [sic], 1823. LexPL.

Hart, Cyrus W. Colloquy on the Immortality of the Soul, with an Essay on Prudence. To which is Added, a Love Touch. 48 pp. Steubenville, O., Printed by James Wilson, 1830. WRHist.

Hinton, Isaac Taylor. A History of Baptism, both from the Inspired and Uninspired Writings. 372 pp. Philadelphia, American Baptist Publication and S. S. Society, n. d. (1840). ChPL.

Holley, Horace. A Discourse Occasioned by the Death of Col: James Morrison, Delivered in the Episcopal Church, Lexington, Kentucky, May 19th, 1823, . . . 37 pp. Lexington, Printed by John Bradford, 1823. ChU, LC, LouPL, NYPL.

Holley, Nathaniel. The Doctrine of the Atonement Explained, in a Sermon Delivered at the New-Jerusalem Temple, in Cincinnati, on the Evening of the 20th of December, 1824. 22 pp. Cincinnati, Morgan & Lodge, Printers, 1825. From *The Cincinnati Literary Gazette*, Feb. 12, 1825.

Howe, E. D. History of Mormonism: or a Faithful Account of that Singular Imposition and Delusion, with Sketches of the Characters of its Propagators. . . . 290 pp. Painesville, O., the Author, 1840. WRHist.

—— Mormonism Unveiled: or, a Faithful Account of that Singular Imposition and Delusion, from its Rise to the Present Time. . . . 290 pp. Painesville, O., the Author, 1834. HistPSO, WRHist, WisH.

Hudson, John. The Peaceful End of the Christian. A Sermon, Delivered in Lebanon, Ohio, Oct. 22nd, 1836. . . . 16 pp. Dayton, O., B. F. Ells, 1837. LaneTS, WRHist.

Jamieson, Milton. A Treatise on the Subject of Baptism; principally Designed as an Exposure of Campbellism. 207, [1] pp. Lexington, Printed by W. M. Todd and W. D. Skillman, 1834. TransylvaniaU.

Jewett, Milo P. The Mode and Subjects of Baptism. 121 pp. Boston, Gould, Kendall and Lincoln, 1839. WRHist.

Kemper, Frederick Augustus. Consolations of the Afflicted, . . . 258 pp. Cincinnati, Printed by Wm. J. Ferris & Co., 1831. CinPL, WRHist.

Kidwell, J. A Series of Strictures on the Subject of Future and Endless Punishment: being the Substance of the Arguments Used in a Public Debate Held at Indianapolis, Jan. 21, 1830, on that Subject, between the Rev. E. Ray and the Publisher. . . . 74 pp. Cincinnati, Printed by S. Tizzard, 1830. WRHist.

MacCalla, William Latta. Remarks on Dr. James Fishback's Philosophy of the Human Mind, in Respect to Religion. 39 pp. Lexington, Printed by M'Call & Downing, for the Author, 1814. ChU.

—— A Sermon, on Prov. iv.23, which was Handed to the West-Lexington Presbytery, by a Student under their Care, in April 1813, and Rejected. It is Accompanied by a Few Notes, . . . To which is Added a Few Remarks on Dr. James Fishback's Philosophy of the Human Mind, in Respect to Religion. 36 pp. Lexington, Printed for the Author by M'Call & Downing, 1814. ChU.

M'Chord, James. The Body of Christ: a Series of Essays on the Scriptural Doctrine of Federal Representation. Corrected, Enlarged and Concluded, from the Evangelical Record and Western Review. . . . Edited by James M'Chord. 264 pp. Lexington, Thomas T. Skillman, 1814. ChU, LexPL, NYPL, TransylvaniaU.

—— A Last Appeal to the "Market-street Presbyterian Church and Congregation." In a Series of Seven Sermons, Predicated on Sketches of the Dispensations of God toward his People. To which are Added The Death of Abel, and The Judgment of Cain; . . . 332 pp. Lexington, T. T. Skillman, 1818. ChU, LexPL, YMML.

—— National Safety: a Sermon, Delivered in the Legislative Hall, before the Hon. the Legislature of Kentucky, . . . 12th January, 1815. . . . 32 pp. Lexington, Thomas T. Skillman, 1815. LaneTS, LC, NYPL, WRHist.

—— A Plea "for the Hope of Israel," — for the Hope of All the World: Delivered on an Appeal before the General Synod of the Associate-Reformed Church. 85 pp. Philadelphia, Published at the Port Folio Office, James Maxwell, Printer, 1817. ChU, LaneTS, WRHist.

—— Sermons on Important Subjects, Selected from the Manuscripts of the Late Rev'd. James M'Chord, . . .

357 pp. Lexington, Printed by Thomas T. Skillman, for the Benefit of the Children of the Author, 1822. ChU, HistPSO, TransylvaniaU.

McCoy, Isaac. History of Baptist Indian Missions: Embracing Remarks on the Former and Present Condition of the Aboriginal Tribes; . . . [4], 611 pp. Washington, William M. Morrison, etc., 1840. ChU, GrandRPL, LC, WRHist, WisH.

M'Farland, John. A Series of Letters, on the Relation, Rights, Privileges and Duties of Baptized Children. 173, [1] pp. Lexington, Printed by Joseph G. Norwood, 1828. ChU, KyStHist, LC.

—— The Signs of the Times, being the Substance of a Discourse Delivered in Chillicothe Ohio, in May Last: and also in Paris, Ky. . . . August 1820. 39 pp. Paris, Ky., Printed by Joel R. Lyle, 1821. CinPL, LaneTS.

M'Farlane, A. The Scriptural Doctrine of Predestination, . . . 2d ed., revised and improved. 47 pp. Cincinnati, M'Millan and Clopper, Printers, 1833. LaneTS.

McGowan, John? Infernal Conference: or, Dialogues of Devils. By the Listener. New ed. 288 pp. (Lexington, Printed by Daniel Bradford, 1804.) ChU (title-page mutilated, but restored).

M'Gready, James. The Posthumous Works of the Reverend and Pious James M'Gready, Late Minister of the Gospel, in Henderson, Kentucky. Edited by the Reverend James Smith. . . . 2 vols. Vol. I, Louisville, Printed by W. W. Worsley, 1831; Vol. II, Nashville, Lowry and Smith, 1833. ChU, LaneTS.

M'Henry, Barnabas. Remarks on Some Passages in a Periodical Work Printed in Lexington, Entitled, 'The Evangelical Record and Western Review:' 50 pp. (Lexington? 1813.) From *Ky. Gaz.*, May 25, 1813.

McIlvaine, Charles Pettit. The Apostolical Commission: the Sermon at the Consecration of the Right Reverend Leonidas Polk, D.D., Missionary Bishop for Arkansas; in Christ Church, Cincinnati, December 9, 1838. 43 pp. Gambier, O., G. W. Myers, 1838. LC, WRHist.

—— A Charge to the Clergy of the Prot. Episc. Church in the State of Ohio, on the Preaching of Christ Crucified; Delivered before the Seventeenth Annual Convention of the Diocese at Chillicothe, September 5th, 1834. 22 pp. Gambier, O., George W. Myers, Printer, 1834. WRHist.

—— Farewell Discourse, Preached in St. Ann's Church, Brooklyn, N. Y. on the 29th of April, 1833, by C. P. McIlvaine, D.D. Bishop of the Protestant Episcopal Church in the State of Ohio. . . . 19 pp. New York, Morgan & Burger, 1833. WRHist.

—— Justification by Faith: a Charge Delivered before the Clergy of the Protestant Episcopal Church in the Diocese of Ohio, . . . Steubenville, September 13, 1839. . . . 156 pp. Columbus, Isaac N. Whiting, 1840. WRHist.

—— The Missionary Character and Duty of the Church: a Sermon, before the Domestic and Foreign Missionary Society of the Protestant Episcopal Church . . . Philadelphia, August 24, 1835. 32 pp. Philadelphia, Printed by Wm. Stavely, 1835. WRHist.

—— The Necessity of Religion to the Prosperity of the Nation: a Sermon Preached . . . in the Chapel of Kenyon College, . . . 31 pp. Gambier, O., George W. Myers, Printer, 1838. WRHist.

—— The Origin and Design of the Christian Ministry: a Sermon Preached at an Ordination, Held . . . at Gambier, . . . October 26, 1839, . . . 22 pp. Gambier, O., G. W. Meyers [sic], 1839. WRHist.

—— The Present Condition and Chief Want of the Church: a Charge to the Clergy of the Prot. Episcopal Church, of Ohio. Delivered before the Nineteenth Annual Convention of the Diocese, at Cleveland, September 9th, 1836, . . . 28 pp. Gambier, O., George W. Myers, Printer, 1836. WRHist.

—— Select Family and Parish Sermons. . . . 2 vols. Columbus, Isaac N. Whiting, 1838. LouPL, WRHist, WisH.

M'Kimmey, William. The Plea of the Innocent, or Hicksiteism: a New Name for Quakerism. . . . Also — a Review of an Epistle of Advice, Issued at Indiana Yearly Meeting, 1827. . . . 61 pp. Richmond, Ind., Finley & Holloway, Printers, 1834. IndStL.

McNemar, Richard. A Concise Answer to the General Inquiry, Who, or what are the Shakers. 10 pp. Union Village, O., 1823. LC, WRHist.

—— The Decision of the Court of Appeals, (in Kentucky) in a Case of Much Interest to Religious Communities in General, and to the Shakers in Particular. . . . Pagination irregular. Dayton, O., 1834. HistPSO, JCrerar, WRHist.

—— Investigator; or a Defence of the Order, Government & Economy of the United Society Called Shakers, against Sundry Charges & Legislative Proceedings. Addressed to the Political World. By the Society of Believers at Pleasant Hill, Ky. . . . 47 pp. Lexington, Printed by Smith & Palmer, 1828. JCrerar, WRHist.

—— The Kentucky Revival, or, a Short History of the Late Extraordinary Out-pouring of the Spirit of God, in the Western States of America, . . . with a Brief Account of the Entrance and Progress of what the World Call Shakerism, among the Subjects of the Late Revival in Ohio and Kentucky. . . . 119 pp. Cincinnati, from the Press of John W. Browne, 1807. WRHist, WisH.

—— Observations on Church Government, by the Presbytery of Springfield. To which is Added, The Last Will and Testament of that Reverend Body: with a Preface and Notes, by the Editor. . . . 23 pp. Cincinnati, from the Press of John W. Browne, Office of Liberty Hall, 1807. ChU. 23 pp. Cincinnati, Printed; Albany, Reprinted, by E. and E. Hosford, 1808. WRHist, WisH.

—— (in part?). The Other Side of the Question. In Three Parts. . . . III. An Account of the Proceedings of Abram Van Vleet, Esq. and his Associates, against the Said United Society at Union Village, Ohio. . . . 164, vii pp. Cincinnati, Looker, Reynolds & Co., Printers, 1819. WRHist, WisH.

—— A Review of the most Important Events Relating to the Rise and Progress of the United Society of Believers in the West; with Sundry Other Documents Connected with the History of the Society. Collected from Various Journals, by E. Wright. . . . 56 pp. Union Village, O., 1831. WRHist.

—— A Series of Lectures on Orthodoxy and Heterodoxy, in Allusion to the Testimony of Christ's Second Appearing. Introduced by a Reply to Sundry Defamatory Letters Written by A. M. Bolton, late, a Catechumen in the United Society at Union Village. Designed for the Edification of Young Believers. By E. W. . . . 12 pp. Dayton, O., 1832. WRHist.

—— Shakerism Detected [a Pamphlet Published by col. James Smith, of Kentucky]. Examined and Refuted in Five Propositions; Published at Lebanon (O) and Lexington (K) in 1811. By Richard M'Namer [*sic*]. . . . (Reprinted by Request). 12, [1] pp. Watervliet, O., May 8, 1833. (First square brackets are in original.) WRHist.

—— The Western Review, or a Memorial of the Labors of our Parents and Ministers, in Founding the Church in the West. By Eleazar Wright, Recorder. . . .24 pp. Watervliet, O., 1834. WRHist.

——, and Calvin Morrell. An Address, to the State of Ohio, Protesting against a Certain Clause in the Militia Law, . . . 24 pp. Lebanon, O., Printed by George Smith, March, 1818. WRHist.

Mahan, Asa. Principles of Christian Union, and Church Fellowship. A Sermon, . . . Preached at Oberlin, May 1836. . . . 32 pp. Elyria, O., A. Burrell, Printer, n. d. WRHist.

—— Scripture Doctrine of Christian Perfection; with Other Kindred Subjects, Illustrated and Confirmed in a Series of Discourses . . . 237 pp. Boston, D. S. King, 1839. WRHist.

—— Tracts on Health . . . No. 12. Physical and Moral Law equally Obligatory. Abstract of an Address, Delivered . . . Feb. 12, 1839, at . . . Boston, . . . 8 pp. N. p., n. d. WRHist.

Marshall, Humphrey. The Letter of a Private Student, or an Examination of the "Evidences of Christianity" as Exhibited and Argued, at Cincinnati, April, 1829; by the Rev. Alexander Campbell, in a Debate with Mr. Robert Owen. iv, 60 pp. Frankfort, Printed by J. H. Holeman, 1830. ChU.

Marshall, S. V. A Discourse on the Best Method of Preserving the Peace and Union of the Presbyterian Church in the United States. Delivered before the West-Lexington Presbytery, . . . April 1, 1835. 22 pp. Lexington, Printed by Wm. D. Skillman, 1835. LaneTS, LexPL.

Matthews, John. The Influence of the Bible in Improving the Understanding and Moral Character. . . . Philadelphia, Harrison Hall, 1833. From *The Western Monthly Magazine*, II, 381 (July, 1834).

Mentor, or Dialogues, between a Parent and Children, on Some of the Duties, Amusements, Pursuits and Relations of Life. 203 pp. Lexington, Printed by Thomas Smith, 1828. ChU. For attribution of the book to an anonymous gentleman of Lexington, see *Ky. Reporter*, June 11, 1828.

Merrill, David. An Oration Delivered before the Mechanic's Institute, and the Teachers and Scholars of the Sabbath Schools of Urbana, Ohio: . . . 14 pp. Urbana, O., 1838. From *The Hesperian*, I, 494 (Oct., 1838).

Monfort, David. A Farewell Sermon, Delivered at Bethel, . . . Eleventh of November, 1827. . . . 12 pp. Oxford, O., J. D. Smith, Printer, 1828. LaneTS.

—— A Reply to the Review of the Rev. A. R. Hinckley, of Sermons on Christian Baptism. . . . 25 pp. Indianapolis, Printed by Stacy & Williams, 1840. IndStL.

—— A Sermon on Justification, from Romans III. 24. . . . 35 pp. Indianapolis, Printed by Douglass and Maguire, 1831. IndStL, LaneTS.

—— Two Sermons on Christian Baptism; Delivered in Franklin, Indiana, July, 1838, . . . 46 pp. Cincinnati, Hefley, Hubbell & Co., Printers, 1839. LaneTS.

Moore, Joshua. A Discourse, Delivered at the Councilhouse, Detroit, before the Legislative Council of Michigan Territory, June 21, 1824. 27 pp. Detroit, Printed by Sheldon & Reed, n. d. (1824?). BurColl.

Moreland, John R. To the Members of Mount-Pleasant

Church, 12 pp. N. p. (Cynthiana, Ky.?), n. d. (1821?). CinPL.

Morris, B. F., and James M. Ray. Addresses, Delivered at the Sunday School Celebration of the Fifty-fourth Anniversary of American Independence, in Indianapolis, on Saturday, the 3d of July, 1830. 20 pp. Indianapolis, Printed by Douglass and Maguire, 1830. IndStL.

Nelson, David. An Appeal to the Church, in Behalf of a Dying Race, from the Mission Institute, near Quincy, Illinois. 23, [1] pp. New York, John S. Taylor, 1838. LaneTS, LexPL.

—— The Cause and Cure of Infidelity: with an Account of the Author's Conversion. 353, [6] pp. New York, John S. Taylor, 1838. WisH.

—— Meditations on Various Religious Subjects, at the Conclusion of which is Affixed a Treatise on Some Important Diseases, . . . 300 pp. Louisville, 1828. ChU, HistPSO.

O'Kane, John, and T. W. Haynes. Report of the Debate on Baptism, which was Held at Bellville, Hendricks County, Ind., from 4th to 7th September, 1839, between John O'Kane, of Crawfordsville, Ia. and T. W. Haynes, Editor of the Regular Baptist, Taken down and Engrossed by A. E. Drapier. . . . 140 pp. Indianapolis, the Reporter, January, 1840. IndStL.

Olmstead, Charles G. The Bible, its Own Refutation. Louisville, 1836. From *The Western Messenger*, III, 453 (Feb., 1837).

Orchard, Isaac. A Summary of Scripture Texts, . . . 46 pp. Hanover, Ind., Printed by Morrow & Newell, 1836. LaneTS.

Original Sermons; by Presbyterian Ministers, in the Mississippi Valley. . . . 309, [1] pp. Cincinnati, M'Millan & Clopper, 1833. ChU.

Overstreet, J. H.   A General Replication to the Rev. William Adams & Co.   36, [1] pp.   Louisville, S. Penn, Jr., Printer, 1824.   ChU.

—— The Secret of Church Secrets, Unsecreted.   .   .   .   24 pp.   Louisville, S. Penn, Jr., Printer, 1824.   ChU.

Owen, Robert.   Debate on the Evidences of Christianity; Containing an Examination of "the Social System," and of All the Systems of Scepticism of Ancient and Modern Times.   Held in the City of Cincinnati, Ohio, in April, 1829; between Robert Owen & Alexander Campbell.   Reported by Charles H. Simms, Esq.   With an Appendix, Written by the Parties.   2d ed.   2 vols.   Cincinnati, Robinson and Fairbank, 1829.   (Title-pages of the two volumes differ slightly.)   ChU, CinPL.

—— Robert Owen's Opening Speech, and his Reply to the Rev. Alex. Campbell, in the Recent Public Discussion in Cincinnati, to Prove that the Principles of All Religions are Erroneous, and that their Practice is Injurious to the Human Race.   Also, Mr. Owen's Memorial to the Republic of Mexico,   .   .   .   227 pp. and additional pages irregularly numbered.   Cincinnati, for Robert Owen, 1829.   ColU, JCrerar, WRHist, WisH.

Owen, Robert Dale. Letters Addressed to William Gibbons, of Wilmington, Del. in Reply to "An Exposition of Modern Scepticism;" together with an Address to the Society of Friends, and a Letter to Eli Hilles, Benj. Ferris and Others.   .   .   .   24 pp.   Philadelphia, J. A. M'Clintock, 1830.   WisH.

Paxton, J. D.   Letters on Slavery; Addressed to the Cumberland Congregation, Virginia.   By J. D. Paxton, their Former Pastor.   viii, 207 pp.   Lexington, Abraham T. Skillman, 1833.   CinPL, WRHist.

Phillips, William.   Campbellism Exposed; or, Strictures

on the Peculiar Tenets of Alexander Campbell. 267 pp. Cincinnati, Poe and Hitchcock, for the Methodist Episcopal Church, 1861. (Advertisement dated 1837.) WRHist.

Potts, William S. Importance of Early Education and Family Government, and Obligations of Parents to Sunday Schools. An Annual Sermon, Preached at St. Louis, July 17, 1831. For the Presbyterian Sunday School Society of St. Louis. 20 pp. St. Louis, Printed at the St. Louis Times Office, 1831. IllU.

Pratt, Parley Parker. History of the Late Persecution Inflicted by the State of Missouri upon the Mormons, in which Ten Thousand American Citizens were Robbed, Plundered, and Driven from the State . . . Detroit, Dawson and Bates, Printers, 1839. From MS. copyright record for the District of Michigan, 1824-1857; MS. entry dated Sept. 30, 1839. 39, [1] pp. Mexico, N. Y., Reprinted at the Office of the Oswego Co. Democrat, 1840. WisH.

—— Late Persecution of the Church of Jesus Christ, of Latter Day Saints. Ten Thousand American Citizens Robbed, Plundered, and Banished; Others Imprisoned, and Others Martyred for their Religion. With a Sketch of their Rise, Progress and Doctrine. . . . Written in Prison. 215, [1] pp. New York, J. W. Harrison, Printer, 1840. WRHist, WisH.

—— Mormonism Unveiled: Zion's Watchman Unmasked, and its Editor, Mr. L. R. Sunderland, Exposed: Truth Vindicated: the Devil Mad, and Priestcraft in Danger! 46 pp. New York, Printed for the Publisher, 1838. WRHist.

—— A Voice of Warning, and Instruction to All People, or an Introduction to the Faith and Doctrine of the

Church of Jesus Christ, of Latter Day Saints. 2d ed.,
revised. 216 pp. New York, J. W. Harrison, Printer,
1839. WRHist, WisH.

Public Discourses, Delivered (in Substance) at Union Vil-
lage, August, 1823, and Prepared for Publication. By
Order of the Ministry. . . . 36 pp. N. p., n. d.
WisH.

Purcell, John B., and Alexander Campbell. A Debate on
the Roman Catholic Religion: Held in the Sycamore-
street Meeting House, Cincinnati, from the 13th to the
21st of January, 1837. Between Alexander Campbell,
of Bethany, Virginia, and the Rt. Rev. John B. Purcell,
Bishop of Cincinnati. Taken down by Reporters, and
Revised by the Parties. . . . 359 pp. Cincinnati,
J. A. James & Co., 1837. ChU, CinPL, WRHist.

Rankin, Adam. Dialogues, Pleasant and Interesting, upon
the All-important Question in Church Government, What
are the Legitimate Terms of Admission to Visible
Church Communion? 350 pp. Lexington, Printed for
the Author, 1819. ChU, LexPL, TransylvaniaU.

—— A Process in the Transilvania Presbytery, &c. Containing: 1st. The Charges, Depositions and Defence in
which the Defendent is Led occasionally to Handle the
much Debated Subject of Psalmody. 2d. His Reasons
for Declining, Any Farther Connections with the Body to
which he Belonged. 3d. His Present Plan of Proceeding,
with the Pastoral Charge. 4th. His Belief, and that of
his People, concerning the Articles of Faith, Contended
between the Reformed Associate Sinod; and the Sinod
of New York and Philadelphia. 5th. An Appendix on a
Late Performance of the Rev. Mr. John Black of Marsh
Creek, Pennsylvania. By Adam Rankin, Pastor, at Lexington: Kentucky. 96 pp. Lexington, Maxwell &
Cooch, n. d. (1793). ChU, LexPL, LC.

—— Rankin's Second Process. To All the Faithful in Christ Jesus, but especially to the Associate Reformed Church in North America; and still more so, to his Dear Flock of Mount Zion, Lexington, Ky. 23 pp. Lexington, Printed at the Office of the Kentucky Gazette, by Jno. Norvell, 1818. CinPL.

—— A Reply to A Narrative of Mr. Adam Rankin's Trial &c. lately Published by Order of the Transylvania Presbytery. 71 pp. Lexington, Printed by J. Bradford, 1794. LC.

—— A Review of the Noted Revival in Kentucky, . . . (Lexington? Printed at the Office of the Kentucky Gazette? 1802.) From *Ky. Gaz.*, May 21 and 28, and June 1, 1802. 78, [1] pp. Washington and Pittsburg, Printed by John Israel, 1802. CinPL. 70 pp. N. p., Printed in the Year 1803, for the Purchaser. MercLStL, WRHist.

Rankin, John. A Present to Families: a Practical Work on the Covenant of Grace, as Given to Abraham. . . . 160 pp. Ripley, O., C. Edwards, 1840. CinPL, LaneTS, WRHist.

—— A Sermon on the Divinity of the Saviour. 23 pp. Augusta (Ky.?), Andrews, Printer, 1830. LaneTS.

Rice, David. An Epistle to the Citizens of Kentucky, Professing Christianity; especially to those that are, or have been, Denominated Presbyterians. 1805. From R. H. Bishop, *An Outline of the History of the Church in the State of Kentucky*, 1824, p. 321. Reprinted *ibid.*, pp. 321-340.

—— An Essay on Baptism. 82 pp. Baltimore, Printed by William Goddard, 1789. LC.

—— A Lecture on the Divine Decrees. 1791. From Bishop, *op. cit.*, p. 113.

—— A Second Epistle to the Citizens of Kentucky Professing the Christian Religion, especially those who are, or have been, Denominated Presbyterians. 2d ed. 32 pp. Raleigh, Printed by W. Boylan, 1809. From LC card.

—— A Sermon, on the Present Revival of Religion, &c. in this Country: Preached at the Opening of the Kentucky Synod. 43 pp. Washington, ''(Geo.)'', Reprinted at the Monitor Press, 1804. ChU, NYPL.

Rice, Nathan L. An Account of the Law-suit Instituted by Rev. G. A. M. Elder, President of St. Joseph's College, against Rev. N. L. Rice, Presbyterian Minister, for a Pretended Libel . . . 192 pp. Louisville, D. Holcomb & Co., Printers, 1837. WRHist.

—— Election: a Scripture Doctrine. 22 pp. Louisville, S. Penn, Jr., Printer, 1834. LaneTS.

—— Infallibility of the Church, Tested by Scripture; together with a Short Essay on the Uncertainty of Salvation in the Church of Rome. 38 pp. Bardstown, Ky., Printed by Jones & Bell, 1834. LaneTS.

Robbins, Samuel P. An Address, to ''The Society in Marietta, for the Promotion of Good Morals.'' Delivered at their Annual Meeting, June 5th, 1815. 14 pp. Marietta, O., Printed by T. & D. H. Buell and R. Prentiss, 1815. HistPSO, WRHist.

Robbins, Thomas. A Sermon Delivered at the Ordination of the Rev. Samuel P. Robbins, to the Pastoral Care of the First Church and Society in Marietta, State of Ohio, Jan. 8th. 1806. 18 pp. Marietta, O., Printed by Samuel Fairlamb, n. d. (1806). From Thomson.

Robertson, Th. R. A Paraphrase on the Vision of Daniel, and Revelation of St. John the Divine. 12 pp. Lawrenceburg, Ind., Printed by D. V. Culley, 1826. ChU.

Root, David. A Discourse Delivered in the Second Presbyterian Church, Cincinnati, Aug. 31, 1828. Occasioned by the Death of Robert Wallace, Senior, . . . 12 pp. Cincinnati, Printed by S. J. Browne, 1828. HistPSO.

Russell, Joshua T. The Christian's Dying Conflict, Victory and Triumph. A Sermon, Delivered in the First Presbyterian Church, Louisville, Ky. . . . May 11th, 1834. . . . 16 pp. Louisville, Prentice & Johnson, Printers, 1834. LouPL.

Scank, Philemon. A Few Chapters to Brother Jonathan, concerning "Infallibility, &c." or, Strictures on Nathan L. Rice's "Defence of Protestantism," &c. &c. &c. 145, 34 pp. Louisville, for the Author, 1835. ChU.

Scott, Job. The Baptism of Christ, a Gospel Ordinance, being altogether Inward and Spiritual: . . . 138 pp. Wilmington, O., Printed by Rice Gaddis for John Hunt, 1817. WRHist.

Scott, John W. The Cholera, God's Scourge for the Chastisement of the Nations: a Discourse Delivered on the Occasion of a Fast Observed in Reference to the Approach of the Epidemic, Oxford, Ohio, August 16th, 1833. 15 pp. Oxford, O., W. W. Bishop, 1833. LaneTS, WRHist.

Scott, Walter. A Discourse on the Holy Spirit. 2d ed., enlarged and improved. 24 pp. Bethany, Va., Printed by Alexander Campbell, 1831. WRHist.

—— The Gospel Restored. A Discourse of the True Gospel of Jesus Christ, in which the Facts, Principles, Duties, and Privileges of Christianity are Arranged, Defined, and Discussed, . . . The Evangelist for the Current Year. 576 pp. Cincinnati, O. H. Donogh, 1836. LaneTS, TransylvaniaU, WRHist.

A Series of Miscellaneous Letters, from a Father to his Children. By a Layman. 144 pp. South Hanover, Ind., James Morrow, 1835. IndStL.

A Series of Questions on the Scriptures and Religious Subjects; . . . 24 pp. Paris, Ky., Printed by Joel R. Lyle, 1820. ChU.

Shepard, Enoch. Thoughts, on the Prophecies; Applicable to the Times: . . . 157 pp. Marietta, O., Printed for the Author, by Joseph Israel, 1812. WRHist. From copy supplied by W. H. Cathcart, Western Reserve Historical Society.

Slave Holding. A Disqualification for Church Fellowships a Letter to Dr. Joshua L. Wilson and the First Presbyterian Church, Cincinnati. "By a Brother." . . . 8 pp. N. p. (Cincinnati, Monthly Concert of Prayer for the Enslaved), n. d. LC, WRHist, WisH.

Sleigh, Joseph. Campbellism Unmasked, or, Spurious Gospels Exposed. Being the Substance of a Discourse Delivered . . . in Cincinnati, . . . July 8, 1834. . . . 16 pp. Cincinnati, Allen & Disney, Printers, 1834. LaneTS.

Smith, Henry. The Fears of the Wicked Reasonable. A Sermon, Preached in the Library Hall, Marietta, Tuesday Evening, February 10, 1835. On Proverbs X. xxiv. 17 pp. Marietta, O., Printed by Pazzi Lapham, 1835. HistPSO, WRHist.

Smith, James. Remarkable Occurrences lately Discovered among the People Called Shakers, of a Treasonous and Barbarous Nature; or, Shakerism Developed. 22 pp. Carthage, Tenn., Printed by William Moore, 1810. WRHist.

Smith, Nathaniel R. Moral Miscellanies: Including, I. A Defence of Christianity; or, Infidelity Disarmed. II. Original Moral Essays. . . . Original Poems. By a Layman. From printed title-page in MS. copyright record for District of Ohio, 1806-1828; MS. entry dated Nov. 8, 1817.

Smith, Thomas. A Sermon, Delivered in Madisonville, Hop-
kins County, Ky. on the One Supreme God, and His Son
Jesus Christ; August 20th, 1821. 40 pp. N. p., D. S.
Patton, Printer, 1821. TransylvaniaU.

Some Strictures on Church Government, in Answer to a
Late Publication on that Subject, by Rev. Lorenzo Dow.
. . . 34 pp. Cincinnati, Abbott Goddard, 1823.
HistPSO.

Sparrow, William. A Reply to the Charges and Accusa-
tions of the Rt. Rev. Philander Chase, D. D. 35 pp.
Gambier, O., Printed at the Office of the Observer, 1832.
LC, WRHist.

Springer, Cornelius. A Review of the Late Decision of
the Supreme Court of Ohio, which has Went virtually
to Incorporate the Methodist Episcopal Church in the
United States:—. . . Shewing that the Creation of
Such a Corporation, . . . is a Dangerous Engine in
a Free Government. 71, [1] pp. Cincinnati, 1832.
LexPL.

Steele, J. The Substance of an Address, . . . In the
Associate Reformed Synod of the West, . . . Steu-
benville; . . . October 16th, 1829, on the Question of
Making the Holding of Slaves, a Term of Communion in
the Church. 43, [1] pp. Washington, O., Printed by
Hamilton Robb, 1830. LC, WRHist, WisH.

Steele, Samuel. A Sermon on Christian Baptism, Shewing the Apostolic Practice, both as to Subjects and Mode.
50 pp. Lexington, Printed by Joseph G. Norwood, 1828.
LaneTS.

Stevenson, Edward. The Exposer of "Sectarian Stratagem" Exposed. 64 pp. Lexington, J. Clarke & Co.,
Printers, 1836. ChU.

Stiles, Joseph C. A Letter to Alexander Campbell, in

Reply to an Article in the Millenial Harbinger, . . . 57 pp. Lexington, Lexington Intelligencer, Print., 1838. ChU.

—— Reply to an Article in the June Number of the Millenial Harbinger. 55, [1] pp. Frankfort, A. G. Hodges, Printer, 1838. ChU.

Stone, Barton Warren. An Address to the Christian Churches in Kentucky, Tennessee & Ohio, on Several Important Doctrines of Religion. 108 pp. Nashville, Tenn., Printed by M. [?] & J. Norvell, 1814. CinPL, LaneTS. 2d ed., corrected and enlarged. v, 102 pp. Lexington, Printed by I. T. Cavins & Co., 1821. LexPL.

—— Letters. 1805. From John P. Campbell, *Vindex*, 1806, p. 53. *Cf.* also *Ky. Gaz.*, July 23, 1805; and R. H. Bishop, *An Outline of the History of the Church in the State of Kentucky*, 1824, p. 137.

—— Letters to James Blythe, D. D. Designed as a Reply to the Arguments of Thomas Cleland, D. D. against my Address, 2d. Edition, on the Doctrine of Trinity, the Son of God, Atonement, &c. 163, [1] pp. Lexington, Printed by William Tanner, 1824. ChU, CinPL, LexPL, WisH.

—— A Letter to Mr. John R. Moreland, in Reply to his Pamphlet. 14 pp. Lexington, Printed at the Office of the Public Advertiser, 1821. CinPL, TransylvaniaU.

Strictures on the Rev. Mr. Blythe's Fast Day Sermon; by Americanus. (Lexington? 1815?) From *Ky. Gaz.*, Mar. 27, 1815.

Strong, T. Episcopal Tract — No. 1. Candid Examination of the Episcopal Church, in Two Letters to a Friend. 23 pp. Lexington, Printed by William G. Hunt, 1821. WisH.

Swartzell, William. Mormonism Exposed, being a Journal of a Residence in Missouri from the 28th of May to the

20th of August, 1838, together with an Appendix, Containing the Revelation concerning the Golden Bible, . . . 48 pp. Pekin, O., the Author, 1840. MoHist.

Taylor, Caleb Jarvis. News from the Infernal Regions. Lexington, 1803. From *Methodist Quarterly Review,* XLI, 404 (July, 1859).

Taylor, John. History of Clear Creek Church; and Campbellism Exposed. 60 pp. Frankfort, Printed by A. G. Hodges, 1830. ChU, LC.

Thomas, David. The Observer, Trying the Great Reformation in this State, and Proving it to have been originally a Work of Divine Power. With a Survey of Several Objections to the Contrary, as being chiefly Comprised in Mr. Rankin's Review of the Noted Revival, lately Published. From *Ky. Gaz.,* Oct. 5 and 12, 1802.

Thompson, Wilson. Simple Truth, Illustrated in Eight Short Discourses, on the System of Salvation . . . 124 pp. Lebanon, O., Printed by William A. Camron, for the Author, 1821. WRHist.

—— The Triumphs of Truth, or the Scripture a Sure Guide to Zion's Pilgrims; . . . 252 pp. Lebanon, O., Printed by Camron and Sellers, for the Author, 1825. HistPSO.

Tresize, Thomas. The Christians' Guide. Being a Collection of Scripture Texts, on almost Every Subject; . . . without Note or Comment. . . . 216 pp. Zanesville, O., 1819. WRHist.

Trial of the Rev. Lyman Beecher, D. D. before the Presbytery of Cincinnati, on the Charge of Heresy. Reported for the New-York Observer. 83 pp. New York, Sold by the Principal Booksellers, 1835. ColU, NewL, WRHist.

Tucker, Levi. Lectures on the Nature and Dangerous Tendency of Modern Infidelity: Delivered to the Young

Men, in the First Baptist Church in the City of Cleveland, Ohio, . . . 189 pp. Cleveland, Francis B. Penniman, 1837. HistPSO.

Useful Discovery, in a Letter Addressed to the Rev. Mr. C—— and Mr. M——, . . . [Signed "HARDENED SINNERS and CARNAL PROFESSORS *of all sorts.*"] From *The Evangelical Record and Western Review,* I, 49 (Feb., 1812).

Valuable Extracts from Sundry Writers (on Various Subjects) Congenial to the Faith of the Gospel. For the Refutation of Bigotry and Infidelity. . . . Pagination irregular. Dayton, O., 1835. WRHist.

Van Vleet, Abram. An Account of the Conduct of the Shakers. Lebanon, O., Van Vleet & Camron, 1818. From *The Other Side of the Question,* 1819, p. 3.

A Vindication of the Truth, being a Review of a Sermon Delivered by Joshua L. Wilson, D. D., . . . By a Member of the Enon Baptist Church, in Cincinnati. 38 pp. N. p. (Cincinnati), Morgan, Fisher, & L'Hommedieu, Printers, February, 1828. WRHist.

Walker, James. A Discourse, Delivered at the Ordination of the Rev. Ephraim Peabody, over the First Congregational Church in Cincinnati, May 20, 1832. 45 pp. Cincinnati, Hubbard and Edmands, 1832. WRHist.

Walker, John. A Treatise on Baptism: being a Reply to a Book Entitled A Debate on Christian Baptism, between Mr. John Walker & Alexander Campbell, . . . June, 1820. To which is Added a Letter to the Rev. Samuel Ralston. [2], 274, [1] pp. Mountpleasant, O., B. Wright & B. Bates, Printers, 1824. WRHist.

——, and Alexander Campbell. Infant Sprinkling Proved to be a Human Tradition; being the Substance of a Debate on Christian Baptism, between Mr. John Walker, a Minister of the Secession, and Alexander

Campbell, V. D. M. a Regular Baptist Minister; Held at Mount Pleasant, . . . Ohio, . . . June 1820, . . . [2], 216 pp. Steubenville, O., Printed by James Wilson, 1820. TransylvaniaU, WRHist.

West, George Montgomery. Address of the Rev. George Montgomery West, A. M., Chaplain to the Bishop of Ohio, on the Completion of his Mission to Europe, . . . 9 pp. N. p., 1830. HistPSO.

—— Pope Peter the First, versus All his Infallible Successors, being a Letter Addressed to "J. K. L." . . . 15 pp. London, Printed at the School-press, Gower's Walk, 1829. HistPSO.

—— Substance of a Discourse, Delivered in St. Mark's Church, Liverpool, on Sunday, the 22d of February, 1829, by the Rev. George Montgomery West, A. M., Chaplain to the Bishop of Ohio, on the Subject of his Mission to this Country. . . . 47 pp. Liverpool, Printed and Sold by Thos. Kaye, n. d. HistPSO.

—— Substance of a Discourse Delivered in Stokesley Church, Cleveland, Yorkshire, . . . 1829, . . . on the Subject of his Mission to this Country. . . . 36 pp. London, J. & C. Rivington, etc., 1829. HistPSO.

Wilson, Joshua Lacy. Episcopal Methodism; or Dagonism Exhibited. In Five Scenes. . . . 82 pp. Cincinnati, Printed by J. Carpenter & Co., 1811. ChU, WRHist.

—— The Faith Kept: or Recollections of Rev. Daniel Hayden, . . . 12 pp. Cincinnati, Printed by James and Gazlay, 1835. WRHist.

—— Four Propositions Sustained against the Claims of the American Home Missionary Society. 19 pp. Cincinnati, Published for the Author, Robinson & Fairbank, Printers, 1831. BurColl, WRHist.

—— Imputation of Sin and Righteousness. A Sermon

from Rom. 5 : 18, 19. 21 pp. Hanover, Ind., Printed
at the Hanover College Press, 1835. LaneTS.

—— A Letter Addressed to R. H. Bishop, D. D., President
of Miami University, on the Subject of his ''Plea for
United Christian Action ;'' . . . 14 pp. Cincinnati,
Lodge, L'Hommedieu & Co., Printers, 1835. CinPL,
LaneTS, NYPL, WRHist.

—— One Proposition Sustained against the New School.
16 pp. Cincinnati, Printed by Lodge, L'Hommedieu
and Co., 1835. LaneTS.

—— Relation and Duties of Servants and Masters ; . . .
32 pp. Cincinnati, Isaac Hefley & Co., 1839. ChU,
WRHist.

—— The Testimony of Three who Bear Witness in Earth,
on the Fact and Mode of Purification : a Sermon Delivered in Lebanon, Ohio, August 19, 1827. 14 pp. Cincinnati, Printed by Morgan, Fisher, and L'Hommedieu,
1827. LaneTS.

—— War, the Work of the Lord, and the Coward Cursed ;
a Sermon, . . . 12 pp. Cincinnati, Printed by J.
Carpenter & Co., 1812. WRHist. 12 pp. Cincinnati,
Printed ; Concord, N. H., Reprinted by I. and W. R.
Hill, 1812. LC, WRHist. 12 pp. Plattsburg, N. Y.,
Reprinted by A. C. Flagg, 1812. WRHist.

—— Wilson's Plea in the Case of Lyman Beecher, D. D.,
Made before the Synod of Cincinnati, October, 1835.
120 pp. Cincinnati, Printed by R. P. Brooks, April,
1837. LaneTS, WRHist.

——, and David Nelson. A Correspondence between Reverend David Nelson, M.D. and J. L. Wilson. . . .
12 pp. Cincinnati (Lodge, L'Hommedieu & Co., Printers), 1834. WRHist.

Wilson, Robert G. The Great Question Answered : or, the
Pure Doctrines of the Cross, Exhibited and Explained.
In Two Parts. . . . 23 pp. Chillicothe, Reprinted

at the Office of the Weekly Recorder, by John Andrews, 1814. WRHist.

—— The Nature and Duty of Rejoicing in the Lord. A Sermon Preached in Chillicothe, February 8th, 1815. In Grateful Remembrance of the Victory Obtained by Major General Jackson over the British Forces, at New-Orleans on the 8th ultimo. 21 pp. Chillicothe, Printed by John Andrews, 1815. ChU.

Woods, John. Shakerism Unmasked, or, a Narrative, Showing the Entrance of the Shakers into the Western Country, their Stratagems and Devices, Discipline and Economy; . . . 84 pp. Paris, Ky., Office of the Western Observer, 1826. LC.

Woodward, E. A Brief View of Methodist Episcopacy, in which their Arbitrary and Unscriptural Form of Government as Laid down in the Discipline of 1828, is clearly Brought to Light. 40 pp. Lexington, Printed by Herndon & Savary, 1831. ChU.

Wylie, Andrew. The Blessedness of the Pious Dead, a Sermon Preached April 12th, 1829, on the Occasion of the Death of Mrs. Elizabeth Brady. 28 pp. New York, John P. Haven, 1829. IndStL.

—— The Danger and Duty of the Young, a Sermon, Preached to the Senior Class . . . Indiana College. 15 pp. Pittsburg, Printed by William Allinder, 1837. IndStL.

—— The Perfect Man; a Sermon Occasioned by the Death of Jonathan Nichols, President of the Board of Trustees of Indiana College. 22 pp. Bloomington, Ind., Printed at the Office of the Equator, 1839. IndStL.

—— Religion and State; not Church and State. A Sermon on Psalm 11, 10-12. Delivered, July Fourth 1830. In the Hall of the Indiana College, Bloomington; . . . 16 pp. N. p., n. d. IU.

—— Sectarianism is Heresy, [?] in Three Parts, in which are

Shewn, its Nature, Evils, and Remedy: . . . 132 pp. Bloomington, Ind., 1840. IndStL, IU, LaneTS.

—— Sermon on the Subject of the Union of Christians for the Conversion of the World, Delivered in Madison, Ia., April 20, 1834, . . . 17 pp. Madison, Ind., Printed by J. Lodge & E. Patrick, 1834. IU.

Youngs, Benjamin Seth. The Testimony of Christ's Second Appearing Containing a General Statement of All Things Pertaining to the Faith and Practice of the Church of God in this Latter-day . . . 400, [2] pp. (Pagination varies in different copies.) Lebanon, O., from the Press of John M'Clean, 1808. LexPL, LC, WRHist. 3d ed., corrected and improved. xxvi, 573, [3] pp. Union Village, O., B. Fisher and A. Burnett, Printers, 1823. WRHist, WisH.

—— Transactions of the Ohio Mob, Called in the Public Papers, "An Expedition against the Shakers." 11 pp. N. p., n. d. (1810?). LC, WRHist, WisH.

III. Popular Accounts of Trials and Public Appeals Relating to Them

Argument on Behalf of the Claimants in the Claim of the Representatives of Jaques Clamorgan, to a Tract on the Rivers Cuivre and Dardenne, in the State of Missouri. 19 pp. N. p., n. d. MoHist.

Beauchamp, Jereboam, and Ann Beauchamp. The Confession of Jereboam O. Beauchamp. Who was Executed at Frankfort, Ky. on the 7th of July, 1826. For the Murder of Col. Solomon P. Sharp, a Member of the Legislature, and Late Attorney General of Ky. Written by himself, . . . To which is Added, Some Poetical Pieces, Written by Mrs. Ann Beauchamp, . . . 134 pp. Bloomfield, Ky., Printed for the Publisher, 1826. ChU.

A Concise Statement of the Trial & Confession of William Clutter, who was Executed on Friday the 8th June, 1810, at Boone Court-house, Kentucky, for the Murder of John Farmer. To which is Prefixed a Short Sketch of his Life. . . . 8 pp. Cincinnati, John W. Browne & Company, 1810. ChU.

Examination of the Decision of Judge James Clark; in the Case of Williams against Blair. 48 pp. Frankfort, Printed by J. H. Holeman, 1822. TransylvaniaU.

Gazlay, James. Report of the Case of Thomas Graham, of Cincinnati, in the State of Ohio, Indicted for Perjury, . . . Reported by a Gentleman of the Bar, . . . 22 pp. Cincinnati, Stephen Curcier, 1821. WRHist.

Goodenow, John M. Historical Record of the Proceedings of the Court of Common Pleas, and 'the Bar' of Hamilton County, Ohio, in Reference to the Appointment of Clerk of Said Court; 1833 and 1834; . . . xvi, 171 pp. Cincinnati, 1834. HistPSO, WRHist, WisH.

Graham, Thomas. Villany Unmasked. A Reply by Thomas Graham, to a Pretended Report of his Case, by James W. Gazlay, alias "a Gentleman of the Bar." 40 pp. Cincinnati, Printed by Morgan, Lodge & Co., 1821. WRHist.

Hammond, Charles. The State of the Case and Argument for the Appellants, in the Case of the Bank of the United States, versus the Auditor and Treasurer of the State of Ohio, and Others, in the Supreme Court of the United States. 98 pp. Cincinnati, Morgan and Lodge, Printers, 1823. WRHist.

Lincoln, William S. Alton Trials: . . . for the Crime of Riot, Committed on the Night of the 7th of November, 1837, while Engaged in Defending a Printing Press, from an Attack Made on it at that Time, by an Armed Mob. . . . Also, the Trial . . . for a Riot Committed in Alton, on the Night of the 7th of November, 1837, in unlawfully and forcibly Entering the Warehouse of Godfrey, Gilman & Co., and Breaking up and Destroying a Printing Press. Written out from Notes Taken at the Time of the Trial, . . . 158 pp. New York, John F. Trow, 1838. WRHist, WisH.

Lockwood, R. A. Speech of R. A. Lockwood, Esq., Delivered in Defence of J. H. W. Frank, at the October Term of the Tippecanoe Circuit Court, 1837. 76 pp. Indianapolis, Bolton and Livingston, 1837. IndStL.

Marshall, Humphrey. A Report of the Case, Nicholds, &c. against Wells; being that of a Treasury Warrant, Opposed to a County Court Pre-emption; as Argued and Adjudged in the Court of Appeals. State of Kentucky. 66 pp. Frankfort, Printed by James M. Bradford, 1803. ChU, TransylvaniaU.

Nelson, T. Somers. A Full and Accurate Report of the Trial of William P. Darnes, on an Indictment Found by the Grand Jury of the County of St. Louis, at the September Term, 1840, . . . by a Member of the St. Louis Bar. 248 pp. St. Louis, at All Booksellers, 1840. From copy supplied by William Clark Breckenridge.

Papers Relating to the Clamorgan Grant. 41 pp. N. p., n. d. MoHist, WRHist.

Reid, Joseph B., and Henry R. Reeder. Trial of Rev. John B. Mahan, for Felony. In the Mason Circuit Court of Kentucky. . . . November, 1838. Reported by Joseph B. Reid and Henry R. Reeder, Esqs. 88 pp. Cincinnati, Samuel A. Alley, Printer, 1838. ChU, WRHist.

Sharp, Leander J. Vindication of the Character of the Late Col. Solomon P. Sharp, from the Calumnies Published against him since his Murder, by Patrick Darby and Jereboam O. Beauchamp. 140 pp. Frankfort, Printed by Amos Kendall and Company, 1827. ChU.

Smith, Jesse. Trial of Samuel Daviess, for the Murder of Henry Pendleton Smith, at a Court Held in Harrodsburg, September Term, 1818; . . . 104 pp. Frankfort, Printed by Kendall and Russells, 1819. ChU.

Sundry Letters and Petitions Addressed to His Excellency James Garrard, Esq. Governor of Kentucky: Relative to the Case of Henry Field. 32 pp. (1799? — lower part of title-page missing.) WisH.

Title Papers of the Clamorgan Grant, of 536,904 Arpens of Alluvial Lands in Missouri and Arkansas. 24 pp. New York, Printed by T. Snowden, 1837. MoHist, WRHist.

Turner, G. (joint author). The Trial of Charles Vattier, Convicted of the Crime of Burglary and Larceny, for Stealing from the Office of the Receiver of Public Monies, for the District of Cincinnati, . . . Reported from Notes Taken in Court, by Two Gentlemen of Law-knowledge . . . lvii, 153, [1] pp. Cincinnati, David L. Carney, 1807. Title from printed title-page in MS. record of copyrights for District of Ohio, 1806-1828; MS. entry dated July 21, Thirty-third year of the Independence of the United States. Here G. Turner is named as "part reporter and Sole proprietor." Paging from restored copy in WRHist.

Vaughan, John C. Argument of John C. Vaughan, Esq., at the Trial of the Rev. John B. Mahan, for Felony, in the Mason Circuit Court of Kentucky, . . . 1838. 21 pp. Cincinnati, Samuel A. Alley, Printer, 1838. WRHist.

IV. MISCELLANEOUS DEBATE AND PROPAGANDA

Baird, H. S. An Address, Delivered at a Public Installation of the Officers of Menomine Lodge, at Green-Bay, Michigan, December 27th, A. L. 5826. 18 pp. Detroit, Sheldon and Wells, 1827. WisH.

Bates, Frederick. An Oration, Delivered before Saint Louis Lodge, No. 111. At the Town of Saint Louis . . . the 9th Day of November, 1808, . . . St. Louis, Printed by Joseph Charless, 1809. From copy (made from an auction catalogue facsimile) supplied by William Clark Breckenridge.

Burgess, Dyer. Solomon's Temple Haunted, or Free Masonry, the Man of Sin, in the Temple of God. An Address Delivered by the Rev. Dyer Burgess, at the Anti-Masonic Meeting, Held at the Court House, West Union, Adams County, Ohio, on the 1st of June 1830. 12 pp. N. p., n. d. LaneTS.

Burnet, George W. An Oration, Delivered to the Masonic Society in Cincinnati, on the Anniversary of St. John, the Evangelist. . . . December 27th, A. L. 5798. 15 pp. Cincinnati, Printed by Joseph Carpenter, 1799. From Thomson.

Caldwell, Charles. A Discourse on the Vice of Gambling, Delivered, by Appointment, to the Anti-gambling Society of Transylvania University, November 2nd and 3rd, 1835, . . . 59 pp. Lexington, J. Clarke & Co., Printers, 1835. ChU.

—— Thoughts on Schools of Medicine, their Means of Instruction, and Modes of Administration, with References to the Schools of Louisville and Lexington. 31 pp. Louisville, Prentice and Weissinger, 1837. ChU.

—— Thoughts on the Impolicy of Multiplying Schools of Medicine. 35 pp. Lexington, Printed by J. Clarke & Co., 1834. ChU.

Chase, Philander. Christianity and Masonry Reconciled. A Sermon, Preached before . . . the Grand Lodge of Ohio, in Chillicothe, . . . 1817. Also before the Most Excellent Grand Chapter of the Same State, in Columbus, . . . 1817. 23 pp. Columbus, Printed by Ezra Griswold, Jun., 1818. WRHist.

Cincinnati Whig and Commercial Intelligencer — Extra. An Inquiry into the Causes that have Retarded the Prosperity of the Medical College of Ohio. 42 pp. N. p., n. d. LaneTS.

Cross, James Conquest. Refutation of Charges Made by Dr. Caldwell, through the Columns of the Louisville Journal, against Professor James C. Cross, of Transylvania University. 15 pp. Lexington, Observer & Reporter Print, 1838. WisH.

——Thoughts on the Policy of Establishing a School of Medicine in Louisville, together with a Sketch of the Present Condition and Future Prospects of the Medical Department of Transylvania University. 113 pp. Lexington, Printed by N. L. Finnell, 1834. LexPL.

Curtis, H. B. An Oration Delivered before the Mansfield Lodge, No. 35, at Mansfield, Ohio, . . . June 25, 1827. From *The Western Monthly Review*, I, 192 (July, 1827). Copy in WRHist not collated.

Davies, Samuel W. A Refutation of Sundry Unfounded Accusations, Contained in Letters and Communications, from Dr. Daniel Drake, to a Committee of the Third District Medical Society. To the Public. 8 pp. N. p. (Cincinnati?), n. d. (1833?). Smith, WRHist.

Drake, Daniel. An Appeal to the Justice of the Intelligent and Respectable People of Lexington. 23 pp. Cincinnati, Looker, Reynolds & Co., Printers, 1818. HistPSO.

—— Communication from Doctor Drake. To the Honorable the General Assembly of the State of Ohio. 20 pp. N. p., n. d. (1833?). HistPSO.

—— A Discourse on Intemperance; Delivered at Cincinnati, March 1, 1828, before the Agricultural Society of Hamilton County, and subsequently Pronounced, by Request, to a Popular Audience. 96 pp. Cincinnati, Looker & Reynolds, Printers, 1828. HistPSO, NYPL, WRHist.

—— Extracts, from the Western Journal of the Medical and Physical Sciences. . . . Addressed to the Legislators, Editors, Physicians, and Students of Medicine, of Ohio, . . . Cincinnati, Jan. 8, 1834. 7 pp. N. p. (Cincinnati?), n. d. (1834?). WRHist.

—— A Narrative of the Rise and Fall of the Medical College of Ohio. 42 pp. Cincinnati, Looker & Reynolds, Printers, 1822. Harvard, HistPSO.

—— ? The People's Doctors; a Review, by 'the People's Friend.' . . . 60 pp. Cincinnati, Printed and Published for the Use of the People, 1829. HistPSO.

—— A Second Appeal to the Justice of the Intelligent and Respectable People of Lexington. 34 pp. Cincinnati, Looker, Reynolds & Co., Printers, 1818. CinPL, HistPSO, WRHist.

Foster, Fisher A. Popular Virtue Essential to Popular Freedom. The Substance of an Address, Delivered before the Zanesville Temperance Society, February 23d, 1836. 16 pp. Zanesville, O., Printed by Parke and Bennett, 1836. WRHist.

Harrison, John P. Intellectual and Moral Benefits Resulting to Young Men from Connection with the Temperance Society. 12 pp. Louisville, 1834. From Smith catalogue.

Haskin, J. J. Haskin's Defence of his Conduct and Opinions in Relation to Dr. John A. Tomlinson, in Reply to an Attack Made upon him by Doctor Tomlinson, in a Pamphlet recently Published, Entitled "Vindication," &c. 53, [1] pp. Danville, Ky., Printed at the Office of the Olive Branch, 1823. ChU.

Henry, John F. An Exposure of the Conduct, of the Trustees and Professors of the Medical College of Ohio, and of the Hospital or Township Trustees, in Relation to John F. Henry, M. D. 20, [2] pp. Cincinnati, Wood & Stratton, Printers, 1833. Smith, WRHist.

Hersey, Thomas. Clericus, Esculapius, and Scepticus, vs. Col. M. Jewett and his Chemical Preparations. In Two Parts. . . . 180 pp. Columbus, 1835. HistPSO, LC, WRHist.

Hunt, William Gibbes. A Masonic Oration, Pronounced before the Companions of the Royal Arch Chapter, . . . at Lexington, Kentucky, on the 27th Day of December, A. L. 5816, . . . 12 pp. Lexington, Printed by Thomas T. Skillman, 1817. ChU.

Jackson, David. To the Public. 22 pp. N. p., n. d. (1826?). ChU.

Kendall, Amos. An Address on the Principles of Masonry, Delivered in the Church at Frankfort, Kentucky, . . . 1823, . . . 14 pp. Frankfort, Printed by Amos Kendall and Company, 1823. TransylvaniaU.

The Literary Pamphleteer, Containing: Some Observations on the Best Mode of Promoting the Cause of Literature in the State of Kentucky; and a Review of the Late Administration of the Transylvania University. . . . Humbly Addressed to the Citizens and Legislature of Kentucky, . . . Nos. I-VI, 16 pp. each. Paris, Ky., Lyle & Keenon, 1823. ChU, WisH (lacks Nos. III and V).

McCalla, John M. Address Delivered at the Celebration of the Fiftieth Anniversary of the Lexington Light Infantry Company. 16 pp. Lexington, J. C. Noble, Printer, 1839. ChU.

Maclure, William. Opinions on Various Subjects, Dedicated to the Industrious Producers. 3 vols. New Harmony, Ind., Printed at the School Press, 1831-1838. IU, TransylvaniaU, WRHist. Copies vary.

Mayo, H. B. An Address Delivered in the Presbyterian Church, Oxford, at the Request of the Oxford Temperance Society August 2, 1838, . . . 18 pp. Oxford, O., Printed by R. H. Bishop, Jun., 1838. WRHist.

Moore, James, and Cary L. Clarke. Masonic Constitutions, or Illustrations of Masonry; Compiled by the Direction of the Grand Lodge of Kentucky, . . . 192 pp. Lexington, Printed by Daniel Bradford, 1808. LexPL, LC. 2d ed. 218 pp. Lexington, Printed by Worsley & Smith, 1818. LC, TransylvaniaU.

Owen, Robert. Oration, Containing a Declaration of Mental Independence, Delivered in the Public Hall, at New-Harmony, Ind., by Robert Owen, at the Celebration of the Fourth of July, 1826. 4 pp. N. p., n. d. WRHist.

The Plan of Reform in Transylvania University. Two Letters. One Addressed to the Academical Faculty and Board of Trustees; the Other to Horace Holley, L. L. D. [sic] President. . . . By Omicron. From the Country — a Friend to Reform. 16 pp. Lexington, 1824. ChU, WisH.

President Holley — not the Transylvania University, in a Letter to William Gibbes Hunt, Esq. in Consequence of the Attacks Made by him in his "Appeal," Published in the Western Monitor of this Place, March 2d, 1824. By Forthcoming. 18 pp. Lexington, Ky., Printed by J. M. M'Calla, 1824. LexPL.

Rankin, John. A Review of the Statement of the Faculty of Lane Seminary, in Relation to the Recent Difficulties in that Institution; . . . 8 pp. Ripley, O., the Author, Campbell & Palmer, Printers, 1835. WRHist, WisH.

Report of the Committee Appointed by the Citizens of Cincinnati, April 26, 1838, to Enquire into the Causes of the Explosion of the Moselle, . . . 76 pp. Cincinnati, Alexander Flash, 1838. HistPSO, WRHist.

Schoolcraft, Henry Rowe. An Address Delivered before the Chippewa County Temperance Society, on the Influence of Ardent Spirits, on the Condition of the North

American Indians. . . . May 8th, 1832. 13 pp. Detroit, Printed by Geo. L. Whitney, 1832. BurColl.

Smith, Delazon. A History of Oberlin, or New Lights of the West. Embracing the Conduct and Character of the Officers and Students of the Institution; . . . 82 pp. Cleveland, S. Underhill & Son, Printers, 1837. From LC card. In WRHist.

A Statement of the Reasons which Induced the Students of Lane Seminary, to Dissolve their Connection with that Institution. 28 pp. Cincinnati, 1834. WRHist.

Storer, Bellamy. An Address Delivered before the Cincinnati Temperance Society, on the Twenty-sixth Day of February, 1833, . . . 16 pp. Cincinnati, Printed by F. S. Benton, 1833. WRHist.

Tannehill, Wilkins. The Masonic Manual, or, Freemasonry Illustrated; . . . 2d ed. 390 pp. Louisville, W. Harrison Johnston, Printer, 1840. ChU.

Thornton, Tho. Towles. Oration, on Behalf of the Paris Artillery Company, Delivered at Paris, Ky. on the 4th Day of July, 1835. 27 pp. Paris, Ky., Printed at the Western Citizen Office, 1835. LaneTS.

Tipton, John. Oration Delivered before Wayne Lodge No. 25, at Fort Wayne, Indiana, . . . June 24, 5825. 12 pp. N. p. (Vevay, Ind., Printed by Wm. C. Keen), n. d. IndStL.

Turner, George. An Oration, Pronounced before the Washington Benevolent Society of the County of Washington, State of Ohio, on the 22d. February, 1817. 12 pp. Marietta, O., Printed by Royal Prentiss, 1817. WRHist.

Yandell, Lunsford P. A Narrative of the Dissolution of the Medical Faculty of Transylvania University. 31, 10 pp. Nashville, Tenn., W. Hasell Hunt, Printer, 1837. ChU, IU.

Young, John C. An Address on Temperance; Delivered at the Court House in Lexington, Ky. 28 pp. Lexington, Printed for the Society, by T. T. & W. D. Skillman, 1834. LaneTS.

CHAPTER V

SCHOLARLY WRITINGS AND SCHOOLBOOKS

I. History

Atwater, Caleb. The General Character, Present and Future Prospects of the People of Ohio. An Address Delivered at the United States' Court House, . . . in Columbus, Ohio, December, 1826. 21 pp. Columbus, Printed by P. H. Olmsted & Co., 1827. IU, LaneTS, NYPL, WRHist.

—— A History of the State of Ohio, Natural and Civil. 403 pp. Cincinnati, Glezen & Shepard, n. d. (1838). ChU, CinPL, WRHist.

Balestier, Joseph N. The Annals of Chicago; a Lecture Delivered before the Chicago Lyceum, January 21, 1840. 24 pp. Chicago, Edward H. Rudd, Printer, 1840. WisH.

Biddle, John. A Discourse, Delivered on the Anniversary of the Historical Society of Michigan, September, 1832. . . . 31 pp. Detroit, Printed by Geo. L. Whitney, 1832. BurColl, WRHist.

Bishop, Robert Hamilton. An Outline of the History of the Church in the State of Kentucky, during a Period of Forty Years: Containing the Memoirs of Rev. David Rice, . . . 420 pp. Lexington, Thomas T. Skillman, 1824. ChU, CinPL, HistPSO, IU, LexPL, LouPL, NYPL, WRHist.

Bullard, Artemas. Historical Sketch of the First Presbyterian Church in Saint Louis. A Sermon, Preached in the First Presbyterian Church of Saint Louis, Missouri, on the First Sabbath of 1839.   24 pp.   St. Louis, Churchill & Ramsey, Printers, 1839.   WisH.

Butler, Mann. An Appeal from the Misrepresentations of James Hall, respecting the History of Kentucky and the West. . . . 32 pp. Frankfort, Printed by Albert G. Hodges, 1837. ChU, LC, WisH.

—— A History of the Commonwealth of Kentucky. xi, 396 pp. Louisville, Wilcox, Dickerman & Co., for the Author, 1834. ChU, CinPL, IU, LexPL, LC, LouPL, TransylvaniaU, WRHist, WisH.

Cass, Lewis. A Discourse, Delivered at the First Meeting of the Historical Society of Michigan. September 18, 1829. Published at their Request. 52 pp. Detroit, Printed by Geo. L. Whitney, 1830. BurColl, CinPL, NewL.

—— A Discourse Pronounced at the Capitol of the United States, in the Hall of Representatives, before the American Historical Society, January 30, 1836, . . . 58 pp. Washington, 1836. BurColl, ChU, CinPL, IU, LC, WRHist, WisH.

Celebration of the Forty-fifth Anniversary of the First Settlement of Cincinnati and the Miami Country, on the 26th Day of December, 1833, by Natives of Ohio. 52 pp. Cincinnati, Shreve & Gallagher, 1834. HistPSO, WRHist, WisH.

Celebration of the Forty-seventh Anniversary of the First Settlement of the State of Ohio, by Native Citizens. 74 pp. Cincinnati, Printed by Lodge, L'Hommedieu and Co., 1835. WRHist, WisH.

Celebration, upon the Battle Ground, of the Twenty-fourth Anniversary of the Battle of Tippecanoe. . . . Lafayette, Indiana, November 9, 1835. 24 pp. N. p., n. d. HistPSO.

Chase, Salmon P. A Sketch of the History of Ohio. 40 pp. Cincinnati, Corey and Fairbank, 1833. WRHist, WisH.

Conover, James F., and Thomas Shreve. Oration, on the History of the First Discovery and Settlement of the New World, with Especial Reference to the Mississippi Valley, etc., Delivered before the Cincinnati Literary Society, at its Fourth Anniversary Celebration, by James F. Conover, Esq. An Ode, Delivered on the Same Occasion, by Mr. Thomas H. Shreve. 32 pp. Cincinnati, Published by the Society, and Josiah Drake, 1835. HistPSO.

Dickey, John M. A Brief History of the Presbyterian Church in the State of Indiana, . . . 24 pp. Madison, Ind., Printed by C. P. J. Arion, n. d. (1828?). From photostat copy (IndStL) of original in possession of the Presbyterian Historical Society, Philadelphia.

Drown, Solomon. An Oration, Delivered at Marietta, April 7, 1789, in Commemoration of the Commencement of the Settlement Formed by the Ohio Company. 17 pp. Worcester, Mass., Printed by Isaiah Thomas, 1789. CinPL, LC, NYPL, WRHist.

Ells, B. F. A History of the Romish Inquisition. Compiled from Various Authors. 120 pp. Hanover, Ind., Monfort & M'Millan, Printers, 1835. Harvard, IndStL, WRHist.

Finley, James B. History of the Wyandott Mission, at Upper Sandusky, Ohio, under the Direction of the Methodist Episcopal Church. 432 pp. Cincinnati, J. F. Wright and L. Swormstedt, 1840. NYPL, WRHist, WisH.

Flint, Timothy. Indian Wars of the West; Containing Biographical Sketches of those Pioneers who Headed the Western Settlers in Repelling the Attacks of the Savages, together with a View of the Character, Manners, Monuments, and Antiquities of the West rn Indians. 240 pp. Cincinnati, E. H. Flint, 1833. BurColl, ChU, CinPL, ColU, HistPSO, IndStL, IU, KyStL, NewL, NYPL, OhioStL, WRHist, WisH, YMML.

Griswold, Stanley. The Exploits of our Fathers, or a Concise History of the Military Events of our Revolutionary War an Oration Delivered at Cincinnati (Ohio) July 3d, 1813 . . . 27 pp. Cincinnati, Printed by J. Carpenter & Co., n. d. HistPSO.

Hall, James. An Address Delivered before the Antiquarian and Historical Society of Illinois, at its Second Annual Meeting, in December, 1828, by James Hall, President of the Society. 20 pp. Vandalia, Ill., Printed by Robert Blackwell, 1829. WisH.

——, and Thomas L. McKenney. History of the Indian Tribes of North America, with Biographical Sketches and Anecdotes of the Principal Chiefs. Embellished with One Hundred and Twenty Portraits, from the Indian Gallery in the Department of War, at Washington. 3 vols. Philadelphia, Edward C. Biddle, 1836-1844. (Vol. I dated 1836.) WRHist.

Historical and Philosophical Society of Ohio. Circular. The Historical and Philosophical Society of Ohio, to ——. 8 pp. N. p., n. d. (1832?). WisH (title-page lacking?).

A History of the Destruction of Jerusalem, and the Desolation of Palestine, . . . Compiled from Milman, by a Citizen of Ohio. With Maps and Engravings. 432 pp. Steubenville, O., J. & B. Turnbull, 1833. From copy supplied by William Clark Breckenridge.

Lanman, James H. History of Michigan, Civil and Topographical, in a Compendious Form; with a View of the

Surrounding Lakes. xvi, 397, [1] pp. New York, E. French, 1839. BurColl, LC, WRHist.

Law, John. Address Delivered before the Vincennes Historical and Antiquarian Society, February 22, 1839. 48 pp. Louisville, Prentice and Weissinger, Printers, 1839. BurColl, ColU, IndStL, LC, NYPL, WRHist, WisH.

M'Afee, Robert B. History of the Late War in the Western Country, Comprising a Full Account of All the Transactions in that Quarter, from the Commencement of Hostilities at Tippecanoe, to the Termination of the Contest at New Orleans on the Return of Peace. viii, 534, [1] pp. Lexington, Worsley & Smith, 1816. ChU, CinPL, ColU, IndStL, KyStL, LC, OhioStL, WRHist, WisH, YMML.

M'Clung, John A. Sketches of Western Adventure: Containing an Account of the most Interesting Incidents Connected with the Settlement of the West, from 1755 to 1794: . . . 360 pp. Maysville, Ky., L. Collins, 1832. ChU, LC, WRHist. 360 pp. Philadelphia, Grigg & Elliot, 1832. LC, NYPL, WisH.

Marshall, Humphrey. The History of Kentucky. Exhibiting an Account of the Modern Discovery; Settlement; Progressive Improvement; Civil and Military Transactions; and the Present State of the Country. 2 vols. Frankfort, Geo: S. Robinson, Printer, 1824. ChU, CinPL, ColU, IndStL, IU, LC, NYPL, OhioStL, WRHist, WisH, YMML.

—— The History of Kentucky. Including an Account of the Discovery — Settlement — Progressive Improvement — Political and Military Events — and Present State of the Country. In Two Volumes. Vol. I, 5, [1], 407 pp. No more published. Frankfort, Printed by Henry Gore, 1812. ChU, CinPL, KyStL, WRHist, WisH.

Metcalf, Samuel L.   A Collection of Some of the most Interesting Narratives of Indian Warfare in the West, Containing an Account of the Adventures of Colonel Daniel Boone, one of the First Settlers of Kentucky, . . . To which is Added, an Account of the Expeditions of Genl's Harmer, Scott, Wilkinson, St. Clair, & Wayne. The Whole Compiled from the Best Authorities, . . . 270 pp. Lexington, Printed by William G. Hunt, 1821. ChU, CinPL, LC, WRHist, WisH.

Morehead, James Turner.   An Address in Commemoration of the First Settlement of Kentucky: Delivered at Boonesborough the 25th May, 1840, . . . 181 pp. Frankfort, A. G. Hodges, 1840. BurColl, ChU, LexPL, LC, NYPL, WisH.

Proceedings of the Buckeye Celebration, in Commemoration of the Day on which General St. Clair Named 'Fort Hamilton'; at Hamilton, Ohio, on the Thirtieth Day of September, 1835. 60 pp. N. p., n. d. WisH.

Ripley, Charles.   An Oration, on the Colonization of New England, Delivered December 22, 1838, before the Pilgrim Society of Louisville. 44 pp. Louisville, Prentice and Weissinger, 1839. MoHist.

Ruter, Martin. A Concise History of the Christian Church, from its First Establishment to the Present Time; . . . Compiled from the Works of Dr. G. Gregory, with Numerous Additions and Improvements. 447 pp. New York, B. Waugh and T. Mason, for the Methodist Episcopal Church, 1834. HistPSO.

—— The Martyrs, or a History of Persecution, from the Commencement of Christianity to the Present Time: . . . Compiled from the Works of Fox and Others. 561, [3] pp. Cincinnati, R. Houck, 1830. WRHist. 561, [3] pp. Cincinnati, E. Deming, Printer, etc., 1834. WRHist.

Schoolcraft, Henry Rowe. A Discourse, Delivered on the Anniversary of the Historical Society of Michigan, June 4, 1830. . . . 44 pp. Detroit, Geo. L. Whitney, 1830. BurColl, NYPL, WRHist, WisH.

Smith, James. A Treatise, on the Mode and Manner of Indian War, their Tactics, Discipline and Encampments, the Various Methods they Practise, . . . Also — a Brief Account of Twenty-three Campaigns, Carried on against the Indians with the Events, since the Year 1755; Gov. Harrison's Included. By Col. James Smith. Likewise — Some Abstracts Selected from his Journal, while in Captivity with the Indians, Relative to the Wars: which was Published Many Years Ago, but Few of them now to be Found. 59 pp. Paris, Ky., Printed by Joel R. Lyle, 1812. ChU, WisH.

Stipp, G. W. The Western Miscellany, or, Accounts Historical, Biographical, and Amusing. Compiled by G. W. Stipp. 224 pp. Xenia, O., Printed for the Compiler, 1827. WRHist, WisH.

Tappan, Benjamin. A Discourse Delivered before the Historical & Philosophical Society of Ohio, at the Annual Meeting of Said Society, in Columbus, December 22, 1832. 16 pp. Columbus, J. R. Emrie, Printer, 1833. LC, WRHist, WisH.

Taylor, John. A History of Ten Baptist Churches, of which the Author has been alternately a Member: in which will be Seen something of a Journal of the Author's Life, for More than Fifty Years. Also: a Comment on Some Parts of Scripture; . . . 300 pp. Frankfort, Printed by J. H. Holeman, 1823. ChU, TransylvaniaU, WisH.

Wakefield, John A. History of the War between the United States and the Sac and Fox Nations of Indians, . . . in the Years Eighteen Hundred and Twenty-

seven, Thirty-one, and Thirty-two. x, 142 pp. Jacksonville, Ill., Printed by Calvin Goudy, 1834. ChU, LC,
WisH.

Walker, Timothy. Annual Discourse, Delivered before the
Ohio Historical and Philosophical Society, at Columbus,
on the 23d of December, 1837. 27 pp. Cincinnati, A.
Flash, 1838. LC, WRHist, WisH.

—— Discourse on the History and General Character of
the State of Ohio, before the Ohio Historical and Philosophical Society. 27 pp. Columbus, 1838. From
Thomson.

Whiting, Henry. A Discourse, Delivered on the Anniversary of the Historical Society of Michigan, June, 1831.
40 pp. Detroit, Printed by Geo. L. Whitney, 1831.
WRHist.

Wickliffe, Robert, Jr. ? Machiavel's Political Discourses
upon the First Decade of Livy. Interspersed with Various Reflections. 29 pp. Louisville, Prentice and Weissinger, 1840. ChU.

Wylie, Andrew. A Discourse Delivered before the Indiana Historical Society, in the Hall of the House of
Representatives at its Annual Meeting, on Saturday,
11th, Dec. 1831. 26 pp. Indianapolis, A. F. Morrison,
Printer, 1831. HistPSO, IndStL, WisH.

Zeisberger, David. The History of our Lord and Saviour
Jesus Christ: Comprehending All that the Four Evan-
gelists have Recorded concerning Him; . . . By the
Rev. Samuel Lieberkuhn, M.A. Translated into the Delaware Indian Language by the Rev. David Zeisberger,
Missionary of the United Brethren. viii, 222 pp. New
York, Printed by Daniel Fanshaw, 1821. (Zeisberger's
address to the Indians is dated Goshen, on the Muskingum, 23d May, 1806.) WRHist.

II. Biography

Black Hawk. Life of Ma-Ka-Tai-Me-She-Kia-Kiak or Black Hawk, Embracing the Tradition of his Nation — . . . With an Account of the Cause and General History of the Late War, his Surrender . . . and Travels through the United States. Dictated by himself. J. B. Patterson, of Rock Island, Ill. Editor and Proprietor. 155 pp. Boston, Russell, Odiorne & Metcalf, etc., 1834. CinPL, LC, WRHist.

Caldwell, Charles. A Discourse Commemorative of Philip Syng Physick, M. D. Prepared by Appointment of the Faculty and Class of the Louisville Medical Institute, and Delivered January 12th, 1838. 41 pp. Louisville, Prentice & Weissinger, 1838. ChU, IU.

—— A Discourse on the Genius and Character of the Rev. Horace Holley, LL.D. Late President of Transylvania University, . . . viii, 294 pp. Boston, Hilliard, Gray, Little, and Wilkins, 1828. HistPSO, JCrerar, LouPL, NYPL, USBurEd, WRHist, WisH.

Campbell, John Wilson. Biographical Sketches; with Other Literary Remains of the Late John W. Campbell, Judge of the United States Court for the District of Ohio. Compiled by his Widow. [4], 279 pp. Columbus, Printed for the Publisher by Scott & Gallagher, 1838. ChU, CinPL, HistPSO, NYPL, WRHist, WisH.

Corry, William M. Eulogy on William M'Millan, Esq. Pronounced . . . October 28, 1837. . . . 41 pp. Cincinnati, 1838. CinPL, WRHist, WisH.

Dawson, Moses. A Historical Narrative of the Civil and Military Services of Major-General William H. Harrison, and a Vindication of his Character and Conduct as a Statesman, a Citizen, and a Soldier. . . . viii, 464, [8] pp. Cincinnati, Printed by M. Dawson, 1824. ChU, CinPL, ColU, IndStL, LC, NewL, WRHist, WisH.

—— Sketches of the Life of Martin Van Buren, President of the United States . . . 216 pp. Cincinnati, J. W. Ely, 1840. CinPL, WRHist, WisH.

Drake, Benjamin. The Life and Adventures of Black Hawk: with Sketches of Keokuk, the Sac and Fox Indians, and the Late Black Hawk War. 252 pp. Cincinnati, George Conclin, 1838. HistPSO, WRHist. 288 pp. Cincinnati, George Conclin, 1839. ChU, CinPL, LC, WisH.

Filson, John. Life and Adventures of Colonel Daniel Boon, the First White Settler of the State of Kentucky. . . . Annexed, is an Eulogy on Col. Boon, and Choice of Life, by Lord Byron. 36 pp. Brooklyn, C. Wilder, 1823. NewL, WisH.

Flint, Timothy. Biographical Memoir of Daniel Boone, the First Settler of Kentucky. Interspersed with Incidents in the Early Annals of the Country. 267 pp. Cincinnati, N. & G. Guilford & Co., 1833. LC, NewL, WisH. 252 pp. Cincinnati, George Conclin, 1836. LexPL.

Gano, John. Biographical Memoirs of the Late Rev. John Gano, of Frankfort, (Kentucky.) Formerly of the City of New-York. Written principally by himself. 151 pp. New York, John Tiebout, 1806. ChU, LC, WRHist.

Glass, Francis. Georgii Washingtonii, Americæ Septentrionalis Civitatum Foederatarum Præsidis primi, vita, Francisco Glass, A. M. Ohioensi, litteris Latinis conscripta. . . . 223 pp. Neo-Eboracopoli, typis Fratrum Harperorum, MDCCCXXXV. HistPSO, IU, LC, WRHist, WisH.

Hall, James. A Memoir of the Public Services of William Henry Harrison, of Ohio. 323 pp. Philadelphia, Edward C. Biddle, 1836. BurColl, CinPL, HistPSO, IndStL, IU, LC, NewL, WRHist, WisH.

Hart, Cyrus W. Essay on Industry, and Biographical Sketches of Theopholus Radclipp and Emma Jones. By a Member of the Bar. 60 pp. Steubenville, O., Printed by James Wilson, 1835. HistPSO.

Howard, Jacob Merritt. A Discourse on the Life and Character of Washington, Delivered before the Detroit Young Men's Society, Feb. 22, 1839, . . . 32 pp. Detroit, Harsha & Bates, Printers, 1839. BurColl.

Johnson, Richard M. Outlines of the Life and Public Services, Civil and Military, of William Henry Harrison, of Ohio. . . . 21 pp. Washington, Thomas Allen, 1840. CinPL.

The Life of Bonaparte, Late Emperor of the French, &c. &c. &c. from his Birth until his Departure to the Island of St. Helena. By a Citizen of the United States. 257 pp. Salem, Ind., Printed by Patrick & Booth, 1818. IndStL, LC, MercLStL.

Lucas, John B. C. Biography of Charles Lucas, Esq. Late Attorney of the United States for the Missouri Territory. 16 pp. N. p., n. d. (1818?). MercLStL.

Lynd, Samuel W. Memoir of the Rev. William Staughton, D. D. 311, [1] pp. Boston, Lincoln, Edmands, & Co., etc., 1834. From LC card.

McDonald, John. Biographical Sketches of General Nathaniel Massie, General Duncan McArthur, Captain William Wells, and General Simon Kenton: who were Early Settlers in the Western Country. 267 pp. Cincinnati, for the Author, by E. Morgan and Son, 1838. ChU, CinPL, LC, NYPL, WRHist, WisH.

McLean, John. An Eulogy on the Character and Public Services of James Monroe, . . . Delivered in Cincinnati, August 27, 1831, . . . 32 pp. N. p. (Cincinnati), Looker and Reynolds, Printers, 1831. WRHist, WisH.

Marshall, Humphrey. Biography of Henry Clay . . .
By Geo. D. Prentice. Reviewed and Revised by Hum-
phrey Marshall, in Relation to himself and the Late Col.
J. H. Daviess, . . . 24 pp. N. p. (Maysville, Ky.,
Printed at the Monitor Office), n. d. (1832). ChU,
WisH.

Narrative of the Civil and Military Services of Wm. H.
Harrison. Compiled from the most Authentic Authori-
ties. . . . 72 pp. Cincinnati, Printed by Ormsby
H. Donogh, 1836. HistPSO.

Prentice, George Dennison. Biography of Henry Clay.
304 pp. Hartford, Conn., Samuel Hanmer, Jr. and
John Jay Phelps, 1831. ChU, ColU, LC, NYPL, WRHist.

Shaw, John Robert. A Narrative of the Life & Travels of
John Robert Shaw, the Well-digger, now Resident in
Lexington, Kentucky. Written by himself. 180 pp.
Lexington, Printed by Daniel Bradford, 1807. HistPSO,
LC.

A Sketch of the Life and Public Services of William Henry
Harrison. 36 pp. Columbus, Printed by Scott &
Wright, 1836. WRHist.

A Sketch of the Life and Public Services of William Henry
Harrison, with an Appendix Containing the Letters of
his Aids-de-camp John Chambers, John Speed Smith,
Charles S. Todd and John O'Fallon.— . . . 49, [1]
pp. Columbus, I. N. Whiting, 1840. CinPL, HistPSO,
WisH.

Swayze, William. Narrative of William Swayze, Minister
of the Gospel. Written by himself. . . . Volume I.
. . . 216 pp. (No more published?) Cincinnati, R. P.
Thompson, Printer, 1839. WRHist.

Thomas, Ebenezer Smith. Reminiscences of the Last Sixty-
five Years, Commencing with the Battle of Lexington.
Also, Sketches of his Own Life and Times. 2 vols.

Hartford, Conn., Printed by Case, Tiffany and Burnham, for the Author, 1840. ChU, CinPL, ColU, IU, LC, NYPL, WRHist, WisH.

Todd, Charles S., and Benjamin Drake. Sketches of the Civil and Military Services of William Henry Harrison. iii, 165 pp. Cincinnati, U. P. James, 1840. ChU, LC, NYPL, WRHist, WisH.

Walker, William. The Missionary Pioneer, or a Brief Memoir of the Life, Labours, and Death of John Stewart, (Man of Colour,) Founder, under God of the Mission among the Wyandotts at Upper Sandusky, Ohio. 96 pp. New York, Printed by J. C. Totten, 1827. HistPSO, WisH.

Williams, William. Journal of the Life, Travels, and Gospel Labours of William Williams, Dec. A Minister of the Society of Friends. Late of White-water, Indiana. 272 pp. Cincinnati, Lodge, L'Hommedieu, and Hammond, Printers, 1828. ChU, IndStL, WRHist.

III. SCIENCE

Atwater, Caleb. The Writings of Caleb Atwater. 408 pp. Columbus, the Author, Printed by Scott and Wright, 1833. ChU, CinPL, ColU, IndStL, NYPL, WRHist, WisH.

Buchanan, Joseph. The Philosophy of Human Nature. vi, 336 pp. Richmond, Ky., Printed by John A. Grimes, 1812. ChU, CinPL, KyStL, LexPL, LC, NYPL, TransylvaniaU, WisH.

Caldwell, Charles. Elements of Phrenology. viii, 100 pp. Lexington, Printed for the Author by Thomas T. Skillman, 1824. LC. 2d ed., greatly enlarged. viii, 279 pp. Lexington, Printed by A. G. Meriwether, 1827. ChU, CinPL, KyStL, LC, NewL, TransylvaniaU.

—— Essays on Malaria, and Temperament. vii, [2], 300

pp. Lexington, Printed by N. L. Finnell & J. F. Herndon, 1831. ChU, KyStL, LC, TransylvaniaU.

—— Medical and Physical Memoirs, . . . Memoirs I-III. [2], 224 pp. Lexington, Printed at the Office of the Kentucky Whig, 1826. ChU, LC.

—— Medical and Physical Memoirs. Memoirs IV-VI. 85 pp. Lexington, Printed by A. G. Meriwether, 1827. ChU.

—— Outlines of a Course of Lectures on the Institutes of Medicine. x, [1], 188 pp. Lexington, Printed by William Tanner, 1823. ChU, TransylvaniaU.

—— Phrenology Vindicated, and Antiphrenology Unmasked. 156, [1] pp. New York, Samuel Colman, 1838. LC, LouPL.

—— Phrenology Vindicated, in a Series of Remarks, . . . on Article VII, of the November Number, 1834, of the "Christian Examiner" . . . 93 pp. Lexington, J. Clarke & Co., Printers, 1835. Harvard, NewL.

—— Thoughts on Quarantine and Other Sanitary Systems, being an Essay which Received the Prize of the Boylston Medical Committee, of Harvard University, in August, 1834. 72 pp. Boston, Marsh, Capen & Lyon, 1834. LC, WisH.

—— Thoughts on the Changes and their Causes, which are perpetually Occurring in Material Creation. . . . Read in the Lexington Medical Society. From *The Western Monthly Review*, II, 528 (Feb., 1829).

—— Thoughts on the Original Unity of the Human Race. x, 178, [4] pp. New York, E. Bliss, 1830. CinPL, LC, NewL, WisH.

—— Thoughts on the True Mode of Improving the Condition of Man. . . . Read to the Lexington Medical Society, . . . 44 pp. Lexington, Printed by H. Savary & Co., 1833. LaneTS.

Cass, Lewis. An Historical, Geographical and Statistical

Account of the Island of Candia, or Ancient Crete. By the American Minister at Paris . . . 12 pp. Richmond, Va., from the Press of T. W. White, 1839. From LC card.

—— Inquiries respecting the History, Traditions, Languages, Manners, Customs, Religion, &c., of the Indians Living within the United States. 64 pp. Detroit, Printed by Sheldon & Reed, 1823. From *The North American Review*, XLV, 34 (July, 1837).

Cooke, John Esten. Essays on the Autumnal and Winter Epidemics. [2], 188 pp. N. p. (Lexington), Printed by J. G. Norwood, 1829. ChU, TransylvaniaU.

—— A Treatise of Pathology and Therapeutics. . . . In Three Volumes. 2 vols. Lexington, 1828. TransylvaniaU.

Curtis, A. (editor). Discussions between Several Members of the Regular Medical Faculty, and the Thomsonian Botanic Physicians, on the Comparative Merits of their Respective Systems. . . . 400 pp. Columbus, Printed at the Office of the Thomsonian Recorder, by Jonathan Phillips, 1836. HistPSO, WRHist.

Davidson, Richard O. A Disclosure of the Discovery and Invention and a Description of the Plan of Construction and Mode of Operation of the Aerostat; or, a New Mode of Aerostation. 32 pp. St. Louis, 1840. MercLStL.

Delafield, John. An Inquiry into the Origin of the Antiquities of America. By John Delafield Jr. With an Appendix, Containing Notes, and "A View of the Causes of the Superiority of the Men of the Northern over those of the Southern Hemisphere." By James Lakey, M. D. 142 pp. Cincinnati, N. G. Burgess & Co., 1839. WRHist. 142 pp. New York, Colt, Burgess & Co., etc., 1839. ChU, HistPSO, NYPL, WRHist.

Drake, Daniel. An Account of the Epidemic Cholera, as

it Appeared in Cincinnati. . . . Extracted from the Sixth Volume of the Western Journal of Medical and Physical Sciences. 46 pp. Cincinnati, Printed at the Chronicle Office, E. Deming, December 1832. JCrerar.

—— An Anniversary Discourse, on the State and Prospects of the Western Museum Society: Delivered by Appointment, in the Chapel of the Cincinnati College, June 10th, 1820, on the Opening of the Museum. 36 pp. Cincinnati, Printed for the Society, by Looker, Palmer and Reynolds, 1820. HistPSO, LC, WRHist.

—— A Practical Treatise on the History, Prevention, and Treatment of Epidemic Cholera, Designed both for the Profession and the People. 180 pp. Cincinnati, Corey and Fairbank, 1832. CinPL, HistPSO, LexPL, OhioStL, WRHist.

Dupré, E. Atlas of the City and County of St. Louis, by Congressional Townships: . . . No pagination. St. Louis, E. Dupré, 1838. MercLStL.

Dwyer, John H. An Essay on Elocution; with Elucidatory Passages from Various Authors. . . . 300 pp. Cincinnati, Printed by Morgan and Lodge, 1824. CinPL.

Eberle, John. A Treatise on the Diseases and Physical Education of Children, . . . [3], 559 pp. Cincinnati, Corey and Webster, etc., n. d. (1833). CinPL, JCrerar. 2d ed. [3], 559 pp. Cincinnati, Corey and Fairbank, etc., 1834. TransylvaniaU.

—— A Treatise on the Practice of Medicine. 2d ed., revised. 2 vols. Philadelphia, John Grigg, 1831. CinPL.

Flint, Timothy. A Condensed Geography and History of the Western States, or the Mississippi Valley. 2 vols. Cincinnati, E. H. Flint (Vol. I); William M. Farnsworth, Printer (Vol. II), 1828. CinPL, HistPSO, IU, LC, LouPL, NewL, NYPL, WRHist, WisH, YMML.

—— The History and Geography of the Mississippi Valley.

To which is Appended a Condensed Physical Geography of the Atlantic United States, and the Whole American Continent. 2d ed. 2 vols. Cincinnati, E. H. Flint and L. R. Lincoln, 1832. BurColl, ChU, ColU, Harvard, HistPSO, IU, LexPL, LC, WRHist.

—— Lectures upon Natural History, Geology, Chemistry, the Application of Steam, and Interesting Discoveries in the Arts. . . . 408 pp. Boston, Lilly, Wait, Colman, and Holden, etc., 1833. LC, NYPL, WRHist, YMML.

Hance. William. An Address and Lecture, Delivered before the Botanic Society, in Columbus, Ohio. 42 pp. Columbus, H. Howard, 1830. From LC card.

Harrison, John P. Essays and Lectures on Medical Subjects. 192 pp. Philadelphia, J. Crissy, 1835. HistPSO, LC, WRHist.

Harrison, William Henry. A Discourse on the Aborigines of the Valley of the Ohio. . . . 51 pp. Cincinnati (Printed at the Office of the Cincinnati Express), 1838. CinPL, MoHist, NYPL, WRHist. 47 pp. Boston, William D. Ticknor, 1840. WisH.

Hildreth, Samuel P. Address of S. P. Hildreth, M.D., President of the Third Medical Convention of Ohio, Delivered at Cleveland, May 14th, 1839. 33 pp. Cleveland, Penniman & Bemis (1839). From *The North American Review*, XLIX, 506 (Oct., 1839).

Houghton, Douglass (and assistants). Second Annual Report of the State Geologist, of the State of Michigan. Made to the Legislature February 4, 1839. 39, 123 pp. Detroit, John S. Bagg, Printer, 1839. CinPL.

—— State of Michigan. No. 8. In Senate, February 3, 1840. [Third annual report of the State Geologist.] 124 pp. N. p., n. d. CinPL, LC.

Howard, Horton. An Improved System of Botanic Medi-

cine, . . . 2 vols. (only Vol. I published?). Columbus, the Author, 1832. LC, WRHist.

Kinmont, Alexander. Twelve Lectures on the Natural History of Man, and the Rise and Progress of Philosophy.
. . . With a Biographical Sketch of the Author.
. . . viii, 355 pp. Cincinnati, U. P. James, 1839.
ChU, CinPL, HistPSO, LC, WRHist, WisH.

Koch, Albert. A Short Description of the Fossil Remains
Found in the State of Missouri. 8 pp. St. Louis, 1840.
Title supplied by William Clark Breckenridge.

Lapham, I. A. A Catalogue of Plants & Shells, Found in
the Vicinity of Milwaukee, on the West Side of Lake
Michigan. 23 pp. Milwaukee, Printed at the Advertiser Office, 1836. WisH.

—— A Catalogue of Plants, Found in the Vicinity of Milwaukee, Wisconsin Territory. 15 pp. Milwaukee, Printed at the Advertiser Office, 1838. WisH.

Letcher, Montgomery E. Wonderful Discovery! Being
an Account of a Recent Exploration of the Celebrated
Mammoth Cave, in Edmonson County, Kentucky, by Dr.
Rowan, Professor Simmons and Others, of Louisville, to
its Termination in an Inhabited Region, in the Interior of
the Earth! Contained in a Letter from Montgomery E.
Letcher, Esq. one of the Exploring Party, to a Professor
in one of the Eastern Colleges. 24 pp. New York, R.
H. Elton, 1839. WisH.

McBride, James. Symmes's Theory of Concentric Spheres;
Demonstrating that the Earth is Hollow, Habitable within, and widely Open about the Poles. By a Citizen of
the United States. 168 pp. Cincinnati, Morgan, Lodge
and Fisher, 1826. CinPL, NYPL, WRHist.

MacLeod, Donald. Substance of a Discourse on Elocution,
Delivered before the Western Literary Institute . . .

26 pp. Cincinnati, Printed at the Cincinnati Journal Office, 1835. NYPL.

Maclure, William. Essay on the Formation of Rocks, or an Inquiry into the Probable Origin of their Present Form and Structure. 53 pp. New Harmony, Ind., the Author, 1832. WisH.

—— Observations on the Geology of the West India Islands, from Barbadoes to Santa Cruz, Inclusive. 17 pp. New Harmony, Ind., Printed for the Author, 1832. IndStL.

M'Murtrie, Henry. The Animal Kingdom Arranged in Conformity with its Organization, by the Baron Cuvier, . . . Translated from the French, with Notes and Additions, by H. M'Murtrie, M. D. &c. &c. 4 vols. New York, G. & C. & H. Carvill, 1831. ChU.

Mather, William W. First Annual Report on the Geological Survey of the State of Ohio. 134 pp. Columbus, Samuel Medary, Printer, 1838. BurColl, USGeoS, WRHist, WisU.

—— Report on the Geological Reconnoissance of Kentucky, Made in 1838. 40 pp. N. p. (Frankfort), n. d. (1839). From LC card.

—— Second Annual Report on the Geological Survey of the State of Ohio. 286 pp. Columbus, Samuel Medary, Printer, 1838. USGeoS, WRHist, WisU.

—— A Series of Geological Queries, Contained in the First Annual Report on the Geological Survey of Ohio. 13 pp. Columbus, S. Medary, Printer, 1838. From LC card.

Miller, Henry. An Inaugural Thesis on the Relation between the Sanguiferous and Nervous Systems, Submitted to the Examination of the Rev. Horace Holley, A. M; A. A. S. President, the Trustees and Medical Professors

of Transylvania University, on the 12th Day of March,
1822. For the Degree of Doctor of Medicine. 46 pp.
Lexington, Printed by William Gibbes Hunt, 1822. ChU.

Olcott, Charles. Iron Ships. Specifications of Olcott's
newly Invented Self-ballasting Iron Safety Ships. Invented by Charles Olcott, 1815. Patented by him July
13, 1835. . . . 16 pp. Washington, Printed by Duff
Green, 1835. LC, WRHist.

Osgood, Charles. The Causes, Treatment and Cure of
Fever and Ague and Other Diseases of Bilious Climates:
. . . Monroe, Mich., Printed by E. Kendall, 1840.
From MS. copyright record for District of Michigan,
1824-1857; MS. entry dated Oct. 9, 1840.

Owen, David Dale. Catalogue of Mineralogical and Geological Specimens, at New-Harmony, Indiana. Collected
in Various Parts of Europe and America, by William
Maclure, . . . 15, [1] pp. New Harmony, Ind.,
1840. WRHist.

―――― Report of a Geological Exploration of Part of Iowa,
Wisconsin, and Illinois, Made under Instructions from
the Secretary of the Treasury of the United States, in
the Autumn of the Year 1839, . . . [Pp. 9-161 of
H. R. Doc. 239, 26th Congress, First Session.] LexPL,
WisH.

―――― Report of a Geological Reconnoisance of the State of
Indiana; Made in the Year 1837, in Conformity to an
Order of the Legislature. . . . Indianapolis, J. W.
Osborn and J. S. Will[ets], 1839. [Pp. 261-292 in *Doc-
uments of the House of Representatives . . . In-
diana*, 1839.] IndStL.

―――― Second Report of a Geological Survey of the State
of Indiana, Made in the Year 1838, in Conformity to an
Order of the Legislature; . . . 54 pp. Indianapolis,
Osborn and Willets, Printers, 1839. IndStL, LaneTS.

Owen, Robert Dale. Moral Physiology; or, a Brief and Plain Treatise on the Population Question. 72 pp. New York, Wright & Owen, 1831. WisH.

Rafinesque, Constantine S. Ancient History, or Annals of Kentucky; with a Survey of the Ancient Monuments of North America, and a Tabular View of the Principal Languages and Primitive Nations of the Whole Earth. iv, 39 pp. Frankfort, Printed for the Author, 1824. ChU, LexPL, LC, MercLStL, NewL, WisH.

—— Annals of Nature; or, Annual Synopsis of New Genera and Species of Animals, Plants, &c. Discovered in North America. 16 pp. N. p. (Lexington, Printed by T. Smith), n. d. (1820). From LC card.

—— Ichthyologia Ohiensis, or Natural History of the Fishes Inhabiting the River Ohio and its Tributary Streams, Preceded by a Physical Description of the Ohio and its Branches. 90 pp. Lexington, Printed for the Author by W. G. Hunt, 1820. HistPSO, LC, NewL.

—— A Monograph of the Fluviatile Bivalve Shells of the River Ohio, Containing Twelve Genera & Sixty-eight Species. Translated from the French of C. S. Rafinesque, . . . Transylvania University. 72 pp. Philadelphia, J. Dobson, 1832. CinPL, LC, WisH.

—— Prodrome d'une monographie des rosiers de l'Amérique Septentrionale, contenant la description de quinze nouvelles espèces et vingt variétés. . . . Sur le genre Houstania . . . Prodrome d'une monographie de turbinolies fossiles du Kentuki . . . Par MM. C. S. Rafinesque et J. D. Clifford. Extraits de la 14me livraison du 5me tome des Annales générales des sciences physiques. 20 pp. Bruxelles, Impr. de Weissenbruch Père, n. d. (1820?). From LC card.

Reynolds, John N. Remarks on a Review of Symmes' Theory, which Appeared in the American Quarterly Review, by a "Citizen of the United States." 75 pp. Washington, Printed by Gales & Seaton, 1827. From LC card.

Riddell, John Leonard. Memoir on the Nature of Miasm and Contagion. Read before the Cincinnati Medical Society, February, 3, 1836. 20 pp. Cincinnati, Printed by N. S. Johnson, 1836. LaneTS, WRHist.

—— Remarks on the Geological Features of Ohio, and Some of the Desiderata which might be Supplied by a Geological Survey of the State. . . . From the Western Monthly Magazine, for March. 12 pp. N. p., n. d. (1836). USGeoS, WRHist, WisH, WisU.

—— Report of John L. Riddell, M. D. one of the Special Committee Appointed by the Last Legislature to Report on the Method of Obtaining a Complete Geological Survey of the State. 34 pp. N. p., n. d. (1837?). WisU.

—— A Supplementary Catalogue of Ohio Plants. Catalogue and Descriptions Read, and Specimens Exhibited, before the Western Academy of Natural Sciences, March 16, 1836. 28 pp. Cincinnati, N. S. Johnson, Printer, 1836. WisU.

—— A Synopsis of the Flora of the Western States. 116 pp. Cincinnati, E. Deming, 1835. LC, WRHist, WisU.

Robinson, Samuel. A Course of Fifteen Lectures, on Medical Botany, Denominated Thomson's New Theory of Medical Practice; . . . Delivered in Cincinnati, Ohio, . . . 206, [2] pp. Columbus, O., Pike, Platt and Co., 1832. TransylvaniaU, WRHist.

Rosenstein, I. G. Theory and Practice of Homoeopathy. First Part, Containing a Theory of Homoeopathy, with Dietetic Rules, etc. . . . xi, 288 pp. Louisville, Henkle & Logan, Printers, 1840. ChU, LC, NewL.

Ruggles, James. A Universal Language, Formed on Phil-

osophical and Analogical Principles; . . . 175, [4]
pp. Cincinnati, Printed by M'Calla and Davis, 1829.
CinPL, WRHist.

Say, Thomas. American Conchology, or Descriptions of
the Shells of North America. Illustrated by Coloured
Figures from Original Drawings Executed from Nature.
[265?] pp., together with numerous plates. New Harmony, Ind., Printed at the School Press, 1830. ChU,
LC, WRHist.

—— Descriptions of Some New Terrestrial and Fluviatile
Shells of North America. 1829, 1830, 1831. 26 pp.
New Harmony, Ind., 1840. CinPL, IndStL, LC.

—— ? A Glossary to Say's Conchology. 25 pp. New Harmony, Ind., Printed by Richard Beck & James Bennett,
1832. (Date partly mutilated, uncertain.) ChU, LC.

Schoolcraft, Henry Rowe. Algic Researches, Comprising
Inquiries respecting the Mental Characteristics of the
North American Indians. First Series. Indian Tales
and Legends. 2 vols. New York, Harper & Brothers,
1839. BurColl, CinPL, LC, NewL, NYPL, WisH.

—— Annual Report of the Acting Superintendent of Indian Affairs for Michigan, Made to the Bureau of Indian
Affairs at Washington, at the Close of the Fiscal Year,
30th September, 1840. 28 pp. Detroit, Asahel S. Bagg,
Printer, 1840. BurColl, WisH.

—— A Memoir, on the Geological Position of a Fossil
Tree, Discovered in the Secondary Rocks of the River
Des Plaines. Read before the American Geological Society. 18 pp. Albany, N. Y., Printed by E. and E. Hosford, 1822. BurColl, USGeoS.

Shaw, Charles. An Inaugural Dissertation, . . .
Transylvania University, for the Degree of Doctor of
Medicine, . . . 1829. By Charles Shaw, of Jeffer-
son County, Mississippi. 16 pp. Lexington, Printed

at the Transylvania Press, by J. G. Norwood, 1829. TransylvaniaU.

Short, C. W.   A Sketch of the Progress of Botany, in Western America. (From the Transylvania Journal of Medicine, &c. Number XXXIV.) 30 pp. Lexington, J. Clarke & Co., Printers, 1836.   LaneTS.

Sullivant, Joseph.   An Alphabetical Catalogue of Shells, Fossils, Minerals, and Zoophites, in the Cabinet of Joseph Sullivant, Curator of the Philosophical and Historical Society of Ohio. 38 pp.   Columbus, Printed by Cutler and Pilsbury, 1838.   HistPSO.

Sullivant, William S.   A Catalogue of Plants, Native and Naturalized, in the Vicinity of Columbus, Ohio.   63 pp. Columbus, Charles Scott, Printer, 1840.   From Thomson.

Symmes, John Cleves.   Light Gives Light, to Light Discover — "ad infinitum." St. Louis, (Missouri Territory,) North America, April 10, A. D. 1818.   To All the World! . . . N. p. (St. Louis), n. d. (1818). Broadside.   MercLStL.

Thompson, Robert.   Treatise on the Nature and Cure of Prolapsus Uteri, . . . 38, [1] pp.   Columbus, Printed by Cutler and Pilsbury, 1838.   WRHist.

Vethake, John W.   A Discourse on the Western Autumnal Disease.   Read before the Tenth District Medical Society of Ohio; at Chillicothe, May 30th, 1826.   39 pp. Chillicothe, Printed by John Bailhache & Co., 1826. WRHist.

Williams, Ara.   A Universal Vocabulary of Proper Names, Ancient and Modern; . . . 536 pp.   Cincinnati, E. Deming, 1831.   CinPL.

Woodward, Augustus Brevoort.   A System of Universal Science.   371, [2] pp.   Philadelphia, Edward Earle, Harrison Hall, and Moses Thomas, 1816.   BurColl, LC.

Yandell, Lunsford P.   An Address, Delivered before the

Medical Society of Tennessee, at its Eighth Annual Meeting at Nashville, on the 7th of May, 1838. 23 pp. Louisville, Prentice & Weissinger, 1838. ChU.

IV. ADDRESSES BEFORE AGRICULTURAL AND MECHANICAL SOCIETIES

Allan, Chilton. Address of the Hon. Chilton Allan, President of the State Agricultural Society, at its Third Annual Meeting, in the Capitol, on the Second Monday in January, 1840. 32 pp. N. p., n. d. LexPL.

Bebb, William. An Address Delivered before the Butler County Agricultural Society at its First Annual Meeting, . . . 12 pp. Hamilton, O., the Society, Woods & Campbell, Printers, 1831. LaneTS.

Caldwell, Charles. Thoughts on the Character and Standing of the Mechanical Profession: a Discourse, Delivered by Invitation, to the Mechanical Institute of the City of Louisville, January 14, 1840. 34 pp. Louisville, Prentice and Weissinger, 1840. IU, MoSHistS, NewL.

Craig, John D. An Address, Delivered at the Meeting of the Citizens of Cincinnati, Convened for the Purpose of Forming a Mechanic's Institute; . . . 17, 3, 3 pp. Cincinnati, the Ohio Mechanics' Institute, Wm. J. Ferris, Printer, 1829. WRHist. From copy supplied by W. H. Cathcart, Western Reserve Historical Society.

Este, David K. Annual Address before the Agricultural Society of Hamilton County. From *The Western Monthly Review*, III, 103 (Aug., 1829).

Leonard, Benjamin G. An Introductory Discourse, Delivered before the Chillicothe Lyceum and Mechanics' Institute. On the 1st of November, 1833. 61 pp. Chillicothe, Published by Order of the Society, Printed at the Scioto Gazette Office, 1834. WRHist, WisH.

Peers, Benjamin O. An Introductory Lecture, Delivered

before the Lexington Mechanic's Institute June 20, 1829.
32 pp.   N. p. (Lexington), Printed by Jos. G. Norwood,
Printer to the University, 1829.   LexPL.

Short, J. C.   An Address, Delivered before the Hamilton
County Agricultural Society, . . . September, at the
Court House in Cincinnati. . . . 1827. From *The
Western Monthly Review,* I, 304 (Sept., 1827).

Slack, Elijah.   A Discourse on Agricultural Chemistry
Delivered at a Quarterly Meeting of the Hamilton
County Agricultural Society, Held on the 4th of June
1831, . . . 14 pp.   N. p. (Cincinnati, the Society),
n. d.   WRHist.

Smith, Stephen C.   An Oration, Delivered at the Request
of the Committee of Associated Mechanicks, at the New
Meeting House in Marietta, . . . on the Fourth of
July, 1808.   16 pp.   Marietta, Printed by Samuel Fairlamb, 1808.   From Thomson.

Storer, Bellamy.   Address Delivered before the Hamilton
County Agricultural Society, at Carthage, Ohio, Sep-
tember 4th, 1835.   14 pp.   Cincinnati, the Society, 1835.
BurColl, WRHist.

Tracy, W. S.   An Address to the Agricultural Society of
Portage County; Delivered at their Late Annual Fair
and Cattle-show.   12 pp.   Ravenna, O., J. B. Butler,
Printer, 1825.   Smith, WRHist.

V.   COLLEGE ADDRESSES AND DISCUSSIONS OF EDUCATIONAL
PROBLEMS

Allan, James S.   Oration Delivered before the Chamberlain Philosophical and Literary Society of Centre College, on the Fourth of July, 1835.   16 pp.   Cincinnati,
Eli Taylor, 1835.   WRHist.

Allen, James S.   A Discourse Delivered at the Second Anniversary of the Philosophronian Society, of Hanover

College. Sept. 29, 1835. . . . 24 pp. Hanover, Ind., Printed by James Morrow, 1835. LaneTS.

Anderson, Charles. An Address Delivered before the Society of Alumni of Miami University, at their Anniversary, August 13th, 1840: . . . 37 pp. Oxford, O., Printed by John B. Peat, 1840. ChU, WRHist.

Aydelott, Benjamin P. An Address on Collegiate Departments of the English Language and Literature, . . . 21 pp. Cincinnati, Kendall and Henry, Printers, 1838. LaneTS.

—— The Medical Student's Dangers and Means of Safety; a Discourse Preached in Christ Church, Cincinnati, January 9, 1831. 12 pp. Cincinnati, J. Whetstone, Jr., Printer, 1831. WRHist.

—— The Teacher's Encouragements. An Address, Delivered by Appointment at a Meeting of the Teachers of Hamilton County, Ohio, at Carthage, June 27, 1835. 25 pp. Cincinnati, Printed by F. S. Benton, 1835. WRHist.

Baldwin, Elihu W. An Address Delivered in Crawfordsville, Indiana, July 13th, 1836. By Rev. Elihu W. Baldwin, A. M. on Occasion of his Inauguration as President of Wabash College. 33 pp. Cincinnati, Printed by James & Gazlay, 1836. IndStL.

—— Address on the Encouragement of Emulation in the Education of Youth, Delivered before the Education Convention of Indiana. . . . December 27, 1837. . . . 12 pp. Indianapolis, Douglass & Noel, Printers, 1837. IndStL.

Ballantine, E. An Address, Delivered before the Literary Societies of Marietta College, Marietta, Ohio. At the Annual Commencement, August 29, 1840. 19 pp. Marietta, O., Gazette Office, Isaac Maxon, Printer, 1840. WRHist.

Beecher, Catharine. An Essay on the Education of Female Teachers. . . . 22 pp. New York, Van Nostrand & Dwight, etc., 1835. LaneTS, LC.

Beecher, Henry Ward. An Address, Delivered before the Platonean Society of the Indiana Asbury University, September 15, 1840. By Henry Ward Beecher, Pastor of the Second Presbyterian Church, Indianapolis. 28 pp. Indianapolis, Printed by William Stacy, 1840. DePauwU.

Beecher, Lyman. An Address, Delivered at the Tenth Anniversary Celebration of the Union Literary Society of Miami University, September 29, 1835. 44 pp. Cincinnati, Printed at the Cincinnati Journal Office, 1835. ChU, WRHist.

—— A Plea for Colleges. 2d ed. 95 pp. Cincinnati, Truman and Smith, etc., 1836. WRHist.

—— A Plea for the West. 172 pp. Cincinnati, Truman and Smith, 1835. CinPL, ColU, HistPSO, KyStL, NewL, NYPL, WRHist, WisH.

Bell, William Columbus. Analysis of Pope's Essay on Man: to which are Added an Essay on Practical Education, and a Theory of Matter, Motion and Life. 310 pp. Lexington, J. Clarke & Co., Printers, 1836. LC, TransylvaniaU.

Bibb, George M. An Oration, Commemorative of Laying the Corner Stone of the College Edifice of the Louisville Medical Institute, on the 22nd of February, 1838. 29 pp. Louisville, Prentice & Weissinger, 1838. LouPL.

Bishop, Robert Hamilton. An Address Delivered September 25, 1833, to the Graduates of Miami University, . . . 15 pp. Oxford, O., W. W. Bishop, 1833. WRHist, WisH.

—— An Address, Delivered to the Graduates of Miami

University, September 28, 1831. 12 pp. Oxford, O.,
Printed at the Oxford Press, 1831. ChU.

—— An Address Delivered to the Graduates of Miami University, September 26, 1832. 15 pp. Oxford, O., Printed by W. W. Bishop, 1832. LexPL.

—— An Address to the Graduates of Miami University. September 30, 1829. 8 pp. Oxford, O., Printed at the Societies' Press, 1829. WisH.

—— An Address to the Graduates of Miami University, September 30, 1830. 12 pp. Oxford, O., W. W. Bishop, 1830. ChU.

—— An Introductory to a Course of Lectures on History. 16 pp. Lexington, William Tanner, Printer, 1823. WisH.

——, and William Gray, and John Thomson. Addresses, Delivered at Oxford, on the 30th of March, 1825, at the Inauguration of Rev. Robert H. Bishop, as President of the Miami University. Published by Order of the Board of Trustees. 24 pp. Hamilton, O., Printed by James B. Camron, 1825. LaneTS.

Blanchard, J. A Perfect State of Society. Address before the ''Society of Inquiry,'' in Oberlin Collegiate Institute. Delivered at Oberlin, Lorain Co. Ohio, at the Annual Commencement, . . . 1839. 16 pp. Oberlin, O., Printed by James Steele, 1839. LaneTS, LexPL, WRHist.

Bledsoe, Jesse. An Introductory Lecture on the Study of the Law, Delivered in the Chapel of Transylvania University, on Monday, November 4, 1822. 24 pp. Lexington, Printed by Joseph Ficklin, 1822. NYPL.

—— An Introductory Lecture, Preparatory to a Course of Instruction on Common and Statute Law, Delivered in the Chapel of Transylvania University, on Monday,

November 3d, 1823. 24 pp. Lexington, William Tanner, Printer, 1823. WisH.

Bliss, Leonard, Jr. An Address on the Uses of History, Delivered before the Philomathean Society of the Washington County Seminary, at Salem, Ia., March 26th, 1840, . . . 19 pp. Louisville, Prentice and Weissinger, 1840. Harvard, IndStL.

Blythe, James. Inaugural Address, Delivered January 1, 1833. By James Blythe, D. D., at his Inauguration into Office, as President of South Hanover College. 18 pp. Cincinnati, M'Millan and Clopper, Printers, 1833. IndStL.

Brewster, George. Lectures on Education, . . . 359, [1] pp. Columbus, Printed for the Author by John Bailhache, 1833. CinPL, LC, WRHist.

Brown, William. Addresses Delivered in the Hall of the House of Representatives, . . . for the Purpose, among Other Things, of Exhibiting the Importance of Education, . . . 22 pp. Vandalia, Ill., William Hodge, Printer, 1839. WisH.

Butler, J. An Eulogy upon the Character of George Swan. Delivered before the Miami Chapter of the Alpha Delta Phi, by J. Butler. March, 1840. . . . 15 pp. Columbus, Cutler & Wright, Printers, 1840. WRHist.

Butler, Mann. An Address on the Value of the Physical Sciences, Compared with the Other Great Branches of Knowledge: Delivered before the Louisville Lyceum, October 1, 1831. 12 pp. Louisville, Printed by J. W. Palmer, 1831. ChU.

Caldwell, Charles. An Address to the Committees on Education of Both Houses of the Legislature of Kentucky, on the State of the School of Medicine of Transylvania University. 23 pp. Lexington, T. Smith, Printer, 1820. ChU.

—— An Inaugural Address to the College of Physicians & Surgeons of the City of Lexington and the County of Fayette. . . . February 2d, 1836. 38 pp. Lexington, J. Clarke & Co., Printers, 1836. IU.

—— Introductory Address on Independence of Intellect. 49 pp. Lexington. From *The Western Monthly Review*, I, 155 (July, 1827).

—— A Report Made to the Legislature of Kentucky, on the Medical Department of Transylvania University, February 15th, 1836. 34 pp. Lexington, J. Clarke & Co., Printers, 1836. ChU.

—— Thoughts on Physical Education: being a Discourse Delivered to a Convention of Teachers in Lexington, Ky. on the 6th & 7th of Nov. 1833. 133 pp. Boston, Marsh, Capen & Lyon, 1834. LexPL, LC.

—— Thoughts on Popular and Liberal Education, with Some Defense of the English and Saxon Languages, in the Form of an Address to the Philomathean Society of Indiana College; Delivered September 28th, 1836. 73 pp. Lexington, Intelligencer Print, 1836. IndStL, IU.

—— Thoughts on the Spirit of Improvement, . . . being an Address (Delivered April 1st, 1835,) to the Agatheridan and Erosophian Societies of Nashville University. 56 pp. Nashville, Tenn., Printed by S. Nye and Co., 1835. ChU.

Caldwell, William B. Address Delivered before the Graduates of the Erodelphian Society, of the Miami University, at its Fourteenth Anniversary, August 7th, A. D. 1839. 22 pp. Oxford, O., Printed by W. W. Bishop, 1839. HistPSO.

Cass, Lewis. Address of Lewis Cass, of Michigan, LL. D. Delivered, by Appointment, before the Association of the Alumni of Hamilton College, at their Anniversary Meeting, August 25, 1830. Published by Request of the

Association. 40 pp. Utica, N. Y., Press of William Williams, 1830. BurColl, WisH.

Chase, Philander. Defence of Kenyon College: . . . 72 pp. Columbus, Olmsted & Bailhache, Printers, 1831. LC, WRHist.

—— A Plea for the West. . . . 16 pp. Philadelphia, Printed by William Stavely, 1826. HistPSO, WRHist, WisH. 15 pp. Boston, Samuel H. Parker, 1827. BurColl.

—— The Star in the West, or Kenyon College, in the Year of our Lord, 1828. 16 pp. N. p., n. d. LC, WRHist.

Cobb, James D. An Address Delivered before the Epanthean Society of Miami University, on the Occasion of their First Anniversary, August 7th, 1838. 21, [1] pp. Oxford, O., Printed by R. H. Bishop, Jun., 1838. WRHist.

Coit, Thomas W. An Inaugural Address Delivered in the Chapel of Morrison College, November 2, 1835. 38 pp. Lexington, Clarke & Co., Printers, 1835. TransylvaniaU.

Coke, Richard Henry. An Address Delivered before the Graduates of the Erodelphian Society of Miami University, August 9th, 1837. 15 pp. Oxford, O., Printed By R. H. Bishop, Jun., 1837. ChU, IU, WRHist.

Corry, William M. Address Delivered before the Society of the Alumni of Miami University, at their Anniversary, September 22, 1834. 23 pp. Hanover, Ind., Monfort & M'Millan, Printers, 1835. ChU, LaneTS, WRHist.

Cross, James Conquest. An Inaugural Discourse on Medical Eclectism. 20 pp. Cincinnati, Printed by Kendall and Henry, 1835. From LC card.

—— An Inaugural Discourse on the Value of Time, and the Importance of Study to the Physician. 34 pp. Lexington, Finnell & Zimmerman, Printers, 1837. MoStHistS.

Daily, William M. An Address Delivered in the Chapel of St. Charles College, Missouri, March 12th, 1839. 22 pp. St. Louis, C. Keemle, Printer, 1839. LexPL.

—— An Address on Education, Delivered to the Students and Patrons of the Indiana Asbury University, March 27, 1838, . . . 25 pp. Madison, Ind., Printed at the Republican Banner Office, 1838. IU.

Drake, Benjamin. An Address, Delivered on the Sixth Anniversary of the Erodelphian Society of Miami University; September 27, 1831. 15 pp. Cincinnati, Published at the Office of the Cincinnati Chronicle, 1831. LaneTS, WRHist.

—— A Public Oration, Delivered . . . before the Phi Alpha Theta, July 4, 1826. 12 pp. Cincinnati, 1826. From *The North American Review,* XXIII, 498 (Oct., 1826).

Drake, Daniel. Anniversary Address, Delivered to the School of Literature and the Arts, at Cincinnati, November 23, 1814. 12 pp. N. p. (Cincinnati), Printed by Looker and Wallace, n. d. (1814?). HistPSO.

—— Discourse on the History, Character, and Prospects of the West: Delivered to the Union Literary Society of Miami University, Oxford, Ohio, at their Ninth Anniversary, September 23, 1834. 56 pp. Cincinnati, Truman and Smith, 1834. ChU, ColU, LaneTS, NYPL, WRHist, WisH.

—— An Inaugural Discourse on Medical Education; Delivered at the Opening of the Medical College of Ohio, in Cincinnati, November 11th, 1820. 31 pp. Cincinnati, Printed by Looker, Palmer and Reynolds, 1820. NYPL, WRHist, WisH.

—— An Introductory Discourse to a Course of Lectures on Clinical Medicine and Pathological Anatomy; Delivered at the Opening of the New Clinical Amphitheatre of the Louisville Marine-hospital, November 5th, 1840. 16 pp. Louisville, Printed by Prentice and Weissinger, 1840. ChU.

—— An Introductory Lecture, on the Necessity and Value of Professional Industry; Delivered in the Chapel of Transylvania University, November 7th, 1823. 31 pp. Lexington, William Tanner, Printer, 1823. CinPL, NYPL, WRHist, WisH.

—— Practical Essays on Medical Education, and the Medical Profession, in the United States. 104 pp. Cincinnati, Roff & Young, 1832. LC, LouPL, TransylvaniaU, WRHist.

—— Remarks on the Importance of Promoting Literary and Social Concert, in the Valley of the Mississippi, as a Means of Elevating its Character, and Perpetuating the Union. Delivered in the Chapel of Transylvania University, to the Literary Convention of Kentucky, November 8, 1833. 26 pp. N. p. (Louisville), Published by Members of the Convention, at the Office of the Louisville Herald, 1833. ChU, CinPL, WisH.

Eells, Samuel. Address before the Alpha Delta Phi Society, of Miami University, on the Study of the Classics. 42, [1] pp. Cincinnati, Smith, Day and Co., 1836. ChU, IU, LaneTS, WRHist.

—— Address on the Moral Dignity of the Office of the Professional Teacher. 24 pp. Cincinnati, 1837. From *The Hesperian*, I, 79 (May, 1838).

——Oration Delivered before the Biennial Convention of the Alpha Delta Phi Society, (at New Haven, Conn., Aug. 15, 1839,) on the Law and Means of Social Advancement. 69 pp. Cincinnati, Kendall and Henry, Printers, 1839. LexPL, WRHist.

Eliot, William Greenleaf, Jr. Address Delivered before

the Franklin Society of St. Louis, on the Occasion of its First Anniversary, January 7th, 1836. 27 pp. St. Louis, Charless & Paschall, Printers, n. d. (1836). WisH.

Ewing, Thomas. An Address Delivered before the Union Literary Society of Miami University, on the Twenty-fifth of September, at their Anniversary Celebration. 21 pp. Cincinnati, Corey and Fairbank, 1833. ChU, LaneTS, WRHist.

Flint, Joshua B. An Address Delivered to the Students of the Louisville Medical Institute, . . . November 13th, 1838. 31 pp. Louisville, Prentice and Weissenger [*sic*], 1838. ChU, LouPL.

Galloway, Samuel. Address Delivered before the Graduates of the Union Literary Society of Miami University. 28 pp. Springfield, O., 1838. From *The Hesperian*, I, 87 (May, 1838). Copy in WRHist not collated.

Going, Jonathan. The Inaugural Address, at the Anniversary of the Granville Literary & Theological Institution, August 8, 1838, . . . 18 pp. Columbus, Printed by Cutler and Pilsbury, 1839. WRHist, WisH.

Groesbeck, Herman J. Address Delivered at the Second Anniversary Celebration of the Alpha Delta Phi Society of Miami University, August 10th, 1837. 24 pp. Cincinnati, R. P. Brooks & Co., Printers, 1837. ChU, WRHist.

Hall, James. An Address Delivered before the Erodelphian Society of Miami University, on the Twenty-fourth of September, 1833, at their Eighth Anniversary Celebration. 32 pp. Cincinnati, Corey and Fairbank, 1833. ChU, LaneTS, NYPL, WRHist.

Hamline, L. L. Address Delivered by Rev. L. L. Hamline, A. M., of the Ohio Conference, before the Jefferson and Union Literary Societies of Augusta College, August,

1836. 16 pp. Cincinnati, J. F. Wright and L. Swormstedt, at the Methodist Book Room, 1836. LexPL, WRHist.

Harney, John H. Party Spirit. An Address before the Society of Alumni of Hanover College, at their Second Anniversary, Sept. 27, 1837. 14 pp. South Hanover, Ind., James Morrow, Printer, 1837. IndStL.

Harrison, John P. An Address, Delivered at the Twelfth Anniversary Celebration of the Union Literary Society of Miami University, August 8th, 1837. 21 pp. Oxford, O., R. H. Bishop, Jun., 1837. ChU, HistPSO, WRHist.

—— Remarks on the Influence of the Mind upon the Body; an Introductory Lecture, Delivered 27th March, 1827, to a Course of Lectures in the Louisville Hospital. Louisville, W. W. Worsley (1827?). From *The Western Monthly Review*, I, 185 (July, 1827).

Hillyer, Giles M. Address Delivered at the Third Anniversary Celebration of the Alpha Delta Phi Society of Miami University, on the Triumphs of Mind. 30 pp. Cincinnati, L'Hommedieu, & Co., Printers, 1839. ChU.

James, John H. Annual Address Delivered before the Historical and Philosophical Society of Ohio, on the 25th December, 1835; Containing Strictures on the Prevailing Systems of Education. 13 pp. Columbus, Printed by Scott & Gallagher, 1838. WisH.

Johnson, Samuel R. Cautions concerning the Spirit of the Age. An Address Delivered at the Fifth Anniversary of the Western Literary Society of Wabash College, July 9th, 1839, . . . 16 pp. Crawfordsville, Ind., P. J. Bartholomew, Printer, n. d. IndStL.

Kaufmann, Peter. A Treatise on American Education, . . . [1], 50, [2] pp. Canton, O., Printed by Peter Kaufmann and Co., 1839. CinPL.

Kinmont, Alexander. Discourse on the Ends and Uses of

a Liberal Education, Delivered before the Union Literary Society of South-Hanover College, Ia. on the 27th September, 1836; being their Fourth Anniversary. 26 pp. Cincinnati, Smith, Day and Co., 1836. LaneTS, WRHist.
—— Report on the Classics and Mathematics, as a Part of Education Delivered before the Western Literary Institute and College of Professional Teachers, . . . 18 pp. Cincinnati, Printed by James and Gazlay, 1835. Smith.

Lane, Henry S. Address, Delivered before the Western Literary Society, of Wabash College, . . . September 29th, 1835. 23 pp. N. p., n. d. IndStL.

Leavitt, O. S. Strictures on the New School Laws of Ohio and Michigan; with Some General Observations of the Systems of Other States. 31 pp. Cincinnati, Isaac Hefley & Co., Printers, 1839. From Thomson.

Linsley, Joel H. Address Delivered at the Annual Commencement of the Marietta College, Ohio, by Joel H. Linsley, D. D. on Occasion of his Inauguration to the Presidency of that Institution. July 25, 1838. 28 pp. Cincinnati, A. Pugh, Printer, 1838. LaneTS, WRHist.

Locke, John. An Introductory Lecture on Chemistry and Geology: Delivered November 6, 1838, before the Class of the Medical College of Ohio, . . . 18, [1] pp. Cincinnati (Republican Print), 1839. MoStHistS.

Logan, Caleb W. An Address before the Deinologian Literary Society of Centre College, Delivered on the Fourth July, 1838, . . . 19 pp. Danville, Ky., 1838. ChU.

Loomis, Elias. An Inaugural Address, Delivered August 21, 1838. By Elias Loomis, A. M. Professor of Mathematics and Natural Philosophy in Western Reserve College. 38 pp. New York, Printed by John F. Trow, 1838. WRHist.

McArthur, John. An Address Delivered before the Society of Inquiry on Missions of Miami University, Sunday Evening, July 1st, 1838. 19 pp. Oxford, O., R. H. Bishop, Jun., 1838. ChU, WRHist.

—— Address Delivered to the Union Literary Society, of Miami University, at its Fifteenth Anniversary, August 12, 1840. 25 pp. Oxford, O., Printed by John B. Peat, 1840. ChU, HistPSO, WRHist.

Macaulay, D. An Address Delivered by Rev. D. Macaulay, D. D. on the Occasion of his being Inducted into the Office of President of Hanover College, March 28, 1838. . . . 24 pp. South Hanover, Ind., Printed by James Morrow, 1838. IndStL.

M'Dowell, Joseph N. A Valedictory Address, Delivered by Appointment, before the Medical and Philosophical Society of Ohio, at the Close of its Winter Session, February 27, 1830: . . . 12 pp. Cincinnati, March, 1830. ChU.

McIlvaine, Charles Petit. Baccalaureate Discourse, Delivered in Rosse Chapel, Gambier, to the Senior Class of Kenyon College, . . . 1837. 16 pp. Gambier, O., George W. Myers, Printer, 1837. HistPSO, WRHist.

—— The Respectful Address of C. P. M'Ilvaine, D. D., Bishop . . . in the State of Ohio, to All who would Promote the Progress of Learning and Religion in the Western States. 16 pp. New York, Sleight & Van Norden, Printers, 1833. BurColl.

MacMaster, Erasmus D. An Address Delivered to the Candidates for the Degree of Bachelor of Arts, in Hanover College, Indiana, at the Anniversary Commencement, September 25, 1839. 16 pp. Cincinnati, Printed by R. P. Brooks, 1839. IndStL, LaneTS.

—— A Discourse Delivered November 7th, 1838, on the Occasion of the Author's Inauguration as President of Hanover College, Indiana. 36 pp. Hanover, Ind., the

Board of Trustees of the College, 1838. IndStL, IU, LaneTS.

McRae, John J. An Address Delivered before the Graduates of the Erodelphian Society of Miami University, August 8th, 1838. Oxford, O., Printed by R. H. Bishop, Jun., 1838. 21, [1] pp. WRHist.

Mansfield, Edward Deering. A Discourse on the Utility of the Mathematics as a Means of General Education. Delivered before the Western Literary Institute, and College of Professional Teachers, on the 8th of October, 1834, . . . 28 pp. Cincinnati, J. Drake, 1835. From LC card.

—— Lecture on the Qualifications of Teachers Delivered before the College of Professional Teachers at Cincinnati. 23 pp. N. p. (Cincinnati), Printed by N. S. Johnson, 1836. CinPL, WRHist.

—— The Means of Perpetuating Civil Liberty. An Oration, Delivered at the Tenth Anniversary Celebration of the Erodelphian Society of Miami University, . . . 35 pp. Cincinnati, Corey & Webster, 1835. ChU, LaneTS, LC, NYPL, WRHist.

Marshall, Samuel V. The Influence of Letters on the Human Condition. An Address, Delivered before the Louisville Mechanics' Institute, . . . Louisville, Ky., Feb. 11, 1837. 44 pp. Louisville, Parrott, Wampler & Co., Printers, 1837. LaneTS.

Marshall, Thomas A. An Introductory Address, Delivered before the Law Class of Transylvania University, on the 9th of Nov. 1839. 16 pp. Lexington, Finnell & Virden, Printers, 1839. MoStHistS.

Mayes, Daniel. An Address to the Students of Law, in Transylvania University, . . . 1833; . . . 27, [1] pp. Lexington, Printed by Tho: J. Pew, 1833. MoStHistS.

—— An Introductory Lecture, Delivered to the Law Class of Transylvania University, on the 5th November, 1832. 32, 4 pp. Lexington, Printed by H. Savary & Co., 1832. MoStHistS.

Miller, Henry. On the True Value of Experience in Medicine; an Introductory Lecture, Delivered at the Session of the Louisville Medical Institute. For 1838 — '39. 21 pp. Louisville, Prentice & Weissinger, Printers, 1838. LouPL.

—— An Oration, Pronounced on the Anniversary of the ΚΛ Society of Hippocrates, in Lexington, Kentucky. 13 pp. Lexington, Printed by Thomas T. Skillman, 1822. ChU.

Miller, Thomas. An Address Delivered at Columbia, Missouri, November 10th, 1834: by Thomas Miller, A. M. on the Occasion of his Installation as Professor in Columbia College. 22 pp. Columbia, Mo., Printed by Nathaniel Patten, 1834. MoStHistS, WisH.

Minor, James L. [Address at Laying of Cornerstone of University of Missouri, at Columbia, July 4,1840.] 8 pp. N. p., n. d. (Title-page lacking; title improvised.) MoHist.

Mitchell, Thomas Duché. Hints on the Connexion of Labour with Study, as a Preventive of Diseases Peculiar to Students; . . . to which is Appended the Substance of an Introductory Lecture, on Medical Education, Delivered in October, 1831. 85 pp. Cincinnati, Corey, Fairbank, & Co., etc., 1832. From LC card (USBurEd). Also in WRHist.

—— The Tripod of the American Revolution, viz: Voluntary Association, Pledge, and Self-denial; being an Address to the Chamberlain Philosophical and Literary Society of Centre College, Kentucky, Delivered by Appointment, on the 4th of July, 1838, in the Presbyterian Church in Danville; . . . 28 pp. Lexington, Intelligencer Print, 1838. GhU.

Morse, Intrepid. Christian Piety and Knowledge, or Literature & Religion; a Sermon. Preached at the Laying of the Corner-stone of the Theological Seminary & Kenyon College, at Gambier, . . . June 9th, 1827. 24 pp. Steubenville, O., Printed by James Wilson, 1827. WRHist.

Niles, M. A. H. Address before the Society of Alumni of Hanover College, at their First Anniversary, Sept. 25th, 1836. 2d ed. 23 pp. Hanover, Ind., James Morrow, Printer, 1836. IndStL, LaneTS.

Niles, William Woodruff? Ought I to Become a Missionary to the Heathen? An Essay, Read before the "Society of Inquiry" in the Literary and Theological Institution, at South Hanover, Indiana. Accompanying the First Annual Report of the "Committee on Foreign Missions." By a Student. 15 pp. Cincinnati, M'Millan & Clopper, Printers, 1832. IndStL.

Olds, Chauncy N. An Address on the Nature and Cultivation of a Missionary Spirit, Delivered before the Society of Inquiry on Missions of Miami University, Sunday Evening, February 26th, 1837, . . . 22 pp. Oxford, O., Printed by R. H. Bishop, Jun., 1837. ChU, HistPSO, WRHist.

—— A Valedictory Address to the Graduates of the Union Literary Society of Miami University, Delivered August 7th, 1839. 21 pp. Oxford, O., Printed by W. W. Bishop, 1839. ChU, HistPSO, WRHist.

Owen, Robert Dale. Address Touching the Influence and Progress of Literature and the Sciences: Delivered before the Philomathean Society of the Indiana University, at the Annual Commencement, September, 1838. 38 pp. Richmond, Ind., Lynde Elliott, 1838. IndStL, IU.

Oxford Addresses; being the Inaugural Address, and Address to the Graduates of Miami University, of the Years 1829, '30, '31, '32, '33, '34, by R. H. Bishop, D. D. President; Addresses Delivered, on Anniversary Occasions, before the Erodelphian and Union Literary Societies of Miami University; and an Address Delivered at the Anniversary of the Society of the Alumni of Miami University, September 22, 1834, by William M. Corry, A. M. 276 pp. Hanover, Ind., Joseph G. Monfort, Hanover College Press, 1835. ChU, CinPL, USBurEd, WRHist.

Peers, Benjamin O. American Education: or Strictures on the Nature, Necessity, & Practicability of a System of National Education, Suited to the United States. . . . With an Introductory Letter by Francis L. Hawks, D. D. 364 pp. New York, John S. Taylor, 1838. ChU, LC, LouPL.

—— Inaugural Address Delivered at the Opening of Morrison College, Lexington, Kentucky, November 4th, 1833. 30 pp. Lexington, Printed by J. Clarke & Co., 1833. LexPL, LC, TransylvaniaU.

Peixotto, Daniel L. M. Introductory Lecture Delivered at the Willoughby Medical College, of the Willoughby University of Lake Erie, 1836-7; . . . 30, [1] pp. Cleveland, Canfield & Spencer, Printers, 1837. HistPSO.

Perkins, James H. Christian Civilization. An Address Delivered before the Athenian Society of the University of Ohio at Athens, September Sixteenth, 1840. 26 pp. Cincinnati, A. Pugh, Printer, 1840. BurColl, WRHist.

Picket, Albert, Sr. Opening Address at the Sixth Annual Session of the Western Literary Institute and College of Professional Teachers. . . . In October, 1836. 24 pp. Cincinnati, 1836. LaneTS, WRHist.

Pitt, William. Letters to the Honorable James T. Morehead, on Transylvania University, and the Necessity of a System of Education in Kentucky. 28 pp. Smithland, Ky., Charles A. Fuller, 1837. From *The North American Review,* XLIX, 262 (July, 1839).

Pope, John. An Introductory Lecture Delivered before the Students at Law, at the Transylvania University, May, 1814, . . . 12 pp. Lexington, Printed at the Office of the Western Monitor, n. d. WisH.

Post, M. M. Symmetry of Mind: an Address Delivered at Wabash College, before the Philomathean Society, . . . Crawfordsville: 1837. 23 pp. N. p. (Lafayette, Ind.), Printed at the Lafayette Free Press, n. d. IU.

Potts, William S. The Inaugural Address of Rev. William S. Potts, President of Marion College. Delivered . . . Sept. 17, 1835, . . . 16 pp. St. Louis, Printed by R. M. Treadway, 1835. LaneTS, MoHist.

Purcell, John B. The Crescent and the Cross: a Discourse, Delivered before the Miami Society, of Miami University, on the 11th of August, 1840. 27 pp. Oxford, O., Printed by John B. Peat, 1840. ChU, WRHist.

Rennie, John. An Address on Education Delivered at Columbia, Missouri, November 24th, 1835. 14, ii pp. Columbia, Mo., Printed by F. A. Hamilton, 1835. LexPL.

Report of the Committee on Education, of the House of Representatives of Kentucky, on so Much of the Governor's Message as Relates to Schools and Seminaries of Learning. 2d ed. 52 pp. Lexington, Printed by Joseph G. Norwood, 1830. LouPL.

Robertson, George. Address on Behalf of the Deinologian Society of Centre College; Delivered at Danville, Kentucky, on the 4th of July, 1834. 24 pp. Lexington, Printed by T. T. & W. D. Skillman, 1834. ChU, NewL.

—— A Biographical Sketch of the Hon. John Boyle: in an Introductory Lecture to the Law Class of Transylvania, November 7, 1838. 22 pp. Frankfort, A. G. Hodges, Printer, 1838. ChU, LouPL, NewL.

—— Introductory Lecture, Delivered before the Law Class of Transylvania University, November 12th, 1836. 48 pp. Lexington, Intelligencer Print, 1836. LexPL.

—— Introductory Lecture, Delivered in the Chapel of Morrison College, on the 7th of November, 1835, . . . 42 pp. Lexington, J. Clarke & Co., Printers, 1835. LexPL.

Schenck, Robert Cumming. Address, Delivered before the Scholars' Union Society, at the Exhibition of the Springfield Classical School. February 13, 1835. 21 pp. Springfield, O., John M. Gallagher, Printer, 1835. HistPSO.

—— Address Delivered before the Society of Alumni of Miami University, at their Anniversary Meeting, September 27, 1836. 16 pp. Dayton, O., Comlys, Printers, Journal and Advertiser Office, 1837. ChU, HistPSO, WRHist, WisH.

Scott, John W. An Address Delivered before the Athenian Society of Indiana University, at its Anniversary Celebration, September 25th, 1838. 32 pp. Oxford, O., Printed by W. W. Bishop, 1838. IndStL, IU.

—— An Address on Female Education, Delivered at the Close of the Summer Session for 1840, of the Steubenville Female Seminary, . . . 12 pp. Steubenville, O., 1840. WRHist.

—— The Instability and Changes of Earth. A Discourse Delivered in the Chapel of Miami University, on Sabbath, the 15th of July, 1838. 19 pp. Oxford, O., R. H. Bishop, Jr., 1838. From *The Hesperian*, II, 166 (Dec., 1838).

Simpson, M. Address Delivered upon the Author's Installation, as President of the Indiana Asbury University, September 16, A. D. 1840. 40 pp. Indianapolis, Printed by William Stacy, 1840. DePauwU.

Smith, N. R. An Address, Introductory to a Course of Lectures on the Theory and Practice of Medicine. 24 pp. Lexington, Printed at the Observer & Reporter Office, 1838. LexPL.

Staughton, J. M. Address Delivered on the Anniversary of the Union Literary Society of Miami University, September 27, 1831. 23 pp. Cincinnati, W. J. Ferris & Co., Printers, 1831. ChU, LaneTS.

Stowe, Calvin E. Address of Professor C. E. Stowe, before the College of Teachers, in Behalf of the Emigrants' Friend Society, October, 1835. . . . 18, [1] pp. Cincinnati, N. S. Johnson, Printer, 1835. LexPL.

—— The Prussian System of Public Instruction, and its Applicability to the United States. 112 pp. Cincinnati, Truman and Smith, 1836. CinPL, HistPSO, NYPL, WRHist.

—— Queries on Education. 7 pp. N. p. (Cincinnati, Printed by Kendall and Henry), n. d. (1837?). WRHist.

—— Report on Elementary Public Instruction in Europe, Made to the Thirty-sixth General Assembly of the State of Ohio, December 19, 1837. 57 pp. Columbus, Samuel Medary, Printer, 1837. CinPL, LaneTS, LC, NYPL, WRHist.

—— Wisdom and Knowledge the Nation's Stability. An Address Delivered at Crawfordsville, Indiana, July 7, 1840, before the Euphonean [*sic*] Society of Wabash College, . . . Published by the Society. 20 pp. N.

p. (Cincinnati), Printed at the Cincinnati Observer Office, 1840. IndStL, IU.

Telford, Charles L. An Address on Individuality of Character, Delivered before the Miami Chapter of the Alpha Delta Phi Society, at its Fourth Anniversary, Held at Oxford, O. August 6th, 1839. 15 pp. Cincinnati, Printed at the Chronicle Office, 1840. WisH.

Thomas, Frederick William. An Address Delivered before the Erodelphian Society of Miami University, at its Thirteenth Annual Celebration, August 7th, 1838. 22 pp. Oxford, O., Printed by W. W. Bishop, 1838. ChU, HistPSO, WRHist.

Tomlinson, J. S. An Address on the Duties, Difficulties and Rewards of Educated Young Men; Delivered before the Chamberlain and Deinologian Societies of Centre College, September 26, 1839. 23 pp. Frankfort, A. G. Hodges, Printer, 1839. LexPL, MoHist.

—— A Discourse on the Nature and Advantages of a Liberal Education; Delivered at the Annual Commencement of Augusta College, in August, 1838, . . . and, in October Following, before the Kentucky Annual Conference, in Danville, . . . 26 pp. Augusta, Ky., Printed by J. S. Power, 1838. LexPL, LC.

Walker, Timothy. An Address Delivered before the Union Literary Society of Miami University, on the Twenty-fifth of September, at their Anniversary Celebration. 26 pp. Cincinnati, Corey and Fairbank, 1832. LaneTS, WRHist, WisH.

—— Introductory Lecture on the Dignity of the Law as a Profession, Delivered at the Cincinnati College, on the Fourth of November, 1837. 26 pp. Cincinnati, Printed at the Daily Gazette Office, 1837. NYPL, WRHist.

Wallace, David. An Address, Delivered at the Installation of President Simpson, of the Indiana Asbury University,

September 16, 1840. 14 pp. Indianapolis, Printed by William Stacy, 1840. DePauwU.

Wickliffe, Robert, Jr. An Address Delivered on the Occasion of Laying the Corner Stone of the New Medical Hall of Transylvania University, July, 1839. 29, [1] pp. Lexington, Noble & Dunlop, Printers, 1839. From LC card.

—— The Importance of a State University to the Commonwealth of Kentucky. 1839. From *The Hesperian*, III, 444 (Nov., 1839).

Wilson, R. G., and Daniel Read. The Baccalaureate Address, Delivered before the Graduates of the Ohio University, at the Annual Commencement, September, 1836. By the President, R. G. Wilson, D. D. Also, the Address, to the Audience, Delivered at the Same Time. By Daniel Read, Professor of Languages. 21 pp. Athens, O., I. Maxon, Printer, n. d. HistPSO.

Woods, Alva. Intellectual and Moral Culture. A Discourse, Delivered at his Inauguration as President of Transylvania University, October 13th, 1828. 20 pp. Lexington, Joseph G. Norwood, Printer, 1828. ChU, LaneTS, LexPL, LC.

Wright, A. K. An Address Delivered before the Society of Alumni of Western Reserve College. August 25, 1840. 16 pp. Hudson, O., Printed by Charles Aikin, 1840. BurColl.

Wylie, Andrew. An Address, Delivered at Bloomington, October 29, 1829, by the Rev. Andrew Wylie, D. D. on the Occasion of his Inauguration, as President of Indiana College. Published by Order of the Board of Trustees. 30 pp. Indianapolis, Printed by Douglass and Maguire, n. d. IndStL, IU.

—— An Address Delivered before the Philomathean Society of the Wabash College, . . . July 10, 1838.

. . . 24 pp. Bloomington, Ind., Printed at the Franklin Office, n. d.   IndStL, WRHist.

—— Address on the Importance and Best Method of Cultivating the Moral Faculties: Delivered before the Education Convention of Indiana. 19 pp. Indianapolis, Douglass & Noel, Printers, 1838.   IU.

—— Address on the Subject of Common School Education, Delivered before the Convention of the Friends of Education, in Indianapolis, January 3, 1837, . . . 19 pp. Indianapolis, Douglass & Noel, Printers, 1837. IndStL, USBurEd.

—— Address, to the Citizens of Monroe County, and to tme [sic] Members of the County Lyceum. 27 pp. Bloomington, Ind., Printed in the Old College Building, July 4, 1840.   IU.

—— The Baccalaureate Address Delivered to the Senior Class of Indiana University, at the Annual Commencement, September 25, 1839. 21 pp. Bloomington, Ind., Printed at the Equator Office, 1839.   IndStL.

—— Baccalaureate Delivered at the Fifth Commencement of Indiana College, Sept. 24, 1834. 11 pp. N. p., n. d. IU, WRHist.

—— Baccalaureate Delivered to the Senior Class, in the Chapel of Indiana College, on the 25th of September, 1836, . . . 20 pp. Terre Haute, Ind., Printed by J. & T. Dowling, 1836.   IU.

—— A Discourse on Education, Delivered before the Legislature of the State of Indiana, at the Request of the Joint Committees on Education, . . . 23 pp. N. p. (Indianapolis), Smith & Bolton, Printers, 1830.   IndStL, IU.

Yandell, Lunsford P. A Lecture on the Duties of Physicians. Delivered before the Medical Class of Transylvania University, on the 4th and 10th of February,

1837. . . . 26 pp. Lexington, Intelligencer Print, 1837. LexPL.

Young, John C. An Address Delivered before the Union Literary Society of Miami University, at its Thirteenth Annual Celebration, August 8th, 1838. 29 pp. Oxford, O., Printed by W. W. Bishop, 1838. ChU, HistPSO, LaneTS, WRHist.

—— Address of Rev. John C. Young, Delivered at his Inauguration as President of Centre College. Danville, Nov. 18, 1830. 11, [1] pp. Lexington, Printed by T. T. Skillman, 1830. LexPL, LC.

VI. Schoolbooks

Adams, Rufus W. The Young Gentleman and Lady's Explanatory Monitor. A Selection from the Best Authors Extant, upon a New Plan Designed for Schools. 2d ed., revised and corrected. 251 pp. Zanesville, O., D. Chambers, 1815. LC card. 5th ed., improved. 260 pp. Columbus, E. Griswold, Jun., 1818. HistPSO, WRHist.

The American Orator: . . . together with a Selection of the most Eloquent Speeches from the most Distinguished Modern Orators, . . . By a Teacher. 290 pp. (incomplete?). Lexington, Printed and Sold by Joseph Charless, 1807. MoHist.

Bates, Elisha. The Juvenile Expositor, or Child's Dictionary: Designed for the Use of Schools, . . . N. p., n. d. From printed title-page (probably clipped) in copyright record for the District of Ohio, 1806-1828; MS. entry dated Jan., 1820.

—— The Western Preceptor, a Spelling Book, in Two Parts. N. p., n. d. From printed title-page (probably clipped) in MS. copyright record for the District of of Ohio, 1806-1828; MS. entry dated Jan. 26, 1820.

—— The Western Preceptor; a Spelling Book in Two

Parts. Part II. . . . 90 pp. Mountpleasant, O., Elisha Bates, 1821. WRHist.

Battin, Richard. The New Ohio Spelling Book, in Three Parts; . . . N. p., n. d. From printed title-page in copyright book for the District of Ohio, 1806-1828. MS. entry dated May 26, 1819.

Beecher, Catharine. The Moral Instructor; for Schools and Families: Containing Lessons on the Duties of Life, Arranged for Daily Study and Recitation. Also Designed as a Reading Book for Schools. 194 pp. Cincinnati, Truman & Smith, 1838. LC.

——, and Harriet Beecher. Primary Geography for Children, on an Improved Plan, with Twelve Maps, and Numerous Engravings. By C. & H. Beecher, Principals of the Western Female Institute. Cincinnati, Corey & Fairbank. From *The Western Monthly Magazine,* I, 287 (June, 1833).

Benedict, H. T. N. Murray's English Grammar, Revised, . . . By H. T. N. Benedict, Teacher. 192 pp. Frankfort, A. G. Hodges, Printer, 1832. LouPL.

Bishop, Robert Hamilton. Elements of Logic; . . . 2d ed. iv, 175 pp. Oxford, O., W. W. Bishop, 1833. LC, LouPL, WRHist, YMML.

—— Elements of the Science of Government: being an Outline of a Portion of the Studies of the Senior Class in Miami University. 166 pp. Oxford, O., Printed by R. H. Bishop, Jun., 1839. ChU, CinPL, WRHist.

—— A Manual of Logic. 5, 172 pp. Oxford, O., Printed at the Societies' Press, 1831. WRHist.

—— Sketches of the Philosophy of the Bible. . . . iv, [1], 305 pp. Oxford, O., W. W. Bishop, 1833. ChU.

Bliss, Leonard. A Comprehensive Grammar of the English Language: Introductory Lessons. 73, [2] pp. Louisville, Morton and Griswold, 1839. LC.

Bridge, B.   The New American Reader, No. 3.   Comprising Selections in Prose and Verse, for the Use of Schools. 251 pp.   Cincinnati, E. Morgan and Co., 1839.   LC.

—— The New American Speaker: Comprising Elegant Selections . . . 250 pp.   Cincinnati, E. Morgan and Son, etc., 1837.   HistPSO, WRHist.

Brouillett, M. B.?   A Collection of Cotillions, Scotch Reels, &c.   Introduced at the Dancing School of M. B. Brouillett, Logansport Indiana, 1834.   8 pp.   Logansport, Ind., S. Lasselle, Printer, 1834.   IndStL.

Buchanan, Joseph.   A Practical Grammar of the English Language, in Three Parts, Adapted to All Capacities. 140 pp.   Lexington, Printed by William W. Worsley, 1826.   TransylvaniaU.

Chambers, Joseph G.   Elements of Orthography.   Or, an Attempt to Form a Complete System of Letters . . . 2, 13, [1] pp.   Zanesville, O., Printed for the Author, by Sawyer & Chambers, 1812.   From LC card.

The Child's Letter-book: Containing the Alphabet, and Monosyllabic Spelling Tables, Arranged under their Proper Rules.   16 pp.   Chillicothe, Printed at Pumroy's Book and Job Office, 1834.   WRHist.

The Child's Spelling Book; or Michigan Instructor: being a Compilation, from the most Approved Authors, Selected by a Teacher.   Part 1.   12 pp.   Detroit, Printed by James M. Miller, 1809.   BurColl.

Connolly, James L.   Connolly's Arithmetic; or the Ohio Accomptant: . . . 250 pp.   Pittsburg, Cramer & Spear, 1829.   WRHist.

Eberle, John.   Notes of Lectures on the Theory and Practice of Medicine, Delivered in the Jefferson Medical College, at Philadelphia.   2d ed., corrected.   218 pp. Cincinnati, Corey & Fairbank, 1834.   From LC card.

Ellis, William R.   A Mirror to Noah Webster's Spelling

Book; . . . From printed title-page (possibly clipped) in MS. copyright record for District of Ohio, 1806-1828; MS. entry dated May 24, 1820.

Ells, B. F. The Dialogue Grammar; or, Book Instructer. Designed to Teach the English Grammar without a Teacher. South Hanover, Ind., Printed at the Hanover College Press, 1834. From *The Western Monthly Magazine*, III, 253 (Apr., 1835). 2d ed., revised and corrected. 216 pp. Dayton, O., B. F. Ells and E. M. Strong, 1835. WRHist.

Finney, Charles Grandison. Skeletons of a Course of Theological Lectures. Vol. I, 248 pp. Oberlin, James Steele, 1840. ChU, WRHist.

Geography for Children; . . . Designed principally for the Use of Schools. . . . by Abbot Lenglet du Fresnoy, and greatly Augmented and Improved by a Teacher of Kentucky. From *Ky. Gaz.*, Apr. 16, 1806.

Goodenow, John M. Historical Sketches of the Principles and Maxims of American Jurisprudence, in Contrast with the Doctrines of the English Common Law on the Subject of Crimes and Punishments: . . . vii, [1], 426, vi pp. Steubenville, O., Printed by James Wilson, 1819. WRHist.

Guilford, Nathan. The Western Spelling Book; . . . 144 pp. Cincinnati, N. & G. Guilford, etc., 1831. NYPL.

Guthrie, Jesse. The American School-master's Assistant; being a Compendious System of Vulgar and Decimal Arithmetic; . . . viii, 235 pp. Lexington, Maccoun, Tilford & Co., 1810. WRHist. 4th ed., revised and corrected. vi ? 202 pp. Paris, Ky., the Rev. John Lyle, 1817. Smith.

Hall, James. The Western Reader; a Series of Useful Lessons, Designed to Succeed Corey and Fairbank's Elementary Reader. Selected and Arranged . . . 216 pp. Cincinnati, Corey and Fairbank, and Hubbard and Edmunds [*sic*], 1833. CinPL, LouPL, NYPL, WRHist.

Harney, John H. An Algebra upon the Inductive Method of Instruction. 288 pp. Louisville, Morton & Griswold, n.d. (1840). ChU, WRHist.

Holloway, Robert S. An Easy and Lucid Guide to a Knowledge of English Grammar, . . . 204 pp. St. Clairsville, O., Printed for the Author, by Horton J. Howard, 1833. CinPL, WRHist.

Houseworth, Henry. Federurbian, or United States Lessons; Intended to Promote Learning and a Knowledge of Republican Principles, in the Minds of our Youth. . . . 144 pp. Philomath, Ind., the Author, Printed by W. E. Johnston, 1839. IndStL, LC.

Hunt, William Gibbes (editor)? Græca Minora. (Lexington, 1823?) From *The Cincinnati Literary Gazette*, Jan. 1, 1824.

The Kentucky Preceptor. (Lexington ? Joseph Charless ? 1806?) From *Ky. Gaz.*, Sept. 22, 1806.

Kilbourn, John. Columbian Geography; or a Description of the United States of America. . . . 228 pp. Chillicothe, Printed by Nashee & Denny, 1815. HistPSO, WRHist.

—— A Geography of the State of Ohio. Designed for Common Schools. 72 pp. Columbus, E. Glover, 1830. From LC card.

—— Introduction to Geography and Astronomy; . . . 6th ed. 24 pp. Columbus, the Author, July, 1826. WRHist.

Leeson, Richard L. A School Book for Militia, in which Tacticks are Explained by the Shape of Human Feet, with Notes of Explanation. 67 pp. Centreville, Ind., Printed by John Scott, for the Author, 1826. IndStL.

The Liberal Primer, or Child's First Book. (Philomath, Ind., 1833.) From *The Sentinel, and Star in the West*, Feb. 16, 1833.

Locke, John. An English Grammar for Children; According to the Elementary Method of Pestalozzi; . . . 228 pp. Cincinnati, W. M. & O. Farnsworth, Jr., Printers, 1827. From LC card.

—— Outlines of Botany. From *The Western Monthly Review*, I, 101 (June, 1827).

—— Problems to Illustrate the most Important Principles of Geography and Astronomy, . . . 14 pp. Cincinnati, Morgan, Fisher and L'Hommedieu, 1828. From LC card.

M'Cullough, Samuel D. Picture of the Heavens, for the Use of Schools and Private Families; . . . 143 pp., with additional matter irregularly paged. Lexington, 1840. LexPL.

M'Donald, James. A New Pronouncing Spelling Book, and Concise Expositor of the English Language. . . . 156 pp. Georgetown, Ky., Printed by Thomas Henderson, 1815. ChU.

—— A New Spelling-book, with Expositor, Adapted to the Different Classes of Learners, . . . xiii, 194 pp. Shelbyville, Ky., Printed by George C. Smoot, 1815. ChU, KyStL.

M'Guffey, William Holmes. The Eclectic Primer: for Young Children. Designed to Precede W. H. M'Guffey's Eclectic Readers. 35, [1] pp. Cincinnati, Truman and Smith, n. d. (1837). WRHist. For attribution to M'Guffey, see M'Guffey, *The Eclectic Third Reader*, 1837, advertisement on back cover.

—— Eclectic First Reader, with Pictures. (Cincinnati, Truman and Smith.) From M'Guffey, *The Eclectic*

Third Reader, 1837, advertisement on back cover. *Cf.* also advertisement following p. 165, *ibid.* Two different forms of the title are given, and probably neither is accurate.

—— The Eclectic Second Reader: Consisting of Progressive Lessons in Reading and Spelling. For the Younger Classes in Schools. With Engravings. 168 pp. Cincinnati, Truman and Smith, n. d. (1836). LC. Revised and Improved Edition of the Eclectic Second Reader; . . . 168 pp. Cincinnati, Truman and Smith, n. d. (1838). LC.

—— The Eclectic Third Reader; Containing Selections in Prose and Poetry, from the Best American and English Writers. With Plain Rules for Reading, and Directions for Avoiding Common Errors. 165, [8] pp. Cincinnati, Truman and Smith, 1837. LC, HistPSO. Revised and Improved Eclectic Third Reader; . . . 165 pp. Cincinnati, Truman and Smith, 1838. WRHist. 26th ed. 165 pp. Cincinnati, Truman and Smith, 1840. WRHist.

—— The Eclectic Fourth Reader; Containing Elegant Extracts in Prose and Poetry, from the Best American and English Writers. With Copious Rules for Reading, and Directions for Avoiding Common Errors. viii, 279 pp. Cincinnati, Truman and Smith, 1837. From copy of original in the library of Miami University, furnished by E. A. F. Porter and H. C. Minnich. The Eclectic Fourth Reader: . . . Enlarged and Improved. Stereotype Edition. 324 pp. Cincinnati, Truman and Smith, 1838. WRHist. 14th ed. 324 pp. Cincinnati, Truman and Smith, 1840. CinPL.

Mansfield, Edward Deering. The Political Grammar of the United States; or, a Complete View of the Theory and Practice of the General and State Governments, . . . 275 pp. New York, Harper & Brothers, 1834. ColU, HistPSO, LexPL, NYPL, WRHist.

Marshall, Humphrey. A Treatise on the Writ of Right. 55 pp. N. p., n. d. (1817?). TransylvaniaU.

Mather, W. W. Elements of Geology, . . . 2d ed. 286 pp. New York, the American Common School Union, 1838. ChU.

Mitchell, Ormsby McKnight. The Works of Quinctilian, Digested and Prepared for the Use of the American Public. Cincinnati (1833 ?). From *The Western Monthly Magazine*, I, 286 (June, 1833).

Mitchell, Thomas Duché. A Cursory View of the History of Chemical Science, and Some of its more Important Uses to the Physician: being an Introductory, to the Course of Lectures, for the Session 1837-8. 22 pp. Lexington, Finnell & Zimmerman, Printers, 1837. ChU.

—— Elements of Chemical Philosophy, on the Basis of Reid, . . . xvi, 553 pp. Cincinnati, Corey & Fairbank, etc., 1832. HistPSO.

Nast, William. The Greek Verb Taught in a Simple and Fundamental Manner According to the Greek Tables of D. Friederich Thiersch . . . with Alterations, Additions and Selections . . . 56 pp. Gambier, O., George W. Myers, Printer, 1835. LexPL.

Niles, M. A. H. Elements of Latin Grammar; with a New Arrangement of Syntax, Compiled from Zumpt's, Adam's, and the Port-Royal Latin Grammars. viii, 91, [2] pp. South Hanover, Ind., Morrow and Bayless, 1834. IndStL.

Parke, Uriah. . . . The Farmers' and Mechanics' Practical Arithmetic, . . . 178 pp. Zanesville, O., A. Lippitt, 1839. From LC card.

—— Parke's Series, No. 3. Key to the Farmers' & Mechanics' Practical Arithmetic: in which the most Difficult Problems are Solved, . . . 130, [1] pp. Zanesville, O., Arnold Lippitt, 1840. WRHist.

Paul, René. Elements of Arithmetic. vi, [2], 160 pp. St. Louis, Printed by Ford & Orr, 1823. LC, MercLStL.

Picket, Albert, and John W. Picket. Introduction to Picket's Expositor; Containing Exercises in English Etymology, Definition and Reading: being the Sequel to the Author's Spelling Book; and Part I. — of the New Juvenile Instructor. 192 pp. Cincinnati, Josiah Drake, 1834. WRHist. 216 pp. Cincinnati, C. P. Barnes, and C. Cropper, 1837. CinPL.

—— The New Juvenile Expositor or Rational Reader, and Key to the Juvenile Spelling Book: . . . being American School Class Book No. 4. 384 pp. Cincinnati, Picket & Co., etc., 1831. CinPL.

—— Picket's Class-book, No. 2. The New Juvenile Reader: . . . 192 pp. Cincinnati, C. P. Barnes, etc., 1837. CinPL.

—— Picket's Class-book, No. 3. The Reader: Containing Pieces in Prose and Verse; Designed for the Higher Classes. 214 pp. (incomplete). Cincinnati, C. P. Barnes, 1836. CinPL.

The Picture Reader; Designed as a First Reading Book, for Young Masters and Misses. By a Friend to Youth. 48 pp. Cincinnati, Truman, Smith & Co., 1833. WRHist.

Ray, Joseph. Ray's Eclectic Arithmetic, on the Inductive and Analytic Methods of Instruction. Designed for Common Schools and Academies. 239 pp. Cincinnati, Truman and Smith, 1837. From LC card.

—— Ray's Little Arithmetic. . . . (Cincinnati, Truman and Smith, 1834?) From *Cinc. Daily Gaz.*, Mar.

28, 1834. *Cf.* also William Holmes M'Guffey, *The Eclectic Third Reader*, 1837, "Advertisement" following p. 165.

—— Ray's Tables and Rules, in Arithmetic, for Children. (Cincinnati, Truman and Smith.) From William Holmes M'Guffey, *The Eclectic Third Reader*, "Advertisement" following p. 165.

Ruter, Martin. An Easy Entrance into the Sacred Language, being a Concise Hebrew Grammar without Points. 96 pp. Cincinnati, 1824. From Smith catalogue.

—— An Easy Introduction to the Study of Arithmetick, Suitable for Young Beginners, . . . From *Ky. Reporter,* Dec. 23, 1829.

—— The Juvenile Arithmetick, and Scholar's Guide; . . . Illustrated by Numerous Questions Similar to those of Pestalozzi. 216 pp. Cincinnati, N. & G. Guilford, 1827. From LC card.

—— The New American Primer, and Juvenile Preceptor: Containing Easy Lessons for Spelling, Reading, and Recitation, together with a Short Scriptural Catechism. . . . N. p. (Cincinnati), n. d. (1821 or 1822). From printed title-page (possibly clipped) in MS. copyright record for District of Ohio, 1806-1828; MS. entry dated Oct. 9, 1821. *Cf.* also *Liberty Hall*, Jan. 9, 1822.

—— New American Spelling Book. From *Liberty Hall*, Mar. 27, 1827.

Shinn, Joshua. The New Ohio Arithmetic, or a New and Complete Calculator; Adapted to the Juvenile Understanding. . . . 251, [1] pp. New-Garden, the Author, 1828. WRHist.

—— Shinn's Arithmetick, or Federal Calculator; . . . to which is Added a Course of Book-keeping, by Single Entry. . . . 3d ed., corrected and revised. 206, [1] pp. St. Clairsville, O., Shinn & Grewell, 1836. WRHist.

Shreve, Joseph. The Speller's Guide, a Spelling Book on a New Plan; with Reading Lessons . . . 2d ed., corrected and improved. 167 pp. Buffaloe, Va., Jackson & Harvey, 1824. From LC card. In WRHist.

Slack, Elijah. A Key to the Technical Language and a Few Other Difficulties of Chemistry; or Chemical Nomenclature. (Cincinnati? 1828?) From *The Western Monthly Review*, I, 693 (Mar., 1828).

Stowe, Calvin Ellis. Introduction to the Criticism and Interpretation of the Bible, Designed for the Use of Theological Students, Bible Classes, and High Schools. 2 vols. Cincinnati, Corey, Fairbank & Webster, 1835. ChU (Vol. II lacking).

Talbott, John L.? Key to the Western Practical Arithmetic, by John L. Talbott. . . . 196 pp. Cincinnati, Ephraim Morgan and Son, 1838. WRHist.

—— The Western Practical Arithmetic, . . . to which is Added a Short System of Book-keeping, . . . 182, [12] pp. Cincinnati, Morgan and Sanxay, etc., 1836 (entered 1833). WRHist.

Walker, Timothy. Elements of Geometry, . . . 132 pp. Philadelphia, J. Kay, Jun. & Brother, etc., 1835. From LC card.

—— Introduction to American Law, Designed as a First Book for Students. xxiv, 679 pp. Philadelphia, P. H. Nicklin & T. Johnson, 1837. YMML.

The Western Primer, or Introduction to Webster's Spelling Book. Illustrated with Seventy-seven Wood Cuts. 35 pp. Cincinnati, Corey and Fairbank, 1833. IllStHist.

Wilson, George. The American Class-reader. From *Detroit Daily Advertiser,* July 6, 1836.

—— A Practical and Theoretical System of Arithmetic. From *Detroit Daily Advertiser*, July 6, 1836. 5th ed., revised and corrected. Canandagua, N. Y., 1838. From

MS. copyright record for District of Michigan, 1824-1857; MS. entry No. 17.

Wilson, Samuel. The Kentucky English Grammar. From *Ky. Gaz.*, Aug. 8, 1798. For later editions, see above, Chapter V, footnotes 54 and 55.

—— The New American Rational Spelling-book: Comprising, the Elements of the English Language . . . 122 pp. Lexington, Printed by William W. Worsley, 1810. From LC card.

—— The Polyanthos; or Kentucky Elegant Selections; Consisting of Essays, Orations, Dialogues, and Historical Anecdotes. The Whole Extracted from the most Celebrated Authors, . . . For the Use of Schools. From prospectus in *Ky. Gaz.*, Nov. 29, 1803. But possibly not published. See above, Chapter V, footnote 60.

Zeisberger, David. Essay of a Delaware-Indian and English Spelling-book, for the Use of the Schools of the Christian Indians on Muskingum River. 113 pp. Philadelphia, Henry Miller, 1776. WRHist.

VII. POPULAR MANUALS

Adams, Rufus W. A Dissertation. Designed for the Yeomanry of the Western Country, Containing a Correct Description of the Best Method of Making Butter and Cheese; . . . 36 pp. Marietta, O., Printed at the Office of the American Friend, n. d. HistPSO.

—— The Farmer's Assistant, Containing a Correct Description of the Best Methods of Raising & Keeping Cows, & Making Butter and Cheese . . . 48 pp. Marietta, O., S. Fairlamp, 1814. From LC card.

Barnum, H. L. Farmer's Farrier, . . . 108 pp. Cincinnati, A. B. Roff, 1831. HistPSO, WRHist.

Benezet, Anthony A. The Family Physician; . . . Calculated particularly for the Inhabitants of the Western Country, and for those who Navigate its Waters. . . . With Original Remarks. By a Graduate of the Pennsylvania University, . . . Who has for Years been Acquainted with the Modes of Living, and with the Diseases of the West. 562 pp. Cincinnati, W. Hill Woodward, n. d. (1826). HistPSO.

Boucherie, Anthony. The Art of Making Whiskey, . . . (Lexington, W. W. Worsley, 1819). From *Ky. Reporter,* Mar. 24, 1819.

Bourne, A. The Surveyor's Pocket-book, Containing Brief Statements of Mathematical Principles, . . . Compiled from Various Sources, . . . 147, [1] pp. Chillicothe, I. N. Pumroy, 1834. WRHist.

Bradford, John. The General Instructor: or the Office, Duty, and Authority of Justices of the Peace, Sheriffs, Coroners and Constables, in the State of Kentucky. . . . xii, 252 pp. Lexington, Printed by John Bradford, 1800. KyStHist.

Burris, William. The Farmer's Farrier Book, . . . Wilmington, O., Rice Gaddis, Printer, 1819. From printed title-page in copyright book for the District of Ohio, 1806-1828.

Cain, John. The Officer's Guide and Farmer's Manual, . . . 347 pp. Indianapolis, Printed by Douglass and Maguire, 1832. IndStL.

Carter, Richard. A Short Sketch of the Author's Life, and Adventures from his Youth until 1818, in the First Part. In Part Second, a Valuable, Vegetable, Medical Prescription, with a Table of Detergent and Corroborant Medicines . . . 461 pp. Versailles, Ky., Printed by John H. Wilkins, 1825. ChU.

Conway, Miles W. Geodœsia, or a Treatise of Practical Surveying, . . . 60 pp. Lexington, Printed by D. Bradford, 1807. From LC card.

Dufour, John James. The American Vine-dresser's Guide, . . . 314, [3] pp. Cincinnati, Printed by S. J. Browne, 1826. CinPL, HistPSO, IndStL.

Ellsworth, Henry William. The American Swine Breeder, a Practical Treatise . . . 304 pp. Boston, Weeks, Jordan and Company, etc., 1840. ColU, LC.

An Essay on the Importance and the Best Mode of Converting Grain into Spirit, . . . (Lexington? W. W. Worsley? 1823.) From *Ky. Reporter*, Nov. 24, 1823.

The Farmer's Guide, and Western Agriculturist. By Several Eminent Practical Farmers of the West. . . . 367 pp. Cincinnati, Buckley, Deforest and Co., 1832. WRHist.

Gazlay, James W. A Treatise on Horses, . . . Compiled from the most Approved Authorities. From *The Western Monthly Review*, I, 192 (July, 1827).

Gazlay, Theodore. The Practical Printers' Assistant: . . . 135 pp. Cincinnati, J. A. James & Co., 1836. From LC card.

Hooper, Edward James. The Practical Farmer, Gardener and Housewife; . . . 544 pp. Cincinnati, Geo. Conclin, 1839. WRHist. 544 pp. Cincinnati, Geo. Conclin, 1840. CinPL, WRHist.

The Indiana Justice, and Farmer's Scrivener: . . . By a Gentleman of the Bar. 168, xl, 5 pp. Indianapolis, Smith and Bolton, 1822. IndStL.

Latta, Samuel A. The Ladies' Guide to Health. . . . 286 pp. Cincinnati, Printed by E. Morgan & Co., 1840. CinPL.

Longgley, John B. The Youth's Companion, or a Historical Dictionary; . . . Originally Compiled by Ezra Sampson, . . . Carefully Revised and Abridged, and Calculated for the Use of Schools and Private Individuals in the Western Country: . . . 300 pp. St. Clairsville, O., Printed for the Compiler by Horton J. Howard, 1832. WRHist.

M'Dougal, John. The Farmer's Assistant, or Every Man his Own Lawyer. 304 pp. Chillicothe, Printed by James Barnes, 1813. HistPSO, WRHist.

Messenger, John. A Manual; or Hand Book, Intended for Convenience in Practical Surveying: . . . From MS. copyright record for District of Illinois, 1821-1848; MS. entry dated Aug. 24, 1821.

The Ohio Officer's Guide, and Clerk's Companion. . . . By a Member of the Bar. xii, 308 pp. (pagination irregular). Steubenville, O., J. & B. Turnbull, 1832. HistPSO, WRHist.

Ruble, Thomas White. The American Medical Guide for the Use of Families, in Two Parts, . . . 222 pp. Richmond, Ky., Printed by E. Harris, for the Author, 1810. ChU.

Scraps, or Food for a Rainy Day, and the Farmer's Pocket Companion: in Five Parts. Compiled, Revised, and Embodied by a Hooshier. 178 pp. Indianapolis, Printed for the Publisher, 1836. IndStL.

Selman, S. H. The Indian Guide to Health, or a Valuable Vegetable Medical Prescription, . . . 200 pp. Columbus, Ind., Printed by James M'Call, Herald Office, 1836. IndStL.

Smith, Peter. The Indian Doctor's Dispensatory, being Father Smith's Advice respecting Diseases and their Cure, . . . Designed for the Benefit of his Children, his Friends, and the Public, but more especially the Citizens of the Western Parts of the United States of America. . . . Cincinnati, 1812. From printed title-page in MS. copyright record for the District of Ohio, 1806-1828. For reprint of 1813 edition, see *Bulletin of the Lloyd Library*, No. 2, 1901.

Swan, Joseph. A Treatise on the Law Relating to the Powers and Duties of Justices of the Peace, and Constables, in the State of Ohio: . . . xviii, 582 pp. Columbus, Isaac N. Whiting, 1837. WRHist.

Swigert, Jacob. The Kentucky Justice; . . . 3d ed. viii, 328 pp. Frankfort, 1838. LouPL.

Van Vleet, Abram. The Ohio Justice and Township Officers' Assistant, . . . 222, [1], 76, iv pp. Lebanon, O., the Author, 1821. WRHist.

Wallis, William. The Western Gentleman's Farrier, . . . 171, [4] pp. Troy, O., John T. Tullis, 1838. HistPSO, WRHist.

The Western Agriculturist, and Practical Farmer's Guide. Prepared under the Superintendence of the Hamilton County Agricultural Society. 367 pp. Cincinnati, Robinson and Fairbank, 1830. LC, TransylvaniaU, WRHist.

Wilcox, P. B. Practical Forms in Actions, Personal and Real, and in Chancery: with Notes, &c. iv, 496 pp. Columbus, Isaac N. Whiting, 1833. WRHist.

VIII. Almanacs

Almanac, for the States of Ohio, Kentucky, and Indiana, for the Year of our Lord 1831; . . . By Oner R. Powell. No pagination. Cincinnati, William Conclin, n. d. WRHist.

An Almanack, for the Year 1801; . . . No pagination. Frankfort, Printed by William Hunter, n. d. LouPL.

Almanac, for the Year of our Lord 1816, . . . No pagination. Georgetown, Ky., Henderson and Reed, 1816. WisH.

Almanac for the Year of our Lord, 1816, . . . [No. 1.] 36 pp. Hamilton, O., Printed at the 'Intelligencer' Office, n. d. HistPSO.

The American Farmer's Almanac, for the Year of our
Lord 1815 . . . No pagination. Lexington, Sold by
W. Essex & Son, and H. C. Sleight, n. d. LouPL, WisH.

Astronomical Diary. The Ohio Almanack, for the Year
of our Lord 1840: . . . [Vol. I, No. 1.] 4, [12] pp.
Cleveland, Sanford & Lott, n. d. WRHist.

Browne's Western Calendar, or the Cincinnati Almanac,
for the Year of our Lord Eighteen Hundred & Six.
(Title-page lacking, supplied by WRHist.) WRHist.
Cf. also Liberty Hall, Nov. 12, 1805. For the years 1807-
1808 (WRHist), 1809 (HistPSO), 1810 (advertised in
Liberty Hall, Sept. 27, 1809), 1811 (HistPSO), 1812
(HistPSO, WRHist), and 1813 (HistPSO).

Charless' Kentucky, Tennessee & Ohio Almanack for the
Year of our Lord 1804: . . . No pagination. Lexington, Printed and Sold by Joseph Charless, n. d. ChU.
For the years 1805 (LexPL), 1806 (LouPL, WisH), and
1807 (ChU, LouPL, WRHist).

Charless' Missouri & Illinois Magazine Almanac, for 1818.
(St. Louis.) From Mo. Gaz., Nov. 22, 1817. For the
years 1819 (advertised in Mo. Gaz.), 1823-1825 (MoHist),
1826-1829 (advertised in Mo. Rep.), 1831 (MercLStL),
1832-1834 (advertised in Mo. Rep.), 1835 (MoHist), and
1836 (advertised in Sangamo Journal).

The Chillicothe Almanac, for the Year of our Lord 1819,
. . . No. I. . . . 48 pp. Chillicothe, Geo. Nashee,
at the Office of the Supporter, n. d. WRHist. Nos.
II-IV, for the years 1820-1822. WRHist.

The Christian Almanac, for Kentucky, for the Year of our
Lord and Saviour Jesus Christ, 1829, . . . 36 pp.
Lexington, the American Tract Society, etc., n. d.
HistPSO, LexPL. For the years 1831 and 1835-1840.
LexPL, LouPL (for 1838 only).

The Christian Almanac, for Ohio, Kentucky, & Indiana,

for . . . 1830: . . . 36 pp. Cincinnati, the American Tract Society, n. d. LexPL, WRHist. For the year 1833. HistPSO.

The Christian Almanac for the Western Reserve . . . for . . . 1831: . . . Vol. II, No. 4. 36, [2] pp. Cleveland, the American Tract Society, n. d. WRHist. For the years 1832 (at Hudson), 1835-1836 (at Hudson), and 1839 (at Cleveland). WRHist.

The Cincinnati Almanac: No. 1: . . . for . . . 1820: . . . 53, [1] pp. Cincinnati, Mason and Palmer, at the Office of the Western Spy, n. d. CinPL.

The Columbus Almanack, for . . . 1821; . . . By William Lusk. No. V. 24 pp. Columbus, the Author, Monitor Office, n. d. WRHist. Nos. X, XI, XVII, and 18, for the years 1827-1828 and 1834-1835. WRHist.

Cummins' Missouri and Illinois Magazine Almanac, for . . . 1821 . . . No. I. No pagination. St. Louis, Printed and Sold by J. C. Cummins, at the Missouri Gazette Office, n. d. MoHist. No. II, for the year 1822. MoHist.

Detroit Almanac and Michigan Register for 1838. (Detroit.) From *Detroit Free Press*, Oct. 25, 1837.

Education Almanac. (Cincinnati, c. 1817 ff. ?) From *The North American Review*, XLVII, 48 (July, 1838).

The Farmer's Almanac, for . . . 1812. (Lexington.) From *Ky. Gaz.*, Oct. 1, 1811. For the years 1816, at Lexington (WisH, LouPL) ; 1819-1821, at Cincinnati (HistPSO) ; 1822-1824, at Lexington (WisH) ; 1826 and 1828, at Lexington (advertised in *Ky. Reporter*) ; 1829-1830, at Lexington (LouPL) ; 1831, at Lexington (advertised in *Ky. Reporter*) ; 1832, at Cincinnati (WRHist) ; and 1840, at Cleveland (WRHist).

The Freeman's Almanack, or, Farmer's Calendar, for
. . . 1823. . . . No pagination. Cincinnati,
Oliver Farnsworth & Co., n. d. HistPSO, WRHist. For
the years 1824-1835 (HistPSO — except 1833 and 1835;
WRHist — except 1829 and 1834); 1837-1840 (Smith —
except 1837; WRHist — except 1839).

Johnson & Warner's Kentucky Almanac, for . . .
1810 . . . No pagination. Lexington, Johnson &
Warner, n. d. WisH. For 1811 (WisH).

The Kentucke Almanack, for the Year of our Lord 1788.
(Lexington.) From *The Kentucke Gazette*, Jan. 5,
1788. Probably printed during the autumn of 1787 (see
ibid., Oct. 13, 1787). For the years 1790 and 1794 (advertised in *Ky. Gaz.*), 1795 (LexPL), 1796-1800 (advertised in *Ky. Gaz.*), 1801 (HistPSO), 1802 (LouPL),
1803 (Smith), 1804 (LouPL), 1805 (advertised in *Ky.
Gaz.*), 1806-1810 and 1815-1821 (WisH), and 1822-1824
(advertised in *Ky. Reporter*).

The Kentucky Farmer's Almanac, for . . . 1810;
. . . No pagination. Lexington, Printed by Wm. W.
Worsley, n. d. LouPL, WisH. For the years 1811-1815
(LouPL — except 1815; WisH); 1817-1818, at George-
town, Ky. (WisH), and 1822, at Frankfort (LouPL).

The Liberal Almanac: for . . . 1839 . . . Vol. I,
No. 1. 24 pp. Cleveland, James S. Underhill, 1838.
WRHist.

Louisville Almanac for 1834. (Louisville.) From *Daily
Lou. Pub. Adv.*, Nov. 6, 1833. Exact title not given.
For the years 1835-1836 (advertised in *Lou. Pub. Adv.*).

The Magazine Almanac for . . . 1838, . . . By
W. Lusk. No pagination. Columbus, E. Glover,
Printer, n. d. WRHist.

Michigan Almanac for 1834. (Detroit.) From *Detroit*

Journal and Michigan Advertiser, Dec. 11, 1833. Exact title probably not given. For the years 1836 (advertised in *Detroit Daily Free Press*) and 1840 (advertised in *Detroit Free Press*).

Michigan Register and Farmers' Calendar, for . . . 1831: . . . No pagination. Detroit, Geo. L. Whitney, n. d. BurColl.

The Missouri Farmer's Almanac and Repository of Useful Knowledge, for . . . 1839: . . . No pagination. St. Louis, J. C. Dinnies & Co., n. d. MercLStL.

The Ohio Almanac, for the Year of our Lord, 1806. . . . By Robert Stubbs, . . . No pagination. Cincinnati, Printed by Joseph Carpenter, n. d. HistPSO. For the years 1810, 1812, and 1814-1816 (HistPSO, WRHist — except 1812 and 1816).

The Ohio Register, and Western Calendar; . . . for . . . 1817. By William Lusk. To be Continued annually. No. I. 58 pp. (incomplete ?). Columbus, P. H. Olmsted and Co., n. d. WRHist. Nos. II and V, for the years 1818 and 1821. WRHist.

Poor Richard's Almanac, for . . . 1835: . . . Astronomical Calculations by Joseph Ray, . . . To be Continued annually. 24 pp. Cincinnati, Truman and Smith, n. d. WRHist.

The West Country Almanac for 1833. Intended expressly for the Farmers of the Mississippi Valley: . . . 36 pp. Cincinnati, Hubbard and Edmands, 1833. HistPSO.

The Western Almanack, for . . . 1817, . . . 36 pp. Cincinnati, Printed by Williams & Mason, at the Office of the Western Spy, n. d. HistPSO. For the years 1818 (HistPSO, WRHist); 1819 (Smith); 1828 and 1830-1831, at Cleveland (WRHist); 1832, at Cincinnati (Smith); 1835, at Columbus (WRHist); and 1840, at Detroit (advertised in *Detroit Free Press,* Sept. 10, 1839).

The Western Almanack, and Michigan Register, for . . . 1826: . . . No pagination. Detroit, Printed by Chipman & Seymour, n. d. DetroitPL. For the year 1827 (advertised in *Michigan Herald,* Jan. 3, 1827).

The Western Calendar; or, Cincinnati Almanac, for . . . 1816, . . . 32 pp. Cincinnati, Printed by Morgan, Williams, & Co., n. d. WRHist.

The Western Comic Almanac: . . . 1834. 48 pp. Cincinnati, N. & G. Guilford & Co. and Hubbard & Edmands, n. d. Smith, WRHist. For the years 1835-1836 (HistPSO) and 1837 (Smith, WRHist).

The Western Farmer's Almanac, for the Year 1809, . . . No pagination. Lexington, Maccoun, Tilford and Co., n. d. WisH.

Western Farmers' Almanac for 1822. (Louisville.) From *Lou. Pub. Adv.,* Nov. 14, 1821. (Exact title probably not given.) For the years 1823 — No. 2 — and 1824 (advertised in *Lou. Pub. Adv.*) ; and 1825-1827 (WisH). For the years 1824-1827, at Lexington (LouPL).

The Western Farmer's Almanac, for . . . 1839: . . . No. XIII. 58 pp. (incomplete). Steubenville, O., James Turnbull, n. d. WRHist.

The Western Reserve Almanac, for . . . 1825: . . . No pagination. Painesville, O., Printed and Sold by E. D. Howe, n. d. WRHist. For the years 1826, 1831, 1835, and 1837-1839 (issues for 1835 and later published at Cleveland). WRHist.

The Western Reserve Magazine Almanac, for . . . 1816. . . . By John Armstrong, . . . No pagination. Warren, O., James White & Co., n. d. WRHist.

The Western Temperance Almanac, for . . . 1835:

. . . 23, [1] pp. Cincinnati, Truman & Smith, n. d. HistPSO.

Worsley & Smith's Kentucky Almanac, and Farmer's Calendar, for . . . 1819: . . . 33, [3] pp. Lexington, Printed at the Office of the Kentucky Reporter, n. d. LouPL, WisH.

CHAPTER VI

FICTION

Burt, Robert. The Scourge of the Ocean. 2 vols. Philadelphia, 1837. From *A Catalogue of Books Belonging to the Young Mens' [sic] Mercantile Library Association of Cincinnati*, n. d. (1838?), No. 1131.

Drake, Benjamin. Tales and Sketches, from the Queen City. 180 pp. Cincinnati, E. Morgan and Co., 1838. ChU, CinPL, LC, WRHist, WisH, YMML.

Flint, Timothy (translator and adapter). The Bachelor Reclaimed, or Celibacy Vanquished. From the French. 288 pp. Philadelphia, Key & Biddle, 1834. WRHist.

—— Francis Berrian, or the Mexican Patriot. . . . 2 vols. Boston, Cummings, Hilliard, and Company, 1826. ColU, HistPSO, WRHist.

—— George Mason, the Young Backwoodsman; or 'Don't Give up the Ship.' A Story of the Mississippi. By the Author of 'Francis Berrian.' 167 pp. Boston, Hilliard, Gray, Little, and Wilkins, 1829. HistPSO, LC.

—— The Life and Adventures of Arthur Clenning. . . . By the Author of "Recollections of Ten Years in the Valley of the Mississippi," "Francis Berrian," &c. 2 vols. Philadelphia, Towar & Hogan, 1828. CinPL, LC, WRHist.

—— The Lost Child. Boston, Putnam & Hunt. From *The North American Review*, XXX, 564 (Apr., 1830).

—— The Shoshonee Valley; a Romance. . . . By the Author of Francis Berrian. 2 vols. Cincinnati, E. H.

Flint, 1830. CinPL, LC, NewL, NYPL, WRHist, YMML.

Ganilh, Anthony. The Novel without a Title. Being a Peep at the West, through the Grate of a Confessional. By the Author of the Quarteroon. Cincinnati, 1835. From *The Western Monthly Magazine*, III, 393 (June, 1835).

Hall, James. The Harpe's Head; a Legend of Kentucky. 256, 36 pp. Philadelphia, Key & Biddle, 1833. Hist-PSO, IU, LC, MoHist, WRHist, WisH.

—— Kentucky. A Tale. 2 vols. London, A. K. Newman and Co., 1834. LC, WisH.

—— Legends of the West. 265 pp. Philadelphia, Harrison Hall, 1832. LC, WRHist. 2d ed. [2], 267 pp. Philadelphia, Key & Biddle, 1833. HistPSO, IU, WRHist, WisH.

—— The Soldier's Bride and Other Tales. 272 pp. Philadelphia, Key and Biddle, 1833. HistPSO, LC.

—— Tales of the Border. 276 pp. Philadelphia, Harrison Hall, 1835. BurColl, LC, WRHist.

Hentz, Caroline Lee. Lovell's Folly. A Novel, . . . 333 pp. Cincinnati, Hubbard and Edmands, 1833. LC.

Kirkland, Caroline M. A New Home — who'll Follow? or, Glimpses of Western Life. By Mrs. Mary Clavers. An Actual Settler. . . . 317, [2] pp. New York, C. S. Francis, etc., 1839. BurColl, ColU, NYPL. 4th ed., revised. 298, [4] pp. New York, C. S. Francis & Co., etc., 1850. IU, WRHist.

M'Clung, John A. Camden; a Tale of the South. . . . 2 vols. Philadelphia, Carey & Lea, 1830. ChU.

Souvenir of the Lakes. (Detroit, Office of the Detroit Journal and Michigan Advertiser, 1831.) From *Detroit Journal and Michigan Advertiser*, Jan. 5, 1831.

Thomas, Frederick William. Clinton Bradshaw; or, the

Adventures of a Lawyer. 2 vols. Philadelphia, Carey, Lea & Blanchard, 1835. LC, YMML.

—— East and West. A Novel. By the Author of "Clinton Bradshaw." 2 vols. Philadelphia, Carey, Lea & Blanchard, 1836. LC, OhioStL.

—— Howard Pinckney. A Novel. By the Author of "Clinton Bradshaw," "East and West," etc., etc. 2 vols. Philadelphia, Lea and Blanchard, 1840. LC, NYPL.

The Western Souvenir, a Christmas and New Year's Gift for 1829. Edited by James Hall. 324 pp. Cincinnati, N. and G. Guilford, n. d. (1829). CinPL, HistPSO, WRHist, WisH.

Wilkinson, Henriette. The Treasure, or Hours in Solitude. . . . Being a Selection of the Best of Pieces from Different Good Authors; with a Few Originals. 211 pp. Cincinnati, Printed by E. Morgan and Co., 1838. Smith, WRHist.

CHAPTER VII

POETRY

I. Songbooks

The American Minstrel. (Cincinnati, U. P. James, 1840.) From *The Daily Chronicle*, June 1, 1840.

Carden, Allen D. The Missouri Harmony, or a Choice Collection of Psalm Tunes, Hymns and Anthems, Selected from the most Eminent Authors, . . . By Allen D. Carden, St. Louis. Published by the Compiler. 200 pp. Cincinnati, Morgan, Lodge & Co., 1820. From Ernst C. Krohn, "A Century of Missouri Music," in *The Missouri Historical Review*, XVII, 134 (Jan., 1923). 199, [1] pp. Cincinnati, Drake and Conclin, 1827. MoHist. Revised and improved. 199, [1] pp. Cincinnati, Morgan and Sanxay, 1832. WRHist. 200, 40 pp. Cincinnati, E. Morgan and Co., 1839. WRHist.

Cleland, Thomas. Evangelical Hymns, for Private, Family, Social, and Public Worship; Selected from Various Authors. Pagination irregular. Lexington, T. T. Skillman, 1825. ChU, KyStL. 2d ed., improved. 436 pp. Lexington, T. T. Skillman, 1828. ChU, KyStL.

The Columbian Harmonist. (Cincinnati, Coleman & Phillips? 1816.) From *Liberty Hall*, Sept. 2, 1816. For ascription of the book to Timothy Flint as compiler, see above, Chapter VII, footnote 38.

Downs, William. A New Kentucky Composition of Hymns and Spiritual Songs; together with a Few Odes, Poems,

Elegies, &c. 389, [2] pp. Frankfort, Gerard & Berry, Printers, 1816. ChU, KyStL.

Gallaher, James. New Select Hymns, Designed to Accompany Watts' Psalms and Hymns. 220 pp. Cincinnati, Corey & Fairbank, 1835. HistPSO.

—— The Psalms, Hymns, and Spiritual Songs of Isaac Watts, D. D.; to which is Added, a New Selection of between Two and Three Hundred Hymns from the Best Authors, . . . Cincinnati, Corey and Fairbank, 1835. From *The Western Monthly Magazine*, III, 310 (May, 1835).

Goddard, Abbott. A Selection of Hymns and Spiritual Songs, Designed for the Use of the Pious. . . . Cincinnati, Abbott Goddard, 1823. From printed title-page in MS. copyright record for the District of Ohio, 1806-1828.

Granade, John A. The Pilgrim's Songster. (Lexington? 1804.) From *Ky. Gaz.*, May 8, 1804. *Cf. ibid.*, Jan. 10, 1804.

Graves, Absalom. Hymns and Psalms. 415, 6 pp. (incomplete). (Lexington? 1825?) ChU (title-page lacking).

The Harrison and Log Cabin Song Book. 105, [3] pp. Columbus, I. N. Whiting, 1840. CinPL, HistPSO, WRHist.

James, U. P. The Eolian Songster, a Choice Collection of the most Popular Sentimental, Patriotic, Naval, and Comic Songs. With Music. 252, [5] pp. Cincinnati, U. P. James, n. d. (first published 1832?). CinPL.

Knight, W. C. The Juvenile Harmony, or, a Choice Collection of Psalm Tunes, Hymns and Anthems, Selected from the most Eminent Authors, . . . 5th ed. 130 pp. (incomplete?). Cincinnati, Morgan & Sanxay, 1831 (first entered in 1825). HistPSO, WRHist.

McNemar, Richard. A Selection of Hymns and Poems;
for the Use of Believers. Collected from Sundry Authors. By Philos Harmoniæ . . . 180, [4] pp.
Watervliet, O., 1833. WRHist.

Metcalf, Samuel L. The Kentucky Harmonist, being a
Choice Selection of Sacred Music, . . . 2d ed. 130,
[2] pp. Cincinnati, for the Author, Morgan, Lodge and
Co., Printers, 1820. Library of Samuel M. Wilson, Lexington, Ky.

Miller, H. A New Selection of Psalms, Hymns and Spiritual Songs, from the Best Authors, Designed for the Use
of Conference Meetings Private Circles, and Congre-
gations. 9th ed. Pagination incomplete. Cincinnati,
Printed by Morgan and Sanxay, 1831 (first entered in
1826). WRHist.

A Selection of Hymns and Spiritual Songs, from the Best
Authors. Together with a Number never before Printed.
. . . 331 pp. Lexington, Printed by J. Charless,
1803. ChU.

Snyder, W. B., and W. L. Chappell. The Western Lyre;
a New Selection of Sacred Music, from the Best Authors;
Including a Number of New and Original Tunes, with a
Concise Introduction to the Art of Singing. Pagination
incomplete. Cincinnati, W. L. Chappell, n. d. (1831).
Smith.

The Tippecanoe Song Book. 64 pp. Cincinnati, U. P.
James, 1840. From *Cinc. Daily Gaz.*, May 30, 1840.

The United States Songster. A Choice Selection of about
One Hundred and Seventy of the most Popular Songs:
Including nearly All the Songs Contained in the Ameri-
can Songster. . . . 223 pp. Cincinnati, U. P.
James, n. d. (entered 1836, but this copy probably much
later). CinPL.

Wells, David. A New Collection of Hymns and Spiritual
Songs, . . . From *Ky. Gaz.*, Nov. 5, 1811.

II. Miscellaneous Verse

Bates, Elisha. The Retrospect: or Reflections on the Goodness of Providence, in the Works of Creation, Redemption, &c. &c. 28 pp. Mountpleasant, O., the Author, 1825. WRHist. 24 pp. Mountpleasant, O., the Author, E. Harris, Printer, 1830. WRHist.

Beach, Samuel B. Escalala: an American Tale. 109 pp. Utica, N. Y., William Williams, 1824. ColU, LC.

Braddock's Defeat; or, the First Field of the West; a Poem. By a Citizen of the West. With Historical Notes. St. Louis, 1839. From Thomson.

Chandler, Elizabeth Margaret. The Poetical Works of Elizabeth Margaret Chandler: with a Memoir of her Life and Character, by Benjamin Lundy. . . . 180 pp. Philadelphia, Lemuel Howell, 1836. ChU, NYPL, WRHist.

Coffeen, John F. The Fate of Genius, and Other Poems. 72 pp. Cincinnati, Alexander Flash, 1835. BrownU.

Curry, Otway. The Lore of the Past, a Poem; Delivered before the Union Literary Society of Hanover College, Ind. at their Fifth Anniversary, September 26, 1837. 23 pp. Cincinnati, R. P. Brooks & Co., Printers, 1838. LexPL, WRHist.

The Dagon of Calvinism, or the Moloch of Decrees; a Poem, in Three Cantos. To which is Annexed a Song of Reason. By the Same. 46 pp. N. p. (Cincinnati?), Printed for the Author, n. d. (1811?). ChU, WRHist. 95 pp. N. p., Printed for the Publisher, 1827. LC.

Depeyster, A. S. Miscellanies, by an Officer. Volume I. 277 pp. Dumfries, Printed by C. Munro, 1813. BurColl.

Emmons, Richard ? The Battle of Bunker Hill, or the Temple of Liberty; an Historic Poem in Four Cantos. . . . 10th ed. (first entered in 1839). Boston, 1859. ChU.

—— Battle of the Thames; being the Seventeenth Canto of an Epic Poem, Entitled the Fredoniad. 37 pp. Lexington, Printed at the Gazette Office, 1822. ChU.

——? The Battle of the Thames, October 5, 1813; from an Unpublished Poem, Entitled Tecumseh, by a Young American. 15 pp. New York, the Log Cabin Office, 1840. BrownU.

—— An Epick Poem in Commemoration of Gen. Andrew Jackson's Victory on the Eighth of January, 1815. 33 pp. Boston, Published for the Author, by William Emmons, 1827. LC.

—— The Fredoniad: or, Independence Preserved. An Epick Poem on the Late War of 1812. Vols. I, II, IV. Boston, William Emmons, for the Author, 1827. ChU, LC, NewL. Vol. III, 295 pp. Boston, Printed by Munroe & Francis, for the Author, 1827. ChU, CinPL, LC, NewL. 2d ed. 4 vols. Philadelphia, William Emmons, 1830. BurColl, CinPL, LC. 3d ed. 4 vols. Philadelphia, William Emmons, 1832. WisH (Vol. I only).

—— The National Jubilee, and Other Miscellaneous Poems. 47, [32] pp. Washington, F. S. Myer, Printer, 1830. Harvard.

Gallagher, William D. Erato, Number I. 36 pp. Cincinnati, Josiah Drake, 1835. CinPL, OhioStL.

—— Erato, Number II. 60 pp. Cincinnati, Alexander Flash, 1835. CinPL, HistPSO, OhioStL, WisH, YMML.

—— Erato, Number III. 60 pp. Cincinnati, Alexander Flash, 1837. OhioStL, WisH.

Ganilh, Anthony. The Quarteroon, a Poem. Cincinnati, 1834. From *The Western Monthly Magazine*, II, 557 (Oct., 1834).

Genin, Thomas H. The Napolead, in Twelve Books; . . . 342 pp. St. Clairsville, O., Printed by Horton J. Howard, 1833. ChU, ColU, HistPSO, NYPL, WRHist.

Guest, Moses. Poems on Several Occasions. To which are Annexed, Extracts from a Journal Kept by the Author while he Followed the Sea, and during a Journey from New-Brunswick, in New-Jersey, to Montreal and Quebec. 160 pp. Cincinnati, Looker & Reynolds, 1823. BrownU, CinPL, LC, WRHist. 2d ed. 158 pp. Cincinnati, Looker & Reynolds, 1824. ChU, NYPL.

Harney, John Milton. Crystalina; a Fairy Tale. By an American. [1], 112 pp. New York, Printed by George F. Hopkins, 1816. LC, LouPL, NYPL, WisH.

Hunn, Anthony. Sin and Redemption. A Religious Poem, . . . 25 pp. Lexington, Printed by W. W. Worsley, 1812. NYPL.

Johnson, Thomas, Jr. [The Kentucky M]iscellany. 4th ed. 36 pp. Lexington, Printed at the Advertiser Office, 1821. ChU. For earlier editions, see above, Chapter VII, footnotes 51 and 53.

Jones, Charles A. The Outlaw, and Other Poems. 72 pp. Cincinnati, Josiah Drake, 1835. CinPL, HistPSO, WRHist.

Lard, Mrs. The Banks of the Ohio. A Poem. 12 pp. Windsor, Vt., Printed by Simeon Ide, 1823. HistPSO.

Lilla; or, the Offering. By "D'Orval." 12 pp. Lexington, J. C. Noble, 1838. From *The Hesperian*, II, 331 (Feb., 1839).

Littell, William. Festoons of Fancy, Consisting of Compositions Amatory, Sentimental and Humorous, in Verse and Prose. 179, [1]pp. Louisville, from the Press of William Farquar, 1814. ChU.

McCracken, Robert. Original Miscellaneous Poems Containing the Reflections of the Author, on the Incidents of his Own Life, and on a Variety of Other Subjects during his Few Leizure Moments . . . 2d ed. (Detroit? 1837?) From MS. copyright record for the District of Michigan, 1824-1857. MS. entry dated July 7, 1837.

McNemar, Richard. A Little Selection of Choice Poetry New and Old, Doctrinal and Devotional. Submitted to the Patronage of the Pious, by E. W. (C. S.) . . . 16, [4 irregularly paged] pp. Watervliet, O., 1835. WRHist.

Marshall, Humphrey. The Aliens: a Patriotic Poem, by H. Marshall, a Senator of the United States. . . . 24 pp. Philadelphia, for the Author, 1798. (Mutilated; place, publisher, and date restored.) LC.

New Years Address, by the Carrier of the Oracle, to his Patrons. 6 pp. Lawrenceburg, Ind., January 1st, 1823. IndStL.

The Old Man's Story of the Rock. A Poem. . . . 15 pp. Lancaster, O., Wright and Mœller, Printers, 1838. Logansport Public Library.

Peirce (or Pierce?), Thomas. The Muse of Hesperia. A Poetic Reverie. . . . 52 pp. Cincinnati, the Philomathic Society, 1823. HistPSO.

—— The Odes of Horace in Cincinnati; as Published in the "Western Spy and Literary Cadet," during the Year 1821. 117 pp. Cincinnati, Printed at Harrison's Press, 1822. BrownU, HistPSO, WRHist.

Pratt, Parley P. The Millenium, and Other Poems: to which is Annexed, a Treatise on the Regeneration and Eternal Duration of Matter. iv, [2], 148 pp. New York, Printed by W. Molineux, 1840. WisH.

Schoolcraft, Henry Rowe. Transallegania, or the Groans of Missouri. A Poem. 24 pp. New York, the Author, 1820. LC, NYPL.

——, and Henry Whiting? The Rise of the West, or a Prospect of the Mississippi Valley. By H. R. S. A Retrospect: or the Ages of Michigan. By H. W. 36

pp. Detroit, Geo. L. Whitney, 1830. From transcript of title-page in BurColl.

Shreve, Joseph. Poems on the Conclusion of the Winter Schools at Salem, at the Close of the Winters 1831 and 1832. By the Teacher. Published by the Pupils. 21 pp. New Lisbon, John Watt, Printer, 1832. WRHist.

Thomas, Frederick W. The Emigrant, or Reflections while Descending the Ohio. A Poem. . . . 48 pp. Cincinnati, Alexander Flash, 1833. CinPL, OhioStL, WRHist.

Thompson, G. Burton. An Address of G. Burton Thompson, Esq. of Cincinnati, Ohio, to the Citizens of Mercer County, Kentucky. To which is Prefixed a Short Poem, Written by himself, Induced by his Reflections upon the Death of his Wife and Six Infants. . . . 22, [1] pp. Harrodsburg, Ky., Printed by William Tanner, 1829. ChU.

Toulmin, J. R. A Little Poem on Peace & War. Second Edition Corrected. To which is Added, Two Lesser Poems. (Lexington, Office of the Kentucky Gazette? 1803.) From *Ky. Gaz.*, Mar. 29, 1803.

Umphraville, Angus. Missourian Lays, and Other Western Ditties. 72 pp. St. Louis, Isaac N. Henry & Co., 1821. MercLStL, OhioStL.

Wallace, William Ross. The Battle of Tippecanoe, Triumphs of Science, and Other Poems. 105, [1] pp. Cincinnati, P. McFarlin, 1837. CinPL, IndStL, OhioStL.

—— The Triumphs of Science, a Poem, Delivered before the Whig Society of Hanover College, . . . 1836. 24 pp. Louisville, Printed at the Office of the Western Presbyterian Herald, 1837. LaneTS.

Ward, James Warner. Yorick, and Other Poems. 71 pp. Cleveland, Sanford and Lott, 1838. WRHist.

Welsh, Joseph S.   Harp of the West: a Volume of Poems,
    . . . 204 pp. Cincinnati, Printed by Dawson and
    Fisher, 1839. IndStL.
Whiting, Henry. The Age of Steam, by ———— Anony-
    mous, Esq. 16 pp. Detroit (Printed at the Journal
    Office), 1830. BurColl.
—— The Emigrant. A Poem. . . . 27 pp. Detroit,
    Printed by Sheldon & Reed, 1819. BurColl.
—— Ontwa, the Son of the Forest. A Poem. 136 pp.
    New York, Wiley and Halsted, 1822. BurColl, WisH.
—— Sannillac, a Poem. . . . With Notes by Lewis
    Cass and Henry R. Schoolcraft, Esqs. iv, 155 pp. Bos-
    ton, Carter, Hendee and Babcock, 1831. BurColl, NYPL,
    WisH.
Wilson, Samuel.   Chelys Hesperia, carmina quædam anni-
    versaria, et alia, numeris Latinis Sapphicis modulata,
    continens, cum notis aliquot adjectis. Auctore S. Wilson
    A. M. . . . 23 pp. Lexingtoniæ, typis T. Smith,
    1825. Library of Samuel M. Wilson, Lexington, Ky.
Worth, Gorham. American Bards: a Modern Poem, in
    Three Parts. . . . 52 pp. N. p. ("West of the
    Mountains"), 1819. BrownU, HistPSO.

CHAPTER VIII

DRAMA

(For sources of the history of Western drama, see bibliographies for earlier chapters, especially Chapters I-III.)

Published Plays

Emmons, Richard. Tecumseh: or, the Battle of the Thames, a National Drama, in Five Acts. 36 pp. New York, Elton & Harrison, 1836. WRHist.

Jones, Abram. Love in Jeopardy, a Tragic Comedy. (Lexington? 1810.) From *Ky. Gaz.*, Nov. 6, 1810.

Nelson, T. Somers. Loss and Gai[n] a Comedy, in Five Acts. . . . Dedicated to the St. Louis Thespian Association. 108 pp. St. Louis, Meech & Dinnies, 1835. From photostat copy in library of William Clark Breckenridge, St. Louis.

Owen, Robert Dale. Pocahontas: a Historical Drama, in Five Acts; with an Introductory Essay and Notes. By a Citizen of the West. 240 pp. New York, George Dearborn, 1837. ChU, CinPL, ColU, IndStL, LC, WRHist.

Wallace, William Ross. Leila, or the Siege of Grenada: a Melo-drama, in Three Acts from E. L. Bulwer's Novel of that Title. 45, [2] pp. Lexington, J. C. Noble, 1838. ChU.

Wetmore, Alphonso. The Pedlar: a Farce in Three Acts. Written for the St. Louis Thespians, by whom it was Performed with Great Applause. 34, [1] pp. St. Louis, John A. Paxton, 1821. MercLStL.

CHAPTER IX

THE VOGUE OF BRITISH AND EASTERN WRITERS

(See bibliographies for earlier chapters.)

INDEX

The index includes no references to preface or bibliographies. Nor does it include the names of Middle Western states (too often mentioned for practical indexing); names denoting sections of the United States (e.g., *the West*), except *New England*; or such general and frequently recurring geographical terms as *America*, *Europe*, *Atlantic*, and *Pacific*. With these exceptions, I have attempted to list all proper names used in the book.

Works cited in the footnotes as *op. cit.* are so marked in the index, and are to be found through reference to the name of the author. Works cited in the footnotes as *ibid.* are indexed by title. All references to footnotes are followed by the abbreviation *n.* except when several consecutive page numbers are united in a single entry. A dash denotes repetition of only the first word in the preceding entry. Certain ligatures have necessarily been printed here as separate letters.

Abaellino (Dunlap), I, 418
Abbot, The (Sir Walter Scott), II, 21, 22
Abdy, E. S., I, 171n.
Abolition Intelligencer, I, 194, 194n.
Abolition Society of Paint Valley, I, 217
"Abstract of the Journal of a Mission, An" (Maccluer), I, 97
Academic Institute, I, 239
Academic Pioneer, The, I, 66n., 199, 239
Account of a Voyage up the Mississippi, An, I, 87
Account of Expeditions, An, I, 87
Account of Monsieur de la Salle's Last Expedition, An, I, 81
Account of the Conduct of the Shakers, An (Van Vleet), I, 226
Account of the Law-suit Instituted by Rev. G. A. M. Elder, An (Nathan L. Rice), I, 230
Account of the Louisville City School, An, 52n.
Account of the Remarkable Occurrences in the Life and Travels of Col. James Smith, An, I, 92

Achilles, I, 77
Act Incorporating the City of Cincinnati, An, I, 437n.
Act of Incorporation (Kentucky Historical Society), I, 238n.
Act Passed at the First Session of the Fourth Congress, An, I, 70
Adair, manager of Detroit Museum, I, 411
Adams, John, I, 27n., 164n.
——, J. Q., I, 231
——, Rufus W., I, 265, 265n.
Address Delivered before the Antiquarian and Historical Society of Illinois, An (James Hall), I, 237
Address Delivered before the Union Literary Society of Miami University, An (Young), I, 208n.
Address Delivered before the Vincennes Historical and Antiquarian Society (Law), I, 236
Address of G. Burton Thompson, An, I, 422
Address to the Christian Churches, An (Barton W. Stone), I, 223
Address to the Churches on the Subject of Slavery, An, I, 217

Address to the Farmers of Great Britain, An (Birkbeck), I, 125

"Address to the Reader" (Guest), I, 337n.

Adelgitha (M. G. Lewis), I, 416

Adelphi Theatre, Louisville, I, 407, 450, 451

Adonais (Shelley), II, 29

Adrian, Mich., I, 26n.

"Adventures of Daniel Boone, The" (Daniel Bryan), I, 122n.

"Adventures of Gilbert Imlay, The," I, 122n.

"Adventures with the Indians," I, 167

Advertiser Office, Lexington, I, 320n.

Age of Steam, The (Whiting), I, 347

Alabama, I, 380

Albany, N. Y., I, 25n., 368n., 369n.

—— Theatre, I, 367, 368n.

Albion (England), I, 331

——, Ill., I, 34

Alcott, Bronson, I, 182

Alethian Critic, I, 189

Alexander I, Czar, I, 335

Algic, word, I, 241

Algic Researches (Schoolcraft), I, 241

Alien and Sedition Laws, I, 211

Allegheny Mountains, I, 13, 104n., 125, 128, 173, 241, 247, 364, 368n.; II, 34

Allen, I. M., I, 44n.

——, J. H., I, 184n.

——, Nathaniel, I, 23n.

Allibone, S. Austin, I, 296n., 297n., 300n., 347n.

All the World's a Stage, I, 353

Almack's, I, 125n.

Alman, A., I, 426, 426n.

Almoner, The, I, 189

Alps, II, 20

Alton, Ill., I, 34, 153, 218

Alumni and Former Student Catalogue of Miami University, The, I, 60n.

Alvord, Clarence, I, 31n., 34n.

Ambleside, England, I, 181n.

Ambrosio, or the Monk (M. G. Lewis), I, 416

America, and the American Church (Caswall), I, 16n. and as *op. cit.*, 126

American Almanac, The, I, 40n., 45n., 55n., 61n., 63n., 65, 67n., 135n., 156n.

American Antiquarian Society, I, 240

American Ballads and Songs (Pound), I, 310n.

American Bards (Worth), I, 323, 323n., 324n.; II, 19, 19n. and as *op. cit.*

American Book Company, I, 267

—— Bottom, I, 6n., 34, 283

American Conchology (Say), I, 257

American Gazetteer, The (Morse), I, 128

American Historical Review, The, I, 15n., 86n., 101n.

American Minstrel, The, I, 318

American Quarterly Review, The, I, 91n., 94n., 109

American Revolution: *see* Revolutionary War

—— Theatre, Louisville, I, 388, 406, 406n., 419, 452-454

—— Theatre, New Orleans, I, 381, 404

Americans, The (Calvin Colton), I, 109

"Americans and their Detractors, The," I, 111

Americans as they are, The (Postl), I, 74n.

Americans in their Moral, Social, and Political Relations, The (Grund), I, 78n.

American Western University, I, 61

Amphitheatre, Cincinnati, I, 382, 383, 403, 447, 448, 449, 450

——, Louisville, I, 449, 450

Amphlett, William, I, 129

Amulet, The, II, 4n.

"Amusements of Earlier Days in Detroit" (Burton), I, 361n.

Anacreon, II, 9, 9n.

Analysis of Pope's Essay on Man (W. C. Bell), I, 262; II, 8, 8n.

Animal Magnetism (Inchbald), I, 415n.

Annales générales des sciences physiques, I, 257n.

Annals of Chicago, The (Balestier), I, 35n., 397n.
"Annals of the Shop" (Wetmore), I, 283
Ann Arbor, Mich., I, 25n.
Anne of Geierstein (Sir Walter Scott), II, 13n.
Annual Register, The (Western Literary Institute), I, 66n., 239
Anti-conspirator, The, I, 201
Antiquarian and Historical Society of Illinois, I, 237
Aplington, Kate, I, 308n.
Apollo, god, I, 323, 324
Apology, An, I, 222
Apology for Calvinism, An (Bishop), I, 223
Appalachian Mountains, I, 104n.
Appeal from the Misrepresentations of James Hall, An (Mann Butler), I, 246
Appeal to the People of Illinois, An (Birkbeck), I, 216
Appeal to the Public, An, I, 228
Apprentices' Library, Cincinnati, I, 68
Arabian transparencies, I, 431
Archaeologia Americana, I, 135n., 240, 240n.
Archbold, A., I, 392, 447
Areopagitica (Milton), I, 218
Arfwedson, C. D., I, 102
Arianism, I, 219
Aristotle, II, 9
Arius, I, 190
Arminianism, I, 219, 225
Arnold, William, I, 392, 449
Asbury, Francis, I, 19n., 23n., 41n., 47n., 50, 50n., 98
Ashe, Thomas, I, 58n., 75n., 102, 103, 103n., 104, 104n., 105, 106, 114
Asia, I, 83n., 292
Associate Methodist Church, I, 228
——— Reformed Church, I, 191, 222, 223, 224
Astley's Amphitheatre, London, I, 383
Astoria (Irving), I, 291
Astorian expedition, I, 99

As you Like it (Shakespeare), I, 414n.
Atala, I, 423
Atala (Chateaubriand), I, 90, 289, 345
Athens, Greece, I, 408
——— of the West, I, 28
———, O., I, 60
Atherton, Miss, II, 19
Atlantic Souvenir, The, I, 422; II, 37n.
Atwater, Caleb, I, 53n., 123, 128, 166, 168, 236, 240, 245, 245n.
——— Street, Detroit, I, 409
Audubon, John James, I, 99, 100
Aufforderung und Erklärung in Betreff einer Auswanderung im Groszen aus Deutschland, I, 19n.
"August" (Gallagher), I, 341n., 342
Aurora, goddess, I, 335
Ausflug nach den Felsen-Gebirgen, Ein (Wislizenus), I, 21n.
"Author's Own Epitaph, The" (Thomas Johnson), I, 322
Autobiography (Caldwell), I, 256n.
Autobiography (James B. Finley), I, 48n.
Autobiography of Joseph Jefferson, The, I, 396n. and as *op. cit.*
Aztecs, I, 240

"BABY in the Woods," I, 393
Babylon, I, 77
"Backwoodsman, The" (James Hall), I, 277, 280
Badin, Stephen T., I, 12n., 230, 230n.
Bailey, Dr., I, 197
———, John, I, 225, 226
——— & Rogers, I, 387, 455
Balbec (Heliopolis), I, 79
Baldwin, Theron, I, 62n.
Balestier, Joseph, I, 35n., 397n.
Balize, the, I, 381n.
Ball, Henry L., I, 143n.
"Ballads and Rhymes from Kentucky" (Kittredge), I, 311n.
Ballantynes, of Edinburgh, II, 16, 16n.
Baltimore, Md., I, 27n., 219, 324, 324n.

Banks of the Ohio, The (Lard), I, 348, 348n.
Baptist Advocate, The, I, 191
Baptists, I, 42, 43, 44, 45, 49, 51, 63, 191
Baptists in America, The (Cox and Hoby), I, 98
Barataria, Isle of, I, 82n.
"Barbara Allen," I, 310
Barbiere di Siviglia, Il (Rossini), I, 419
Bardstown, Ky., I, 39, 40n., 230
Barlow, Joel, I, 330, 331, 332, 335; II, 19, 31
"Baron de Lahontan, Le" (Roy), I, 82n.
Barrett: *see* Blissett
Barry, Phillips, I, 311n.
Bassanio, I, 379n.
Bates, Elisha, I, 157, 190, 191, 229
―― & Surtees, I, 388, 405
Battery, New York, I, 36n.
Battle Ground, Ind., I, 338
Battle of Bunker Hill, The, I, 332
"Battle of Point Pleasant, The," I, 308
Battle of the Thames (Richard Emmons), I, 329, 329n., 333
Battle of the Thames, The, I, 333
Battle of Tippecanoe, The (William Ross Wallace), I, 338; II, 20n.
Bazaar, Mrs. Trollope's, I, 110
Beach, Samuel, I, 346, 346n.; II, 20
Beale, actor, I, 368n.
Beall, Benjamin, I, 320n.
Beatty, Charles, I, 97
Beauchamp, Jereboam, I, 73
Beauties of the Hon. Henry Clay, The, I, 210n.
Beckford, Henry, I, 298
――, Ralph, I, 298
Bédier, Joseph, I, 91n.
Beecher, Catharine, I, 267
――, Edward, I, 153n., 218
――, Harriet: *see also* Harriet Beecher Stowe, I, 173, 287
――, Lyman, I, 62, 67, 224, 225
―― family, I, 51
Bee Hunter, The, I, 427, 427n.
Beggar's Opera, The (Gay), I, 414
Beggs, S. R., I, 50n.

Beginnings of Literary Culture in the Ohio Valley (Venable), I, 70n., 104n., 138n. and as *op. cit.*, 236n., 296n., 323n., 357n.; II, 32n. and as *op. cit.*
Belden, H. M., I, 311n.
Bell, Thomas H., I, 196
――, William C., I, 262; II, 8, 8n.
Bellefontaine, Ill., I, 34
Belle's Stratagem, The (Cowley), I, 415
Belleville, Ill., I, 21n.
Bellini, Vincenzo, I, 419
Beltrami, Constantino, I, 89
Benedict, H. T. M., I, 264
Benning, Thomas R., I, 134n.
Benton, Thomas Hart, I, 209
Beppo (Byron), II, 14
Bericht über eine Reise (Duden), I, 3n.
Bernhard, Duke of Saxe-Weimar, I, 33n., 41n., 102, 240, 240n.
Berquin, M., I, 12n.
Berrian, Francis, I, 288
Bertram (Maturin), I, 374n., 416
Betterton (Thomas H. Shreve), I, 301, 301n.
Bible, I, 162, 189, 222, 227, 262, 335
"Bible, The," I, 269
"Bibliography of American Newspapers, 1690-1820" (Brigham), I, 135n.
Bickley, John, I, 133n.
Biddle, James W., I, 7n.
――, John, I, 237
――, Richard, I, 108n.
Billy Earthquake, I, 73
"Billy Moody" (Peirce), I, 327; II, 20
Bingham, Caleb, I, 74n.
Biographical Memoir of Daniel Boone (Timothy Flint), I, 251
"Biographical Sketches," I, 176
Biographical Sketches (John McDonald), I, 250, 250n., 251, 251n.
Biographical Sketches (John W. Campbell), I, 251
Biography of Henry Clay (Prentice), I, 252
Bird, Robert Montgomery, I, 73, 421

Birkbeck, Morris, I, 31n., 105, 106, 113, 124, 125, 125n., 216, 279, 290, 303

Birney, Gillespie, and Company, I, 320n.

———, James G., I, 217, 218, 218n.

———, William, I, 218n.

Bishop, Robert Hamilton, I, 50n., 59, 60, 67, 77n., 215n., 219n., 222n., 223, 223n., 224n., 239, 248, 270

Bishop Chase's Defence of himself, I, 229

Black-eyed Susan (Jerrold), I, 416

Black Hawk, I, 248, 249

——— War, I, 23, 35

Blackwell, Robert, I, 172

——— & Hall, I, 172

Blackwood's Edinburgh Magazine, I, 5n., 112, 112n.; II, 3, 3n.

Blaike, theatrical manager, I, 394, 455, 456

Blakely, American naval officer, I, 331

Blake, William, I, 2

Blanchard, theatrical manager, I, 378, 443

———, Charles, I, 39n.

Blanche of Devan, II, 20

Blane, William N., I, 32n., 103n., 114, 115n.; II, 13n.

Blazeaway, I, 299

Blennerhasset Island, I, 347

Bliss, Leonard, I, 264, 264n.

Blissett, actor, I, 367n.

Blois, J. T., I, 10n., 17n., 20n., 26n., 40n., 62n., 129

Bloomington, Ind., I, 61, 187

Blue Beard (Colman), I, 416n.

Blue Devils, The (Colman), I, 416n.

Blunt, Edmund M., I, 129

Blythe, actor, I, 374n.

———, James, I, 59, 189, 248

Boatman's Magazine, The I, 74n.

Body of Christ, The (M'Chord), I, 224

Bolanus, I, 256

Bold Throw for a Husband, A (Cowley), I, 415n.

Bold Throw for a Wife, A (Centlivre), I, 415n.

Book of Mormon, I, 232

Boone, Daniel, I, 2, 13, 22n., 94, 122, 122n., 243, 251, 274, 278, 347; II, 14

Boon House, in Kentucky, I, 299

Booth, Junius B., I, 399, 399n.

Bossu, Jean Bernard, I, 79, 83, 83n., 84

Boston, Mass., I, 11n., 58, 147n., 190, 253n., 291n., 329n., 368n., 423

——— Arena Company, I, 452

——— Circus, I, 453

Boswell, James, I, 1, 4n.

Boswell's Life of Johnson, I, 4n., 5n.

Botanical Luminary, I, 199

Botanico-medical Recorder, The, I, 198

Bourdin, Henri, I, 133n.

Bourne, Edward G., I, 86n.

Bowness, England, I, 181n.

Boylston Medical Committee, I, 255

Brackenridge, H. M., I, 8n., 9n., 90, 90n., 95, 99, 124, 276n., 304, 304n.

———, Hugh H., I, 276

Bradbury, John, I, 8n., 99, 256, 304, 304n.

Bradford, Daniel, I, 133n., 134n., 146, 164, 165

———, Fielding, I, 133

———, Fielding, Jr., I, 134n.

———, John, I, 70, 132, 133, 133n., 134n., 153, 164; II, 4n.

Bradsher, Earl L., II, 2n.

Breckenridge, William Clark, I, 21n., 307n.

Brewster, George, I, 262

Brickibus, M. D., Professor, I, 326

Bride of Abydos, The (Dimond), I, 417

Bridge, B., I, 267

Brief History of the Church of Christ of Latter Day Saints, A (Corrill), I, 232

Brigand, The, I, 420

Brigham, Clarence S., I, 135n., 136n., 139n., 141n., 156n.

"Bright Star" (John Keats), I, 181n.

Brissot, J. P., I, 114n.

Bristed, John, I, 72n., 76n.; II, 2, 2n.
Britain: see Great Britain
British: see also English and Great Britain, I, 6, 45n., 85, 104, 112, 115n., 119, 247, 250, 294, 295, 315, 332; II, 30
———— authors: see also English authors, I, 113, 128, 180, 266, 343; II, 1-30, 31
"British Ballads in the Cumberland Mountains" (Shearin), I, 311n.
British Isles: see Great Britain
———— magazines, I, 5n., 111, 170, 306; II, 3, 27
———— travellers, I, 5, 102-117, 125, 405n.
Broken Sword, The (Dimond), I, 416, 428
Brooklyn, N. Y., I, 122n.
Brooks, R. P., I, 184n.
Brookville, Ind., I, 363
Brown, Austin H., I, 425n.
————, J. Purdy, I, 382, 383, 383n., 384n., 387, 401, 447, 448, 449, 450
————, O. W., I, 387, 454
————, O. W., & Co., I, 453
————, Paul, I, 33n.
————, Samuel R., I, 12n., 28n., 36n., 129, 142n.
————, T. Allston, I, 381, 381n.
———— County, O., I, 216
———— University, I, 333n.
Browne, John W., I, 136n., 137, 137n.
————, John W., & Company, I, 228
————, Samuel J., I, 137n.
Brown's Amphitheatre, Lexington, I, 448, 449
———— equestrian company: see also J. Purdy Brown and O. W. Brown, I, 451
Brussels, I, 257
Bruté, Bishop, I, 39
Brutus (Payne), I, 417n.
Bryan, Daniel, I, 122n.
Bryant, William Cullen, I, 15n.; II, 31, 35
Buchanan, Joseph, I, 261, 263
Buck, Solon J., I, 14n., 16n., 34n.

Buckeye and Cincinnati Mirror, The, I, 163
Buckstone, J. B., I, 420
Buffalo, N. Y., I, 18, 24, 25n., 391, 394
Bullard, Artemas, I, 39n.
Bullock, William, I, 125, 125n.
Bulwer-Lytton, Edward, I, 131, 417, 426, 427
Bunn, Matthew, I, 308, 308n.
Burgess, Dyer, I, 201, 235
————, N. G., & Co., I, 71
"Burial of the Minnisink" (Longfellow), II, 37n.
Burke, William, I, 228
Burnet, Isaac G., I, 137n.
————, Jacob, I, 238
Burns, Robert, II, 2, 11, 11n., 12n., 29
Burr, Aaron, I, 213; II, 17
Burrows and Tunis, I, 378, 443
Burt, Robert, I, 301
Burton, Clarence M., I, 6n., 10n., 361n.
———— Collection, Public Library, Detroit, I, 11n., 12n., 261n., 347n.
Burton's Gentleman's Magazine, I, 340n.
Busseron Creek, Ind., I, 41n.
Busy Body, The (Centlivre), I, 353, 415n.
Butler, Mann, I, 59, 85n., 122n., 144n., 179, 206, 206n., 243, 243n., 244, 246
————, Samuel, author of Hudibras, I, 326
Buttrick, Tilly, I, 121
By-laws and Ordinances of the City of Detroit, I, 362n., 391n.
Byron, George Gordon, Lord, I, 2, 31n., 111, 122n., 131, 167, 276, 278, 298, 299, 321, 323, 327, 328, 338, 339, 347, 417; II, 1, 2, 11-23, 27, 28, 31

CABELL, theatrical manager, I, 387, 451
———— & Forrest, I, 387, 450
Cadillac, Antoine de la Mothe, I, 36
Cadiz, O., I, 191
"Cadwallen" (Gallagher), I, 342n.

Cahokia, village, I, 6, 34
Cain (Byron), II, 14
Cain Ridge, in Kentucky, I, 46, 47, 47n.
Cake, Julius, I, 299
Caldwell, Charles, I, 58n., 59, 59n., 67, 206, 206n., 254, 255, 256n.; II, 7n.
———, James, I, 366n., 381, 381n., 382, 384, 385, 385n., 386, 386n., 387, 388, 404, 405, 406, 407, 408, 432, 434, 446-450, 452
California, I, 292
"Calomel," I, 310n.
Calvin, John, I, 219
Calvinism, I, 189, 222
Calvinists, I, 204, 229
Cambridge History of American Literature, The (William P. Trent and others), I, 276n., 311n., 425n.
Camden (M'Clung), I, 294, 295, 295n.; II, 18, 35n.
Camden, S. C., I, 294
Campaign, The, I, 159
Campbell, Alexander, I, 44, 223, 224, 231n., 233
———, John P., I, 223
———, John W., I, 251
———, Olive Dame, I, 311n.
———, Thomas, II, 2, 19
Campbellism Exposed (William Phillips), I, 229
Campus Martius, I, 166n.
Canada, I, 11n., 84, 92, 142n.
Canadian frontier, I, 115
——— "patriots," I, 435
Canadians, I, 31, 304, 307
Cane Ridge: *see* Cain Ridge
Canton, O., I, 20n., 21n.
Cape Girardeau, Mo., I, 376
Capitolium, I, 166n.
Captain Bonneville (Irving), I, 291
Carden, Allen D., I, 316n.
Cargill, actor, I, 368n.
Carlyle, Thomas, I, 79, 83, 84n., 177, 180; II, 12n., 30, 30n.
Carmelite, The (Cumberland), I, 415n.
Carolinas, the I, 13, 14
Carondelet, village, I, 8n., 291
Carpenter, Joseph, I, 136

Carré, Henri, I, 9n.
Carter, John, I, 448
Carthage, Ill., I, 202
Cartwright, Peter, I, 50, 226, 227, 227n., 228n.
Carver, Jonathan, I, 86, 86n.
Cass, Lewis, I, 76, 88, 94n., 96, 96n., 130, 130n., 237, 241, 242; II, 34
Casseday, Ben, I, 73n.
Casseday's History of Louisville, I, 73n.
Cass Street, Detroit, I, 362, 409
Castle of Indolence, The (James Thomson), I, 116
Castle Spectre, The (M. G. Lewis), I, 416
Caswall, Henry, I, 16n., 28n., 45n., 64, 64n., 126
Catalogue of Books Belonging to the Library of the Philomathesian Society of Kenyon College, A, II, 24n.
Catalogue of Books Belonging to the Young Mens' Mercantile Library Association of Cincinnati, A, I, 68n., 301n.; II, 3n., 25n.
Catalogue of Mineralogical and Geological Specimens (David Dale Owen), I, 258
Catalogue of the Books, Belonging to the Lexington Library Company, A, I, 68n.
Catalogue of the Books Contained in the Library of Miami University, A, II, 3n.
Catalogue of the Books in the Lexington Library, II, 9n., 12n., 24n.
Catalogue of the . . . Erodelphian Society of Miami University, A, II, 25n.
Catalogue of the Harris Collection of American Poetry, A (Stockbridge), I, 333n.; II, 31n.
Catalogue of the Officers and Students in Indiana University, I, 61n.
Catalogue of the Officers and Students of Hanover College, I, 63n.
Catalogue of the Officers and Students of Illinois College, I, 62n.
Catalogue of the Officers and Students of Miami University, I, 60n.

Catalogue of the Officers and Students of Transylvania University, A, I, 59n.
Catalogue of the Ohio State Library, II, 25n.
Catalogue of the Transylvania Law Class, I, 60n.
Catalogue of Valuable Books, A, II, 24n.
Catharine and Petruchio (Shakespeare), I, 371n., 413, 414n.
Cathcart, W. H., I, 355n.
Catholepistemiad, or University of Michigania, I, 61, 166n.
Catholic periodicals, I, 21n., 158
Catholics, I, 38, 39, 39n., 40, 43, 63, 174, 204, 230, 231
Catholic Telegraph, The, I, 158
Cauthorn, Henry S., I, 138n., 236n.
Cave-in-Rock, on the Ohio, I, 103, 347
Cavins, I. T., I, 134n.
Celeste, Mlle., I, 399, 400
Centennial History of Cincinnati (Greve), I, 316n.
Centinel of the North-Western Territory, The, I, 23n., 24n., 27n., 52n., 70, 135, 136n., 147n., 149n., 211n.; II, 4n., 9n., 11n.
Centlivre, Susanna, I, 414, 415n.
Chactas, I, 90
Chaldean Magi, I, 431
Chambers & Knapp, I, 141n.
———, Harris & Knapp, I, 141n.
———, Knapp & Co., I, 140, 141n.
Chandler, Elizabeth M., I, 337n.
Channing, W. H., I, 51, 183, 183n.
"Chanson de l'année du coup" (Trudeau), I, 307
Chapman family (actors), I, 397, 397n.
Chappell, W. L., I, 317
"Chapter on Autography, A" (Poe), I, 339n.
"Characters at the Hotel" (Peirce), I, 326
Charless, Edward, I, 140n.
———, Edward, & Co., I, 140n.
———, & Paschall, I, 141n.
———, Edw., and Paschall, N., I, 141n.

———, Joseph, I, 139, 139n., 140, 140n., 152
Charless' Kentucky, Tennessee, and Ohio Almanac, I, 139n.
Charles the Second (Payne), I, 417
Charleston, S. C., I, 366
Charlevoix, Pierre, I, 82n., 84, 86n., 95, 425
Chase, Philander, I, 45n., 46n., 62, 229, 235
———, Salmon P., I, 245, 245n.
———, Samuel, I, 229
Chateaubriand, François René, I, 2, 3n., 90, 91, 91n., 118, 284, 288, 289, 344, 345, 423, 425
Chaucer, Geoffrey, II, 4, 4n.
Cherry and Fair Star, I, 420
Chevalier, Michel, I, 78, 78n., 101
Cheyenne Indians, I, 293
Chicago, Ill., I, 25n., 35, 35n., 88, 249n., 364, 396
———, University of, I, 320n., 333n., 358n.
Chicago American, I, 148n.
Child, Francis James, I, 311n.
"Childe Harold" (Gallagher), II, 20
"Childe Harold" (William Ross Wallace), I, 338; II, 20n.
Childe Harold (Byron), II, 17, 20
Child of Nature, The (Inchbald), I, 415n.
Children in the Wood (Morton), I, 416
Chillicothe, O., I, 23n., 30, 97, 136n., 192, 234; II, 4n.
China, I, 83, 292
Chinard, Gilbert, I, 90n., 91n.
Chinese, I, 291
"Chinese Philosopher, The," I, 162
Chouteau family, I, 8
"Christabel" (Coleridge), II, 24
Christian Intelligencer, The, I, 191
Christianity and Masonry Reconciled (Philander Chase), I, 235
Christian Messenger, The, I, 192
Christian Panoplist, The, I, 192
Christian Register, The, I, 189, 189n., 190, 190n.
Christians, I, 277
"Christians," or Disciples of Christ, I, 223, 226

Christian Traveller, The (Isaac Reed), I, 55n., 98

Christliche Apologet, Der, I, 21n.

Chronicles of the North American Savages, I, 202

Church Street, St. Louis, I, 360, 407, 446

Cincinnati, O., I, 19-21, 23-30, 37-40, 51-53, 66, 68, 70, 71n., 103, 105, 108, 110, 112, 115-117, 119, 123, 125, 125n., 126, 127, 135-137, 144, 147n., 152, 155-158, 163, 166n., 172, 172n., 174, 176, 178, 183-186, 188, 191, 192, 195-201, 209-212, 217, 218n., 225, 227, 227n., 231, 232, 233, 239, 240, 251, 252, 255, 262, 265, 272, 282, 287, 288, 293, 296, 296n., 297n., 301, 316-318, 325-327, 337, 337n., 354, 355, 356, 357, 361, 365-368, 373, 374, 378-391, 393n., 396, 398-400, 402, 406n., 412, 413, 413n., 421-428, 430-434, 436, 437, 440-457; II, 2, 3, 3n., 5, 5n., 6n., 11-13, 15, 26, 30n., 34, 36

———, City Clerk, I, 357n., 437n., 444

——— College, I, 196, 256, 327n.

Cincinnati, Covington, Newport and Fulton Directory, The, I, 29n.

Cincinnati Daily Gazette, I, 21n., 37n., 52n., 68n., 74n., 110n., 137n., 231n., 249n., 291n., 297n., 317n., 357n., 381n., 385n., 386n., 388n., 396n., 398n., 400n., 404n., 406n., 424n., 425n., 426n., 427n., 429n., 430n., 432n., 435n., 437n., 439n., 448-455, 457; II, 6n., 16n., 24n.

Cincinnati Directory, The, I, 29n., 71n., 403n., 404n.

Cincinnati Exchange, I, 405, 453

Cincinnati in 1826 (Benjamin Drake and Mansfield), I, 403n.

Cincinnati in 1841 (Cist), I, 29n. and as *op. cit.,* 156n. and as *op. cit.,* 239n.; II, 2n.

Cincinnati Literary Gazette, The, I, 162, 162n., 163n., 195n., 271n., 445; II, 14n., 16n., 23n., 24n.

Cincinnati Medical College, I, 258

Cincinnati Mirror and Ladies' Parterre, The, I, 163, 188, 282n., 339n., 404n., 423n.; II, 6n., 11n., 20n., 36n.

Cincinnati Mirror, and Western Gazette of Literature and Science, The, I, 163, 188

Cincinnati Miscellany, The, I, 74n., 75n.

Cincinnati Public Library, I, 318n.

———Theatre (name not always applied to the same building), I, 260n., 352, 354, 357n., 378, 379, 385, 386, 402, 404, 405, 434, 443-448, 450-452; II, 5n.

Cinderella (Rossini), I, 419, 419n., 429

Cipriani, John, I, 365, 366

———, Mary, I, 365, 367

Circleville, O., I, 240

Circus, Louisville, I, 406, 406n.

Cist, Charles, I, 29n., 37n., 68n., 156n., 157n., 158n., 184n., 185n., 186n., 192n., 239n.; II, 2n.

Citizens' Theatre, Cincinnati, I, 402, 450

City Free School, Louisville, I, 52n.

——— Hotel, St. Louis, I, 377, 407, 443

"City Lawyers" (Peirce), I, 326

City of Detroit, The, I, 6n., 361n.

"City Poets" (Peirce), I, 326, 327; II, 19

City School, Lexington, I, 52n.

——— Theatre, Cincinnati (name not always applied to the same building), I, 403, 405, 445, 452, 453, 454

——— Theatre, Detroit, I, 363, 394, 410, 452-457

——— Theatre, Louisville, I, 386n., 399n., 405, 405n., 406n., 419, 424n., 448-457

Civil War, American, I, 302, 310n.

Clari (Payne), I, 417

Clark, theatrical manager, I, 457

———, Christopher, I, 226

———, George Rogers, I, 97

———, William, I, 324, 325n.

Clarke, James Freeman, I, 51, 179n., 182, 182n., 183, 183n., 184, 184n.; II, 28

Clavers, Mrs. Mary, I, 285

Clay, Henry, I, 150, 209, 210n., 215, 224, 252, 266; II, 36

Cleland, T. H., I, 227n.

———, Thomas, I, 223, 224, 227, 227n.

Clenning, Arthur, I, 289, 290

Cleveland, C. C., I, 43n., 47n., 48n., 49n.

———, O., I, 30, 391, 392, 395, 396

Cleveland Academy, I, 262

Cleveland Liberalist, I, 161

Clinton Bradshaw (Frederick W. Thomas), I, 179, 297, 297n., 298n.

Clio (Percival), I, 339; II, 32

Cobb, Dr., I, 197

Cobbett, William, I, 32n., 106, 114n., 125

Coggeshall, William T., I, 154n., 296n., 301n., 327n., 350n.; II, 21n.

Coil, Hearty, I, 299

Colby, John, I, 49, 49n.

Cole, theatrical manager, I, 454

Coleman, Charles W., I, 302n.

———, Elisha, I, 134n.

Coleridge, Samuel Taylor, I, 180; II, 23, 24, 25, 25n., 26, 28

Colhoun, member of Stephen Long's expedition, I, 88

Collection of Some of the most Interesting Narratives of Indian Warfare, A (Metcalf), I, 247

Collection of the Acts of Virginia and Kentucky, Relative to Louisville, A, I, 438n.

College Mirror, The, I, 201

Collins, actor, I, 367, 368n.

———, of Collins & Jones, I, 378

———, Lewis, I, 39n., 43n.

———, S. H., I, 129

——— & Jones, I, 378, 379, 380, 381, 401, 402, 443-445

Collot, Victor, I, 8n., 100, 101, 101n.

Colman, George, the Younger, I, 371n., 415, 416n., 419

"Colonization of the West, 1820-1830, The" (F. J. Turner), I, 15n.

Colton, Calvin, I, 8n., 96, 109, 129, 261n.

———, Joseph, I, 129

Columbia, goddess, I, 328, 330, 331, 332

———, Mo., I, 36

Columbiad, The (Hunn), I, 329n.

Columbian Geography (Kilbourn), I, 270

Columbian Harmonist, The (Timothy Flint), I, 316, 316n.

Columbian Magazine, The, I, 164

Columbia River, I, 77

——— Street, Cincinnati, I, 378, 443

——— Street Theatre, Cincinnati, I, 385, 402, 404, 443, 447-451

Columbus, Christopher, I, 331

———, Ky., I, 381

———, O., I, 21n., 30, 177, 198, 199, 238, 253, 265, 318, 396

Colvin, Sidney, I, 181n.

Commerce, Ill., I, 194

Commercial Bulletin, I, 360n., 431n., 435n., 452

Commercial Daily Advertiser, The, I, 155

Commercial Register, I, 155

Commons, John R., I, 61n.

Common School Advocate, I, 199

Common School Advocate, The, I, 200

Common School Journal, The, I, 200

Commonwealth, The, I, 122n.

Compendium of the Enumeration of the Inhabitants and Statistics of the United States, I, 156n.

Complete Poems of Edgar Allan Poe, The, I, 297n., 340n.

Comprehensive Grammar, A (Bliss), I, 264, 264n.

Comprehensive History of the Disciples of Christ, A (W. T. Moore), I, 45n.

Concert Hall, St. Louis, I, 408, 457

Concise Account, A (Rogers), I, 85

Concise Answer, A, I, 226

Concise History of the Christian Church, A (Ruter), I, 248

Condensed Geography and History of the Western States, A (Timothy Flint), I, 127, 246, 261, 294

Cone, Spencer W., I, 340n.

Congregational Church, I, 62

Congress, of the United States, I, 210, 210n., 259

"Conqueror Worm, The" (Poe), I, 340

Conrad, II, 23

"Consequences of Idleness, The," I, 269

Constitution and By-laws of the Historical Society of Michigan, I, 237n.

Constitution of the French Moral and Benevolent Society, The, MS., I, 12n.

Continuation of the Narrative of the Indian Charity-school, A (Wheelock), I, 97n.

Cook, Dan'l P., & Co., I, 141

Cooke, John Esten, I, 197, 198, 256

Coolidge, J. K., I, 160

Cooper, James Fenimore, I, 3n., 96, 272, 276, 284, 286, 295, 301, 418, 426; II, 2, 2n., 31, 34, 35

———, Thomas Abthorpe, I, 398, 398n., 399, 400

Corey and Fairbank, I, 172n., 175n.

Corin, I, 112

Coriolanus (Shakespeare), I, 414n.

Corneille, Pierre, I, 418, 418n.

Corporation of the Town of Detroit, I, 10n.

Correct View, A (Schermerhorn and Mills), I, 98

Correspondence between George Nicholas, of Kentucky, and Robert G. Harper, I, 212

Correspondence of Thomas Carlyle and Ralph Waldo Emerson, The, 84n.

Corrill, John, I, 232

Corsair, The (Byron), I, 417; II, 23

"Corsair," the, II, 15

Corwin, Moses B., I, 253

"Cosmopolite," I, 226

Cossack hetman, I, 430

Country Girl, The (Wycherley, Garrick), I, 414n., 415n.

Country Wife, The (Wycherley), I, 414n.

Court House, Lexington, I, 353, 401

——— House, St. Louis, I, 358

Court of Appeals, in Kentucky, I, 159, 213, 214

Cowdery, Oliver, I, 193, 232

Cowell, Joseph, I, 319n., 357n., 380n., 384n., 447, 448

Cowley, Hannah, I, 415, 415n.

Cowper, William, II, 2, 11, 11n.

Cox, F. A., I, 98

Coxe, Daniel, I, 85

Coxshaw, printer, I, 11n.

Crab Orchard, Ky., I, 23

Crabbe, George, II, 25

Craig, Elijah, I, 51n.

———, Parkers & Co., I, 144

Craighead, T. B., I, 223

Cramer, Zadock, I, 103, 103n., 104n.

Crampton & Smiths, I, 446

Cranch, Christopher P., II, 27

Crane, publisher, I, 136n.

———, Ichabod, I, 285

Creek Indians, I, 308

Cresap, Colonel, I, 85

Crèvecœur, St. Jean de, I, 133n.

Crihfield, Arthur, I, 192

Critic, The (Sheridan), I, 415, 415n.

Critical Dictionary, A (Allibone), I, 296n. and as *op. cit.*, 347n.

"Critical Evaluation of the Sources for Western History" (Quaife), I, 86n.

"Criticism of Pedobaptists, Refuted, The" (Downs), I, 315n.

Croghan, George, I, 85, 244

Crothers, Samuel, I, 217, 234

Crow, John Finley, I, 194

Crusoe, Robinson, I, 289, 430

Cry from the Wilderness, A (Dow), I, 226

Crystalina (John M. Harney), I, 336, 337n.

Cumberland, Richard, I, 415, 415n.

——— River, I, 376

Cuming, Fortescue, I, 74n.

Cummins, James C., I, 140n.

Cunningham, J., I, 134n.

Cupid, god, I, 74

Cure for the Heartache, A (Morton), I, 416

Curry, Otway, I, 177, 266, 275, 339, 342; II, 28

Cyclopaedia of American Literature (Duyckinck), I, 296n.
Cynthiana, Ky., I, 364, 364n.

DAGON *of Calvinism, The*, I, 227, 228
Daily Chronicle, The, I, 317n., 318n.; II, 30n.
Daily Cincinnati Gazette, The, I, 136, 137n., 153, 155, 195n., 380n., 383n., 399n., 403n., 422n., 426n., 428n., 429n., 430n., 432n., 435n., 446-448; II, 10n., 36
Daily Cleveland Herald, I, 155
Daily Louisville Public Advertiser, I, 155, 386n., 400n., 427n., 430n., 432n., 448-451; II, 4n., 36n.
Daily Missouri Republican, I, 25n., 37n., 140, 140n., 396n., 400n., 453, 455, 457
Dallas, friend of Byron, II, 1
Dalton, Mr. and Mrs., I, 360n.
"Dandy, The" (Peirce), I, 326
Dandyism: see also Modern Fashions, 422n.
Daniel Boone, I, 421
Danville, Ky., I, 28, 214, 223, 320, 320n., 321, 322
"Dark Maid of Illinois, The" (James Hall), I, 281
Darwin, Charles, I, 262
"Dash down the Harp" (William Ross Wallace), I, 339
Daveiss, Joseph H., I, 213
Dawning of Music, The (Heinrich), I, 318
Dawson, Moses, I, 252, 253, 253n., 254, 254n.
Dawson's Schoolhouse, Cincinnati, I, 378, 443
Day after the Wedding, The, I, 420
Dayton, O., I, 30, 161, 364, 364n.
"Dead Husband, The" (Wetmore), I, 283
Deaf and Dumb (Holcroft), I, 415, 416n.
Dean, theatrical manager, I, 387, 393n., 396, 454
Dean, Julia, I, 369n.
Dean, Mrs. (Julia Drake), I, 368n., 398

Dean & McKinney, I, 393, 394, 394n., 451-453
Death of André, The (Dunlap), I, 418
Debate on the Evidences of Christianity (Alexander Campbell and Robert Owen), I, 233
Debate on the Roman Catholic Religion, A (Alexander Campbell and Purcell), I, 231
Decalves, Don Alonzo, I, 93
Defence of Kenyon College (Philander Chase), I, 229
"Defense of the Medical Profession" (Caldwell), I, 255
Defoe, Daniel, I, 94, 289
Delafield, John, I, 242
De Lara (Hentz), I, 423
Delaware Indians, I, 40n., 85, 96, 97
Delawares, King of the, I, 97
Delcamp, Mary Estelle, I, 51n., 52n.
De Menil, Alexander Nicolas, I, 302n.
Democracy in America (Tocqueville), I, 22n., 101
Democracy in America. Part the Second (Tocqueville), II, 6n.
Denison University, I, 63
Denny, Fanny (Mrs. Alexander Drake), I, 369n., 398
DePauw University, I, 63
Depeyster, A. S., I, 343, 344, 344n.
De Prefontaine, theatrical manager, I, 452
D'Eres, Charles Dennis Rusoe, I, 93
Description de la Louisiane (Hennepin), I, 80, 81
"Description of the Antiquities Discovered in the Western Country, A" (Atwater), I, 240
Description of the English Province of Carolana, A (Coxe), I, 85
Descriptions of Some New Terrestrial and Fluviatile Shells (Say), I, 258
Detroit, Mich., I, 3n., 6, 9n., 10, 10n., 11, 11n., 12n., 17n., 24, 25n., 27n., 36, 38, 39, 40n., 52, 70, 85, 87, 88, 93, 141, 142, 151, 166n., 237, 286, 307, 330, 343, 347, 357, 361, 362, 363n., 390, 391-395, 402,

409-413, 424, 429, 433, 435, 438, 440-457; II, 12n., 13, 24
—————— Book Store, II, 3n.
—————— Branch of the University of Michigan, I, 62, 363n.
Detroit Courier, I, 52n., 435n., 450
Detroit Daily Advertiser, I, 18n., 25n., 28n., 199n., 218n., 452; II, 16n.
Detroit Daily Free Press, I, 148n., 155, 410n., 452; II, 3n., 12n., 15n., 24n.
Detroit Daily Tribune, The, I, 392n., 395n., 409n., 446
Detroit Debating Society, I, 201
Detroit Free Press, I, 26n., 62n., 151, 363n., 396n., 429n., 430n., 453-457; II, 6n.
Detroit Gazette, I, 9n., 10n., 11n., 24n., 28n., 36n., 38n., 52n., 61n., 94n., 142-143, 155n., 261n., 307n., 344n., 346n., 362n.; II, 10n., 13n., 14n., 15n., 16n., 24n., 32n., 35n.
Detroit Journal and Courier, II, 16n.
Detroit Journal and Michigan Advertiser, I, 17n., 25n., 52n., 145n., 151, 151n., 237n., 287n., 410n., 435n., 450, 451; II, 10n., 16n.
Detroit Lyceum, I, 9n.
—————— National Theatre: *see also* National Theatre, Detroit, I, 394, 410, 455
Detroit, Past and Present (Trowbridge), I, 362n.
Detroit Post and Tribune, I, 307n.
Detroit, Public Library of, I, 237n., 261n., 347n.
—————— Thespian Society, I, 362
Detroit Tribune, The, I, 362n.
Deutsche Element, Das (Körner), I, 19n., 21n.
Deutsche Franklin, Der, I, 21n.
Deutsche in Nord Amerika, Der, I, 19n.
Deutscher Anzeiger des Westens, I, 21n.
D'Grushe, actor, I, 375n.
Dhu, Roderick, I, 345; II, 18
Dial, The, I, 183, 183n.
Dialogue between Calvinists and Arminians, A, I, 227n.

Dialogue Grammar, The (B. F. Ells), I, 264
Dialogue, on Commonwealths, A (Paul Brown), I, 33n.
Dialogues, Pleasant and Interesting (Adam Rankin), I, 222
Diary in America, A (Marryat), I, 14n. and as *op. cit.*, 117; II, 15n.
Dibdin, Thomas, I, 417, 420
Dickens, Charles, I, 298; II, 30, 30n.
Digest of the Statute Law of Kentucky, A (Littell and Swigert), I, 75n.
Dillon, John B., I, 275
Dimond, William, I, 416, 417
Dionne, N. - E., I, 11n.
Directory of the City of Detroit (MacCabe), I, 411n.
Directory of the City of Lexington (MacCabe), I, 26n. and as *op. cit.*
Disciples of Christ, I, 42, 44, 191, 223
Discourse Delivered before the Historical & Philosophical Society of Ohio, A (Tappan), I, 238
Discourse on Intemperance, A (Daniel Drake), I, 234
Discourse on the Aborigines, A (William Henry Harrison, I, 242
Discourse on the Genius and Character of the Rev. Horace Holley, A (Charles Caldwell), I, 58n. and as *op. cit.*, 206n., 254; II, 7n.
Discourse on the History, Character, and Prospects of the West (Daniel Drake), I, 123, 207n., 272; II, 34n.
Discovery, Settlement and Present State of Kentucke, The (Filson), I, 121, 242, 251
Disseminator of Useful Knowledge, The, I, 201
"Distribution of Happiness," I, 265
Divinity College address, Emerson's, II, 38
Doctrine and Covenants of the Church of the Latter Day Saints, I, 232
Doctrine and Discipline of Divorce, The (Milton), II, 5n.
"Doctrine of Endless Miseries Investigated, The," I, 189

Dodsleys, publishers, I, 84
Doige, Mrs., I, 367
Domestic Manners ("Fitzblue"), I, 110
Domestic Manners (Trollope), I, 108-111, 115 and as *op. cit.*, 131, 293n., 329n.; II, 7n. and as *op. cit.*
Don Juan (Byron), I, 31n., 122n.; II, 14, 14n., 20, 22, 23
Don't Give up the Ship (Timothy Flint), I, 290n.
Doric architecture, I, 404
Douglas, theatrical manager, I, 365, 366, 367, 369, 395, 440
——— Ellen, I, 345
Douglas (Home), I, 415, 415n.
Dow, Lorenzo, I, 49, 50n., 226, 227n.
Downs, William, I, 314, 314n.
Drake, Alexander, I, 368n., 398, 446
———, Mrs. Alexander, I, 369n., 387, 398, 398n., 406n., 425, 455
———, Benjamin, I, 249, 253, 266, 275, 283, 403n.
———, Charles D., I, 179
———, Daniel, I, 59, 123, 135n., 136n., 195, 195n., 196, 196n., 198, 206, 207, 207n., 234, 235, 239, 240, 245, 255, 272, 356; II, 34n.
———, James, I, 368n.
———, Julia, I, 368n., 398
———, Martha, I, 368n.
———, Samuel, I, 358, 364, 366-373, 376-378, 380, 380n., 381-383, 385, 395, 396, 398, 399n., 401, 405-407, 428, 434, 436, 437, 440, 442-450
———, Samuel, Jr., I, 368n.
Dramatic Life (Ludlow), I, 24n. and as *op. cit.*, 353n. and as *op. cit.*, 368n. and as *op. cit.*, 370n. and as *op. cit.*, 411n. and as *op. cit.*
Dramatist, The (Frederick Reynolds), I, 416
Drayton, Daniel, I, 1
Drayton (Thomas H. Shreve), I, 301
Drumm, Stella M., I, 11n.
Drury Lane Theatre, I, 417
Dryden, John, I, 414; II, 8, 9

Du Bourg, Bishop, I, 12n.
Dubuque, Ia., I, 40n.
Du Buque Visitor, I, 143
Duddon sonnets, Wordsworth's, II, 25n.
Duden, Gottfried, I, 3n., 20n.
Du Fresnoy, geographer, I, 270
Dumilieu & Charles, I, 403, 444
Duncan, James, I, 216
———, Mathew, I, 141, 141n.
Dunkers, I, 20n.
Dunlap, William, I, 353n., 361n., 366n., 417
Dunlavy, John, I, 222, 223, 225, 226
Durango, I, 288
Durrett Collection, I, 320n., 333n.
Dusky, I, 294
Duyckinck, Evert A., I, 296n.
———, George L., I, 296n.
Dwight, Timothy, I, 331
Dwyer, theatrical manager, I, 445
Dyke, Mrs. R., I, 426

"EACH and All" (Emerson), I, 182
"Each in All" (Emerson), I, 182n.
Eagle, Ill., I, 34
——— Circus Co., I, 453
——— Street Theatre, Buffalo, N. Y., I, 394
Early American Plays (Wegelin), I, 361n.
"Early Camp-meeting Song Writers, The" (B. St. James Fry), I, 312n.
Early Days in Detroit (Friend Palmer), I, 392n. and as *op. cit.*
Early Days in Lafayette, Indiana, MS. (Sample), I, 363n.
"Early Drama, The" (Quinn), I, 425n.
Early Life of Lexington, The, MS. (Delcamp), I, 51n.
"Early Schooling in Detroit" (Burton), I, 6n.
East and South, I, 427
East and West (Frederick W. Thomas), I, 297n., 298, 298n., 300; II, 15, 15n.
Eastin, Augustine, I, 229
Easy and Lucid Guide, An (Holloway), I, 264

Eberle, John, I, 197, 198, 256
———, Powell & Co., I, 393, 410, 451
Eclectic First Reader, The (M'Guffey), I, 267n., 268
Eclectic Fourth Reader, The (M'Guffey), I, 268, 269
Eclectic Second Reader, The (M'Guffey), I, 268
Eclectic Series, I, 267
Eclectic Third Reader, The (M'Guffey), I, 267-269
Economic and Social Beginnings of Michigan (George N. Fuller), I, 17n. and as *op. cit.*, 263n.
Eden, garden, I, 116, 118, 326
Edinburgh, Scotland, II, 12, 13
Edinburgh Review, The I, 1, 5n., 111, 111n., 112, 307n.; II, 3, 3n., 12n., 19
Edinburgh, University of, I, 60
"Editor's Budget," I, 176
"Edwin and Edelia", I, 154n.
"Effects of Rashness," I, 269
Eggleston, Edward, I, 65, 283, 286
Egyptian architecture, I, 38
——— Hall, I, 125n.
Elba, Island of, I, 334
Elders' Journal, I, 193
El Dorado, I, 1
Elements of Chemical Philosophy (Thomas D. Mitchell), I, 270
Elements of Geology (W. W. Mather), I, 270
Elements of Latin Grammar (Niles), I, 271
Elements of Logic (Bishop), I, 270
Elements of the Science of Government (Bishop), I, 270
El Hyder, I, 420
Eliot, William G., I, 183n.
Elizabethan age, I, 414
Elizabethtown, Ky., I, 395
"Ellen Douglas", the, II, 15
Elliott, R., I, 11n.
Ells, B. F., I, 248, 249, 264
"Eloquence of the West" (Maffitt), I, 206n.
Emerson, Ralph Waldo, I, 79, 83, 84n., 182, 182n., 183n.; II, 32, 37, 38

Emigrant, The (Frederick W. Thomas), I, 297n., 347, 347n.; II, 20
Emigrant, The (Henry Whiting), I, 347
"Emigrants, The" (James Hall), I, 279
Emigrants, The (Imlay), I, 287n.
"Emigrant's Abode in Ohio, The" (Timothy Flint), I, 266
Emigrant's Directory to the Western States, The (Amphlett), I, 129
Emigrant's Guide to the United States, The (S. H. Collins), I, 129
Emigrant's Guide to the United States, The (Holditch), I, 129
"Émigrés français en Amérique, Les" (Carré), I, 9n.
Emmons, Richard, I, 328-333, 334, 336, 343, 424, 424n.; II, 4, 31
———, William, I, 332n., 333n.
Encyclopaedia Britannica, The, II, 13n.
End Moor, England, I, 181n.
England: *see also* Great Britain, I, 45n., 58, 94, 97, 102, 111, 113, 125, 125n., 126, 149, 167, 173, 180, 191, 202, 351, 398; II, 1, 24
English: *see also* British, I, 6, 10n., 18n., 22n., 34, 45, 62, 64, 84n., 86, 98, 99, 102, 104n., 111, 113, 113n., 129, 163, 284, 286, 294
——— authors: *see also* British authors, I, 110, 177, 267, 273, 298, 416; II, 2, 3, 10, 14, 27, 28, 32
English Bards and Scotch Reviewers (Byron), I, 323; II, 19
English constitution, I, 111
English Folk Songs from the Southern Appalachians (Olive Dame Campbell and Cecil J. Sharp), I, 311n.
English Grammar for Children, An (John Locke), I, 264
English immigrants, I, 7, 9, 18, 105, 106, 107, 124, 125, 216, 279, 280, 361
——— language, I, 10, 12, 12n., 20, 21n., 32, 51, 52n., 58, 58n., 80, 81, 83, 84, 84n., 85, 96, 96n., 99, 100, 114n., 142, 142n., 166n.,

209, 257, 257n., 271, 278, 304, 307, 336, 419; II, 6, 8, 9
—————— literature: *see also* British authors and English authors, I, 71, 111n., 167, 174, 289, 309, 310, 310n., 429; II, 3, 4, 4n., 5, 7
—————— Prairie settlements, I, 18n., 34, 107, 113n., 114; II, 1
—————— travellers: *see also* British travellers, I, 116, 118, 210n.; II, 14
Eolian Songster, The (U. P. James), I, 318
Epick Poem in Commemoration of Gen. Andrew Jackson's Victory, An (Richard Emmons), I, 330n.
"Epigram on William Hudson" (Thomas Johnson), I, 321
Episcopalians, I, 45n., 46n.
Episcopal Methodism (Joshua L. Wilson), I, 227n., 228
Epistle from William, An (Littell), I, 214
Epistle to the Citizens of Kentucky, An (David Rice), I, 219, 219n.
Epitres et evangiles, I, 12n.
Erato (Gallagher), I, 339-342; II, 20, 32, 35
Erectheum, Athens, I, 408
Erie Canal, I, 17
—————, Lake, I, 24, 85, 88, 149n.
Errand Boy, The, I, 192
Erstes Uebungsbuechlein fuer Kinder (Steines), I, 21n.
Esarey, Logan, I, 115n.
Escalala (Samuel Beach), I, 346; II, 20
Essay of a Delaware-Indian and English Spelling-book (Zeisberger), I, 271
Essay on Baptism, An (David Rice), I, 219
Essay on Federalism, An (Daveiss), I, 213
Essay on Man, An (Pope), II, 7, 8
Essay on the Formation of Rocks (Maclure), I, 258
"Essay on the Life and Writings of Pope" (Villemain), II, 7n.
"Essays", I, 176

Essays (Elizabeth M. Chandler), I, 337, 337n.
Essays and Lectures on Medical Subjects (John P. Harrison), I, 256
Essays on Malaria (Caldwell), I, 255
Essays to Do Good (Cotton Mather), II, 31
Études critiques (Bédier), I, 91n.
Eugene Aram (drama), I, 427
Evangelical Record, The, I, 189, 227n., 228n.
Evangelist, The, I, 192, 192n.
Evans, Estwick, I, 8n., 74n., 118, 119, 362, 362n., 433, 433n.
Evening and Morning Star, I, 193, 193n.
Every one Has his Faults (Inchbald), I, 415n.
Ewing, John, I, 363n.
Excursion through the United States and Canada, An (Blane), I, 32n., 103n., 114 and as *op. cit.*; II, 13n.
Expansion of New England, The (Mathews), I, 17n.
Extracts (Elisha Bates), I, 229
Extra Equator, The, I, 187

FACTS *and Conditions of Progress* (Gallagher), I, 239n.
Facts Relative to the Expulsion of the Mormons (John P. Greene), I, 232
"Fair Margaret and Sweet William", I, 310
Falls of St. Anthony, I, 344, 381n.
—————— of St. Mary, I, 87
—————— of the Ohio, I, 85, 103
Familiar Dialogue, A (Cleland), I, 227
Family Book, The, I, 12n.
Family Jars, I, 420
Family Magazine, The, I, 185, 185n., 186, 306n.
Fanaticism Exposed (John Bailey), I, 225
Farmer, Silas, I, 11n., 361, 361n., 392, 448, 451
Farmer's Library, The, I, 140n.
Farmer's Reporter, I, 200
Farrar Street, Detroit, I, 410, 451
Farrell, Robert, I, 450
Farren, stage manager, I, 457

Far West, Mo., I, 193
Far West, The (Flagg), I, 7n. and as *op. cit.*, 124, 237n., 316n.; II, 17n.
Fatherland, German, I, 19
Faust, Albert B., I, 20n.
Faustus (Soane and Terry? from Goethe), I, 419
Faux, William, I, 32n., 75, 75n., 107
Fearon, Henry B., I, 105, 105n., 106; II, 2, 2n., 3n.
"Fearon's Falsehoods", I, 106
Featherstonhaugh, George W., I, 85n.
Federurbian (Houseworth), I, 266, 267, 267n.
Ferguson, actor, I, 367
Ferrall, Simon A., I, 33n., 48n., 74n., 408, 408n.
Festoons of Fancy (Littell), I, 214n., 336
Few Chapters to Brother Jonathan, A, I, 230
Ficklin, Joseph, I, 134n.
Field, Matthew, I, 454
Fielding, Henry, I, 414, 415n., 418
Fifth Street, Cincinnati, I, 448
—— Street, Louisville, I, 407
Fifty Years as a Presiding Elder (Cartwright), I, 227n. and as *op. cit.*
Filson, John, I, 121, 122n., 123, 242, 243, 244, 251
"Fine Arts", I, 163
Fink, Mike, I, 73, 275n., 306
Finley, James B., I, 47, 48n., 97, 229n.
——, James C., I, 196
——, John, I, 154n., 349
First Annual Catalogue of the Officers and Students of Indiana Asbury University, I, 63n.
First Annual Report of the Superintendent of Common Schools (Ohio), I, 54n.
First Catalogues and Circulars of the Botanical Garden of Transylvania University (Rafinesque), I, 257
First Century of German Printing in America, The (Seidensticker), I, 20n.

"First Theatrical Company in Detroit, The", I, 409n.
Fisher, Brownlow, I, 137n.
——, Charles, I, 230
——, Clara, I, 399, 400
Fitzblue, Lucretia, I, 110
Fitzhurst, Miss, II, 18
Fitzhursts, the, I, 299
Fitz-James, James, I, 345; II, 18
Flaget, Bishop, I, 39
Flagg, Edmund, I, 7n., 8n., 9n., 17n., 20n., 39n., 62n., 124, 163, 237n., 316, 316n.; II, 17, 17n., 37
Flash, Ryder & Co., I, 175n.
Fletcher, John, I, 414
Flint, E. H., I, 291n.
——, James, I, 46n., 48n., 74n.; II, 3n., 13, 13n.
——, Timothy, I, 14n., 16n., 28n., 36n., 48n., 72n., 95, 126-127, 168-171, 173, 176, 205-206, 246, 251, 253n., 261, 261n., 266, 275, 282, 283, 287-296, 300, 316, 316n., 332; II, 7n., 10, 10n., 17, 18, 27n., 35, 35n.
Floating Beacon, The, I, 428
Floating Theatre, I, 397, 397n.
Florence, O., I, 201
Flower, Richard, I, 125
Flying Dutchman, The, I, 428
Forbes, actor, I, 387, 452
Forest Knight, The, I, 427
Forest of Rosenwald, The, I, 416n.
Forget me not, II, 4n.
Forrest, Edwin, I, 379, 379n., 380n., 397, 399, 399n., 400, 422, 445
——, William S., I, 392, 392n., 409
Fort Jefferson, I, 308
—— Massac, I, 101
—— Pitt, I, 9n., 124
Ft. St. Peter, I, 89
Fort Snelling, I, 22
—— Strother, I, 310n.
—— Sumpter, I, 310n.
Forty Etchings (Basil Hall), I, 108
Forty Thieves, The (Colman), I, 416n.
Fosdick, Mrs. (Julia Drake), I, 398
Foster, reprinter of *Blackwood's*, II, 3

Foundling of the Forest, The (Dimond), I, 371n., 416
Fourth of July addresses, I, 179, 208, 265
———— Street, Cincinnati, I, 388, 405, 454
———— Street, Louisville, I, 405, 448
Fox, Charles James, I, 164
————, John, I, 20n., 248
———— River, I, 25n., 82, 86, 344
France, I, 6n., 34, 101, 130, 149, 166n., 211
France, its King, Court, and Government (Cass), I, 76n., 130, 130n.
Francis Berrian (Timothy Flint), I, 288, 288n., 289, 293, 300; II, 18, 27n.
Frankfort, Ky., I, 28, 106, 123n., 135, 147n., 159, 213, 214, 243, 357, 365, 366, 367n., 368n., 369n., 370, 371, 372, 372n., 380, 380n., 395; II, 11n.
———— Theatre, I, 368n., 369, 370
"Franklin of Cincinnati," I, 206, 356
Frederick the Great, of Prussia, I, 294
Fredonia, goddess, I, 330, 332
Fredoniad, The (Richard Emmons), I, 329-333, 336
Free Enquirer, The, I, 160n.
Freeman, Edmund, I, 136n.
———— & Carpenter, I, 136, 136n.
————, S., and Son, I, 136n.
Freemans, publishers, I, 135
Freeman's Journal, I, 135, 135n., 136, 136n., 147n., 148n.
Free School, Detroit, 52n.
Freiheitsbote für Illinois, Der, I, 21n.
Freischütz, Der (Weber), I, 419
French: *see also* French travellers, etc., I, 13, 39, 86, 90, 95n., 212, 336, 361n.
———— and Indian War: *see also* Seven Years' War, I, 91, 92
———— language, I, 10, 10n., 11n., 12n., 52, 52n., 81, 84, 85, 109n., 122n., 142, 142n., 166n., 167, 257, 304; II, 6n.

———— literature, I, 79, 87, 293, 344, 418, 425
———— Revolution, I, 6n., 283
———— settlers, I, 4, 6-13, 18n., 20, 31, 34, 35, 36, 36n., 105, 124, 142, 236, 246, 254n., 279, 281, 361
———— travellers, I, 38, 46, 80-85, 90, 100-102
"French Village, The" (James Hall), I, 275
Friday, Crusoe's servant, I, 289
Friends, or Quakers, I, 15n., 45, 158, 190, 194, 230, 337; II, 36
Frontier State, The (Pease), I, 34n.
Front Street, Cincinnati, I, 136n.
Fry, B. St. James, I, 312n.
————, Joseph R., I, 175, 175n.
Full and Impartial Account of the Company of Mississipi, A, I, 85
Fuller, George N., I, 17n., 36n., 263n.
————, H. H., I, 391, 392, 395, 409, 446
————, Margaret, I, 182
Fürstenwärther, M. von, I, 19n.

GABRIEL, angel, I, 335
———— (in *Lamorah*), I, 423
Galerie historique (Dionne), I, 11n.
Gallagher, William Davis, I, 176, 177, 178n., 179, 188, 239n., 301n., 339-343; II, 20, 26, 32-36
———— and Shreve, I, 184n.
Gallaher, James, I, 317
Galland, J., I, 202
Galland's Iowa Emigrant, I, 129
Gallipolis, O., I, 4, 8, 9, 124
Gambier Observer, The, I, 158
Garrett, L., I, 48n.
Garrick, David, I, 413, 414n., 415, 415n.
Gay, John, I, 414
Gazette de la Louisiana, I, 11n.
Gazetteer of Illinois, A (J. M. Peck), I, 39n., 129
Gazetteer of the State of Michigan (Blois), I, 10n. and as *op. cit.*, 129
Gazetteer of the State of Missouri

(Wetmore), I, 111n., 129, 283, 421

Gazette française, La, I, 11n.

General Character, Present and Future Prospects of the People of Ohio, The (Atwater), I, 124, 236

General Convention of the Teachers of the Western Country I, 66, 199, 239

"General Preface," I, 179n.

General Synod of the Associate Reformed Church, I, 222

Genin, Thomas H., I, 328, 333-336, 343; II, 4, 31

Genius of Universal Emancipation, I, 194

Gentlemen Amateurs, Cincinnati, I, 357n.

Geography Made Easy (Morse), I, 263

George III, of England, I, 337

George Balcombe (Tucker), I, 302, 302n.

George Barnwell (Lillo), I, 414, 415n., 434

George Caleb Bingham (Shapley), I, 74n.

George Mason (Timothy Flint), I, 290, 290n., 291n.

Georgetown, Ky., I, 144, 192, 396

———, O., I, 217

——— College, I, 63

Georgii Washingtonii, . . . vita (Glass), I, 254, 254n.

German Element, The (Faust), I, 20n.

German immigrants, I, 18-21, 29, 31, 37, 40

——— language, I, 19-20, 96, 167; II, 30

——— literature, I, 418; II, 30

Germantown, O., I, 20n.

German travellers, I, 64, 102

Germany, I, 19

Geschichte des Bisthums Cincinnati (Friedrich Reese), I, 21n.

"G. G. F.," I, 427

Gibault, Father, I, 38

Gieszen, Germany, I, 19n.

Gill, tavern-keeper, I, 322

Gilman, Chandler R., I, 17n., 18n., 95, 119

Giron's Ball Room, Lexington, I, 402, 451

Girtys, outlaws, I, 72

Gist, Christopher, I, 85

Glass, Francis, I, 254, 254n.

Globe Theatre, Cincinnati, I, 379, 403, 422, 422n., 445

"Goblet, The" (William Ross Wallace), I, 339

Godman, John D., I, 195, 198

Godwin, Parke, I, 15n.; II, 35n.

Goethe, Johann Wolfgang von, I, 339, 419

Goforth, Dr., I, 103, 104n.

Goldsmith, Oliver, I, 154, 162, 415, 415n.

"Good-bye, Proud World!" (Emerson), I, 183

Goodenow, John M., I, 270

"Goodness of God, The," I, 269

Goshen, village, I, 271n.

Gospel Herald, The, I, 192

"Gospel Invitation," I, 269

Gospel of the Jubilee, The (Crothers), I, 217

Gothic architecture, I, 38

Gould, Hannah, II, 31, 32, 32n.

"Grace Extempore, A" (Thomas Johnson), I, 322

Graeca Minora, I, 271

Graeme, Malcom, I, 345

Graham's Lady's and Gentleman's Magazine, I, 340n.

Graham's Magazine, I, 340n.

Granade, John A., I, 312, 312n., 313

Granville Literary and Theological Institution, I, 63

Gratiot (State) Street, Detroit, I, 451

Gray, theatrical manager, I, 384

——— & Rowe, I, 430, 448

Great Britain: *see also* England, Scotland, and British, I, 27n., 29, 85, 105, 112, 114, 147n., 311n., 323; II, 2

——— Crossing, Ky., I, 329n.

——— Lakes, I, 4, 17, 25, 80, 82, 83, 85, 95, 118, 344, 391

Great Revival in the West, The

(Cleveland), I, 43n. and as *op. cit.*

"Great Unknown," I, 167

Greece, II, 20

"Greedy Girl, The," I, 268

Greek architecture, I, 38

———— language, I, 51, 58, 166n., 167; II, 8

Greeks, I, 356n., 435

Greek Verb, The (Nast), I, 271

Green Bay, Wis., I, 143

Green-Bay Intelligencer, I, 143, 153, 153n.

Greene, J., I, 457

————, John P., I, 232

————, Nathanael, I, 295

Greenfield Temperance Society, I, 234

Green Tree Tavern, St. Louis, I, 407, 442

Greenville, Tenn., I, 194, 194n.

Gregory, G., I, 249

Greve, Charles T., I, 316n.

Greyslaer (Hoffman), I, 73

Gridiron, The, I, 161, 364n.

Griswold Street, Detroit, I, 411

Gross, Dr., I, 197

Grund, Francis, I, 78, 78n.

"G. T. D.," I, 179n.

Guerin, Bertrand, I, 230

Guest, Moses, I, 337, 337n.

Guide for Emigrants, A (J. M. Peck), I, 129

Guilford, Nathan, I, 53, 275

Gulliverian romance, I, 260

Guthrie, actor, I, 374n.

Guy Mannering (Terry), I, 417

Hackett, James H., I, 400

Hale, Edward Everett, I, 179n.

Halkett, John, I, 425

Hall, Basil, I, 108

————, Baynard R., I, 55n.

————, B. F., I, 192

————, Frederick, I, 26n.

————, Harvey, I, 29n.

————, James, I, 22n., 72, 77, 77n., 94n., 95, 104n., 126-128, 171-177, 179, 237, 246, 246n., 250, 253, 253n., 261n., 265, 266n., 272, 274-284, 287, 293, 295, 296, 296n.,

300, 304, 305, 305n., 310, 310n., 311n., 343n.; II, 17, 17n., 18, 20, 20n., 27n.

Halleck, Fitz-Greene, I, 267; II, 31, 33

Hamilton, Alexander, II, 17

————, Thomas, I, 74n., 113

———— College, I, 64

Hamlet (Shakespeare), I, 413, 414n.; II, 4n.

Hammond, Charles, I, 136, 136n., 137n., 153, 245, 297n.

————, Thomas, I, 137n.

Handing, Ky., I, 66n.

Hanover College, I, 59, 63

Hardin, Colonel, II, 18

————, Benjamin, I, 215

———— County, Ky., I, 314

Harmonie, Ind., I, 21n., 31, 32, 41, 114

Harney, John M., I, 275, 336, 337n.

Harold, Childe, I, 347

Harper, J. Henry, II, 2n.

Harpes, outlaws, I, 295, 296

Harpe's Head, The (Hall), I, 72, 295, 296n.

Harp of the West (Welsh), I, 348-349

Harris, Thaddeus, I, 120

————, William Tell, I, 32n., 41n., 114

Harrison, John P., I, 256

————, William Henry, I, 21n., 115n., 238, 242, 247, 252, 253, 254, 318, 333, 338

Harrison and Log Cabin Song Book, The, I, 318

Harrison Songs, I, 318

Harrodsburg, Ky., I, 28, 198, 422

———— Springs, Ky., I, 396

Hartley, David, I, 262

Harvard College, I, 64

———— University, I, 255

Hawkins and Eldridge, I, 450

Hawley, Zerah, I, 76, 76n., 120

Hawthorne, Nathaniel, I, 177; II, 31, 34, 37

Haynes, N. S., I, 192n.

Heart of Midlothian, The (Dibdin), I, 417

Hebrew language, I, 271

Hebrew Melodies (Byron), II, 13

Heckewelder, John, I, 40, 40n., 96, 97, 271n.; II, 34

Heidelberg, Germany, I, 21n.

Heinrich, A. P., I, 318

Heir at Law, The (Colman), I, 416n.

Heitman, Francis B., I, 355n.

Helvétius, Claude, I, 164

Hemans, Felicia, I, 131; II, 10, 10n., 11, 32

Hennepin, Louis, I, 80, 81, 81n., 82, 83, 84, 95

Henry, actor, I, 374n., 376

———, John F., I, 235

Henry IV (Shakespeare), I, 414n.

Hentz, Caroline Lee, I, 282, 300, 385n., 423, 423n.; II, 20

Herald of Literature and Science, The, I, 201

Hercules, I, 430

Heretic Detector, The, I, 192

Hersey, Thomas, I, 198

Hesperia, Muse of, I, 328

Hesperian, The, I, 72n., 150n., 177-178, 210n., 231n., 273, 282n., 294n.; II, 28, 28n., 30, 30n., 33n., 34n., 37, 37n.

He would be a Soldier, I, 353

Hiawatha (Longfellow), I, 241

Hicksites, I, 191

Higher Education in Indiana (Woodburn), I, 54n. and as *op. cit.*

Highlanders, Scotch, II, 18

Highlands of Scotland, I, 181n.

Hildreth, Richard, I, 253, 253n.

———, S. P., I, 238

Hill, F. S., I, 386, 452

———, G. B., I, 4n.

Hilson, theatrical manager, I, 386, 450

Hinde, Thomas S., I, 312, 312n.

Hinshaw, Lydia, I, 309n.

Histoire de la Louisiane (LePage du Pratz), I, 84

Histoire et description generale de la Nouvelle France (Charlevoix), I, 82n., 84

Historical and Philosophical Society of Ashtabula County, I, 239

——— and Philosophical Society of Ohio, I, 136n., 237, 242

Historical and Scientific Sketches of Michigan, I, 237, 241, 242

Historical Collections of Ohio (Henry Howe), I, 30n.

Historical Collections of the Great West (Henry Howe), I, 304n.

Historical Narrative, A (Dawson), I, 252, 253

Historical Register (Heitman), I, 355n.

Historical Sketch (Baldwin), I, 62n.

Historical Sketch (Bullard), I, 39n.

Historical Sketches (Goodenow), I, 270

Historical Sketches of Kentucky (Lewis Collins), I, 39n. and as *op. cit.*

Historical Society of Indiana, I, 237

——— Society of Michigan, I, 237

History and Geography of the Mississippi Valley, The (Timothy Flint), I, 14n. and as *op. cit.*

"History in Kentucky Folk Song" (Shearin), I, 311n.

History of Cosmopolite (Dow), I, 226

History of Detroit, The (Farmer), I, 11n., 361n. and as *op. cit.*

History of Higher Education in Michigan (McLaughlin), I, 61n.

History of Higher Education in Ohio, The (George W. Knight and Commons), I, 61n.

History of James Jaquith, The, I, 66n.

History of Kentucky, The (Humphrey Marshall), I, 242, 243n.

History of Lexington (Ranck), I, 68n.

History of Louisiana, or of the Western Parts of Virginia and Carolina, The (Le Page du Pratz), I, 84, 85n.

History of Michigan (Lanman), I, 7n., 245

History of Mormonism (E. D. Howe), I, 231, 231n.

History of Ohio (Randall and Ryan), I, 40n.

History of Printing in America, The (Isaiah Thomas), I, 135n.

History of Saint Louis (Scharf), I, 53n. and as *op. cit.*, 302n.

History of the American Stage (T. Allston Brown), I, 381n.

History of the American Theatre, A (Dunlap), I, 353n. and as *op. cit.*

History of the Catholic Church in Indiana (Charles Blanchard), I, 39n.

"History of the 'Chanson de l'année du coup' " (Wilson Primm), I, 307n.

History of the City of Vincennes, A (Cauthorn), I, 138n.

History of the Commonwealth of Kentucky, A (Butler), I, 85n., 122n., 144n., 206n., 243-244

History of the Disciples of Christ in Illinois (Haynes), I, 192n.

"History of the Educational Legislation in Ohio from 1803 to 1850" (Edward A. Miller), I, 68n.

History of the Indian Tribes of North America (James Hall and McKenney), I, 95, 250

History of the Late War (M'Afee), I, 243, 247, 247n., 248n.

History of the McGuffey Readers, A (Vail), I, 267n.

History of the Romish Inquisition, A (Ells), I, 249

History of the Southern Baptists (Riley), I, 43n.

History of the State of Ohio, A (Atwater), I, 245, 245n.

History of the War between the United States and the Sac and Fox Nations of Indians (Wakefield), I, 247

History of the Wyandott Mission (James B. Finley), I, 97

Hobhouse, John Cam, I, 327

Hoby, J., I, 98

Hoffman, Charles Fenno, I, 10n., 16n., 18n., 35n., 36n., 73, 119

Hogarth, William, I, 326

Hogg, James, II, 16n., 25

Hoher Zweck und Bestimmung der Harmonie, I, 21n.

Holcroft, Thomas, I, 415, 416n.

Holditch, Robert, I, 129

Holley, Horace, I, 58, 59, 60, 67, 206

Holloway, Robert S., I, 264

Holmes, Oliver Wendell, I, 182, 338; II, 31, 36

"Holy Fair, The" (Burns), II, 11n.

Home, John, I, 415, 415n.

Homer, I, 78, 335, 336; II, 9

Honey Moon, The (Tobin), 383n.

Hood's Comic Annual, II, 4n.

Hoosier, The, I, 427, 427n.

"Hoosier Listening Post, A" (Rabb), I, 363n., 396n., 425n.

Hoosiers, I, 350

"Hoosier's Nest, The" (John Finley), I, 154n., 349

Hopkinsville, Ky., I, 395

Horace, poet, II, 9

"Horace in Cincinnati," I, 379

"Horace in Lexington," II, 9

Horsley, Samuel, I, 190

Hoskins, Nathan, I, 121

Houghton, Douglas, I, 258

———, Lord, I, 181n.

House of Harper, The (Harper), II, 2n.

Houseworth, Henry, I, 266, 267n.

Howard, Horton J., I, 201

Howard Pinckney (Frederick W. Thomas), I, 297n., 299; II, 18, 19n.

Howe, magazine editor, I, 183n.

———, E. D., I, 231

———, Henry, I, 30n., 304n.

———, O. D., I, 231n.

Hudson, William, I, 321

———, O., I, 62

Hugo, Victor, I, 418

Hulbert, Archer B., I, 30n.

Hull, William, I, 10n.

Hulme, Thomas, I, 32n., 114

"Humble-bee, The" (Emerson): *see also* "To the Humble-bee," II, 38

Hume, David, I, 262

Humphrey, E. P., I, 227n.

Hunn, Anthony, I, 19n., 198, 329n.

Hunt, Leigh, II, 25

———, William Gibbes, I, 166, 201, 201n., 271

———, Wilson P., I, 95, 99, 304

Hunter, John Dunn, I, 94, 94n.

———, Miles, I, 132, 133n.

————, W., I, 192
———— and Beaumont, I, 135
Hunter of the Alps, The (Dimond),
I, 416
Hunter of the West, The, I, 421
"Hunters of Kentucky, The" (Wood-
worth), I, 319n.
Huntington, actor, I, 366
Huron, Lake, I, 82, 85, 119, 345
Hurons, Queen of, I, 9
Hutchins, Thomas, I, 97
Huzzah for the Boys of the West, I,
421
"Hymn on the Seasons, A" (James
Thomson), II, 11n.
"Hymn to Apollo" (John Keats), I,
181n.
"Hyperion" (John Keats), I, 341n.
Hyperion (Longfellow), I, 177

ICHTHYOLOGIA *Ohiensis* (Rafinesque),
I, 257
"Icolmkill, Staffa, and Fingal's Cave"
(John Keats), I, 181
"Idle Boy Reformed, The," I, 268
Idler, The, I, 79
Illinois Anti-slavery Convention, I,
218
———— College, I, 62
———— Conference (Methodist), I,
49n.
Illinois Country, The (Clarence Al-
vord), I, 31n. and as *op. cit.*
Illinois Herald, The, I, 141
Illinois in 1818 (Solon J. Buck), I,
14n. and as *op. cit.*
Illinois in 1837, I, 35n., 129
Illinois Intelligencer, The, I, 141; II,
14n.
Illinois Monthly Magazine, I, 170,
171, 172, 172n., 173, 174, 175n.,
293n., 310n.
Illinois River, I, 81, 82, 83, 86, 88,
104n.
———— Valley, 94, 95
Imlay, Gilbert, I, 122, 122n., 128,
242, 287n.
"Importance of well Spent Youth,"
I, 269
Incas, Indians, I, 240

Inchbald, Elizabeth, I, 415, 415n.,
418
Incognito, The, I, 427, 427n.
Independence, Mo., I, 36, 193
Independent Botanic Register, The,
I, 198, 199n.
Independent Gazetteer, I, 139
Independent Press, I, 379n., 422n.,
430n., 432n., 433n., 444-446
Indiana Asbury University, I, 63
Indiana Catholic, The, I, 254n.
Indiana College, I, 61
Indiana Gazette, I, 137, 138, 141,
145n., 146n., 148n., 149
Indiana Gazetteer, The (John Scott),
I, 129
Indianapolis, Ind., I, 31, 191, 229,
237, 350, 363, 396, 425n.
Indianapolis Journal, I, 154n.
Indianapolis Star, The, I, 363n.,
396n., 425n.
Indiana Seminary, I, 61
———— State Library, I, 41n., 237n.,
363n.
———— University, I, 61, 67
Indiana University Bulletin, I, 61n.
Indiana University Studies, I, 122n.
Indian Department, United States, I,
250
"Indian Hater, The" (James Hall),
I, 276, 280, 281
"Indian Legend of Hiawatha, The"
(Stith Thompson), I, 241
"Indian News," I, 23n.
Indians, American, I, 3n., 5n., 7,
18n., 22, 23, 30, 35, 38, 80, 81,
84-98, 105, 115n., 119, 144, 204,
236, 239-242, 244, 245, 247-250,
271, 271n., 274, 276, 278-283, 286,
291-293, 296, 307, 308, 318, 337,
338, 342-347, 349, 422-425; II,
18, 20, 34
"Indian Wife's Lament, The" (James
Hall), I, 280, 310
Infallibility of the Church (Nathan
L. Rice), I, 230
"Infant's Grave, The" (H. D. Lit-
tle), I, 266
Ingersoll, David, I, 426
———— & Dyke, I, 387, 454
Inkle and Yarico (Colman), I, 416n.

Inquiry into the Origin of the Antiquities of America, An (Delafield), I, 242
Introduction to American Law (Timothy Walker), I, 270
Introduction to Geography and Astronomy (Kilbourn), I, 270
Introductory to a Course of Lectures on History, An (Bishop), I, 77n.
Investigator, I, 226
Investigator and Expositor, I, 195
Iowa, State University of, I, 309n.
Ireland (Maffitt), I, 206n.
Irish immigrants, I, 40
Irish Tutor, The, I, 420
Irish Widow, The (Garrick), I, 415n.
Iron Chest, The (Colman), I, 416n.
Irving, Washington, I, 115, 119, 291, 418; II, 31, 33, 37
Isabella (Southerne), I, 414n.
Isherwood, Henry, I, 394, 410, 455
——, H., & Co., I, 455
——, W., I, 455, 456
Island, The (Byron), II, 14, 14n., 23
"Isle of Yellow Sands, The" (James Hall), I, 280
Israelites, I, 97
Italia, II, 20
Italian language and literature, I, 167, 419, 419n.
—— Opera Company, I, 419n.
Italians, I, 89, 419n.
"Italy" (William Ross Wallace), I, 339
Ivanhoe (Sir Walter Scott), II, 13, 21
Ivanhoe, or the Jew of York, I, 417

JACKSON, Andrew, I, 215, 308, 309, 309n., 310n.
Jacksonville, Ill., I, 15n., 192, 200
Jacobean dramatists, I, 414
Jacobs, Bela, I, 98
James, actor, I, 365, 374n.
"James Bird," I, 310n.
James, Edwin, I, 87, 94
James Freeman Clarke, I, 179n., 183n., 184n.
James G. Birney and his Times (William Birney), I, 218n.

James, J. A., I, 186n.
——, J. A., & Co., I, 318n.
——, John H., I, 245n.
——, U. P., I, 71, 317, 318
Jameson, Anna B., I, 7n.
Jamestown, Va., I, 425
Jamieson, Milton, I, 224
Jane Shore (Rowe), I, 365, 414, 415n.
Jaquith, James, I, 65n.
Jefferson, actor, I, 367
——, Joseph, I, 396n., 397n.
——, Thomas, I, 27n., 88, 164, 211, 212, 213
——, Mo., I, 36
——, O., I, 239
—— Avenue, Detroit, I, 411, 451
—— County, O., I, 194n.
—— Street, Louisville, I, 383, 405, 406, 406n., 447, 448
Jeffrey, Francis, II, 27, 28
Jennings, Robert L., I, 159n.
Jerrold, Douglas, I, 416
Jessy, I, 292
Jesuit order, I, 63, 95
Jesuit Relations and Allied Documents, The (Thwaites), I, 96n.
Jew, The (Cumberland), I, 415, 415n.
Jewett, Isaac A., I, 273n., 281
Jewett's Advertiser, I, 199
Job, Book of, I, 180; II, 12n.
Jodolet (René Paul, from Molière?), I, 418, 425
"John Anderson my Jo," tune of, I, 307
John Bull (Colman), I, 416n.
John Bull in America (Paulding), I, 22n., 113n.; II, 1
Johnson, Samuel, I, 1, 4n., 78, 79, 320n.; II, 8, 9n.
——, Thomas, I, 69n., 320-323, 325, 339, 343, 349
Johnston, G. W., I, 363n.
Joliet, Louis, I, 80
"Jollie Thresherman, The," I, 309, 309n., 310n.
Jonathan in England (Colman), I, 416n.
Jones, actor, I, 366

————, of Collins & Jones, I, 378, 429, 443

————, Abram, I, 421

————, Charles A., I, 347, 348

————, David, I, 97

Journal, Cincinnati newspaper, I, 158

Journal, Louisville newspaper, I, 150, 151

"Journal" (Byron), II, 1

"Journal" (Croghan), I, 85, 244

"Journal, The" (Hulme), I, 32n., 114

"Journal" (Schoolcraft), I, 86n.

Journal historique (Charlevoix), I, 84

Journal of American Folk-lore, The, I, 311n.

Journal of a Residence and Tour (Abdy), I, 171n.

Journal of a Tour, A (Hawley), I, 76n., 120

Journal of a Tour, The (Thaddeus Harris), I, 120

Journal of a Tour from Lake-George, A (Zophar Roberts), I, 117

Journal of a Tour to the Hebrides, The (Boswell), I, 1

Journal of a Two Months Tour, The (Beatty), I, 97

Journal of a Voyage to North-America (Charlevoix), I, 84

Journal of a Voyage up the River Missouri (H. M. Brackenridge), I, 95, 124, 304n.

Journal of the Adventures of Matthew Bunn, A, I, 92

Journal of the Historical and Philosophical Society of Ohio, I, 238n.

Journal of the Last Voyage Performed by Monsr. de la Sale, A (Joutel), I, 82

Journal of the Proceedings of the Common Council (Detroit), I, 9n., 391n., 392, 392n., 393, 393n., 394n., 438n., 446-447, 449-457

Journal of the Rev. Francis Asbury, The, I, 19n. and as *op. cit.*, 98

Journal of the Senate (Missouri), I, 62n.

Journal of Travels into the Arkansa Territory, A (Nuttall), I, 99

Journal of Two Campaigns, A (Adam Walker), I, 92

Journal of Two Visits, A (David Jones), I, 97

Journals (Rogers), I, 85

Journey in North America, A (Collot), I, 8n., 100

Joutel, Henri, I, 82

Jove, god, I, 335

Judson, Miss, I, 299

Julia, Lake, I, 89

Julius Caesar (Shakespeare), I, 414n.

Jupiter, god, I, 321

Juvenile Forget me not, II, 4n.

Juvenile Harmony, The (W. C. Knight), I, 317

Juvenile Museum, The, I, 201

KAINTUCKY (Kentucky), I, 15n.

Kalamazoo, Mich., I, 62

Kamschatka (Kamchatka), I, 119

Kaskaskia, village, I, 6, 34, 141, 144

Kean, Charles, I, 399

Keating, William, I 86n., 87, 88

Keats, George, I, 180, 181n., 303

————, Georgiana, I, 125n., 181n., 303

————, John, I, 125n., 180, 181, 181n., 303, 341n., 351; II, 23, 24, 25n., 28, 29

————, Tom, I, 181n., 303

"Keats in the Wordsworth Country," I, 181n.

Keemle, Charles, I, 24n., 25n., 35n., 53n., 163, 172, 382, 407n.

Keepsake, The, II, 4n.

Kendal, England, I, 191

Kenilworth (Sir Walter Scott), II, 13, 21

Kennedy, actor, I, 366, 367

Kenney, James, I, 420

Kentucke Almanack, The, I, 69, 70n.

Kentucke Gazette, The, I, 51n., 69, 69n., 132, 133, 133n., 135n., 144, 145, 145n., 147n., 149, 156; II, 4n., 11n.

Kentuckian, The, I, 420

Kentuckians in History and Literature (J. W. Townsend), I, 320n.

Kentucky Abolition Society, I, 194

Kentucky a Pioneer Commonwealth (Shaler), I, 13n.

Kentucky. A Tale (James Hall), I, 72, 295

Kentucky Colonization Society, I, 217

Kentucky English Grammar, The (Samuel Wilson), I, 263, 264

Kentucky Gazette, The, I, 23n., 24n., 27n., 51n., 52n., 54n., 58n., 69n., 70n., 132-135, 138n., 139, 139n., 144n., 145, 145n., 146, 146n., 148n., 149, 149n., 152n., 153, 158n., 164, 164n., 165n., 189n., 198n., 206n., 212n., 220n., 263n., 264n., 270n., 312n., 316n., 320n., 336n., 353n., 354n., 364, 364n., 365-368, 370n., 371n., 372n., 395n., 396n., 401n., 402n., 421n., 426n., 429n., 431n., 434n., 435n., 440-443, 445-446, 452-455; II, 4n., 8n., 9n., 10n., 11n., 12n., 13n., 16n., 24n., 32n., 35n.

Kentucky Harmonist, The (Metcalf), I, 316

Kentucky Historical Society, I, 238

Kentucky in American Letters (J. W. Townsend), I, 320n.

Kentucky Miscellany, The (Thomas Johnson), I, 69n., 319-323, 325

Kentucky Penitentiary, I, 151

Kentucky Reporter, I, 134n., 168n., 215, 259n., 379n., 380n., 399n., 401n., 442, 444-446, 448; II, 13n., 14n., 16n., 24n., 36n.

Kentucky Resolutions, I, 211

Kentucky Revival, I, 41, 46, 188

Kentucky Revival, The (McNemar), I, 225

Kentucky Rifle, The, I, 421

Kentucky State Historical Society, I, 238n.

Kenyon College, I, 62, 271

Keokuk, Chief, I, 249

Ker, Henry, I, 121

Kidwell, J., I, 229

Kilbourn, John, I, 129, 270

Kilgore, Charles, I, 355n.

Killgore, amateur theatrical manager, I, 355n.

Kimball, D., I, 152

"Kind Little Girl, The," I, 268

King, actor, I, 375n.

———, John, I, 143

King John (Shakespeare), I, 414n.

"King John and the Bishop," I, 311n.

King Lear (Shakespeare), I, 414, 414n.

Kinmont, Alexander, I, 200, 239, 262

Kirkham, Samuel, I, 263

Kirkland, Caroline M., I, 66n., 284-286, 288, 321

Kirkpatrick, John E., I, 287n., 290n., 316n.

Kirtland, O., I, 42, 193, 193n., 231, 232

Kittredge, George L., I, 311n.

Kleine Sammlung harmonischer Lieder, Eine, I, 21n.

Knight, Mrs., I, 399

———, George W., I, 61n.

———, W. C., I, 317

Knowles, James Sheridan, I, 416, 416n.

Koch & Riley, I, 457

Körner (Koerner), G., I, 15n., 19n., 20n., 21n., 28n., 209, 209n.

Kotzebue, August von, I, 414, 418

"Kubla Khan" (Coleridge), II, 24

Ku-ku, city, I, 260

Kwasind, I, 241

LA CHINE, village, I, 83

Lady and the Devil, The (Dimond), I, 416

"Lady Isabel and the Elf Knight," I, 310

Lady of Lyons, The (Bulwer), I, 417

Lady of the Lake, II, 18

Lady of the Lake, The (melodrama), I, 417, 428

Lady of the Lake, The (Sir Walter Scott), I, 345; II, 12, 18

"Lady of the Lake," the, II, 15

La Fayette, Marquis de, I, 6n., 52n., 101

Lafayette, Ind., I, 363

Lafayette in America (Levasseur), I, 6n. and as *op. cit.*, 101

Lahontan, Baron, I, 82, 82n., 83, 84, 86, 86n.

Lake County, O., I, 42

Lakeside Press, Chicago, I, 249n.

Lakey, James, I, 242

Lamb, Charles, I, 177, 417

Lament of Tasso, The (Byron), II, 13, 14n.

L'ame penitente, I, 11n.

L'Amérique et la rêve exotique (Chinard), I, 90n.

Lamorah, I, 423

Lamorah, or the Western Wild (Hentz), I, 282, 423; II, 20

Lamp, The, I, 19n., 164n.

Lancaster, O., I, 19n.

Lancastrian schools, I, 52

Landino, I, 292

Landon, Letitia E., II, 11

Landscape Annual, II, 4n.

Lane Theological Seminary, I, 62, 67

Lanman, James H., I, 7n., 245

Lapham, I. A., I, 258

Lard, Mrs., I, 348, 348n.

La Salle, René Robert Cavelier, Sieur de, I, 6, 80, 81, 82, 83

Last Appeal, A (M'Chord), I, 224

Last Days of Pompeii, The (Bulwer), I, 417

"Last of the Boatmen, The" (Neville), I, 275, 306n.

Last of the Mohicans, The (drama), I, 418

Last Will and Testament, The, I, 222

Late Persecution of the Church of Jesus Christ (Pratt), I, 232

Latin, I, 12n., 51, 52n., 58, 166n., 167, 254, 256, 271; II, 8

Latrobe, Charles, I, 15n., 35n., 111n., 115

Latter Day Saints: see also Mormons, I, 42

Latter Day Saints' Messenger and Advocate, I, 193, 193n.

Laugh when you can (Frederick Reynolds), I, 416

Law, John, I, 236

Laws of the Territory (North-West Territory), I, 70

Lea, Albert M., I, 129

"Leatherwood God, The" (Taneyhill), I, 46n.

Lebanon, Ky., I, 51n.

———, O., I, 41

Leclair, Antoine, I, 249

Lecture on the Divine Decrees, A (David Rice), I, 219

Lectures on Education (Brewster), I, 262

Lectures upon Natural History (Timothy Flint), I, 261, 261n.

Legends of a Log Cabin (Gilman), I, 18n.

Legends of the West (James Hall), I, 276-279, 279n., 281, 282, 310n., 311n.

Leggett, William, I, 422

Leila (William Ross Wallace), I, 417, 426, 426n., 454

Leona of Athens (Mrs. Alexander Drake), I, 425

Le Page du Pratz, I, 84, 85n.

Lesueur, Charles, I, 33

Letcher, Montgomery, I, 260

Lethbridge, Caroline, I, 294, 295

———, Simon, I, 294

Lethe, river, I, 327

Letter from George Nicholas, A, I, 211

Letter on Colonization (James G. Birney), I, 217

Letters (Barton W. Stone), I, 223

Letters, Conversations and Recollections (Coleridge), II, 26

Letters from America (James Flint), I, 46n. and as *op. cit.*; II, 3n. and as *op. cit.*

Letters from Illinois (Birkbeck), I, 125

Letters from Lexington and the Illinois (Flower), I, 125

Letters from Palestine (J. D. Paxton), I, 130

Letters from the East and from the West (Frederick Hall), I, 26n.

Letters from the Illinois (Flower), I, 125

"Letters from Theodoric to Aspasia," I, 187

Letters from the West (James Hall), I, 77n., 104n., 127, 275, 305n.; II, 17n., 27n.

Letters from the West (Ogden), I, 121

Letters of Gen. Adair & Gen. Jackson, I, 215

Letters of John Keats, I, 181n.

"Letters on Cincinnati," I, 168

Letters on Slavery (J. D. Paxton), I, 217

Letters on Slavery (John Rankin), I, 216

Letters on the Divine Unity (Eastin), I, 229

Letters to Barton W. Stone (Cleland), I, 224

Letters to James Blythe (Barton W. Stone), I, 224

Letters to the Honorable James T. Morehead, I, 54n.

"Lettre à M. Le Chevalier de Boufflers" (Lezay-Marnezia), I, 9n.

Lettres à Sophie (Aimé Martin), I, 261

Lettres d'un cultivateur américain (Crèvecœur), I, 133n.

Lettres écrites des rives de l'Ohio, I, 9n., 12n.

Lettsom, John Coakley, I, 86n.

Levasseur, A., I, 6n., 8n., 9n., 52n., 101

Lewis, Mr. and Mrs., I, 369n.

——, General, I, 308

——, Hannah, I, 92, 93

——, M. G., I, 330, 416

——, Meriwether, I, 88

——, Samuel, I, 55n.

—— and Clark's expedition, I, 87, 88

Lexington, Ky., I, 26-28, 42n., 51-52, 70, 76, 92, 106, 107, 132, 135, 138-139, 158, 165, 168, 187, 189, 192, 195, 197, 201, 212, 215, 219, 220, 224, 229, 256, 257, 262, 263n., 319, 320n., 329n., 352-354, 357, 361, 364-369, 371-375, 378-380, 387, 390, 391, 395, 396, 398n., 401, 402, 412, 413, 413n., 421, 421n., 426, 429, 434, 435, 436, 436n., 440-457; II, 4n., 8, 8n., 9, 9n., 11n., 12, 13, 14n., 24, 31, 31n.

——, Board of Trustees of, I, 436n., 445

——, City Clerk of, I, 436n., 445

—— Grammar School, I, 51n.

Lexington Intelligencer, I, 431n., 454, 455

Lexington Library, I, 67; II, 12, 24

Lexington Observer, and Kentucky Reporter, I, 449, 451-452

Lexington Public Library, I, 51n., 354n.

—— Theatre, I, 366, 367, 368, 368n., 369, 370, 387, 440, 453, 454, 455

Lezay-Marnezia, I, 8, 9n., 12n.

L'Hommedieu, R. F., I, 137n.

——, S. S., I, 137n.

Liberty Hall, I, 27n., 68n., 136, 137, 137n., 144n., 152, 152n., 154n., 168n., 230n., 260n., 271n., 316n., 337n., 356n., 357n., 364n., 365n., 367n., 373n., 378n., 379n., 403n., 431n., 432n., 434n., 435n., 436n., 437n., 440-445; II, 6n., 9n., 10n., 11n., 12n., 16n., 24n., 31n., 32n.

Library of Congress, I, 297n.

Licht im Abendlande, I, 19n.

Licking River, I, 166n.

Life and Adventures of Arthur Clenning, The (Timothy Flint), I, 261n., 289, 289n., 290, 293, 300; II, 10n.

Life and Adventures of Black Hawk, The (Benjamin Drake), I, 249

Life and Adventures of Jonathan Jefferson Whitlaw, The (Trollope), I, 110n.

Life and Letters of John Greenleaf Whittier (Pickard), II, 36n.

Life, Experience, and Travels of John Colby, The, I, 49n., 98

Life in Cincinnati, I, 421

Life, Letters, and Literary Remains, of John Keats (Lord Houghton), I, 181n.

Life of Andrew Jackson (Parton), I, 310n.

Life of Bonaparte, The, I, 254

Life of Ma-Ka-Tai-Me-She-Kia-Kiak (Black Hawk), I, 249

Life of Robert Burns (Lockhart), II, 12n.

Life of Travels and Researches, A (Rafinesque), I, 168n.

Life on the Lakes (Chandler R. Gilman), I, 17n., 119

Lights and Shadows of American Life (Mitford), I, 275n.

Lillibridge, G. R., I, 148n.

Lillo, George, I, 414, 415n.

Limestone, Ky.: *see also* Maysville, I, 24n., 28, 369n.

―――― Street, Lexington, I, 448

Lincoln, Abraham, I, 22n., 396n.

―――― County, Ky., I, 19n., 164n.

Lindsay, William, I, 396

"Lines Written on the Bank of the Mississippi" (Umphraville), II, 19

L'inganno felice (Rossini), I, 419

Lion of the West, The, I, 420

Lisa, Manuel, I, 95, 304

"Literary Essay on Shakespeare, A" (Villemain), II, 6n.

Literary Focus, The, I, 187, 187n.

"Literary Notices," I, 343n.

Literary Register, The, I, 163

Literary Souvenir, The, II, 4n.

Literature of the Louisiana Territory, The (De Menil), I, 302n.

Littell, William, I, 75n., 213, 214, 214n., 336

Little, actor, I, 367

―――― , H. D., I, 266

"Little Idle Boy, The," I, 268

"Little Musgrave and Lady Barnard," I, 310

Liverpool, England, I, 381n.

Liverpool Museum, I, 104n.

Locke, Dr., I, 197

―――― , John, English philosopher, I, 262

―――― , John, Western writer, I, 264, 270

Lockhart, J. G., I, 111n.; II, 12n., 16n.

Locust Street, St. Louis, I, 407

Lodge, James, I, 137n.

Logan, James, I, 35n.

Logansport, Ind., I, 363

Logansport Herald, The, I, 363n., 425n.

London, England, I, 15n., 72, 77, 80, 81, 82, 111n., 129, 147n., 215n., 250, 290n., 295, 383, 398n.

Long, Stephen, I, 87, 88, 89

Longfellow, H. W., I, 177, 241, 241n.; II, 31, 34, 37

Long River, I, 82n.

Longue, La Riviere; *see* Long River

Looker, James H., I, 137n.

―――― & Reynolds, I, 137n.

"Lord Byron's Exit from Earth," II, 16n.

"Lord's Prayer, The," I, 268

Lore of the Past, The (Curry), I, 339

Losantiville: *see also* Cincinnati, I, 29n., 166n.

Loss and Gain (T. Somers Nelson), I, 422

Lost Child, The (Timothy Flint), I, 290

Lottery Ticket, The, I, 420

Louis XIV, of France, I, 6n.

―――― XVI, of France, I, 166n.

Louisiana, state, I, 376n.

―――― , province and territory, I, 6, 82, 83n., 87, 139, 212, 361

Louisiana Gazette, I, 10n., 11n., 99n., 140n., 145n.

Louisiana Herald, I, 140n.

Louisiane, La, I, 79

Louis Philippe, I, 76, 130

Louisville, Ky., I, 26n., 28, 31, 37, 51, 52, 103, 107, 124, 127, 133n., 139n., 140n., 150, 161, 166n., 176, 178, 180, 181n., 183n., 184, 184n., 196, 197, 206n., 209, 237, 238, 256, 264, 303, 357, 358, 358n., 361, 367, 367n., 368n., 369, 369n., 370, 372, 372n., 373, 375n., 377-380, 380n., 382-391, 395, 396, 398, 398n., 399, 399n., 400, 402, 405-407, 412, 413, 413n., 419, 419n., 421, 424, 424n., 427, 427n., 431n., 432, 437, 437n., 440-457; II, 13, 14, 14n., 28

―――― , Board of Trustees, I, 437n.

―――― , Clerks of the Boards of Aldermen and Councilmen, I, 139n., 437n.

Louisville Daily Focus, I, 398n., 449

Louisville Directory, The, I, 357n., 405n.

Louisville Gazette, I, 139

Louisville Hotel, I, 406

Louisville Journal of Medicine and Surgery, I, 196

Louisville Literary News-letter, I, 163, 164n., 456; II, 37, 37n.

Louisville Public Advertiser, I, 37n., 52n., 69n., 151, 151n., 155, 183n., 184n., 244n., 318n., 358n., 379n., 383n., 384n., 398n., 399n., 405n., 406n., 419n., 424n., 430n., 431n., 433n., 437n., 443-449, 451-455, 457; II, 10n., 14n., 32n., 33n., 35n.

Louisville Public Library, I, 68
——— Theatre, I, 368n., 369, 370, 398n., 433, 440

Louisville Weekly Public Advertiser, I, 446

"Love" (Coleridge), II, 24, 24n.

Love à la mode, I 353

Love in Humble Life (Payne), I, 417n.

Love in Jeopardy (Abram Jones), I, 421

Lovejoy, Elijah P., I, 152, 153, 161, 218, 218n., 435

Love Laughs at Locksmiths (Colman), I, 416n.

Lovell's Folly (Hentz), I, 300

Lovers' Vows (Inchbald, from Kotzebue), I, 415n., 418

Love's Labour's Lost (Shakespeare), I, 414n.

Lowell, James R., I, 341

Lucifer, I, 48

Ludlow, actor, I, 368n.
———, N. M., I, 24n., 36n., 353n., 359n., 364-366, 368-378, 380-385, 387-390, 395, 396n., 401n., 403n., 406-409, 411n., 430n., 432, 432n., 438n., 442-444, 447-449, 451-455, 457
——— and Brown, I, 403, 447
——— & Smith, I, 360, 387, 389, 427, 452-455, 457
——— and Vos, I, 443

Lundy, Benjamin, I, 194, 337, 338n.

Lutherans, I, 204

Lying Valet, The (Garrick), I, 415, 415n.

Lyons, France, I, 8

Lyrical Ballads (Coleridge and Wordsworth), II, 24

Lysicrates, monument of, I, 408

M'AFEE, Robert B., I, 243, 247, 247n.

Macbeth (Shakespeare), I, 413, 414n.

McBride, James, I, 238, 260, 260n.

MacCabe, J. P. B., I, 26n., 52n., 411n.

M'Call, John, I, 70

M'Calla, John M., I, 134n.

M'Chord, James, I, 224, 224n.

Maccluer, David, I, 97

M'Clung, John A., I, 247, 266, 294, 295, 295n.; II, 18, 35, 35n.

McCormack, T. J., I, 15n.

M'Cullough, Samuel D., I, 270, 354n.

McDonald, John, I, 250, 250n., 251

M'Donald, William, I, 23n.

M'Farland, John, I, 248

MacGlashan, Marschael, I, 453

M'Guffey, William Holmes, I, 60, 200, 239, 267, 267n., 268, 268n., 269

McIlvaine, Charles Pettit, I, 67, 242

Mackay, M., I, 291

McKenney, Thomas L., I, 95, 250

Mackenzie & Jefferson, I, 387, 396, 457

M'Kimmey, William, I, 229

McKinney, D. D., I, 394, 454

McKinstrey, David, I, 394, 394n., 410, 411n.

McKnight, Sheldon, I, 143n.

McLaughlin, Andrew C., I, 61n.

MacLean, J. P., I, 41n., 42n., 226n., 317n.

Maclure, William, I, 33, 234, 258

Macluria, I, 160

M'Murtrie, Henry, I, 405n.

McNemar, Richard, I, 41, 222, 223, 225, 226, 317

Macomb, Alexander, I, 362, 424

Madison, Ind., I, 31, 199
———, Wis., I, 37

Maffitt, John N., I, 205, 206n.

Magee, William, I, 190

Magruder, A. B., I, 164, 165, 165n., 212

Main Street, Cincinnati, I, 402, 405, 448, 453, 454

—— Street, Lexington, I, 220
—— Street, Louisville, I, 407, 421
Major, Samuel, I, 135n.
Malone, John, I, 361n.
Mandeville, Sir John, I, 82
Manfred (Byron), II, 2, 13, 14n., 17
Manifesto, The (Dunlavy), I, 226
Manlius, pseudonym, I, 150
Manners and Customs of Several Indian Tribes (Hunter), I, 94
"Man of Destiny," II, 20
Mansfield, Edward D., I, 104, 186, 196n., 234n., 239, 270, 356n., 403n.
Manual for Emigrants to America (Calvin Colton), I, 129
Manual of Logic, A (Bishop), I, 270
Marble, Dan, I, 400
Marco Savona, I, 427
Marie Antoinette, Queen, I, 166n.
Marietta, O., I, 9n., 30, 30n., 75n., 120, 166n., 179, 208
Market Street, Louisville, I, 406, 407
"Marmion," the, II, 15
Marnezia: *see* Lezay-Marnezia
Marquette, Jacques, I, 6, 38, 80, 81, 95
Marriwood, Penitence, I, 300, 301
Marriwoods, the, I, 301
Marryat, Frederick, I, 14n., 22, 22n., 117, 163; II, 14, 14n., 15n., 30, 30n.
Mars, god, I, 335
Marsh, actor, I, 366
——, theatrical manager, I, 454
Marshall, theatrical manager, I, 453
——, Humphrey, I, 242, 243, 243n., 244
——, James B., I, 176
Marsh and Eaton, I, 394, 454
Martha, Doña, I, 288, 289
Martin, actor, I, 374n.
——, Aimé, I, 261
Martineau, Harriet, I, 35n., 38n., 76n., 116, 210n., 272; II, 2, 3n., 10, 10n., 23, 23n., 30, 30n.
Martyrs, The (Ruter), I, 248
Maryland, I, 15n., 16, 39, 85
"Mary, the Maid of the Inn" (Southey), I, 417
Mason, James M., I, 196

Masonic Hall, Lexington, I, 401, 402, 402n., 448, 452
Masonic Miscellany, The, I, 201, 201n.
Masonry, I, 201, 235, 359n., 435
"Masque of the Red Death, The" (Poe), I, 340
Massachusetts, I, 15n., 56, 56n., 127
Massinger, Philip, I, 414
Mather, Cotton, II, 31, 31n.
——, W. W., I, 258, 270
Mathew Carey (Bradsher), II, 2n.
Mathews, Lois K., I, 17n.
Maturin, Charles, I, 416
Maud, actor, I, 375n.
Maumee River, I, 88
Maxwell, William, I, 135, 135n.
—— & Cooch, I, 220
Maysville, Ky.: *see also* Limestone, I, 28, 396
Mazeppa (Byron), II, 22
Mazeppa (melodrama), I, 417, 430
"Mazeppa," the, II, 15
Medical and Physical Memoirs (Caldwell), I, 255
Medical Friend of the People, I, 198
Medical Institute of the City of Louisville, I, 196
"Medical Topography" (Daniel Drake), I, 255
Medina, playwright, I, 421
Medley, or Monthly Miscellany, The, I, 164, 165, 165n.; II, 8n.
Medora, II, 23
"Medora," the, II, 15
Meigs, R. J., I, 179
Melchior (A. Alman), I, 426
Melish, John, I, 28n., 74n., 114, 128, 367n., 440
Melmoth, the Wanderer (Maturin), I, 416
Melodramatic Theatre, Louisville, I, 383, 406, 447, 448, 452
Membré, Father, I, 81
"Memoir" (Lundy), I, 338n.
"Memoir" (Whitty), I, 297n.
Memoir of the Public Services of William Henry Harrison, A (James Hall), I, 253
Memoirs (D'Eres), I, 93
Memoirs (Koerner), I, 15n. and as *op. cit.,* 20n., 28n., 209n.

Memoirs and Confessions (Ashe), I, 104n.

Memoirs of a Captivity among the Indians (John D. Hunter), I, 94

Memoirs of Mammoth, and Various Other Extraordinary and Stupendous Bones (Ashe), I, 104n.

Memoirs of the Historical Society of Pennsylvania, I, 96n.

Memoirs of the Life and Services of Daniel Drake (Mansfield), I, 196n., 234n., 356n.

Memoirs of the Rev. Thomas Cleland, I, 227n.

Memorable Days in America (Faux), I, 32n. and as *op. cit.*, 107

Men and Manners in America (Hamilton), I, 74n., 113

Ménard family, I, 8

"Mercer Election, The" (Thomas Johnson), I, 320n.

Merchant of Venice, The (Shakespeare), I, 413, 414n.

Meriwether, Albert G., I, 134n.

Meschasipi River: *see* Mississippi River

Messages and Letters of William Henry Harrison, I, 115n.

Metcalf, Samuel L., I, 247, 316

Methodist Episcopal Church, The (Burke), I, 228

Methodist Episcopal Church, Detroit, I, 451, 452

—— General Conference, I, 49

—— newspapers, I, 21n.

—— Protestant Church, I, 228

Methodist Quarterly Review, I, 312n., 313n.

Methodists, I, 18n., 42, 43, 43n., 44, 46, 47, 50, 51, 63, 98, 158, 189, 192, 205, 226, 227, 228, 281, 312, 410

Mettez, Théophile, I, 12n.

Mexico, I, 240, 246, 288

Miami country, I, 260

—— University, I, 59, 60, 67, 163, 187, 199, 248, 267, 270

"Miami Woods" (Gallagher), I, 342

Miami Woods A Golden Wedding and Other Poems (Gallagher), I, 342

Michaux, André, I, 8n., 99, 256

——, François A., I, 46, 99, 256

Michigan, Lake, I, 153, 343

——, Supreme Court of, I, 261

——, University of, I, 61, 62, 363n.

"Michigan Emigrant Song, A," I, 307n.

"Michigan Emigrant's Song, The," I, 307

Michigan Essay, I, 10n., 11n., 142, 147n.

Michigan Historical Collections, I, 286n.

Michilimackinac, island, I, 38, 87, 93, 343

Microscope, The, I, 161, 161n., 162

Middle Ages, I, 346

Middleburg, O., I, 192

Midnight Hour, The (Inchbald), I, 415n.

"Mignon" (Goethe), I, 339

Military Society, Lexington, I, 354

Millenium, The (Pratt), I, 233

Miller, Professor, I, 196

——, Edward A., I, 68n.

——, H., I, 317

——, James M., I, 11n., 142, 142n.

Mills, Samuel J., I, 98

Milton, John, I, 3n., 117, 180, 221, 330, 335; II, 2, 4, 4n., 5, 5n., 7, 8, 12n., 27

Milwaukee, Wis., I, 37, 258

Minister of the Interior (France), I, 99

Minutes City Council, MS., Cincinnati, I, 357n., 437n., 444-452, 454-455, 457

Minutes of the Annual Conferences (1773-1828), I, 43n., 44n.

Minutes of the Annual Conferences (1839-1845), I, 44n.

Minutes of the General Assembly of the Presbyterian Church, I, 44n.

"Miscellaneous," I, 176

Miscellaneous Repository, The, I, 190, 191, 191n.

"Miscellaneous Selections," I, 187

Miscellanies (Depeyster), I, 344n.

"Miscellany," I, 154

Miss in her Teens (Garrick), I, 415n.

Mississippi, I, 376n.

———— River, I, 2, 6, 22, 24, 39, 74, 78, 80-89, 91-94, 104n., 110n., 111, 115, 124, 126, 130, 138, 139, 172, 207, 212, 248, 290, 299, 306, 307, 326, 344, 376, 390; II, 15

———— Valley, I, 4, 5n., 21n., 79, 80, 84n., 127, 207, 297n., 408

Mississippi Valley Historical Review, The, I, 86n. and as *op. cit.*

Missouri River, I, 20n., 22, 77, 83, 85, 86, 87, 88, 95, 99, 104n., 304, 348

———— Valley, I, 126, 346

Missourian Lays (Umphraville), I, 324, 324n., 325n.; II, 19, 19n. and as *op. cit.*

Missouri Fur Company, I, 95

Missouri Gazette, I, 52n., 70, 139, 139n., 140, 140n., 141, 142, 144n., 145n., 147n., 152, 152n., 259n., 325n., 329n., 359n., 360n., 374n., 376n., 407n., 429n., 433n., 435n., 442, 444

Missouri Harmony, The (Carden), I, 316, 316n.

Missouri Historical Society, I, 11n., 374n., 411n.

Missouri Historical Society Collections, I, 308n.

Missouri Republican, I, 21n., 56n., 69n., 140n., 155, 301n., 302n., 360n., 382n., 407n., 408n., 409n., 419n., 421n., 425n., 426n., 427n., 429n., 431n., 432n., 433n., 446, 450-452, 454-455; II, 10n., 14n., 16n., 24n., 27n., 32n., 33n., 34n., 36n., 37n.

Missouri Saturday News, I, 163

Missouri, University of, I, 62

Mr. Birney's Second Letter, I, 217

Mr. H. (Lamb), I, 417

Mitchell, Dr., I, 197

————, O. M., I, 271

————, S. A., I, 128

————, Thomas D., I, 270

Mitford, Mary Russell, I, 275n., 284, 290, 290n.

Mobile, Ala., I, 389, 390

Mock Doctor, The (Fielding), I, 414, 415n., 418

Modern Chivalry (Hugh H. Brackenridge), I, 124, 276n.

Modern Fashions (M. Smith), I, 422

"Modern Schools" (Peirce), I, 326

Mogul Tale, The (Inchbald), I, 415n.

Molière, I, 418, 418n.

Monastery, The (Sir Walter Scott), II, 13, 21

Moncacht-apé, I, 84

Moncrieff, W. T., I, 420

Mondelli, theatrical painter, I, 404

Monograph of the Fluviatile Bivalve Shells, A (Rafinesque), I, 257, 257n.

Monroe, James, I, 115n.

————, Mich., I, 62

Monster, or the Fate of Frankenstein, The, I, 417

Montacute, village, I, 284, 285, 321

———— Female Beneficent Society, I, 285

Montgomery, W., I, 394, 456

Monthly American Journal of Geology and Natural Science, The, I, 85n., 244

Monthly Chronicle, The, I, 186

Montreal, Canada, I, 83, 92, 364, 365, 440

———— Theatre, I, 365n., 375n.

Moore, G. G., I, 186n.

————, Thomas, I, 131; II, 2, 10, 11n., 19, 32

————, W. T., I, 45n.

Moorhead, Dr., I, 197

Moral Advocate, The, I, 190

Moral Instructor, The (Catharine Beecher), I, 267

Moravians, I, 40, 40n., 96, 97

More, Hannah, II, 10

Morgan, actor, I, 367

————, Ephraim, I, 137n.

————, E., & Co., I, 71

———— & Lodge, I, 137n.

————, Palmer & Co., I, 137n.

Mormonism Exposed (Swartzell), I, 233

Mormonism Unveiled (E. D. Howe), I, 231, 231n.

Mormonism Unveiled (Pratt), I, 232

Mormons: *see also* Latter Day Saints, I, 42, 46, 192-194, 231, 232

"Morning of Life, The" (Benjamin Drake), I, 266
Morse, Jedidiah, I, 128, 263
"Mortifications of Vice, The," I, 265
Morton, Thomas, I, 371n., 416
———— & Griswold, I, 184n.
———— & Smith, I, 184n.
Moscow, Russia, I, 431, 431n.
Mountaineers, The (Colman), I, 416n.
Mountain Muse, The (Daniel Bryan), I, 122n.
"Mountain Paths, The" (Gallagher), I, 340, 342 .
Mount Clemens, Mich., I, 346n.
Mountpleasant, O., I, 45, 158, 190, 191, 194, 194n., 201
Mount St. Bernard, drama, I, 418
Much Ado (Shakespeare), I, 414, 414n.
Muddy Run, I, 73
Mueller, theatrical manager, I, 395
Municipal Reference Library, St. Louis, I, 438n.
Murray, Sir Charles Augustus, I, 36n., 115
————, Lindley, I, 263
Murray's English Grammar, I, 264
Muscleshellorum, Professor, I, 256, 326
Muse of Hesperia, The (Peirce), I, 327, 327n.; II, 7n.
Muses, the, I, 206; II, 5n., 7, 28
"Muses, The," I, 154
Museum, Detroit, I, 394, 410, 453-456
————, St. Louis, I, 408, 457
Muskingum River, I, 40n., 85, 96, 97, 271, 271n.
———— Valley, I, 97
Muzzy, theatrical manager, I, 451
———— & Watson, I, 387, 451

NAGLE, Maurice, I, 321
Naples, Italy, I, 430
Napolead, The (Genin), I, 333-336
Napoleon Bonaparte, I, 6n., 254n., 334, 335, 336
Narrative, A (Heckewelder), I, 40n., 96, 271n.
Narrative Journal of Travels (Schoolcraft), I, 88

Narrative of an Expedition through the Upper Mississippi to Itasca Lake (Schoolcraft), I, 88
Narrative of an Expedition to the Source of St. Peter's River (Keating), I, 86n., 88
Narrative of a Tour in North America (Tudor), I, 115
Narrative of Mr. Adam Rankin's Trial, A, I, 220, 221n.
Narrative of Riots at Alton (Edward Beecher), I, 153n., 218
Narrative of the Captivity and Providential Escape of Mrs. Jane Lewis, I, 92
Narrative of the Capture and Providential Escape of Misses Frances and Almira Hall, I, 92
Narrative of the Incidents Attending the Capture, Detention, and Ransom of Charles Johnston, A, I, 92
Narrative of the Late Riotous Proceedings against the Liberty of the Press, in Cincinnati, I, 218n.
Narrative of the Life and Adventures of Matthew Bunn, I, 308n.
Narrative of the Visit to the American Churches, A (Andrew Reed), I, 98
Nashville, Tenn., I, 138n., 372, 374, 376, 378, 382, 384, 390, 395
Nast, William, I, 271
Natchez, Miss., I, 24n., 110n., 163, 382, 390
National Amphitheatre, Cincinnati, I, 454
———— Hotel, St. Louis, I, 419n.
National Jubilee, The (Richard Emmons), I, 333
National Republican, The, I, 327n., 357n.; II, 32n., 35n.
National Republican Party, I, 252
———— Theatre, Cincinnati: see also New National Theatre, I, 388, 426n., 454-455, 457
———— Theatre, Detroit, I, 394, 456, 457
National-Zeitung, Die, I, 20n.
"Native Balladry in America" (Phillips Barry), I, 311n.
Natural and Statistical View (Daniel Drake), I, 123, 135n., 240, 255

Nature and Philosophy, I, 420
Naudowessies, Indians, I, 86
Nauvoo, Ill., I, 42, 194
Navarino (Green Bay), Wis., I, 143
Navigator, The (Cramer), I, 103, 103n. and as *op. cit.*
Negroes, I, 18n., 31, 35n., 319n., 431
Nelson, T. Somers, I, 422
——— County, Ky., I, 329n.
Nepos, Cornelius, II, 9
Nettletongue, Nelly, I, 162
Neuvaine a l'honneur de St. François Xavier, I, 11n.
Neville, Morgan, I, 275, 306n.
New Albany, Ind., I, 31, 161, 254n.
New American Reader, No. 3, The (Bridge), I, 267
New American Speaker, The (Bridge), I, 267
New American Theatre, New Orleans, I, 406
——— Cincinnati Theatre, I, 385, 404, 450
Newburyport, I, 58n., 103n.
New Collection of Hymns, A (David Wells), I, 316
New College, Oxford, I, 110 ,
New Discovery of a Vast Country in America, A (Hennepin), I, 80, 81, 81n.
New England, I, 14-18, 29, 30, 36, 40, 46, 56, 92, 120, 126, 142, 180-183, 205, 206, 252, 300, 306, 307; II, 31, 32, 36, 37
New-England Magazine, The, I, 38n.; II, 36
New England Review, The, I, 150; II, 36
"New England Sketch, A" (Harriet Beecher), I, 287
New Guide, A (J. M. Peck), I, 129
Newhall, John, I, 57n.
New Hampshire, I, 22n.
——— Harmony, Ind., I, 21n., 31, 32, 33n., 52, 160, 160n., 201, 234, 257, 258, 363
New-Harmony and Nashoba Gazette, The, I, 160n.
New-Harmony Community of Equality, the, I, 160

New-Harmony Gazette, The, I, 33n., 159, 159n., 160n., 161n., 363n.; II, 5n., 10n., 16n., 17n., 28n.
New Haven, Conn., I, 263
New Home, A (Kirkland), I, 66n., 284-286
New Hotel, The ("G. G. F."), I, 427, 427n.
New Jersey, I, 15n., 16n., 29, 97, 136n.
——— Jerusalem, I, 42
——— Jerusalem Church, I, 192
New Kentucky Composition of Hymns and Spiritual Songs, A (Downs), I, 314, 314n., 315n., 316n.
New Madrid, Mo., I, 346
"New Moon, The" (James Hall), I, 281
New National Theatre, Cincinnati, I, 388, 389, 405, 454
"New Orleans," the, I, 24
New Orleans, La., I, 25n., 27, 93, 94, 101, 102, 127, 212, 361, 361n., 373, 381, 381n., 382, 385, 386n., 390, 398, 399, 400, 404, 406, 424, 430
———, Battle of, I, 319n., 330, 332
Newport, Ky., I, 259, 357n., 364
New Purchase, The (Baynard R. Hall), I, 55n.
New St. Louis Theatre: *see also* St. Louis Theatre, I, 360, 389, 408, 432, 453, 454, 455
New Select Hymns (Gallaher), I, 317
New Selection of Psalms, Hymns and Spiritual Songs, A (H. Miller), I, 317
New Spain, I, 87, 93
New System of Geography, A (Morse), I, 263
New Theatre, Lexington, I, 353, 401, 402, 440, 452, 453
New Travels (Brissot), I, 114n.
New Travels to the Westward (Decalves), I, 93
New Voyages to North-America (Lahontan), I, 82
New Way to Pay Old Debts, A (Massinger), I, 414n.
New Year's Gift, II, 4n.

New York state, I, 14n., 15n., 16, 17, 17n., 22n., 25n., 29, 36, 40, 42, 56, 56n., 120, 142, 224, 346n.
————, N. Y., I, 25, 37, 105, 109n., 147n., 160n., 210n., 260, 293n., 297n., 329n., 366, 367, 368n., 398n., 399, 424, 425, 425n.; II, 7n., 26, 31
Ney, Marshal, I, 254n.
Niagara Falls, I, 90
Nicholas, George, I, 211
Nicholasville, Ky., I, 396
Nick of the Woods (Bird), I, 73
Nick of the Woods (Medina? from Bird), I, 420
Niles, M. A. H., I, 271
Niles' National Register, I, 15n.
Niles' Weekly Register, I, 14n., 15n., 17n., 18n., 19n., 25n., 26n., 32n., 52n., 54n., 71n., 141n., 170n.
Nineveh, I, 77, 79
Noah, M. M., I, 418
North American Review, The I, 19n., 53n., 54n., 71n., 76n., 81n., 94n., 96n., 181n., 201n., 210n., 242, 250n., 254n., 264n., 282n., 286n., 291n.; II, 30, 34n.
North American Sylva, The (F. A. Michaux), I, 99
North Carolina, I, 14n., 15n.
Northern Reformer, The, I, 192
North-Western Journal, I, 17n.
Northwest Passage, I, 90
North-West Territory, I, 30, 43n., 61, 166n., 208, 212
Norton, Charles Eliot, 84n.
Norvell, John, I, 134n.
————, John, and Co., I, 134n.
————, Joshua, & Co., I, 134n.
———— & Cavins, I, 134n.
Norwegians, I, 346
No Song No Supper, I, 420
Notes of a Journey (Logan), I, 35n.
Notes on a Journey (Birkbeck), I, 31n., 125, 125n.
"Notes on Illinois," I, 171, 172
"Notes on Kentucky" (John Bradford), I, 153, 153n.
"Notes on St. Louis" (John A. Paxton), I, 407n.

Notes on the Western States (James Hall), I, 127, 247n.
Notes on Wisconsin (Lea), I, 129
"Notes sur le voyage de Chateaubriand en Amérique" (Chinard), I, 91n.
Notes upon the Western Country (Hoskins), I, 121
Notices concerning Cincinnati (Daniel Drake), I, 123
Notions of the Americans (James Fenimore Cooper), II, 2n.
Nouvelle decouverte (Hennepin), I, 80
"Novice of Cahokia, The" (Benjamin Drake), I, 283
Nuttall, Thomas, I, 99
Nyon Fils, I, 82n.

Oberlin Collegiate Institute, I, 63
Observations, on a Letter from George Nicholas, I, 212
Observations on Church Government (McNemar), I, 225
Observations on Church Government, by the Presbytery of Springfield, I, 222n.
Observer, Lovejoy's, I, 152, 161, 218, 435
Observer & Reporter, I, 402n., 426n., 453, 454; II, 8n.
Ocean Steam Company, I, 381n.
Odes of Horace in Cincinnati, The (Peirce), I, 257n. and as *op. cit.*, 325-327, 379n.; II, 5n., 9, 19, 20n.
"Ode to Apollo" (John Keats), I, 180, 181n.
Odyssey, I, 79, 83
Œuvres et correspondance inédites (Tocqueville), I, 3n. and as *op. cit.*, 43n., 101
Officia propria pro Dioecesi Ludovicenensi (Du Bourg), I, 12n.
Ogden, George W., I, 121, 121n.
"Ohio" (Guilford), I, 275
Ohio, General Assembly of, I, 259
————, Medical College of, I, 197, 235, 256, 270
Ohio Adler, Der, I, 20n.
Ohio and Michigan Register, I, 201

Ohio Archaeological and Historical Publications, I, 68n.

Ohio Chronik, Die, I, 20n.

Ohio Company, I, 61, 85

Ohio Gazetteer, The (Kilbourn), I, 129

Ohio Medical Repository, The, I, 196

Ohio River, I, 2, 6, 8, 16, 23, 23n., 24, 25, 31, 34, 66n., 74, 78, 83, 83n., 85, 88, 90, 91, 92, 97, 99, 101, 104n., 115, 116, 118, 124, 126, 127, 129, 130, 161, 251, 283, 289, 299, 300, 304, 305, 306, 307, 308, 337, 347, 369n., 376, 390, 423, 430; II, 1, 13, 15, 37

Ohio River, The (Hulbert), I, 30n.

Ohio Staats-Zeitung, I, 21n.

Ohio University, I, 60, 67

———— Valley: see also Ohio River, I, 79, 93, 98, 206, 346, 348, 374

———— Valley Historical Association, *Seventh Annual Report*, I, 311n.

Ohio Valley Historical Series Miscellanies, I, 46n.

O'Keefe, John, I, 354, 416

"Old-Country Ballads in Missouri" (Belden), I, 311n.

"Old Ironsides" (Holmes), I, 338; II, 36

"Old Maid of St. Louis, The" (Umphraville), I, 325

Old Salt-house Theatre, St. Louis, I, 360, 382, 385, 389, 407, 408, 446, 448, 450-452

"Old Wisdom," I, 132

Olive Street, St. Louis, I, 389, 407, 408, 453

Oliver Twist (Dickens), I, 298

Olney Hymns (Cowper and Newton), II, 11n.

"On Contentment" I, 265

"On Maurice Nagle, Esq." (Thomas Johnson), I, 321

"On the Immortality of the Soul," I, 265

"On the Re-launching of the Constitution" (William Ross Wallace), I, 338

Ontwa (Henry Whiting), I, 344, 345, 345n.; II, 20

"On Viewing the Falls of Ohio" (Guest), I, 337

"Oolemba in Cincinnati" (Timothy Flint), I, 275, 283

Opinions on Various Subjects (Maclure), I, 234, 234n.

"Oral Literature" (Pound), I, 311n.

Oration, Containing a Declaration of Mental Independence (Robert Owen), I, 234

Oration, Delivered at Marietta, An (Varnum and others), I, 209n.

Ordinance of 1787, I, 53

Ordinances of the Borough of Vincennes, I, 439n.

Oregon River, I, 291

"Original Communications," I, 187

"Original Essays," I, 163

Origine et progrès de la mission du Kentucky (Badin), I, 12n.

"Origin, Manners, Customs, Religion, and Language of the Indians" (Carver), I, 86

Orkneys, islands, I, 112

Ornemens de la memoire, Les, I, 11n.

Ornithological Biography (Audubon), I, 100

Orpheus, I, 321

Osages, Indians, I, 94

Osborn, publisher, I, 138n.

————, Selleck, I, 324; II, 31, 32, 32n.

Osceola (Lewis F. Thomas), I, 424, 424n.

Ostroklotz, island, I, 292

Othello (Shakespeare), I, 413, 414n.

Other Side of the Question, The (McNemar), I, 226

Otway, Thomas, I, 414

Our Mutual Friend (Dickens), I, 298

"Our Western Land" (Gallagher), I, 342n.

Outlaw, The (Charles A. Jones), I, 347

Outline of the History of the Church in the State of Kentucky, An (Bishop), I, 50n., 215n. and as op. cit., 248

"Outlines of a Plan for Cooperative Associations" (Rafinesque), I, 160

Outlines of Botany (John Locke), I, 270

Ovid, II, 9

Owen, David Dale, I, 258

———, Robert, I, 31, 32, 33n., 159, 233, 234

———, Robert Dale, I, 159, 159n., 425

———, William, I, 159, 159n., 160

——— family, I, 33

Oxford, O., I, 60, 199

———, University of, I, 110

Ozark Mountains, I, 283

PAGES *from the Early History of the West and North-West* (Beggs), I, 50n.

Pagoda Theatre, Louisville, I, 407, 453

Paincourt, I, 8n.

Paine, Thomas, II, 1

"Pains of Sleep, The" (Coleridge), II, 24, 25

Palladium, The, I, 135, 147n., 148n.; II, 11n., 12n.

Palmer, Friend, I, 363n., 392, 392n., 393, 393n., 446

———, Thomas, I, 137n., 159n.

Pandemonium, I, 330

Pansa, Sancho, I, 82n.

Paradise, I, 277

Paradise Lost (Milton), I, 3n., 117

Paradise Regained (Milton), I, 221

Paris, France, I, 8, 11n., 12n., 77, 80, 147n., 234

———, Ky., I, 135, 396, 421

Parke, Benjamin, I, 237

Parker, theatrical manager, I, 395

———, Amos, I, 121

———, Samuel, I, 121

——— & Mueller, I, 395, 457

"Parnassiad," I, 154

Parsons, theatrical manager, I, 392, 448, 452, 454, 455

——— & Dean, I, 393, 410, 450

Partisan Leader, The (Tucker), I, 302, 302n.

Partizan, The, I, 427

Parton, James, I, 310n.

"Passionate Boy, The," I, 268

"Pastoral Elegy," I, 310n.

"Pathetic Piece. The Close of Life," I, 265

"Patience under Provocation," I, 265

Patriot, The, I, 159

Patterson, J. B., I, 249

Pattie, James O., I, 94

Pauguk, I, 241

Paul, René, I, 418, 418n., 425

Paulding, J. K., I, 22n., 113, 113n., 272, 420; II, 1

Paul Jones, I, 418

Paup-Puk-Keewiss, I, 241

Pavilion Theatre, Cincinnati, I, 379, 403, 434, 444, 445, 454

Pawnee Hard-Heart, I, 96; II, 34

Paxton, J. D., I, 130, 217

———, John A., I, 325n., 407n.

Payne, John Howard, I, 417, 417n.

Peabody, Elizabeth, I, 182

———, Ephraim, I, 51, 183, 183n., 342

Pearl Street, Cincinnati, I, 405, 453

Pearman, theatrical manager, I, 448

Pease, Theodore, I, 34n.

Peck, John M., I, 39n., 51, 129, 163, 244n.

Pedestrious Tour, A (Evans), I, 8n. and as *op. cit.*, 118, 118n., 362n.

Pedlar, The (Wetmore), I, 421, 421n.

Pedro, Don, I, 288

Peeping Tom (Garrick), I, 415n.

Pegasus, I, 326

Peirce, Thomas, I, 256, 257, 257n., 261n., 325-327, 343, 379, 379n.; II, 5n., 7, 7n., 9, 19, 20, 20n.

Pelagian Detected, The (John P. Campbell), I, 223

Pelagianism, I, 219, 225

Pelham, William, I, 159n.

Pendleton, Miss, I, 296

Peniston, Francis, I, 139, 140n.

Penn, Shadrach, I, 151, 155

Pennsylvania, I, 14n., 15n., 16, 16n., 18, 29, 32, 40n., 56, 56n., 96, 276

Pentland & Norris, I, 454

People's Presidential Candidate, The (Richard Hildreth), I, 253n.

Pepin's equestrian company, I, 445

Percival, James Gates, I, 267, 339; II, 31, 32

Perkins, James H., I, 51, 72n., 183, 183n., 238, 342; II, 12n., 20, 27

Perrin, William Henry, I, 135n.

Personal Narrative of James O. Pattie, The, I, 94, 127

"Pete Featherton" (James Hall), I, 276, 280

Peter, Robert, I, 60n., 197

Peter Wilkins, I, 420

Petit catachisme historique, I, 12n.

Petrie, Miss, I, 400

Pew, Thomas J., I, 134n.

Peyton, actor, I, 375n.

Phantom Ship, The (Marryat), I, 163

Philadelphia, Pa., I, 6n., 14n., 27, 27n., 37, 77, 133n., 139, 144, 147n., 164, 195, 215, 301n., 329, 367, 368n., 374, 398n.; II, 15n.

"Philadelphia," the, I, 429

"Philadelphia Dun, The" (James Hall), I, 280n.

Philadelphiensis, pseudonym, I, 150

Philanthropist, The, I, 157

Phillips, theatrical manager, I, 374

———, William, I, 224, 229

"Philomathic Prize Poem" (Peirce), I, 327n.

Philomathic Society, I, 327n.

Philos Harmoniae, I, 317

Philosophy of Human Nature, The (Buchanan), I, 262

Phoebus Apollo: *see also* Apollo, I, 335

Phrenology Vindicated (Caldwell), I, 256

Pickard, Samuel T., II, 36n.

Picket, Albert, Sr., I, 239, 269

———, John W., I, 200, 269

Picture of Cincinnati, I, 15n., 16n., 20n., 25n., 27n., 54n., 67n., 68n., 71n.; II, 15n.

Picture of the Heavens (M'Cullough), I, 270

Picture Reader, The, I, 269

Pierce, Thomas: *see* Thomas Peirce

Pierre, I, 281

Pike, Zebulon M., I, 87, 89

Pilgrimage, A (Beltrami), I, 89

Pilgrims of the Plains (Aplington), I, 308n.

Pilgrim's Songster, The (Granade), I, 312

Pinckney, Howard, I, 299; II, 18, 19

"Pioneer, The" (James Hall), I, 281

Pioneer Collections. Report of the Pioneer Society of the State of Michigan, I, 307n.

Pioneer Life in Kentucky (Daniel Drake), I, 123

Pioneer Press of Kentucky, The (Perrin), I, 135n.

Piper, E. F., I, 309n., 310n.

Pirate, The (Sir Walter Scott), II, 21

Pitt, William, I, 54n.

Pittman, Philip, I, 8n., 85

Pittsburg, Pa., I, 23n., 24, 24n., 25n., 40n., 85, 87, 102, 133n., 147n., 367, 368n., 441

Pizarro (Kotzebue), I, 354n., 414, 418

Placide, Jane, I, 400

Plain Narrative of the Uncommon Sufferings, and Remarkable Deliverance of Thomas Brown, A, I, 91

Plain Tale, A, I, 213

Planché, J. R., I, 420

"Planting of Literary Institutions at Vincennes, Indiana" (Cauthorn), I, 138n., 236n.

Plato, I, 187

Plea of the Innocent, The (M'Kimmey), I, 230

Pleasant Hill, Ky., I, 41, 226

Plebius, pseudonym, I, 150

Plumbe, John, I, 37n., 143n.

Pocahontas, I, 423

Pocahontas (Robert Dale Owen), I, 424

Pocock, playwright, I, 417

Poe, Edgar Allan, I, 73, 297n., 338n., 339, 339n., 340, 340n.; II, 32

Poems (Holmes), II, 36

Poems (Maffitt), I, 206n.

Poems, chiefly Lyrical (Tennyson), II, 29

Poems on Several Occasions (Guest), I, 337, 337n.

"Poetical Asylum," I, 154

Poetical Works of Elizabeth Margaret Chandler, The, I, 337, 338n.

"Poetry," I, 176

Poets and Poetry of the West, The (Coggeshall), I, 154n., 296n. and as *op. cit.*, 327n. and as *op. cit.*; II, 21n.

"Poet's Banquet, The" (Peirce), I, 327

"Poet's Corner," I, 154

Poland, I, 347

Polar expedition, Symmes's, I, 435

"Policy of France toward the Mississippi Valley, The" (Turner), I, 101n.

Polish Chiefs, The, I, 297n.

"Politian" (Poe), I, 73

Political Characters of John Adams and Thomas Jefferson, The (Magruder), I, 164n.

Political, Commercial and Moral Reflections (Magruder), I, 212

Political Grammar of the United States, The (Mansfield), I, 270

Political Transactions in and concerning Kentucky (Littell), I, 213, 214

Polyanthos, The (Samuel Wilson), I, 264

Pontiac, Mich., I, 26n., 43n., 62

Pontiac (Macomb), I, 423

Poor Gentleman, The (Colman), I, 416n.

Poor Soldier, The (O'Keefe), I, 354, 355, 371n., 416

Pope, Alexander, I, 328, 349; II, 6, 7, 7n., 8, 9

Pope, the, I, 217

"Possessions of God, The" (William Ross Wallace), I, 339

Post, Christian, I, 40, 40n.

Postl, Karl, I, 64, 64n., 74n., 102

Postmaster General, American, I, 27n.

Potomac River, I, 85

Potter, J. S., I, 387, 452, 453

———, J. S., & Co., I, 452

——— & Waters, I, 387, 405, 453, 454

Poulson, C. A., I, 257n.

Pound, Louise, I, 310n., 311n.

"Poverty and Knowledge" (Perkins), II, 21n.

Powers, Benjamin F., I, 137n.

Pownall, Thomas, I, 85

Practical Grammar, A (Buchanan), I, 263

Practical Treatise, A (Daniel Drake), I, 255

Prairie, The (Cooper), I, 272; II, 34

Pratt, Parley P., I, 232, 233

Précieuses ridicules, Les (Molière), I, 418n.

Precursor, The, I, 192

"Preface to the Fourth Edition" (Kirkland), I, 286n.

Prentice, George D., I, 150, 151, 163, 252, 266, 342; II, 36

Presbyterians, I, 42-44, 46, 49, 50, 62, 63, 98, 216, 217, 219, 222-225, 230, 248, 317

Present State of the European Settlements on the Missisippi, The (Pittman), I, 8n., 85

Price, William, I, 160

Priestley, Joseph, I, 58

Primary Geography for Children (Catharine and Harriet Beecher), I, 270

Primm, Wilson, I, 307n.

Princeton College, I, 64

"Principles and Articles of Association of a Cooperative Community," I, 160

Pritchard, Mrs., I, 400

Proceedings and Transactions of the Royal Society of Canada, I, 82n.

Proceedings of the American Antiquarian Society, I, 135n. and as *op. cit.*

Proceedings of the American Philosophical Society, I, 8n.

Proceedings of the Board of Managers of the Western Methodist Historical Society, I, 239n.

Proceedings of the Corporation of the Town of Cincinnati, I, 436n.

Proceedings of the General Convention of Western Baptists, I, 49n.

Proceedings of the Ill. Anti-slavery Convention, I, 218n.

Process in the Transilvania Presbytery, A (Adam Rankin), I, 70n., 220, 222

Prophecy of Dante, The (Byron), II, 22, 22n.

Prose Writings (Bryant), I, 15n.; II, 35n.

Protestant, Der, I, 21n.

Protestant Episcopal Church, I, 45, 62, 158, 229

Protestants, I, 40, 43, 46, 229, 230

Proteus, god, I, 321

Prothero, Rowland E., II, 13n.

"Proud Ladye, The" (Cone), I, 340n.

Prussian System of Public Instruction, The (Stowe), I, 262

Psalms, the, I, 220, 316

Public Advertiser: see also The Louisville Public Advertiser, I, 155, 358n.

Publications of the Modern Language Association of America, I, 241n.

Pulpit Sketches (Maffitt), I, 206n.

Purcell, John B., I, 233, 239

Purchas, Samuel, I, 425

Putnam & Hunt, I, 291n.

QUAIFE, Milo M., I, 86n., 121n., 249n.

Quakers: *see* Friends

Quarterly Review, The, I, 5n., 103, 111n., 125n.; II, 1, 3, 3n.

Quebec, Canada, I, 93, 364, 365, 440

"Queen City, The" (Benjamin Drake), I, 283

Quincy, Ill., I, 34

Quinn, Arthur Hobson, I, 425n.

"Quinze jours au désert" (Tocqueville), I, 3n., 204

RABB, Kate Milner, I, 363n., 396n., 425n.

Rafinesque, Constantine S., I, 59, 66, 160, 167, 168, 168n., 243, 256, 257, 325, 326

Rail-road from the Banks of the Ohio River, I, 26n.

Ramble of Six Thousand Miles, A (Ferrall), I, 33n. and as *op. cit.*, 408n.

Rambler in North America, The (Latrobe), I, 15n. and as *op cit.*, 111n.

Ranck, G. W., I, 68n.

Randall, E. O., I, 40n.

Randolph Street, Detroit, I, 446

"Rank and Riches," I, 265

Rankin, Adam, I, 70n., 219-222, 248

———, John, I, 216

Rankin's Second Process (Adam Rankin), I, 222

Rape of the Lock, The (Pope), II, 7

Rapp, George, I, 31n., 32, 41, 114

Rawle, William, I, 96n.

Ray, Joseph, I, 269

Raymond and Agnes, I, 416n.

"R. B.," I, 13n., 15n., 74n., 129

Real Principles of Roman Catholics, The (Badin), I, 230

Recollections, MS. (Frederick W. Thomas), I, 297n.

Recollections of Persons and Places in the West (H. M. Brackenridge), I, 8n. and as *op. cit.*, 90n., 124, 276n.

Recollections of the Last Ten Years (Timothy Flint), I, 72n., 126, 293

Recollections of the West (Garrett), I, 48n.

Récollet order, I, 95

Reconciliation (Kotzebue), I, 418

Record 1781-1825 Town of Louisville, MS., I, 139n., 437n.

Records of Lexington, MS., I, 436n., 445, 451

Red River, I, 93

Red Rover, The (melodrama), I, 418, 426, 429

Reed, Andrew, I, 98

———, Ebenezer, I, 11n., 143n.

———, Henry, II, 27

———, Isaac, I, 55n.

Reese, Friedrich, I, 21n.

Reformation, the, I, 204

Reform Bill, English, I, 111

Reformed Gamester, I, 426

Register of Graduates (Indiana University), I, 61n.

Regular Baptist, The, I, 191

Regular Baptist Miscellany, The, I, 191

Religious Examiner, The, I, 191

"Remarkable Escape, A," I, 266

Remarks Made during a Tour (William Tell Harris), I, 32n. and as *op. cit.*, 114

Remarks Made on a Tour to Prairie du Chien (Atwater), I, 124

Remarks on the Catholic and Protestant Religions (Guerin), I, 230

Remarks upon Recent Publications (Samuel Chase), I, 229

"Reminiscence of the Scioto Valley," I, 266

Reminiscences (E. S. Thomas), I, 26n., 155n., 251

Reminiscences of Lexington, MS. (M'Cullough), I, 354n.

Rendezvous, The, I, 420

René, I, 90

Reply to A Narrative of Mr. Adam Rankin's Trial, A (Adam Rankin), I, 221, 221n.

Reply to Strictures on Sketches of the West (James Hall), I, 246

Reply to the Charges and Accusations of the Rt. Rev. Philander Chase, A (Sparrow), I, 229

"Reply to the Letter" (Cartwright), I, 227

"Report" (Samuel Lewis), I, 55n.

Reporter, The, I, 27n., 373n., 435n., 436n., 440-442; II, 12n.

Report of a Missionary Tour (Samuel J. Mills and Daniel Smith), I, 98

Report of the Committee on Education, of the House of Representatives of Kentucky, I, 54n.

Report of the Select Committee, The, I, 213

Report on Elementary Public Instruction in Europe (Stowe), I, 262

Resources of the United States, The (Bristed), I, 72n. and as *op. cit.*; II, 2n.

Response of the Judges of the Court of Appeals, The, I, 215

Restoration playwrights, I, 414

Retrospect of Western Travel (Martineau), I, 38n., 117, 210n.

"Revellers, The" (Gallagher), I, 339, 340

Revenge, The (Edward Young), I, 414, 415n.

Review, The (Colman), I, 416n.

Review of Captain Basil Hall's Travels, A (Richard Biddle), I, 108n.

Review of the Late Decision of the Supreme Court of Ohio, A (Springer), I, 228

Review of the Noted Revival, A (Adam Rankin), I, 222

"Reviews, and Literary Notices," I, 176

Revised and Improved Edition of the Eclectic Second Reader (M'Guffey), I, 268n.

Revised Ordinances of the City of Saint Louis, The, I, 37n., 438n.

Revised Statutes of the State of Indiana, The, I, 75n.

Revolutionary War, American, I, 13, 34, 40n., 101, 102, 104, 236, 294, 295, 301, 337

Revue de Paris, La, I, 9n.

Revue encyclopédique, I, 234

Reynolds, Frederick, I, 416

——, J. N., I, 254n.

——, Sacket, I, 137n.

"Rhodora, The" (Emerson), I, 183

Rice, David, I, 50, 215, 219, 219n., 221, 248

——, Nathan L., I, 230

Richard II (Shakespeare), I, 414n.

Richard III, of England, I, 399

Richard III (Shakespeare), I, 413, 414, 414n.

Richard, Gabriel, I, 11, 11n., 12n.

Richelieu (Bulwer), I, 417

Richland, Iowa, I, 309n.

Richmond, Ind., I, 31, 45

——, Ky., I, 198n., 396

——, Va., I, 13n.

Riddell, John L., I, 258

"Rifle, The" (Leggett), I, 422

Rifle, The (Solon Robinson), I, 422

Rigdon, Sidney, I, 232

Riley, B. F., I, 43n.

Ripley, O., I, 216

Rip Van Winkle (melodrama), I, 418; II, 33

Rise of Methodism in the West, The (Sweet), I, 49n., 50n., 312n.

"Rise of the West, The" (Schoolcraft), I, 346

Rivals, The (Sheridan), I, 415, 415n.

Rivers, Mrs., I, 367
Road to Ruin, The (Holcroft), I, 415, 416n.
Roaster, Tommy, I, 162
Robbers, The (Schiller), I, 419
Robert Owen's Opening Speech, I, 233
"Robert Owen to the Ten Social Colonies," I, 160
Roberts, T. H., I, 161
————, Zophar, I, 117
Robertson, George, I, 215
Robinson, Solon, I, 422
Rob Roy (Pocock), I, 417
Rob Roy (Sir Walter Scott), II, 13
Rochambeau, Jean, I, 101
Rochefoucauld-Liancourt, La, I, 92
Rocky Mountains, I, 36, 36n., 87
Rogers, Robert, I, 85
Roland for an Oliver, A (Morton), I, 416
Roman architecture, I, 431
Roman Catholics: *see* Catholics
Roman Father, The (Whitehead), I, 415
Romeo and Juliet (Shakespeare), I, 413, 414n.
Roosevelt, Theodore, I, 87n., 149n.
Roscian Society, Lexington, I, 354, 365n.
———— Society, St. Louis, I, 359
Rose of the Valley, The, I, 186, 206n.; II, 30n.
Ross, O. B., I, 192
Rossini, Gioachino, I, 419
Rossville, O., I, 217
Rousseau, Jean Jacques, I, 2, 89, 90n., 423, 425
Rovington, I, 301
Rowe, James S., I, 382, 384, 385, 386, 446, 450
————, Nicholas, I, 414, 415n.
Roy, J. -Edmond, I, 82n.
Ruggles, Mrs. H. A., I, 188
————, James, I, 271
Rule a Wife and Have a Wife (John Fletcher), I, 414n.
Russell, John B., I, 184n.
————, Richard, I, 385, 386, 452, 453
———— & Co., I, 452

———— & Rowe, I, 385, 386, 386n., 450-452
Russellville, Ky., I, 141n., 395
Russia, I, 334, 335
Ruter, Martin, I, 248, 269, 271
"R. W. Emerson, and the New School," II, 38n.
Ryan, Daniel J., I, 40n.

SAC and Fox Indians, I, 92, 249
Sacra Via, Marietta, I, 166n.
"Sacred to the Muses," I, 154
Saginaw, Mich., I, 3n.
St. Anne, Church of, at Detroit, I, 38
St. Charles, Mo., I, 20n., 126
St. Clair, Arthur, I, 9, 54n., 101, 308
"St. Clair's Defeat" (Bunn), I, 308
St. Clairsville, O., I, 191, 333
St. Genevieve, village, I, 6, 124
St. Lawrence River, I, 83, 306
St. Louis, Mo., I, 6, 8n., 11n., 12n., 21n., 24, 25, 25n., 35-37, 39, 40n., 52, 69, 70, 88, 95, 99, 124, 126, 139n., 140, 140n., 142, 144, 147n., 152, 163, 172, 184, 188, 259, 259n., 307, 325, 357, 358-361, 372, 374-378, 381, 382, 384, 385, 387-391, 396, 400, 402, 407, 408, 412, 413, 413n., 418, 419n., 421, 422, 425-427, 429, 431n., 432, 433, 435, 438, 438n., 440-457
St. Louis Beacon, I, 360n., 427n., 430n., 435n., 447, 448, 449; II, 4n.
St. Louis Commercial Bulletin, I, 409n., 452
St. Louis County, Mo., I, 302n.
St. Louis Directory, The, I, 24n., 25n., 35n., 53n., 325n., 407n.
St. Louis Enquirer, I, 152
St. Louis Juvenile Thespian Association, I, 421n.
———— Mercantile Library, I, 259n.
———— ordinances, I, 438n.
St. Louis Republic, The, I, 140
St. Louis Theatre, I, 359, 376, 443, 455, 457
———— Thespian Association, I, 422
———— Thespian Society, I, 360
———— Thespian Theatrical Association, I, 360, 407

———— University, I, 63
St. Patrick's Day (Sheridan), I, 415, 415n.
St. Petersburg (Petrograd), Russia, I, 30n., 93
Saint-Pierre, Bernardin de, I, 9, 9n., 289
Salem, Ind., I, 254
Saline, Mich., I, 199
Sallust, II, 9
Salop, county of, England, I, 129
Salt River, I, 73
Sample, Sallie, I, 363n.
Sangamo Journal, I, 25n., 148n., 364n.
Sannillac, I, 345
Sannillac (Henry Whiting), I, 345, 345n.; II, 20
Sardanapalus (Byron), I, 417; II, 14
Sarjent, Abel M., I, 189
Satan, I, 313, 330, 331
Saugrain, Dr., I, 8, 90
Sault Ste. Marie, Mich., I, 94; II, 15
Say, Thomas, I, 33, 88, 160, 257
Scank, Jonathan, I, 231
————, Philemon, I, 231
Scanyawtauragahrooote Indians, I, 93
"Scenery of the Ohio," I, 266
Scharf, J. T., I, 53n., 63n., 302n.
Schermerhorn, John F., I, 98
Schiller, Johann Christoph Friedrich von, I, 419; II, 21
Schoenbrunn, village, I, 40n.
Schoolcraft, Henry Rowe, I, 86n., 88, 89, 94, 95, 128, 237, 240, 241, 346
School for Arrogance, The (Holcroft), I, 416n.
School for Authors, The, I, 358
School for Scandal, The (Sheridan), I, 415, 415n.
Schoolmaster, The, I, 199
School of Industry at New Harmony, Ind., I, 201
Schultz, Christian, I, 103n., 118, 118n.
Schweinitz, Lewis D. de, I, 88
Scio, island, II, 20
Scotch immigrants, I, 32

Scotch-Irish immigrants, I, 14
Scotch novels, I, 167; II, 13
Scotland, I, 343
Scott, John, I, 129
————, Sir Walter, I, 4, 111, 131, 167, 276, 298, 344-346, 417; II, 2, 2n., 11-13, 15-22, 23, 25, 31
————, Walter, the Rev., I, 192
———— & Rule, I, 360, 407, 446
———— & Thorne, I, 387-390, 405, 454-455, 457
Scottish ballads, I, 310
———— Highlanders, I, 337
———— verse, II, 12n.
Scourge of the Ocean, The (Burt), I, 301
Scripture, the, I, 217
Seaborn, Captain Adam, I, 260
Sea Captain, The (Bulwer), I, 417
Sealsfield, Charles: *see* Karl Postl
Seamons, amateur theatrical manager, I, 355n.
"Seat of the Muses," I, 154
Sebastian, Benjamin, I, 213
Second Discourse before the Medical Library Association of Cincinnati (Daniel Drake), I, 196n.
Second Epistle, A (David Rice), I, 219, 219n.
Second Series of a Diary (Marryat), II, 14n., 30n.
Second Street, Cincinnati, I, 402
Sectarianism is Heresy (Wylie), I, 208n., 233
Sedwick, George, I, 191
Seidensticker, Oswald, I, 20n., 21n.
"Selected Poetry," I, 154
"Selected Tales," I, 163
Selection of Hymns and Poems, A (McNemar), I, 317
Selections from the Poetical Literature of the West (Gallagher), I, 342, 342n.
"Select Miscellany," I, 177
Semi-pelagianism I, 219
Semi-weekly Free Press, I, 453
Senex, pseudonym, I, 56n.
Sentinel, and Star in the West, The, I, 158
Series of Strictures, A (Kidwell), I, 229

Serious Expostulation, A (Charles Fisher), I, 230

Sermon at the Opening of the Synod of Kentucky, A (David Rice), I, 219

Sermon on Regeneration, A (Craighead), I, 223

"Sermon on the Mount," I, 269

Seth Way (Snedeker), I, 33n.

Seventh Street, Cincinnati, I, 405, 453, 454

Seven Years' War: *see also* French and Indian War, I, 85

Several Letters (John P. Campbell), I, 223

Sewanee Review, The, I, 311n.

Shaffer, David, I, 29n.

Shakerism, I, 223, 225

Shakerism Detected . . . Examined (McNemar), I, 225

Shakers (United Society of Believers), I, 40, 41, 41n., 42n., 46, 225, 226, 317

Shakers of Ohio (MacLean), I, 41n. and as *op. cit.*

Shakespeare, William, I, 413, 414, 418, 420; II, 4-6, 8, 21

Shakespearean plays: *see also* Shakespeare, I, 399n., 400, 413, 413n., 414, 414n.; II, 5

Shaler, N. S., I, 13n.

Shapley, Fern Rusk, I, 74n.

Sharp, Cecil J., I, 311n.

Shawnee Indians, I, 97, 308

Shawneetown, Ill., I, 34, 88, 216, 305, 306

Shawondasee, I, 241

Shearin, Hubert G., I, 311n.

Shelby, Isaac, I, 247

Shelbyville, Ky., I, 194, 396

Sheldon, John P., I, 143n.

——— & Reed, I, 142, 143n.

Shelley, Mary, I, 416

———, Percy Bysshe, I, 177, 180; II, 23-25, 28, 28n.

Shelton, F. W., I, 109, 110

Shepard and Stearns, I, 184n.

Sheridan, Richard Brinsley, I, 414, 415, 415n., 418

She Stoops to Conquer (Goldsmith), I, 415, 415n.

"She walks in beauty" (Byron), II, 13n.

Shienne (Cheyenne) Indians, I, 292, 293

Shiloah, I, 221

Shirreff, Patrick, I, 109n., 433, 433n.

Shock to Shakerism, A (Christopher Clark), I, 226

Short, Illinois settler, I, 15n.

———, Charles W., I, 197, 258

———, Hark, I, 296

———, Rich, I, 108

Shoshonee Indians, I, 291, 292, 293

Shoshonee Valley, The (Timothy Flint), I, 170n., 291, 291n., 292, 292n., 293, 293n., 294, 300; II, 10n., 35n.

Shotwell, Dr., I, 197

Shreve, Thomas, I, 179, 188, 301, 301n., 342

Shroeder Collection, I, 193n.

Shurtliff, Illinois settler, I, 15n.

Siberia, I, 125n.

Siege of Baltimore, The (Umphraville), I, 324n.

"Silver Mine, The" (James Hall), I, 281

Simms, William Gilmore, I, 73

Sin and Redemption (Hunn), I, 329n.

Sioux Indians, I, 95, 249

"Sir Walter Scott's Family" (Hogg), II, 16n.

Sketch Book, The (Irving), II, 33

"Sketches," I, 176

Sketches of America (Fearon), I, 105n.; II, 2n.

Sketches of a Tour (Cuming), I, 74n.

"Sketches of a Traveller" (Flagg), I, 124

Sketches of Character (Frederick W. Thomas), I, 297n.

Sketches of History, Life, and Manners, in the West (James Hall), I, 94n., 127, 246; II, 17n., 18n.

Sketches of Iowa (Newhall), I, 57n.

Sketches of Iowa and Wisconsin (Plumbe), I, 37n., 143n.

Sketches of Louisville (M'Murtrie), I, 405n.

Sketches of the Civil and Military

Services of William Henry Har-rison (Todd and Benjamin Drake), I, 253

Sketches of the Life of Martin Van Buren (Dawson), I, 254, 254n.

Sketches of Western Adventure (M'-Clung), I, 247, 266, 294, 295n.

Sketches of Western Methodism (James B. Finley), I, 229n.

Sketch of a Journey (Bullock), I, 125

Sketch of the Geographical Rout of a Great Railway, I, 26n.

Sketch of the History of Ohio, A (Salmon P. Chase), I, 245

Sketch of the Life and Labors of Richard McNemar, A (J. P. Mac-Lean), I, 226n., 317n.

Sketch of the Life and Public Ser-vices of William Henry Harrison, A, I, 253

"Sketch of the Political Profile of our Three Presidents" (Daveiss), I, 213

Sketch of the Progress of Botany, A (C. W. Short), I, 258

Skillman, Thomas T., I, 158, 189

Skizze des Lebens und der öffentlichen Dienste von William H. Harrison, Eine, I, 253

Slavery Inconsistent with Justice and Good Policy (David Rice), I, 215, 215n.

Sleigh, Joseph, I, 224

Smart, Robert, I, 393

Smith, actor, Cincinnati, I, 355n.

———, actor, St. Louis, I, 374n.

———, Dr., I, 197

———, Charles, I, 363n.

———, Daniel, I, 98

———, J. Calvin, I, 129

———, Colonel James, I, 225, 226

———, Joseph, I, 42, 193, 232

———, M., I, 422

———, Solomon F., I, 369n., 377n., 378n., 379-381, 389, 389n., 396, 396n., 397n., 398n., 400n., 422, 422n., 428n., 443-446, 449, 452, 454-455

———, Thomas, I, 133n., 168n.

Smyth, J. F. D., I, 102

Snedeker, Caroline Dale, I, 33n.

Snow & Fisk, II, 24n.

Snuffle, Simon, I, 162

Snyder, W. B., I, 317

Soane, playwright, I, 419

Society in America (Martineau), I, 35n., 76n., 116n., 117, 117n., 272; II, 3n. and as *op. cit.*

Society, Manners and Politics in the United States (Chevalier), I, 78n., 101

Socinianism, I, 219

Socini-Arian Detected, The (Thomas Cleland), I, 223

Socinus, I, 190

Sodom and Gomorrah, I, 431, 431n.

Soldier's Bride, The (James Hall), I, 261n., 276, 280, 280n.

Solomon's Temple Haunted (Bur-gess), I, 235

Somnus, I, 350

"Song" (Shelley), II, 28n.

"Song at the Feast of Brougham Castle" (Wordsworth), II, 27n.

Sonnambula, La (Bellini), I, 419

Southerne, Thomas, I, 414

Southern Literary Messenger, The, I, 302n.

Southey, Robert, I, 180, 417; II, 2, 11, 12n., 25

South Seas, I, 260

Souvenir of the Lakes, I, 286, 287n.

Spalding, Josiah, I, 140n.

———, M. J., I, 39n.

———, Solomon, I, 232

Spanier in Peru, Die (Kotzebue), I, 414, 418

Spanish, the, I, 87, 101, 212, 213, 288, 291, 292, 307, 361

——— language, I, 109n.

——— North America, I, 95

Sparrow, William, I, 229

"Spectator, A" I, 152

Spectator, The, I, 162

Spectre Bridegroom, The (farce), I, 418; II, 33

Speeches of Henry Clay, The, I, 210n.

Speech of Salmon P. Chase, I, 218

Speed, Thomas, I, 60n.

Speed the Plough (Morton), I, 371n., 416

Spenser, Edmund, I, 335
Spirit of '76, The, I, 159
"Spirit of the Pestilence" (Whittier), II, 36
Spirit of the West, I, 356n., 368n., 434n.
Spoiled Child, The, I, 420
Springer, Cornelius, I, 228
Springfield, Ill., I, 34, 148n., 364, 364n., 396n.
———— Presbytery, Kentucky, I, 222
Spring Street, Lexington, I, 440
"Squaw Song, The," I, 309, 309n.
Stackpole, Roaring Ralph, I, 73
State of Indiana Delineated, The (Joseph Colton), 129
State Street, Detroit, I, 410, 451
Statistical, Topographical, and Political History of Ohio, A (John H. James), I, 245n.
Statistics of the West (James Hall), I, 127, 246, 246n.
Staughton, Dr., I, 197
Steamboat Hotel, Detroit, I, 392, 393, 409, 446, 448
Stedman, E. C., I, 338n., 339n.
Steele's Western Guide Book, I, 129
Steines, Friedrich, I, 21n.
Steubenville, O., I, 396
Stewart, theological writer, I, 190
Stewart's Kentucky Herald, I, 135, 353n.
Stipp, G. W., I, 153n.
Stockbridge, John C., I, 333n.; II, 31n.
Stone, Barton W., I, 44, 192, 222-224, 226, 248
Stout, Elihu, I, 138, 138n., 363n.
———— & Jennings, I, 138n.
———— & Osborn, I, 138n.
————, Elihu, & Smoot, George C., I, 138n.
————, Elihu, and Son, I, 138n.
Stowe, Calvin, I, 51, 67, 239, 262
————, Harriet Beecher: *see also* Harriet Beecher, I, 110n., 287
Strait-creek, O., I, 216
"Strange fits of passion have I known" (Wordsworth), II, 28
Stranger, The (Kotzebue), I, 418

"Stranger's Grave, The" (Otway Curry), I, 266
Strickland, W. P., I, 48n.
Strictures on African Slavery (Crothers), I, 217
Strictures on Two Letters (John P. Campbell), I, 223
Stuart, James, I, 115, 405n., 432n.
Stuttgard Universal Gazette, The, I, 19n.
Sublime Mountains, I, 93
Such Things are (Inchbald), I, 416n.
Sullens, Zay Rusk, I, 438n.
Sunday News-Tribune, The, I, 363n., 411n.
Superior, Lake, I, 87, 93, 119, 138
Supplementary Catalogue of Ohio Plants, A, I, 258
Supplement to Library Service Published by the Detroit Public Library, I, 12n., 237n.
Supporter, The, II, 4n.
Surprising Account of the Captivity and Escape of Philip M'Donald & Alexander M'Leod, A, I, 93
Sutherland, Lorelly, I, 300, 301
Swan, Eliza, I, 92
Swartzell, William, I, 233
Swedes, the, I, 102
Sweet, W. W., I, 49n., 50n., 312n.
Swigert, Jacob, I, 75n.
Sycamore Street, Cincinnati, I, 382, 388, 402, 403, 405, 447, 448
———— Street Theatre, Cincinnati, I, 449, 454
Sylvester Daggerwood (Colman), I, 416n.
Symmes, John Cleves, I, 258-261, 325, 326, 357n., 435
Symmes's Theory of Concentric Spheres, I, 259n., 260, 260n.
Symzonia, I, 260
Synod, Associate Reformed, in Kentucky, I, 224
———— of Cincinnati, 217, 224
———— of Kentucky, I, 222
Synopsis of the Flora of the Western States, A (Riddell), I, 258
Systematic Catalogue of Books Belonging to the Circulating Library Society of Cincinnati, A, I, 68n.

System of Universal Science, A (Woodward), I, 261, 261n.

TADPOLE, Titus, I, 162
Tailor in Distress, The (Sol Smith), I, 422, 422n.
"Tales," I, 176
Tales and Sketches (Benjamin Drake), I, 283
Tales of the Border (James Hall), I, 22n., 276, 280-281
Tales of the North West, I, 286
Taming of the Shrew, The (Shakespeare), I, 413
Taneyhill, R. H., I, 46n.
Tanner, H. S., I, 128
———, John, I, 94
Tan-tu, village, I, 260
Tartarrac, New Spain, I, 93
Task, The (Cowper), II, 11n.
Taylor, Caleb Jarvis, I, 312n., 313
———, Eli, I, 158, 175n.
Te-cum-seh, I, 94
Tecumseh (Richard Emmons), I, 424
Telltruth, Margaret, I, 162
Tempest, The (Shakespeare), I, 414n.
Templeton, I, 294, 295
Tennessee, I, 15, 138, 280n., 281, 312, 376n., 377, 380
Tennesseean, I, 306
Tennyson, Alfred, Lord, I, 180; II, 4, 29
Terre Haute Prairie, I, 121
Territorial University (Vincennes), I, 61
Territory of Michigan, Supreme Court of, I, 261
Terror, Reign of, I, 211
Terry, playwright, I, 417, 419
Testimony of Christ's Second Appearing, The (Youngs), I, 225
Texas Volunteers, I, 435
Thalaba (Southey), I, 417
Thames River, I, 2
Theatrical Apprenticeship, The (Sol Smith), I, 369n. and as *op. cit.*, 379n., 380n., 396n., 398n., 422n., 443, 444, 446
Theatrical Association, Vincennes, I, 363
Theatrical Management (Sol Smith),

I, 379n., 389n., 396n., 397n., 400n., 422n., 428n., 445, 446, 449, 452, 454, 455
"The heath this night must be my bed" (Sir Walter Scott), II, 12n.
"Themes for Western Fiction" (Jewett), I, 273n.
Therese (Payne), I, 417
Thespian Association, Louisville, I, 358
Thespian Corps, Cincinnati, I, 355-357
——— Corps (professional company), Louisville, I, 358
Thespians, the, St. Louis, I, 360
Thespian Society, Cincinnati, I, 356, 402
——— Society, Detroit, I, 362
——— Society, Lexington, I, 353, 354, 421, 421n.
——— Society, Newport, Ky., I, 260n., 357n., 364n.
——— Society, St. Louis, I, 359, 376, 407
Thespis, I, 352
Third Street, Cincinnati, I, 405, 454
——— Street, Louisville, I, 383, 405, 406, 406n., 447, 448
——— Street, St. Louis, I, 389, 408, 453
Third Triennial Catalogue of the Officers and Graduates of Miami University, I, 60n.
Thirty Years Passed among the Players (Cowell), I, 319n., 357n. and as *op. cit.*
"This is what they Call Eloquence," I, 208n.
Thomas, David, I, 103n., 121
———, Ebenezer S., I, 26n., 155n., 251
———, Frederick W., I, 179, 296-300, 342, 347, 347n., 388n.; II, 15n., 18, 19, 19n., 20
———, Isaiah, I, 135n.
———, Lewis F., I, 407n., 408n., 409n., 424, 446, 447, 451; II, 6n.
Thompson, G. Burton, I, 422
———, Stith, I, 241n.
Thomson, James, II, 7, 11, 11n.
———, Samuel, I, 198

Thomsonian Recorder, The, I, 198, 198n.

Thorne, James, I, 388, 388n.

Thornton, Mr. and Mrs., I, 367

"Thoughts" (Caldwell), I, 255

"Thoughts on Optimism" (Caldwell), I, 255

Thoughts on Quarantine (Caldwell), I, 255

Thoughts on the Destiny of Man, I, 31n.

"Thoughts on the Style and Eloquence of the Pulpit, the Bar, and the Press" (Timothy Flint), I, 205n.

"Thoughts upon the Poetry of Milton," II, 5n.

Three Years in North America (Stuart), I, 115, 405n. and as *op. cit.*

Thwaites, Reuben G., I, 96n.

Tightlace, Timothy, I, 162

Times and Seasons, I, 194

Timothy Flint (Kirkpatrick), I, 287n. and as *op. cit.,* 316n.

Timour the Tartar (M. G. Lewis), I, 416, 420

Tinkerville, I, 284, 321

"Tintern Abbey" (Wordsworth), II, 27

Tippecanoe, Battle of, I, 318

Tippecanoe Song Book, The, I, 317

"To a Dandelion" (Lowell), I, 341

"To an Early Spring Flower" (Gallagher), I, 341

"To Coleridge," II, 26

Tocqueville, Alexis de, I, 3, 3n., 7n., 22n., 43n., 90, 101, 119, 204; II, 6n.

Todd, C. S., I, 247n., 253

Toledo, O., I, 26n.

Tom Thumb the Great (Fielding), I, 414, 415n.

"To my Sister M., with Wordsworth's Poems" (Cranch), II, 27

Tonson, Jacob, I, 81

Tonti (Tonty), Chevalier, I, 82

Tontine Coffee House, Detroit, I, 148n.

Topographical Description, A (Imlay), I, 122, 122n., 242

Topographical Description, A (Pownall), I, 85

"To Posterity" (Peirce), I, 326

Tory party, I, 111, 111n.

"To the Humble-bee" (Emerson), I, 182

"To the Literary Gazette," I, 162n.

"To the Publishers" (Peirce), I, 325n.

ª 'Tother Side of Ohio," I, 120

"To the Virginian Voyage" (Drayton), I, 1

Touchstone, I, 112

Touchy, Nettleton, I, 162

Toulmin, Harry, I, 58

Tour, A (Smyth), I, 102

Tour de Nesle (Hugo), I, 418

Tourists in America, I, 110

Tour of the American Lakes (Calvin Colton), I, 8n., 96n., 261n.

Tour on the Prairies, A (Irving), I, 119

Tour through North America, A (Shirreff), I, 109n., 433n.

Town and Country (Morton), I, 416

Townsend, J. K., I, 121

———, J. W., I, 320n.

Tracy, Joe, I, 369n.

———, Joshua L., I, 175n.

Transactions (Historical and Philosophical Society of Ohio), I, 238

Transactions (Western Literary Institute and College of Professional Teachers), I, 55n., 66n., 199n., 239

Transallegania (Schoolcraft), I, 346

Translation of a Memorial in the French Language, I, 10n.

Transylvania Catalogue of Medical Graduates, I, 60n.

Transylvania Journal of Medicine, The, I, 197

Transylvanian, The, I, 187

Transylvania Presbytery, I, 219, 220, 221

——— Seminary, I, 58

——— University, I, 28, 50, 52n., 58-60, 64, 67, 166, 167, 197, 206, 224, 230, 248, 255-257, 262, 325, 326, 353, 354, 401, 434, 435

Transylvania University (Peter), I, 60n.

Transylvania University, Medical School of, I, 195
Trappists, I, 39
Traveller's Directory, The (Melish), I, 128
Traveller's Guide to and through the State of Ohio (Blunt), I, 129
Travels (Ashe), I, 58n. and as *op. cit.*, 102, 103n., 118
Travels (Bernhard, Duke of Saxe-Weimar), I, 33n. and as *op. cit.*, 240n.
Travels (Bossu), I, 83n., 84
Travels (Bradbury), I, 8n., 99, 304n.
Travels (Carver), I, 86, 86n.
Travels (Basil Hall), I, 108
Travels (Melish), I, 28n. and as *op. cit.*, 114, 367n. and as *op. cit.*
Travels (F. A. Michaux), I, 46n., 99
Travels (Sir Charles Murray), I, 36n., 115
Travels (Schoolcraft), I, 88, 240
Travels (Schultz), I, 103n., 118 and as *op. cit.*
Travels (Rich Short), I, 108
Travels (David Thomas), I, 103n., 121
Treatise of Pathology and Therapeutics, A (Cooke), I, 256
Treatise on Slavery, A (James Duncan), I, 216
Treatise on the Diseases and Physical Education of Children, A (Eberle), I, 256
Treatise on the Practice of Medicine, A (Eberle), I, 256
Tree, Ellen, I, 400
Trial of Charles Vattier, The, I, 355n.
Trial of the Rev. Lyman Beecher, I, 224
Tribune, The (St. Louis), I, 21n.
Triennial Baptist Register, The (I. M. Allen), I, 44n.
Triplett, Philip, I, 215
Tripoli, I, 429
Tripolitan fleet, I, 430
Tristram Shandy (Sterne), I, 162
"Triumphs of Science, The" (William Ross Wallace), I, 338
Triumphs of Science, a Poem, The (William Ross Wallace), I, 338n.

"Trois canards, Les," I, 304
Trojan War, I, 78
Trollope, Frances, I, 29, 37, 108-113, 115, 117, 119, 125n., 131, 285, 293, 293n., 329, 329n., 357, 433; II, 7n., 10, 10n.
"Trollope's Folly," I, 110
Trollopiad, The (Shelton), I, 109
Trotter, George J., I, 134n.
Trowbridge, Charles, I, 361, 362n.
Troy, N. Y., I, 142n.
———, O., I, 195
Trudeau, Jean Baptiste, I, 307
Truman and Smith, I, 71, 267, 269
———, Smith & Co., I, 269; II, 6n.
Trumbull, H., I, 120
"Truth" (Chaucer), II, 4n.
Truth's Advocate, I, 195, 195n.
Tryon & Co., I, 387, 452
Tucker, Nathaniel Beverley, I, 301, 302, 302n.
Tudor, Henry, I, 115
Turco in Italia, Il (Rossini), I, 419
Turkish architecture, I, 38
Turner, Master, I, 375n.
———, Emma, I, 375n.
———, Frederick J., I, 15n., 101n.
———, Sophia, I, 365, 366, 367, 374, 375n.
———, William, I, 359, 365, 365n., 366, 366n., 367, 368, 368n., 369, 370, 373, 374, 374n., 375, 375n., 378, 381, 407, 440, 441, 442
——— & Morgan, I, 373
Turn out, I, 420
Turnpike Gate, The, I, 420
Twain, Mark, pseudonym, I, 73
Twamley, Edna M., I, 286n.
'Twas I (Payne), I, 417
Twelfth Night (Shakespeare), I, 414n.
Twelve Lectures (Kinmont), I, 262
Twelve Months in New-Harmony (Paul Brown), I, 33n.
Twice-told Tales (Hawthorne), I, 177; II, 37
Two Foscari, The (Byron), II, 14
Two Friends, The (Holcroft), I, 416n.
Two Galley Slaves, The (Payne), I, 417n.

Two Gentlemen of Verona, The (Shakespeare), I, 414n.
Two Years' Residence (John Woods), I, 74n.

ULTIMA Thule, II, 15
Umphraville, Angus, I, 324-325, 343; II, 19, 19n., 31, 31n.
Una, I, 116
Unadilla, I, 307n.
Uncas, I, 96; II, 34
Uncle Tom's Cabin (Harriet Beecher Stowe), I, 110n., 173, 270
Underhill, Samuel, I, 161
Union Village, O., I, 41, 41n.
Unitarians, I, 45, 51, 58, 178, 204
United Brethren, I, 20n.
United States Magazine and Democratic Review, The, I, 81n.
United States of North America as they are, The (Postl), I, 64n.
United States Songster, The, I, 318
Universal Educator, I, 199
Universalism, I, 219, 229
Universalists, I, 158
Universal Language, A (Ruggles), I, 271
University Building, Detroit, I, 363, 410
University of California Publications in Modern Philology, I, 91n.
University of Michigan Regents' Proceedings, I, 62n.
"University Report" (University of Missouri), I, 62n.
"Upon Scripture Psalmody" (Adam Rankin), I, 221
Upper Alton, Ill., I, 218
——— Street, Lexington, I, 354n.
Uriel, angel, I, 335
"Ursuline Convent, The" I, 231
Useful Discovery, A, I, 227, 227n.
"Useful Man, The" (James Hall), I, 280
Use of Strong Drink, The (Crothers), I, 234
Usher, Mr. and Mrs., I, 366, 367
———, Luke, I, 368, 368n., 369, 370, 372, 372n., 373, 381, 401, 436n.

———, Noble Luke, I, 353, 366, 368, 368n., 436, 440
Utica, N. Y., I, 142, 142n.
Utrecht, I, 80

VAIL, Henry Hobart, I, 267n.
Valley of the Mississippi, The (Lewis F. Thomas and Wild), I, 407n. and as *op. cit.*; II, 6n.
Van Buren, Martin, I, 254
Vandalia, Ill., I, 34, 141, 171, 172, 177, 237
Van Doren, Carl, II, 31n.
Van Vleet, Abram, I, 226
Varnum, James M., I, 209n.
Vaterlandsfreund, I, 21n.
Vatican, I, 338
Vaughan, actor, I, 367, 369
Vauxhall Gardens, Cincinnati, I, 379, 430, 444
Venable, W. H., I, 70n., 104n., 138n., 178n., 181n., 182n., 236n., 296n., 323n., 357n.; II, 32n., 37n.
Venice Preserved (Otway), I, 414n.
Vermont, I, 121
Versailles, Ky., I, 192, 396
Very, Jones, I, 182
Vesuvius, Mt., I, 430
Vevay, Ind., I, 216
Victorians, the, II, 29
Vide Poche, I, 8n.
Vienna, Austria, I, 21n.
"View of Gen. Jackson's Domestic Relations," I, 195
View of the Climate and Soil of the United States (Volney), I, 7n. and as *op. cit.*, 100n.
View of the Lead Mines of Missouri, A (Schoolcraft), I, 240
View of the President's Conduct, A (Daveiss), I, 213
View of the Valley of the Mississippi ("R. B."), I, 13n. and as *op. cit.*, 129
Views in Theology (Lyman Beecher), I, 224
Views on Lake Erie (S. R. Brown), I, 12n., 36n., 142n.
"Villani" (William Ross Wallace), I, 338
Villemain, A. F., II, 6n., 7n.

Vincennes, Ind., I, 6, 8n., 30, 34, 38, 39, 40n., 41, 41n., 70, 137, 138, 146n., 363, 363n., 377, 377n., 378, 396, 439
―――― Historical and Antiquarian Society, I, 236
Vindex (John P. Campbell), I, 223
"Vindication of the American Indians from the Charge of being Savages" (Calvin Colton), I, 96
"Vindication of the Rev. Mr. Heckewelder's History of the Indian Nations, A" (Rawle), I, 96n.
Vine Street, Cincinnati, I, 453
Virgil, I, 335; II, 9
Virginia, I, 13, 14, 14n., 15n., 16n., 132, 149, 211, 215, 217, 219, 224, 296, 302, 302n., 308, 320n., 425
Virginius (Knowles), I, 416, 416n.
Vision of Columbus, The (Barlow), II, 31
Visit to North America, A (Welby), I, 32n., 106
Visit to the United States, A (Weston), I, 75n., 113
Voice from the West, A (Jacobs), I, 98
Voice of Warning, A (Pratt), I, 232
Voices of the Night (Longfellow), II, 37
Volksblatt, I, 21n.
Volney, Constantin F. C., I, 7, 7n., 8n., 9n., 100, 100n., 101, 425
Vos, John H., I, 359, 359n., 365n., 366, 375n., 376, 377
―――― , Mrs., I, 375n.
Voyages, Travels and Discoveries (Buttrick), I, 121
Voyage to North America, A (G. Taylor), I, 86

WABASH River, I, 30, 31, 88, 96, 104n.
―――― Valley, I, 18n., 41, 54n., 121
Wahrheitsfreund, I, 21n.
Wakefield, John A., I, 247, 248
Walker, Adam, I, 92
―――― , John, I, 224
―――― , Timothy, I, 270
"Walk-in-the-Water," the, I, 24
Wallace, actor, I, 374n.

―――― , Andrew, I, 137n.
―――― , David, I, 137n.
―――― , William Ross, I, 338, 339, 425, 426, 426n., 454; II, 20, 20n., 36
Walnut Street, Cincinnati, I, 378, 405, 443, 453
Wandering Boys, The (Noah), I, 418
Ward, James W., I, 339
War Department, United States, I, 88
Warner, Harriot W., I, 256n.
War of 1812, I, 23, 92, 105, 133n., 247, 315, 324, 328, 330, 354n.
Warren County, O., I, 41
Washington, Bushrod, I, 325
―――― , George, I, 101, 331, 337, 429
―――― , D. C., I, 10n., 27n., 143n., 147n., 210, 250, 302n.
―――― , O., I, 191
"Wasp," the, I, 331
Waters, Samuel, I, 387
Water Street, Cincinnati, I, 378, 443
―――― Street, Lexington, I, 440
Watervliet, O., I, 41, 317
Watts, Isaac, I, 220, 221
Waverley, II, 15
Waverley (Sir Walter Scott), II, 12, 17, 20, 21, 34
Waverley novels, II, 16, 21
Wayne Street, Detroit, I, 361
Ways and Means (Colman), I, 416n.
"We are Seven" (Wordsworth), II, 24
Webster, Daniel, I, 267
Wedding Day, The (Inchbald), I, 415n.
Weekly Reveille, The, I, 307n.
We Fly by Night (Colman), I, 416n.
Wegelin, Oscar, I, 361n.
Welby, Adlard, I, 32n., 106, 107
―――― , Amelia B., I, 342
Wellbred, Julia, I, 162
Welsh, Joseph S., I, 348, 348n., 349
Weltbürger, Der, I, 21n.
Wept of Wish-ton-wish, The (drama), I, 418
Werner (Byron), I, 417
West, G. M., I, 229
Western Academician, The, I, 200

Western Academy of Natural Sciences, I, 239

Western Christian Advocate, I, 158

Western Courier, The, I, 69n., 358n., 367n., 369n., 370n., 371n., 372n., 397n., 431n., 433n., 441, 442

Western Emigrants' Magazine, The, I, 200n., 202

Western Emigration (Trumbull), I, 120

Western Emigration. Narrative of a Tour, I, 120

Western Farmer, The, I, 200

Western Gazetteer, The (S. R. Brown), I, 28n., 129

Western Intelligencer, The, I, 105n., 141, 144n.

Western Journal of Medicine and Surgery, The, I, 196, 196n.

Western Journal of the Medical and Physical Sciences, The, I, 195n., 196

Western Literary Institute and College of Professional Teachers, I, 66, 239

Western Literary Journal and Monthly Review, I, 170n., 178n., 185n.

Western Literary Journal, and Monthly Review, The, I, 175-178; II, 26n.

Western Luminary, The, I, 158

Western Lyre , The (Snyder and Chappell), I, 317

Western Magazine and Review, The, I, 168

Western Medical and Physical Journal, The, I, 196

Western Medical Gazette, The, I, 197, 197n.

Western Medical Reformer, The, I, 198, 198n.

Western Messenger, The, I, 46n., 178-185, 200n., 208n., 238n., 246n.; II, 12n., 26-30, 36-38

Western Methodist Book Concern, I, 229

———— Methodist Historical Society, I, 238

Western Minerva, I, 168, 168n.

Western Mirror, and Ladies' Literary Gazette, I, 188, 188n.

Western Miscellany, The, periodical, I, 191

Western Miscellany, The (Stipp), I, 153n.

Western Monthly Magazine, The, I, 14n., 17n., 26n., 42n., 49n., 50n., 68n., 98n., 104n., 119n., 150n., 171-176, 178, 197n., 199n., 202n., 245n., 264n., 270-271, 273-274, 287n., 297n., 300n., 343n., 348n., 423, 423n.; II, 5n., 20n., 23n., 26n., 27n., 30n., 32n., 34n., 35n.

Western Monthly Magazine, and Literary Journal, The, I, 175, 176, 177n., 183n., 200n., 301n., 424n.; II, 29, 29n.

Western Monthly Review, The, I, 127, 168-170, 205n., 237n., 253n., 260n., 270n., 273, 289n., 290n., 332n.; II, 3n., 6n., 7n., 12n., 34n., 35n.

Western People's Magazine, I, 186, 186n.

"Western Poetry," I, 179

Western Quarterly Journal of Practical Medicine, The, I, 197

Western Quarterly Reporter, The, I, 195

Western Reader, The (James Hall), I, 265, 266n.

Western Religious Magazine, The, I, 191

Western Reserve, I, 17, 76, 120

———— Reserve College, I, 62

———— Reserve Historical Society, I, 231n., 355n.

Western Review and Miscellaneous Magazine, The, I, 165-167, 201, 201n.; II, 7n., 21, 22, 22n., 25n., 33n.

"Western Sketches of Caroline Mathilda (Stansbury) Kirkland, The" (Twamley), I, 286n.

Western Souvenir, The, I, 171n., 275, 275n., 287, 306n.; II, 20n.

Western Spy, The, I, 136, 136n., 139n., 165n., 354n., 355n.

Western Sun, The, I, 41n., 138, 138n., 146n., 230n., 236, 363n., 377n.

Western Tourist and Emigrant's

Guide, The (J. Calvin Smith), I, 129

Western Unitarian Association, I, 184n.

West-Indian, The (Cumberland), I, 415, 415n.

Westland, Das, I, 21n.

West Lexington, Presbytery of, I, 224

Westliche Adler, Der, I, 20n.

Westliche Beobachter, Der, I, 20n.

Westliche Merkur, Der, I, 21n.

Weston, Richard, I, 74, 75n., 113

West's equestrian company, I, 443

West Tennessee Light Infantry, I, 310n.

Westward Ho! (Paulding), I, 272

Wetmore, Alphonso, I, 111n., 129, 163, 283, 421, 421n.

Wheelock, Eleazar, I, 97n.

Wheel of Fortune, The (Cumberland), I, 415n.

Whitby, Richesson, I, 160

Whitehead, William, I, 415

Whitewater, O., I, 41

——— district, Ind., I, 45

Whiting, Henry, I, 237, 344-347; II, 20

———, I. N., I, 318

Whittier, John G., I, 150; II, 31, 36, 36n.

Whitty, J. H., I, 297n., 340n.

Whitwell, Stedman, I, 160

Who's the Dupe? (Cowley), I, 415n.

Who Wants a Guinea? (Colman), I, 416n.

Wickliffe, Charles, I, 134n.

Wife, The (Knowles), I, 416, 416n.

Wild, J. C., I, 407n., 408n., 409n., 446, 447, 451; II, 6n.

Wilkinson, James, I, 87, 213, 243, 244, 320n.

William III, of England, I, 80

Williams, actor, I, 365

———, F. G., I, 232

William Tell (Knowles), I, 416, 416n.

Willis, N. P., II, 31, 32, 33

Will she be Married? (Cowley), I, 415n.

Wilson, Alexander, I, 99, 256

———, Joshua L., I, 227n., 228, 239, 434

———, Samuel, I, 263, 264, 264n.

"Winander Lake and Mountains" (John Keats), I, 181

Winchester, James, I, 115n.

Windsor Forest, I, 116

Winning of the West, The (Roosevelt), I, 87n., 149n.

Winter in the West, A (Hoffman), I, 10n. and as *op. cit.,* 119, 119n.

Winter Studies and Summer Rambles in Canada (Jameson), I, 7n.

Wisconsin, State Historical Society of, I, 123n., 165n., 193n.

Wisconsin in Three Centuries, I, 7n.

Wisconsin River, I, 82, 86, 344

Wislizenus, A., I, 21n.

Witherell, B. F. H., I, 11n.

Withers's Inn, Vincennes, I, 363n.

Wives as they were (Inchbald), I, 415n.

Wona, I, 345

Wonder! The (Centlivre), I, 415n.

Wonderful Discovery! (Letcher), I, 260

Woodberry, G. E., I, 338n., 339n.

Woodbridge Street, Detroit, I, 446

Woodburn, James A., I, 54n., 55n., 58n., 61n.

Woodruff, proprietor of theatre, I, 403

Woods, John, I, 74n.

———, John, of Tennessee, I, 309n., 310n.

"Wood's Execution," I, 308, 309n.

Woodward, Augustus B., I, 261, 261n.

——— Avenue, Detroit, I, 409, 410, 451

Woodworth, Ben, I, 409

———, Samuel, I, 319n.

Woodworth's Hotel, Detroit, I, 393

Wordsworth, William, I, 4, 177, 180, 181n., 342.; II, 23-25, 27-28, 35

Works of Edgar Allan Poe, The, I, 338n., 339n.

Works of Lord Byron. . . . Letters and Journals, The, II, 13n.

Works of Quinctilian, The, I, 271

"Worldly Matters," I, 193

Worsley, William W., I, 133n.
Worth, Gorham, I, 323, 323n., 327;
    II, 19, 19n., 32, 32n., 33, 33n.
Worthington, O., I, 198
———— College, I, 198
Wright, Frances, I, 33, 159n.
————, Guy W., I, 196
————, J. C., I, 137n.
Writings of Caleb Atwater, The, I,
    53n., 240
Wycherley, William, I, 414
Wylie, Andrew, I, 67, 208, 233, 239

X. Y. Z. (Colman), I, 416n.

YALE College, I, 58, 62, 64
———— University, I, 133n.
Yandell, Lunsford P., I, 196, 197
Yankee, I, 18n.
Yankee among the Nullifiers, A, I,
    427

Yazoo Indian, I, 84
Year's Residence, A (Cobbett), I,
    32n., 106n. and as *op. cit.*
Yorick (Ward), I, 339
Young, Edward, I, 414, 415n.
————, John, I, 454
————, John C., I, 208, 208n.
"Young Beichan," I, 310
"Young Charlotte," I, 310n.
Young Gentleman and Lady's Ex-
    planatory Monitor (Rufus W.
    Adams), I, 265, 265n.
Young Men's Mercantile Library,
    Cincinnati, I, 68
Youngs, Benjamin, I, 225
Young Widow, The, I, 420
Youth's Magazine, I, 201
Ypsilanti, Mich., I, 26n.

ZANESVILLE, O., I, 191, 228
Zeisberger, David, I, 40, 40n., 271,
    271n.

COLUMBIA UNIVERSITY PRESS
COLUMBIA UNIVERSITY
NEW YORK

————

FOREIGN AGENT
HUMPHREY MILFORD
AMEN HOUSE, E.C.
LONDON